1985

MILITARY
AIRCRAFT MARKINGS

PETER R. MARCH

D0674613

LONDON

IAN ALLAN LTD

Contents

Photographs by Andrew March, Daniel March, and Peter R. March

This edition published 1985

ISBN 0 7110 1463 9

Published by Ian Allan Ltd, Shepperton, Surrey; and printed by Ian Allan Printing Ltd at their works at Coombelands in Runnymede, England

Cover: SEPECAT Jaguar GR1s of RAF Germany. *Crown Copyright*

Introduction

This sixth edition of *abc Military Aircraft Markings*, a companion to *abc Civil Aircraft Markings*, again sets out to list all current aircraft carrying service serial numbers that are based or might be seen in the British Isles. This includes all Royal Air Force, Royal Navy, Army Air Corps, Ministry of Defence (Procurement Executive) and manufacturers' test aircraft (including those located overseas if they are likely to return to the UK), USAF and USN machines based in the UK, and the current Irish Army Air Corps fleet. There is also coverage of USAF, US Army and USN aircraft normally based in North-West Europe and types that regularly visit from the USA, together with a selection of aircraft from other overseas air arms which might be seen visiting the UK from time to time. Historic aircraft which carry overseas military markings but are based in the UK have been listed in a separate section. Wherever possible the operating units and bases of RAF, RN and Army Air Corps aircraft are detailed together with locations of civilian owned aircraft in military markings.

The term aircraft used here covers powered, manned aeroplanes, helicopters and gliders. It does not include un-manned target drones. The serials listed are in the main those presently displayed on the aircraft, whether it is a primary or a secondary identity such as an RAF Support Command 'M' or Royal Navy 'A' maintenance number. Aircraft used as targets on MoD ranges are generally omitted as access to view these machines is restricted. The serials of some incomplete aircraft have been included, such as the cockpit sections of machines displayed by the RAF Exhibition Flight at Abingdon and significant parts of aircraft held by preservation groups and societies. Where an aircraft on the charge of the fire section has reached a point at which its final destruction seems imminent, then it is deleted from the listing. A new feature for this edition is the inclusion of a list of aircraft that appeared in the last edition, but have now been eliminated.

UK serials are listed in strict alphabetical and numerical order with the manufacturer and type detailed and the owner/operator and location shown for each. If the aircraft has an alternative, previous or current identifying serial or civil registration this is shown in brackets after the type. A cross reference to the many RAF 'M' and RN 'A' numbers is included. Where a serial is omitted in a sequence this indicates that no aircraft is carrying that number at present, having been written off, scrapped, sold abroad or allocated an alternative marking.

The unit code identification for all RAF, RN and AAC aircraft, as recorded up to 31 December, is shown in square brackets after the type. These unit markings are normally carried boldly on the sides of the fuselage or on the aircraft's fin. In the case of RAF and AAC machines currently in service they are usually single or pairs of letters or numbers, while the RN continues to use a well established system of three-figure codes between 000 and 999 together with a fin letter code denoting the aircraft's operational base. RN squadrons, units and bases are allocated blocks of numbers from which individual aircraft codes are issued. Codes change when aircraft move between units and therefore the markings shown in this edition might not be that currently painted on a particular aircraft, having been overtaken by events. To help identification of RN bases and landing platforms on ships a list of tail létter codes with their appropriate name, ship pennant number and type of vessel is included.

Current USAF and USN aircraft based in the UK are listed by type. The serial number actually displayed on the aircraft's tail is shown in full with appropriate fiscal year information also provided. Details of the operating wing and, where possible, the squadron allocation are provided. For European and mainland USA aircraft a similar pattern is followed. The serial numbers of overseas service aircraft are as usually presented on the individual machine or as they are normally identified. Likewise the listed historic aircraft show the number carried on the fuselage as principal means of identification.

Information shown is believed to be correct at 1 January 1985 and the addendum carries any changes noted while the book was in production.

Acknowledgements
The compiler wishes to thank the many people who have taken trouble to send comments, criticism and other useful information following the publication of the previous edition of *abc Military Aircraft Markings*. In particular the following correspondents: J. R. Cross, S. Menges, J. Nairne, S. Newton, K. Sloper, B. Taylor, G. Turner and A. L. Wood.

This compilation has relied heavily on the publications of the following aviation groups and societies: *Air North, Air Scotland* (The West of Scotland Aviation Group), *British Aviation Review* (British Aviation Research Group), *Cotswold Messenger* (Cotswold Aircraft Restoration Group), *Flightpath* (The Cheshire Aviation Society), *Flypast* (Merseyside Aviation Society), *Hawkeye* (Gatwick Aviation Society), *Humberside Air Review* (Humberside Aviation Society), *Irish Air Letter, Osprey* (Solent Aviation Society), *Prestwick Airport Letter* (Prestwick Airport Aviation Group), *Scottish Air News* (Central Scotland Aviation Group), *Skyward* (Westcountry Aviation Society), *South West Aviation News* (South West Aviation Society), *Stansted Aviation Newsletter* (The Stansted Aviation Society), together with these publications: *French Military Aviation* (second edition) by Paul A. Jackson, Midland Counties Publications; *Foreign Military Air Arms to Europe* by S. M. Jessup and A. G. W. Mower, Seefive Publications; *United States Military Aviation: The Air Force* by Robert J. Archer, Midland Counties Publications; *Wrecks and Relics* (9th Edition) by Ken Ellis, Merseyside Aviation Society.

The new edition of *abc Military Aircraft Markings* would not have been possible without considerable research and checking by Wal Gandy, Howard Curtis, Daniel March and John G. Smith.

PRM

Abbreviations

AAC	Army Air Corps	**BATUS**	British Army Training Unit Support
A&AEE	Aeroplane & Armament Experimental Establishment	**BDRF**	Battle Damage Repair Flight
		BDRT	Battle Damage Repair Training
ABS	Air Base Squadron	**BFWF**	Basic Fixed Wing Flight
ACCGS	Air Cadets Central Gliding School	**BGA**	British Gliding Association
ACCS	Airborne Command and Control Squadron	**BHC**	British Hovercraft Corporation
		BP	Boulton & Paul
ACR	Armoured Cavalry Regiment	**BRNC**	Britannia Royal Naval College
AEF	Air Experience Flight	**B-V**	Boeing-Vertol
AES	Air Engineering School	**BW**	Bomber Wing
AETW	Air Engineering Training Wing	**CATCS**	Central Air Traffic Control School
AEW	Airborne Early Warning	**CBAS**	Commando Brigade Air Squadron
AFRES	Air Force Reserve	**CCF**	Combined Cadet Force
AIU	Accident Investigation Unit	**CDE**	Chemical Defence Establishment
AMS	Air Movements School	**CFS**	Central Flying School
ANG	Air National Guard	**CinC**	Commander in Chief
APS	Aircraft Preservation Society	**CSDE**	Central Servicing Development Establishment
ARRS	Aerospace Rescue and Recovery Squadron		
		CTE	Central Training Establishment
ARW/LCF	Advanced Rotary Wing Lynx Conversion Flight	**CTTS**	Civilian Technical Training School
		CV	Chance-Vought
ARWS	Advanced Rotary Wing Squadron	**D-BD**	Dassault-Breguet Dornier
AS&RU	Aircraft Salvage and Repair Unit	**DH**	De Havilland
ATC	Air Training Corps	**DHC**	De Havilland Canada
ATS	Aircrewman Training Squadron	**D&TS**	Development and Trials Squadron
AvCo	Aviation Company	**EE**	English Electric
AW	Armstrong Whitworth Aircraft/Aircraft Workshops	**EMA**	East Midlands Airport
		EoN	Elliot's of Newbury
AW&CW	Airborne Warning & Control Wing	**ETPS**	Empire Test Pilots School
BAC	British Aircraft Corporation	**EWAU**	Electronics Warfare Avionics Unit
BAe	British Aerospace Company	**FAA**	Fleet Air Arm
BAOR	British Army of the Rhine	**FBW**	Fly by wire
BAPC	British Aircraft Preservation Council	**FCS**	Facility Checking Squadron
		FE	Further Education

FF&SS	Fire Fighting & Safety School	**RNEC**	Royal Naval Engineering College
FIS	Fighter Interceptor Squadron	**RNEFTS**	Royal Naval Elementary Flying
Flt	Flight		Training School
FMA	Fabrica Militar de Aviones	**R-R**	Rolls-Royce
FONAC	Flag Officer Naval Air Command	**RS**	Reid & Sigrist
FRADU	Fleet Requirements and Direction	**RS&RE**	Royal Signals and Radar
	Unit		Establishment
FRSB	Fleet Reserve Storage Base	**RW**	Reconnaissance Wing
FSS	Flying Selection School	**SA**	Scottish Aviation
FTS	Flying Training School	**SAH**	School of Air Handling
FW	Foster Wickner	**SAL**	Scottish Aviation Limited
GD	General Dynamics	**SAR**	Search and Rescue
HMS	Her Majesty's Ship	**Saro**	Saunders-Roe
HP	Handley-Page	**SAREW**	Search & Rescue Engineering Wing
HQ	Headquarters	**SARTF**	Search and Rescue Training
HS	Hawker Siddeley		Flight
IAM	Institute of Aviation Medicine	**SCF**	Scout Conversion Flight
IWM	Imperial War Museum	**SHSU**	Sea Harrier Servicing Unit
JATE	Joint Air Transport Establishment	**SKTF**	Sea King Training Flight
JMU	Jaguar Maintenance Unit	**SOS**	Special Operations Squadron
LCF	Lynx Conversion Flight	**SoTT**	School of Technical Training
LTF	Lightning Training Flight	**Sqn**	Squadron
MAS	Military Airlift Squadron	**SRW**	Strategic Reconnaissance Wing
MAW	Military Airlift Wing	**TAS**	Tactical Airlift Squadron
McD	McDonnell Douglas	**TAW**	Tactical Airlift Wing
MGSP	Mobile Glider Servicing Party	**TCW**	Tactical Control Wing
MoD(PE)	Ministry of Defence (Procurement	**Tech Coll**	Technical College
	Executive)	**TFS**	Tactical Fighter Squadron
Mod	Modified	**TFTAS**	Tactical Fighter Training Aggressor
MR	Maritime Reconnaissance		Squadron
MU	Maintenance Unit	**TFW**	Tactical Fighter Wing
NA	North American	**TMTS**	Trade Management Training School
NAF	Naval Air Facility	**TOEU**	Tornado Operational Evaluation
NASU	Naval Air Support Unit		Unit
NHTU	Naval Hovercraft Trials Unit	**TRS**	Tactical Reconnaissance Squadron
OCU	Operational Conversion Unit	**TRW**	Tactical Reconnaissance Wing
OEU	Operation Evaluation Unit	**TTTE**	Tri-national Tornado Training
PAX	Passenger procedural trainer		Establishment
PRU	Photographic Reconnaissance Unit	**TWCU**	Tornado Weapons Conversion Unit
RAE	Royal Aircraft Establishment	**TWU**	Tactical Weapons Unit
RAF	Royal Aircraft Factory/	**UAS**	University Air Squadron
	Royal Air Force	**UK**	United Kingdom
RAFC	Royal Air Force College	**UKAEA**	United Kingdom Energy Authority
RAFGSA	Royal Air Force Gliding and	**US**	United States
	Soaring Association	**USAF**	United States Air Force
RCAF	Royal Canadian Air Force	**USAREUR**	US Army Europe
REME	Royal Electrical & Mechanical	**USN**	United States Navy
	Engineers	**VGS**	Volunteer Gliding School
RM	Royal Marines	**VS**	Vickers-Supermarine
RMC of S	Royal Military College of Science	**WO**	Written off
RN	Royal Navy	**WS**	Westland
RNAS	Royal Naval Air Station	**WW2**	World War II
RNAY	Royal Naval Aircraft Yard		

Note: Whilst every effort has been made to ensure the accuracy of this publication no part of the contents has been obtained from official sources. The compiler will be pleased to continue to receive comments, corrections and further information for inclusion in subsequent editions of *Military Aircraft Markings*.

British Military Aircraft Serials

The Committee of Imperial Defence through its Air Committee introduced a standardised system of numbering aircraft in November 1912. The Air Department of the Admiralty was allocated the first batch 1-200 and used these to cover aircraft already in use and those on order. The Army was issued with the next block from 201-800, which included the number 304 which was given to the Cody Biplane now preserved in the Science Museum. By the outbreak of World War 1 the Royal Navy was on its second batch of serials 801-1600 and this system continued with alternating allocations between the Army and Navy until 1916 when number 10000, a Royal Flying Corps BE2C, was reached.

It was decided not to continue with five digit numbers but instead to start again from 1, prefixing RFC aircraft with the letter A and RNAS aircraft with the prefix N. The RFC allocations commenced with A1 an FE2D and before the end of the year had reached A9999 an Armstrong Whitworth FK8. The next group commenced with B1 and continued in logical sequence through the C, D, E and F prefixes. G was used on a limited basis to identity captured German aircraft, while H was the last block of wartime ordered aircraft. To avoid confusion I was not used, so the new postwar machines were allocated serials in the J range. A further minor change was made in the serial numbering system in August 1929 when it was decided to maintain four numerals after the prefix letter, thus omitting numbers 1 to 999. The new K series therefore commenced at K1000, which was allocated to an AW Atlas.

The Naval N prefix was not used in such a logical way. Blocks of numbers were allocated for specific types of aircraft such as seaplanes or flying boats. By the late 1920s the sequence had largely been used up and a new series using the prefix S was commenced. In 1930 separate naval allocations were stopped and subsequent serials were issued in the 'military' range which had by this time reached the K series. A further change in the pattern of allocations came in the L range. Commencing with L7272 numbers were issued in blocks with smaller blocks of serials between not used. These were known as blackout blocks. As M had already been used as a suffix for Maintenance Command instructional airframes it was not used as a prefix. Although N had previously been used for naval aircraft it was used again for serials allocated from 1937.

With the build-up to World War 2 the rate of allocations quickly accelerated and the prefix R was being used when war was declared. The letters O and Q were not allotted, neither was S which had been used up to S1865 for naval aircraft before integration into the RAF series. By 1940 the serial Z9999 had been reached, as part of a blackout block, with the letters U and Y not used to avoid confusion. The option to recommence serial allocation at A1000 was not taken up; instead it was decided to use an alphabetical two-letter prefix with three numerals running from 100 to 999. Thus AA100 was allocated to a Blenheim IV.

This two-letter, three-numeral serial system which started in 1940 continues today with the current issue being in the ZE range. The letters C, I, O, Q, U and Y were, with one or two exceptions, not used. For various reasons the following letter combinations were not issued: DA, DB, DH, EA, GA to GZ, HA, JE, JH, JJ, NZ and SA to SK. The first postwar serials issued were in the VP range while the end of the WZs had been reached by the Korean War. At the current rate of issue the Z range should last out the remainder of this century.

British Military Aircraft Markings

Serial	Type (alternative identity)	Owner, Operator or Location	Notes
164	Bleriot Type XI (BAPC 106)	RAF Museum, Hendon	
168	Sopwith Tabloid Replica (G-BFDE)	Bomber Command Museum, Hendon	
304	Cody Biplane (BAPC 62)	Science Museum, South Kensington	
433	Bleriot Type XXVII (BAPC 107)	RAF Museum, Hendon	
2345	Vickers FB5 Gunbus Replica (G-ATVP)	RAF Museum, Hendon	
2699	RAF BE2C	Imperial War Museum, Duxford	
3066	Caudron GIII (G-AETA)	RAF Museum, Hendon	
5894	DH2 Replica (G-BFVH)	Russavia, Duxford	
5984	DH2 Replica (BAPC 112)	Leisure Sport/St Just	
6232	RAF BE2C Replica (BAPC 41)	RAF St Athan Historic Aircraft Museum	
8151	Sopwith Baby Replica (BAPC 137)	Leisure Sport, Thorpe Park	
8359	Short 184	FAA Museum, RNAS Yeovilton	
A1325	RAF BE2e	Mosquito Aircraft Museum, London Colney	
A1742	Scout D Replica (BAPC 38)	RAF St Athan Historic Aricraft Collection	
A2416	RAF SE5A Replica	Privately owned, Powerscourt	
A3240	RAF SE5A Replica	Privately owned, Powerscourt	
A4850	RAF SE5A Replica (BAPC176)	South Yorkshire Aviation Society, Worksop	
A5401	RAF SE5A Replica (EI-ARK)	Privately owned, Powerscourt	
A6275	RAF SE5A Replica	Privately owned, Powerscourt	
A8226	Sopwith 1½ Strutter Replica (G-BIDW)	RAF Museum, Hendon	
B1807	Sopwith Pup (G-EAVX)	Privately owned, Keynsham, Avon	
B4863	RAF SE5A Replica (BAPC 113) [G]	Leisure Sport, Thorpe Park	
B7270	Sopwith Camel F1 Replica (G-BFCZ)	Imperial War Museum, Duxford	
C1381	Avro 504K Replica (BAPC177) [G]	RAF Museum Store, Henlow	
C1701	Sopwith Camel F1 Replica (G-AWYY)	FAA Museum, RNAS Yeovilton	
C1904	RAF SE5A Replica (G-PFAP) [OZ]	Privately owned, Bicester	
C4912	Bristol M1c Replica (BAPC 135)	Leisure Sport, Thorpe Park	
D3419	Sopwith Camel F1 Replica (BAPC 59)	RAF St Athan Historic Aircraft Collection	
D5329	Sopwith Dolphin	RAF Museum Store, Cardington	
D7560	Avro 504K	Science Museum, South Kensington	
D8096	Bristol Fighter (G-AEPH) [D]	Shuttleworth Collection, Old Warden	
E449	Avro 504K (G-EBKN)	RAF Museum, Hendon	
E2581	Bristol Fighter	Imperial War Museum, Duxford	
F344	Avro 504K Replica	RAF Museum Store, Henlow	
F373	Avro 504K Replica	RAF Museum Store, Henlow	
F904	RAF SE5A (G-EBIA)	Shuttleworth Collection, Old Warden	
F938	RAF SE5A (G-EBIC)	RAF Museum, Hendon	
F939	RAF SE5A (G-EBIB) [6]	Science Museum, South Kensington	
F943	RAF SE5A Replica (G-BIHF)	Privately owned, Booker (Lady Di)	
F943	RAF SE5A Replica (G-BKDT)	Privately owned, Sherburn	
F1010	DH9A [19]	Bomber Command Museum, Hendon	
F3556	RAF RE8	Imperial War Museum, Duxford	
F5447	RAF SE5A Replica (G-BKER) [N]	Privately owned, Glasgow	
F5459	RAF SE5A Replica (BAPC 142) [Y]	Cornwall Aero Park, Helston	
F-5459	RAF SE5A Replica (G-INNY)	Privately owned, Old Sarum	
F6314	Sopwith Camel [B]	RAF Museum, Hendon	
F8010	RAF SE5A Replica (G-BDWJ) [19]	Privately owned, Booker	

7

Notes	Serial	Type (alternative identity)	Owner, Operator or Location
	F8614	Vickers Vimy Replica (G-AWAU)	Bomber Command Museum, Hendon
	H1968	Avro 504K Replica (BAPC 42)	RAF St Athan Historic Aircraft Collection
	H2311	Avro 504K (G-ABAA)	RAF Museum Store, Henlow
	H5199	Avro 504K (G-ACNB, G-ADEV, E3404)	Shuttleworth Collection, Old Warden
	J7326	DH Humming Bird (G-EBQP)	Russavia Collection, Duxford
	J8067	Pterodactyl 1a	Science Museum, South Kensington
	J9941	Hawker Hart (G-ABMR) [57]	RAF Museum, Cardington
	K1786	Hawker Tomtit (G-AFTA)	Shuttleworth Collection, Old Warden
	K2059	Isaacs Fury (G-PFAR)	Privately owned, Dunkeswell
	K2567	DH Tiger Moth (G-MOTH)	Russavia Collection, Duxford
	K2568	DH Tiger Moth (G-APMM)	Privately owned, Bedford
	K2571	DH Tiger Moth	Privately owned, Lutterworth
	K2572	DH Tiger Moth (G-AOZH)	Privately owned, Shoreham
	K3215	Avro Tutor (G-AHSA)	Shuttleworth Collection, Old Warden
	K4232	Avro Rota (SE-AZB)	RAF Museum, Hendon
	K4235	Avro Rota (G-AHMJ)	Shuttleworth Collection, Old Warden
	K4972	Hawker Hart Trainer IIA (1746M)	RAF Museum, Hendon
	K5054	Supermarine Spitfire replica	Spitfire Society, Southampton
	K5414	Hawker Hind (G-AENP/ BAPC 78)	Shuttleworth Collection, Old Warden
	K6038	Westland Wallace II	RAF Museum Store, Cardington
	K7271	Hawker Fury II Replica (BAPC 148)	RAF Cosford Aerospace Museum
	K8042	Gloster Gladiator (8372M)	Battle of Britain Museum, Hendon
	K9942	VS Spitfire IA (8383M) [SD-V]	RAF Museum, Hendon
	L1592	Hawker Hurricane I [KW-Z]	Science Museum, South Kensington
	L1592	Hawker Hurricane I Replica (BAPC 63) [KW-Z]	Torbay Aircraft Museum, Paignton
	L2301	VS Walrus (G-AIZG)	FAA Museum, RNAS Yeovilton
	L2940	Blackburn Skua	FAA Museum, RNAS Yeovilton
	L5343	Fairey Battle I	RAF St Athan Historic Aircraft Collection
	L6906	Miles Magister (BAPC 44)	Privately owned, Wroughton
	L8032	Gloster Gladiator (G-AMRK)	Shuttleworth Collection, Old Warden
	L8756	Bristol Bolingbroke (RCAF 10001) [XD-E]	Battle of Britain Museum, Hendon
	N220	Supermarine S5 replica (G-BDFF)	Privately owned, St Just
	N248	Supermarine S6A	Southampton Hall of Aviation
	N1671	Boulton Paul Defiant I (8370M) [EW-D]	Battle of Britain Museum, Hendon
	N1854	Fairey Fulmar II (G-AIBE)	FAA Museum, RNAS Yeovilton
	N2078	Sopwith Baby	FAA Museum, RNAS Yeovilton
	N2276	Gloster Sea Gladiator (N5903)	FAA Museum, RNAS Yeovilton
	N3788	Miles Magister (G-AKPF)	Privately owned, Bassingbourn
	N4172	Fairey Albacore [5A]	FAA Museum at St Just
	N4877	Avro Anson I (G-AMDA) [VX-F]	Skyfame Collection, Duxford
	N5180	Sopwith Pup (G-EBKY)	Shuttleworth Collection, Old Warden
	N5182	Sopwith Pup (G-APUP/B5292)	RAF Museum, Hendon
	N5195	Sopwith Pup (G-ABOX)	Privately owned, Blackbushe
	N5430	Sopwith Triplane Replica (G-BHEW)	Privately owned, Old Warden
	N5445	DH Tiger Moth (G-AIXH/DE722)	Privately owned, Little Gransden
	N5492	Sopwith Triplane Replica (BAPC 111)	Leisure Sport, Thorpe Park
	N5628	Gloster Gladiator II	RAF Museum, Hendon
	N5912	Sopwith Triplane (8385M)	RAF Museum, Hendon
	N6452	Sopwith Pup Replica (G-BIAU)	Whitehall Theatre of War, London
	N6466	DH Tiger Moth (G-ANKZ)	Privately owned, Barton
	N6532	DH Tiger Moth (G-ANTS)	Strathallan Aircraft Collection
	N6720	DH Tiger Moth (7014M) [RUO-B]	No 493 Sqn ATC, Kings Heath
	N6812	Sopwith Camel	Imperial War Museum, Lambeth
	N6847	DH Tiger Moth (G-APAL)	Privately owned, Denham

Serial	Type (alternative identity)	Owner, Operator or Location	Notes
N6848	DH Tiger Moth (G-BALX)	Privately owned, Redhill	
N6985	DH Tiger Moth (G-AHMN)	Museum of Army Flying, Middle Wallop	
N8224	DH Tiger Moth (G-AHUR)	Privately owned, Blackbushe	
N9191	DH Tiger (G-ALND)	Privately owned, Shipdham	
N9238	DH Tiger Moth (G-ANEL)	Privately owned, Catterick	
N9389	DH Tiger Moth (G-ANJA)	Privately owned, Shipmeadow, Suffolk	
N9508	DH Tiger Moth (G-APCU)	Privately owned, Hemel Hempstead	
N9510	DH Tiger Moth (G-AOEL)	Royal Scottish Museum of Flight, East Fortune	
N9899	Supermarine Southampton	RAF Museum Store, Cardington	
P2183	Fairey Battle I [36]	RAF St Athan Historic Aircraft Collection	
P2617	Hawker Hurricane I (8373M) [AF-F]	Battle of Britain Museum, Hendon	
P3175	Hawker Hurricane I	Battle of Britain Museum, Hendon	
P6382	Miles Magister (G-AJRS)	Shuttleworth Collection, Old Warden	
P7350	VS Spitfire IIA (G-AWIJ) [SH-D]	RAF Battle of Britain Flight, Coningsby	
P7540	VS Spitfire IIA [DU-W]	Dumfries & Galloway Aviation Museum, Tinwald Downs	
P9390	VS Spitfire I Replica (BAPC 71) [KL-B]	Norfolk & Suffolk Aviation Museum, Flixton	
P9444	VS Spitfire IA [RN-D]	Science Museum, South Kensington	
R1914	Miles Magister (G-AHUJ)	Strathallan Aircraft Collection	
R3950	Fairey Battle I (RCAF 1899)	Strathallan Aircraft Collection	
R4907	DH Tiger Moth (G-ANCS)	Privately owned, Sywell	
R4959	DH Tiger Moth (G-ARAZ)	Privately owned, Goodwood	
R5086	DH Tiger Moth (G-APIH)	Privately owned, Little Gransden	
R5250	DH Tiger Moth (G-AODT)	Privately owned, Swanton Morley	
R5868	Avro Lancaster I (7325M) [PO-S]	Bomber Command Museum, Hendon	
R6915	VS Spitfire I	Imperial War Museum, Lambeth	
R9125	Westland Lysander III (8377M) [LX-L]	Battle of Britain Museum, Hendon	
S1287	Fairey Flycatcher Replica (G-BEYB) [5]	Privately owned, Middle Wallop	
S1595	Supermarine S6B	Science Museum, South Kensington	
S1595	Supermarine S6B Replica (BAPC 156)	Leisure Sport, Thorpe Park	
S4523	Spad VII N2727V)	Imperial War Museum, Duxford	
T5424	DH Tiger Moth (G-AJOA)	Privately owned, Chisledon	
T5493	DH Tiger Moth (G-ANEF)	Privately owned, Cranwell	
T5854	DH Tiger Moth (G-ANKK)	Privately owned, Halfpenny Green	
T6296	DH Tiger Moth (8387M)	RAF Museum, Hendon	
T6313	DH Tiger Moth (G-AHVU)	Privately owned, Denham	
T6553	DH Tiger Moth (G-APIG) [N]	Privately owned, Shoreham	
T6645	DH Tiger Moth (G-AIIZ)	Privately owned, Redhill	
T6818	DH Tiger Moth (G-ANKT)	Shuttleworth Collection, Old Warden	
T7281	DH Tiger Moth (G-ARTL)	Privately owned, Sunderland	
T7404	DH Tiger Moth (G-ANMV)	Privately owned, Compton Abbas	
T7909	DH Tiger Moth (G-ANON)	Privately owned, Sherburn-in-Elmet	
T8191	DH Tiger Moth	RN Historic Flight, RNAS Yeovilton	
T9707	Miles Magister (G-AKKR/8378M)	Manchester Air & Space Museum	
T9738	Miles Magister (G-AKAT)	Newark Air Museum, Winthorpe	
V3388	Airspeed Oxford (G-AHTW)	Skyfame Collection, Duxford	
V7767	Hawker Hurricane Replica (BAPC 72)	Air Museum, North Weald	
V9281	Westland Lysander III (G-BCWL)	Warbirds of GB, Blackbushe	
V9300	Westland Lysander	British Aerial Museum, Duxford	
V9441	Westland Lysander IIIA (RCAF2355/G-AZWT) [AR-A]	Strathallan Aircraft Collection	
W1048	HP Halifax II (8465M) [TL-S]	Bomber Command Museum, Hendon	
W4041	Gloster E28/39 [G]	Science Museum, South Kensington	
W4050	DH Mosquito 1	Mosquito Aircraft Museum, London Colney	
W5856	Fairey Swordfish II	Strathallan Aircraft Collection	

Notes	Serial	Type (alternative identity)	Owner, Operator or Location
	W5984	Fairey Swordfish II (HS618/ A2001) [5H]	FAA Museum, RNAS Yeovilton
	X4590	VS Spitfire I (8384M) [PR-F]	Battle of Britain Museum, Hendon
	Z2033	Fairey Firefly I (G-ASTL)	Skyfame Collection, Duxford
	Z7015	Hawker Sea Hurricane IB (G-BKTH)	Shuttleworth Collection, Duxford
	Z7197	Percival Proctor III (G-AKZN/ 8380M)	RAF St Athan Historic Aircraft Collection
	Z7258	DH Dragon Rapide (G-AHGD)	Privately owned, Booker
	AB910	VS Spitfire VB (G-AISU) [XT-M]	RAF Battle of Britain Flight, Coningsby
	AL246	Grumman Martlet I	FAA Museum, RNAS Yeovilton
	AP507	Cierva C30a (G-ACWP) [KX-P]	Science Museum, South Kensington
	AR213	VS Spitfire IA (G-AIST) [QG-A]	Privately owned, Booker
	AR501	VS Spitfire VC (G-AWII) [NN-D]	Shuttleworth Collection, Duxford
	BB731	DH Tiger Moth (A2126/ G-ADCG)	RNAS Yeovilton, in store
	BB807	Tiger Moth (G-ADWO)	Wessex Aviation Society, Wimborne
	BB814	DH Tiger Moth (G-AFWI)	RN Gliding Club, Lee-on-Solent
	BL614	VS Spitfire VB (AB871/4354M) [ZD-F]	Manchester Air & Space Museum
	BM597	VS Spitfire VB (5713M) [PR-O]	RAF Church Fenton, on gate
	DE208	DH Tiger Moth (G-AGYU)	Privately owned, Nayland
	DE363	DH Tiger Moth (G-ANFC)	Mosquito Aircraft Museum, London Colney
	DE373	DH Tiger Moth T.2 (A680/ A2127)	FAA Museum store, RNAS Yeovilton
	DE623	DH Tiger Moth (G-ANFI)	Privately owned, Little Snoring
	DE673	DH Tiger Moth (G-ADNZ/ 6948M)	Privately owned, Hampton
	DE992	DH Tiger Moth (G-AXXV)	Privately owned, Wellesbourne Mountford
	DF130	DH Tiger Moth (G-BACK)	Privately owned, Laindon
	DF155	DH Tiger Moth (G-ANFV)	Privately owned, Lossiemouth
	DF198	DH Tiger Moth (G-BBRB)	Privately owned, Biggin Hill
	DG202	Gloster F9/40 Meteor (5758M)	RAF Cosford Aerospace Museum
	DG590	Miles Hawk Major (G-ADMW/8379M)	RAF Museum Store, Henlow
	DP872	Fairey Barracuda II	FAA Museum, RNAS Yeovilton
	DR613	FW Wicko GM1 (G-AFJB)	Privately owned, Berkswell
	DR628	Beech D.17s (N18V) [PB-1]	Privately owned, Duxford
	DV372	Avro Lancaster I	Imperial War Museum, Lambeth
	EE531	Gloster Meteor F4 (7090M)	Midland Air Museum, Coventry
	EE549	Gloster Meteor F4 (6372M/ 7008M)	RAF St Athan Historic Aircraft Collection
	EJ693	Hawker Tempest V [SA-J]	RAF Museum Store, Henlow
	EM727	DH Tiger Moth (G-AOXN)	Leicester Aircraft Preservation Group
	EM903	DH Tiger Moth (G-APBI)	Privately owned, Audley End
	EP120	VS Spitfire VB (5377M/8070M) [QV-H]	RAF Wattisham
	EX280	NA Harvard IIB (G-TEAC) [G]	Privately owned, Bourn
	EX976	NA Harvard III	FAA Museum, RNAS Yeovilton
	EZ259	NA Harvard III	Lincolnshire Aviation Museum, Tattershall
	EZ407	NA Harvard III	RN Historic Flight, Lee-on-Solent
	FE992	NA Harvard IIB (G-BDAM)	Privately owned, Goodwood
	FH153	NA Harvard IIB (G-BBHK) [GW-A]	Privately owned, Exeter
	FS728	NA Harvard IIB (G-BAFM)	Privately owned, Goodwood
	FT229	NA Harvard IIB (G-AZKI)	Privately owned, Sandown
	FT239	NA Harvard IV (G-BIWX)	Privately owned, White Waltham
	FT323	NA Harvard IIB (G-AZSC)	Privately owned, Fairoaks
	FT375	NA Harvard IIB	MoD(PE) A&AEE Boscombe Down
	FT391	NA Harvard IIB (G-AZBN)	Privately owned, Staverton
	FX301	NA Harvard IIB (G-JUDI) [FD-NQ]	Privately owned, Ipswich
	FX442	NA Harvard IIB	Privately owned, Bournemouth
	HB275	Beech D18S (N5063N)	Privately owned, White Waltham

Serial	Type (alternative identity)	Owner, Operator or Location	Notes
HB751	Fairchild Argus III (G-BCBL)	Privately owned, Little Gransden	
HD368	NA B-25J Mitchell (N9089Z) [VO-A]	Aces High, Duxford	
HJ711	DH Mosquito NFII [VI-C]	Privately owned, York	
HM354	Percival Proctor III (G-ANPP)	Privately owned, Duxford	
HR723	HP Halifax II	Privately owned, Elvington	
HS503	Fairey Swordfish IV (BAPC 108)	RAF Museum Store, Henlow	
JV482	Grumman Wildcat V	Ulster Aviation Society, Castlereagh	
HS649	VS Spitfire XVIII	Privately owned, Henfield	
HX922	DH Mosquito TT35 (G-AWJV) [EG-F] (really TA634)	Mosquito Aircraft Museum, London Colney	
KB889	Avro Lancaster 10	Warbirds of GB, Blackbushe	
KB976	Avro Lancaster B10 (G-BCOH)	Strathallan Aircraft Collection	
KD431	CV Corsair IV [E2-M]	FAA Museum, RNAS Yeovilton	
KE209	Grumman Hellcat II	FAA Museum, RNAS Yeovilton	
KF183	NA Harvard IIB	MoD(PE) A&AEE Boscombe Down	
KG374	Douglas Dakota C-4 (KN645/8355M)	RAF Cosford Aerospace Museum	
KG374	Douglas Dakota C-4 (TS423/G-DAKS) [YS-L]	Aces High, Duxford	
KH191	Consolidated Liberator [T-18]	Warbirds of GB, Blackbushe	
KK995	Sikorsky Hoverfly I (KL110) [E]	RAF Museum, Hendon	
KN751	Consolidated Liberator VI	RAF Cosford Aerospace Museum	
KP208	Douglas Dakota C-4 [75] [YS]	Airborne Forces Museum, Aldershot	
KX829	Hawker Hurricane IV [JV-I]	Birmingham Museum of Science & Industry	
LA198	VS Spitfire F21 (7118M) [JX-C]	RAF Locking, main gate	
LA226	VS Spitfire F21 (7119M)	RAF Memorial Chapel, Biggin Hill	
LA255	VS Spitfire F21 (6490M) [LX-V]	RAF Wittering	
LA564	VS Seafire F46	Privately owned, Newport Pagnell	
LB312	Taylorcraft Plus D (G-AHXE)	Privately owned, Shoreham	
LB375	Taylorcraft Plus D (G-AHGW)	Privately owned, Coventry	
LF363	Hawker Hurricane IIC [VY-X]	RAF Battle of Britain Flight, Coningsby	
LF738	Hawker Hurricane IIC (5405M)	RAF, Rochester Aircraft Restoration	
LF751	Hawker Hurricane IIC (5466M) [FB-B]	RAF Bentley Priory Society	
LS326	Fairey Swordfish II (G-AJVH) [5A]	RN Historic Flight, RNAS Yeovilton	
LZ551	DH Sea Vampire I	FAA Museum, RNAS Yeovilton	
LZ766	Percival Proctor III (G-ALCK)	Skyfame Collection, Duxford	
MF628	Vickers Wellington T10	Bomber Command Museum, Hendon	
MH434	VS Spitfire IX (G-ASJV) [ZD-B]	Privately owned, Duxford	
MJ627	VS Spitfire TIX (G-ASOZ/G-BMSB)	Privately owned, Coventry	
MJ730	VS Spitfire IX (G-BLAS)	Privately owned, Hastings	
MK356	VS Spitfire IX (5690M) [21-V]	RAF St Athan Historic Aircraft Museum	
ML407	VS Spitfire T9 (G-LFIX)	Privately owned, St Merryn	
ML417	VS Spitfire LFIXe (G-BJSG) [2I-T]	Privately owned, Booker	
ML427	VS Spitfire IX [I-ST]	Birmingham Museum of Science & Industry	
ML796	Short Sunderland V	Imperial War Museum, Duxford	
ML824	Short Sunderland V [NS-Z]	Battle of Britain Museum, Hendon	
MN235	Hawker Typhoon IB	RAF Museum, Hendon	
MP345	Airspeed Oxford (G-AITB/MP425)	RAF Museum Store, Cardington	
MT360	Auster 5 (G-AKWT)	Loughborough & Leicester Aircraft Museum	
MT438	Auster III (G-AREI)	Privately owned, Bodmin	
MT818	VS Spitfire T8 (G-AIDN) [G-M]	Privately owned, Dinas Powis	
MT847	VS Spitfire XIV (6960M)	RAF Cosford Aerospace Museum	
MV154	VS Spitfire VIII (G-BKMI)	British Aerial Museum, Duxford	
MV262	VS Spitfire XIV [42-G]	Warbirds of GB, Blackbushe	
MV293	VS Spitfire XIV (G-SPIT)	Warbirds of GB, Blackbushe	
MV370	VS Spitfire XIV (G-FXIV) [AV-L]	Whitehall Theatre of War, London	
MW100	Avro York C1 (G-AGNV/TS798)	RAF Cosford Aerospace Museum	
NF370	Fairey Swordfish III	Imperial War Museum, Lambeth	

Notes	Serial	Type (alternative identity)	Owner, Operator or Location
	NF389	Fairey Swordfish III [5B]	FAA Museum, Lee-on-Solent
	NF875	DH Dragon Rapide 6 (G-AGTM) [603/CH]	Privately owned, Duxford
	NH238	VS Spitfire IX (N238V/ G-MKIX) [D-A]	Warbirds of GB, Blackbushe
	NH749	VS Spitfire XIV (G-MXIV) [L]	Privately owned, Cranfield
	NH799	VS Spitfire XIV	Warbirds of GB, Blackbushe
	NJ673	Auster 5D (G-AOCR)	Privately owned, Saltby
	NJ695	Auster 4 (G-AJXV)	Privately owned, Tollerton
	NJ703	Auster 5 (G-AKPI)	Privately owned, Doncaster
	NL750	DH Tiger Moth (A2123)	RNAS Yeovilton, in store
	NL985	DH Tiger Moth (7015M)	Lincoln Field Vintage & HAC, Bushey
	NM181	DH Tiger Moth (G-AZGZ)	Privately owned, Little Gransden
	NP181	Percival Proctor IV (G-AOAR)	Lashenden Air Warfare Museum, Headcorn
	NP184	Percival Proctor IV (G-ANYP) [K]	Torbay Aircraft Museum, Paignton
	NP294	Percival Proctor IV	Lincolnshire Aviation Museum, Tattershall
	NP303	Percival Proctor IV (G-ANZJ)	Privately owned, London
	NR747	DH Dragon Rapide (G-AJHO)	Privately owned, Bassingbourn
	NV778	Hawker Tempest V (8386M)	RAF Museum, Hendon
	NX611	Avro Lancaster VII (G-ASXX/ 8375M) [YF-C]	Privately owned, East Kirkby
	PA474	Avro Lancaster I [SR-D]	RAF Battle of Britain Flight, Coningsby
	PG617	DH Tiger Moth (G-AYVY)	Privately owned, Ronaldsway
	PG651	DH Tiger Moth (G-AYUX)	Privately owned, Booker
	PG671	DH Tiger Moth (N82AM) [26]	Privately owned
	PK624	VS Spitfire F22 (8072M) [RAU-T]	RAF Abingdon, at main gate
	PK664	VS Spitfire F22 (7759M) (V6-B)	RAF Binbrook, at main gate
	PK683	VS Spitfire F24 (7150M)	Southampton Hall of Aviation
	PK724	VS Spitfire F24 (7288M)	RAF Museum, Hendon
	PL983	VS Spitfire XI (G-PRXI)	Privately owned, Duxford
	PM631	VS Spitfire XIX [DL-E]	RAF Battle of Britain Flight, Coningsby
	PM651	VS Spitfire XIX (7758M)	RAF Benson, at main gate
	PS853	VS Spitfire XIX	RAF Battle of Britain Flight, Coningsby
	PS915	VS Spitfire XIX (7711M)	RAF Battle of Britain Flight, BAe Preston
	PV202	VS Spitfire TIX (G-TRIX)	Privately owned, Saffron Walden
	PZ865	Hawker Hurricane II (G-AMAU) [JU-Q]	RAF Battle of Britain Flight, Coningsby
	RA848	Slingsby Cadet TXI	Privately owned, Harrogate
	RA854	Slingsby Cadet TXI	Privately owned, Wigan
	RD253	Bristol Beaufighter TFX (7931M)	RAF Museum, Hendon
	RF398	Avro Lincoln B2 (8376M)	RAF Cosford Aerospace Museum
	RG333	Miles Messenger IIA (G-AIEK)	Privately owned, Felton, Bristol
	RG333	Miles Messenger IIA (G-AKEZ)	Torbay Aircraft Museum, Paignton
	RH377	Miles Messenger 4A (G-ALAH)	The Aeroplane Collection, RAF Henlow
	RH378	Miles Messenger IIA (G-AJOE)	Cotswold Aircraft Restoration Group, RAF Innsworth
	RH746	Bristol Brigand TF1	North East Air Museum, Sunderland
	RL962	DH Dragon Rapide (G-AHED)	RAF Museum Store, Cardington
	RM221	Percival Proctor IV (G-ANXR)	Privately owned, Biggin Hill
	RM689	VS Spitfire XIV (G-ALGT) [AP-D]	Rolls-Royce, East Midlands Airport
	RR299	DH Mosquito T3 (G-ASKH) [HT-E]	British Aerospace, Hatfield
	RT520	Auster 4 (G-ALYB)	South Yorkshire A.P.S., Firbeck
	RW382	VS Spitfire XVIe (7245M/ 8075M)	Warbirds of GB, Blackbushe
	RW386	VS Spitfire XVIe (6944M) [RAK-A]	Warbirds of GB, Blackbushe
	RW388	VS Spitfire XVIe (6947M) [U4-U]	R. J. Mitchell Memorial, Hanley, Staffs

D8096 Bristol Fighter; Shuttleworth Collection, Old Warden. *PRM*

N5430 Sopwith Triplane Replica; Privately owned, Old Warden. *PRM*

RM221 Percival Proctor IV; Privately owned, Biggin Hill. *PRM*

TF956 Hawker Sea Fury FB11; RN Historic Flight, RNAS Yeovilton. *PRM*

TJ569 Auster A 5; Museum of Army Flying, Middle Wallop. *PRM*

VP952 DH Devon C2; RAF St Athan Historic Aircraft Collection. *PRM*

Serial	Type (alternative identity)	Owner, Operator or Location	Notes
RW393	VS Spitfire XVIe (7293M) [XT-A]	RAF Turnhouse, at main gate	
SL542	VS Spitfire XVIe (8390M) [4M-N]	RAF Coltishall, at main gate	
SL574	VS Spitfire XVIe (8391M)	RAF Bentley Priory	
SL674	VS Spitfire XVIe (8392M)	RAF Memorial Chapel, Biggin Hill	
SM832	VS Spitfire XIV (G-WWII)	Warbirds of GB, Blackbushe	
SM969	VS Spitfire XVIII (G-BRAF)	Warbirds of GB, Blackbushe	
SX137	VS Seafire XVII	FAA Museum, RNAS Yeovilton	
SX300	VS Seafire XVII (A646)	Privately owned, Warwick	
SX336	VS Seafire XVII (A2055)	Privately owned, Newark	
TA122	DH Mosquito FBVI [UP-G]	Mosquito Aircraft Museum, London Colney	
TA634	DH Mosquito B35 (G-AWJV)	Mosquito Aircraft Museum, London Colney	
TA639	DH Mosquito TT35 (7806M)	RAF Cosford Aerospace Museum	
TA719	DH Mosquito TT35 (G-ASKC) [6T]	Skyfame Collection, Duxford	
TB252	VS Spitfire XVIe (7257M) [GW-H]	RAF Leuchars, at main gate	
TB382	VS Spitfire XVIe (7244M)	RAF Exhibition Flight, Abingdon	
TB752	VS Spitfire XVIe (7256M) [KH-Z]	RAF Manston, Memorial Hall	
TB863	VS Spitfire XVIe (G-CDAN)	Privately owned, Booker	
TD248	VS Spitfire XVIe (7246M) [DW-A]	RAF Sealand, at main gate	
TE184	VS Spitfire XVIe (6850M) [LA-A]	Ulster Folk & Transport Museum, County Down	
TE311	VS Spitfire XVIe (7241M) [AU-Y]	RAF Exhibition Flight, Abingdon	
TE356	VS Spitfire XVIe (6709M/ 7001M)	RAF Scampton	
TE392	VS Spitfire XVIe (7000M)	Warbirds of GB, Blackbushe	
TE462	VS Spitfire XVIe (7243M)	Royal Scottish Museum of Flight, East Fortune	
TE476	VS Spitfire XVIe (7451M/ 8071M)	RAF Northolt at main gate	
TE517	VS Spitfire IX (G-BIXP)	Privately owned, Duxford	
TE566	VS Spitfire IX (G-BLCK)	Privately owned, Hastings	
TF956	Hawker Sea Fury FB11 [123/T]	RN Historic Flight, RNAS Yeovilton	
TG263	Saro SRA1 (G-12-1)	Skyfame Collection, Duxford	
TG511	HP Hastings T5 (8554M)	RAF Cosford Aerospace Museum	
TG517	HP Hastings T5 [517]	Newark Air Museum, Winthorpe	
TG528	HP Hastings C1A	Skyfame Collection, Duxford	
TG536	HP Hastings C1A (8405M)	RAF FF&SS Catterick	
TG568	HP Hastings C1A	RAE Bedford Fire Section	
TJ118	DH Mosquito TT35	Mosquito Aircraft Museum	
TJ138	DH Mosquito B35 (7607M) [V-O]	RAF Museum Store, Swinderby	
TJ343	Auster 5 (G-AJXC)	Privately owned, Popham	
TJ472	Auster AOP5 (BAPC 70)	Royal Scottish Museum of Flight, East Fortune	
TJ569	Auster 5 (G-AKOW)	Museum of Army Flying, Middle Wallop	
TJ672	Auster 5 (G-ANIJ)	Privately owned, Thruxton	
TK777	GAL Hamilcar	Museum of Army Flying, Middle Wallop	
TL615	Airspeed Horsa II	Mosquito Aircraft Museum, London Colney	
TL659	Airspeed Horsa (BAPC 80) [74]	Museum of Army Flying, Middle Wallop	
TV959	DH Mosquito T3 [AF-V]	Imperial War Museum, Lambeth	
TW117	DH Mosquito T3 (7805M)	Bomber Command Museum, Hendon	
TW439	Auster 5 (G-ANRP)	Warnham War Museum, Horsham	
TW536	Auster AOP6 (7704M)	Museum of Army Flying, Middle Wallop	
TW641	Auster AOP6 (G-ATDN)	Privately owned, Biggin Hill	
TX183	Avro Anson C19	Privately owned, Duxford	
TX192	Avro Anson C19	Guernsey Airport Fire Section	
TX213	Avro Anson C19 (G-AWRS)	North East Aircraft Museum, Sunderland	

Notes	Serial	Type (alternative identity)	Owner, Operator or Location
	TX214	Avro Anson C19 (7817M)	RAF Cosford Aerospace Museum
	TX226	Avro Anson C19 (7865M)	Imperial War Museum, Duxford
	TX228	Avro Anson C19	City of Norwich Aviation Museum
	TX235	Avro Anson C19	Torbay Aircraft Museum, Paignton
	VF301	DH Vampire F1 (7060M)	Midland Air Museum, Coventry
	VF516	Auster AOP6 (G-ASMZ)	Privately owned, Middle Wallop
	VH127	Fairey Firefly TT4	FAA Museum, RNAS Yeovilton
	VL348	Avro Anson C19 (G-AVVO)	Newark Air Museum, Winthorpe
	VL349	Avro Anson C19 (G-AWSA)	Norfolk & Suffolk Aviation Museum, Flixton
	VM325	Avro Anson C19	Midland Air Museum, Coventry
	VM360	Avro Anson C19 (G-APHV)	Royal Scottish Museum of Flight, East Fortune
	VM791	Slingsby Cadet TX3 (really XA312)	RAF No 1 MGSP, Halton
	VN148	Grunau Baby	Russavia Collection, Duxford
	VP293	Avro Shackleton T4	Strathallan Aircraft Collection
	VP519	Avro Anson C19 nose only	The Aeroplane Collection, Gtr Manchester
	VP952	DH Devon C2 (8820M)	RAF St Athan Historic Aircraft Collection
	VP955	DH Devon C2 (G-DVON)	Privately owned, Staverton
	VP956	DH Devon C2	No 1404 Sqn ATC, RAF Manston
	VP957	DH Devon C2 (8822M)	RAF BDRT, Bishop's Court, NI
	VP958	DH Devon C2 [DC] (8795M)	RAF CTTS, St Athan
	VP959	DH Devon C2 [L]	MoD(PE) RAE Farnborough
	VP960	DH Devon C2	CTE, RAF Manston
	VP962	DH Devon C2 (G-BLRB)	Privately owned, RAF Kemble
	VP963	DH Devon C2	CTE, RAF Manston
	VP965	DH Devon C2 [DE] (8823M)	RAF Manston Fire Section
	VP968	DH Devon C2	MoD(PE) A&AEE Boscombe Down
	VP971	DH Devon C2 (8824M)	RAF FF&SS, Catterick
	VP973	DH Devon C2 (8512M)	RAF Northolt, ground simulator
	VP975	DH Devon C2 [M]	MoD(PE) RAE Farnborough
	VP976	DH Devon C2 (8784M)	RAF Northolt Fire Section
	VP977	DH Devon C2 (G-ALTS)	RAE West Freugh Fire Section
	VP981	DH Devon C2	RAF Battle of Britain Flight, Scampton
	VR137	Westland Wyvern TF1	FAA Museum, RNAS Yeovilton
	VR249	Percival Prentice T1 (G-APIY) [FA-EL]	Newark Air Museum, Winthorpe
	VR930	Hawker Sea Fury FB11 (8382M)	FAA Museum store, Wroughton
	VS356	Percival Prentice T1 (G-AOLU)	Scottish Aircraft Collection Trust, Perth
	VS562	Avro Anson T21 (8012M)	No 2445 Sqn ATC, RAE Llanbedr
	VS610	Percival Prentice T1 (G-AOKL) [K-L]	Privately owned, Southend
	VS623	Percival Prentice T1 (G-AOKZ)	Midland Air Museum, Coventry
	VT229	Gloster Meteor F4 (7151M) [60]	Newark Air Museum, Winthorpe
	VT260	Gloster Meteor F4 [67] (8813M)	RAF Portreath, for display
	VT409	Fairey Firefly AS5	North East Aircraft Museum, Sunderland
	VT812	DH Vampire F3 (7200M) [N]	RAF Museum, Hendon
	VT921	Grunau Baby	Midland Air Museum, Coventry
	VT935	Boulton Paul P111A	Midland Air Museum, Coventry
	VV106	VS510 (7175M)	RAF Cosford Aerospace Museum
	VV217	DH Vampire FB5 (7323M)	No 301 Sqn ATC, Bury St Edmunds
	VV901	Avro Anson T21	Pennine Aviation Museum, Bacup
	VW453	Gloster Meteor T7 (8703M)	Cotswold Aircraft Restoration Group, RAF Innsworth
	VX250	DH Sea Hornet 21 [48]	Mosquito Aircraft Museum, London Colney
	VX272	Hawker P1052 (7174M)	RAF Cosford Aerospace Museum
	VX275	Slingsby Sedbergh TX1	RAF St Athan
	VX302	Hawker Sea Fury T20 (G-BCOV) [77/M]	Warbirds of GB, Blackbushe
	VX461	DH Vampire FB5 (7646M)	RAF Museum Store, Henlow
	VX573	Vickers Valetta C2 (8389M)	RAF Cosford Aerospace Museum

Serial	Type (alternative identity)	Owner, Operator or Location	Notes
VX577	Vickers Valetta C2	North East Aircraft Museum, Sunderland	
VX580	Vickers Valetta C2	Norfolk & Suffolk Aviation Museum Flixton	
VX595	Westland Dragonfly HR1 [29]	RAF Museum Store, Henlow	
VX653	Hawker Sea Fury FB11	RAF Museum, Hendon	
VZ304	DH Vampire FB5 (7630M) [S]	Privately owned, Bushey	
VZ345	Hawker Sea Fury T20	MoD(PE) ETPS Boscombe Down	
VZ462	Gloster Meteor F8	Second World War Aircraft Preservation Society, Lasham	
VZ467	Gloster Meteor F8 [01]	RAF Shawbury store	
VZ608	Gloster Meteor FR9	Newark Air Museum, Winthorpe	
VZ634	Gloster Meteor T7 (8657M)	No 1331 Sqn ATC, RAF Wattisham	
VZ638	Gloster Meteor T7 (G-JETM)	Brencham Historic Collection, Bournemouth	
VZ728	RS4 Desford Trainer (G-AGOS)	Scottish Aircraft Collection Trust, Perth	
VZ962	Westland Dragonfly HR1	Cornwall Aero Park, Helston	
VZ965	Westland Dragonfly HR5	FAA Museum, at RNAS Culdrose	
WA473	VS Attacker F1 [102/J]	FAA Museum, RNAS Yeovilton	
WA576	Bristol Sycamore 3 (G-ALSS/ 7900M)	Privately owned, East Fortune	
WA577	Bristol Sycamore 3 (G-ALST/ 7718M)	North East Aircraft Museum, Sunderland	
WA591	Gloster Meteor T7 (7917M) [W]	RAF Woodvale, on display	
WA634	Gloster Meteor T7/8	RAF St Athan Historic Aircraft Collection	
WA638	Gloster Meteor T7	Martin Baker Aircraft, Chalgrove	
WA662	Gloster Meteor T7	MoD(PE) RAE Llanbedr	
WA669	Gloster Meteor T7 [02]	RAF Vintage Pair, CFS Scampton	
WA984	Gloster Meteor F8 [A]	Wessex Aviation Society, Wimborne	
WB188	Hawker Hunter F3 (7154M)	RAF St Athan Historic Aircraft Collection	
WB271	Fairey Firefly AS5 [204/R]	RN Historic Flight, RNAS Yeovilton	
WB440	Fairey Firefly AS6	Manchester Air & Space Museum	
WB491	Avro Ashton	Wales Aircraft Museum, Cardiff	
WB530	DH Devon C2 (8825M)	RAF Swinderby, on display	
WB531	DH Devon C2 (G-BLRN)	Privately owned, Staverton	
WB533	DH Devon C2 (G-DEVN) [DA]	British Air Reserve, Lympne	
WB534	DH Devon C2 (G-BLPZ) [DB]	Privately owned, Guernsey	
WB550	DH Chipmunk T10 [F]	RAF FSS, Swinderby	
WB560	DH Chipmunk T10	RAF No 4 AEF, Exeter	
WB565	DH Chipmunk T10 [X]	AAC BFWF, Middle Wallop	
WB567	DH Chipmunk T10	RAF No 12 AEF, Turnhouse	
WB569	DH Chipmunk T10 [2]	RAF No 1 AEF, Manston	
WB575	DH Chipmunk T10 [907]	RN Flying Grading Flt, Plymouth	
WB584	DH Chipmunk T10 PAX (7706M)	RAF No 12 AEF, Turnhouse	
WB586	DH Chipmunk T10 [A]	RAF No 6 AEF, Abingdon	
WB588	DH Chipmunk T10 (G-AOTD)	Shuttleworth Collection, Old Warden	
WB615	DH Chipmunk T10 [E]	AAC BFWF, Middle Wallop	
WB624	DH Chipmunk T10 PAX	The Aeroplane Collection, Warmingham	
WB627	DH Chipmunk T10 [N]	RAF No 5 AEF, Cambridge	
WB645	DH Chipmunk T10 PAX (8218M)	RAFGSA Bicester	
WB647	DH Chipmunk T10 [R]	AAC BFWF, Middle Wallop	
WB652	DH Chipmunk T10 [V]	RAF No 5 AEF, Cambridge	
WB654	DH Chipmunk T10 [14]	RAF No 10 AEF, Woodvale	
WB657	DH Chipmunk T10 [908]	RN Flying Grading Flt, Plymouth	
WB670	DH Chipmunk T10 (8361M)	Newark Air Museum, Winthorpe	
WB671	DH Chipmunk T10 [910]	RN Flying Grading Flt, Plymouth	
WB685	DH Chipmunk T10 PAX	Privately owned, Harrogate	
WB693	DH Chipmunk T10 [S]	AAC BFWF, Middle Wallop	
WB697	DH Chipmunk T10 [O]	RAF No 3 AEF, Filton	
WB739	DH Chipmunk T10 [8]	RAF No 8 AEF, Cosford	
WB754	DH Chipmunk T10 [H]	AAC BFWF, Middle Wallop	
WB758	DH Chipmunk T10 (7729M) [P]	Torbay Aircraft Museum, Paignton	

Notes	Serial	Type (alternative identity)	Owner, Operator or Location
	WB763	DH Chipmunk T10 (G-BBMR) [14]	Southall Technical College
	WB919	Slingsby Sedbergh TXI (G-ALLH)	RAF store, Syerston
	WB920	Slingsby Sedbergh TXI	RAF store, Syerston
	WB922	Slingsby Sedbergh TXI	RAF No 615 VGS, Kenley
	WB923	Slingsby Sedbergh TXI	RAF Cranwell Glider Flight
	WB924	Slingsby Sedbergh TXI	RAF store, Syerston
	WB926	Slingsby Sedbergh TXI	RAF store, Syerston
	WB927	Slingsby Sedbergh TXI	RAF No 615 VGS, Kenley
	WB932	Slingsby Sedbergh TXI	RAF No 615 VGS, Kenley
	WB934	Slingsby Sedbergh TXI [A]	RAF No 618 VGS, West Malling
	WB935	Slingsby Sedbergh TXI	RAF No 631 VGS, Sealand
	WB937	Slingsby Sedbergh TXI	RAF No 643 VGS, Scampton
	WB938	Slingsby Sedbergh TXI	RAF Halton Glider Flight
	WB939	Slingsby Sedbergh TXI	RAF store, Syerston
	WB941	Slingsby Sedbergh TXI	RAF store, Syerston
	WB942	Slingsby Sedbergh TXI	RAF ACCGS/No 644 VGS, Syerston
	WB944	Slingsby Sedbergh TXI	RAF No 622 VGS, Upavon
	WB946	Slingsby Sedbergh TXI	RAF No 631 VGS, Sealand
	WB947	Slingsby Sedbergh TXI	RAF store, Syerston
	WB958	Slingsby Sedbergh TXI	RAF No 621 VGS, Weston-super-Mare
	WB960	Slingsby Sedbergh TXI	RAF No 4 MGSP, Dishforth
	WB961	Slingsby Sedbergh TXI	RAF No 661 VGS, Kirknewton
	WB962	Slingsby Sedbergh TXI	RAF store, Syerston
	WB963	Slingsby Sedbergh TXI	RAF No 618 VGS, West Malling
	WB971	Slingsby Sedbergh TXI	RAF No 631 VGS, Sealand
	WB972	Slingsby Sedbergh TXI	RAF No 626 VGS, Predannack
	WB973	Slingsby Sedbergh TXI	RAF No 634 VGS, St Athan
	WB974	Slingsby Sedbergh TXI	RAF No 663 VGS, Kinloss
	WB975	Slingsby Sedbergh TXI	RAF No 661 VGS, Kirknewton
	WB976	Slingsby Sedbergh TXI	RAF store, Syerston
	WB978	Slingsby Sedbergh TXI	RAF No 643 VGS, Scampton
	WB979	Slingsby Sedbergh TXI	RAF No 663 VGS, Kinloss
	WB980	Slingsby Sedbergh TXI	RAF No 614 VGS, Wethersfield
	WB981	Slingsby Sedbergh TXI	RAF No 631 VGS, Sealand
	WB983	Slingsby Sedbergh TXI	RAF No 634 VGS, St Athan
	WB985	Slingsby Sedbergh TXI	RAF store, Syerston
	WB986	Slingsby Sedbergh TXI	RAF No 614 VGS, Wethersfield
	WB987	Slingsby Sedbergh TXI	RAF No 662 VGS, Arbroath
	WB988	Slingsby Sedbergh TXI	RAF store, Syerston
	WB989	Slingsby Sedbergh TXI	RAF No 631 VGS, Sealand
	WB990	Slingsby Sedbergh TXI	RAF No 622 VGS, Upavon
	WB991	Slingsby Sedbergh TXI	RAF No 621 VGS, Weston-super-Mare
	WB992	Slingsby Sedbergh TXI	RAF store, Syerston
	WB993	Slingsby Sedbergh TXI	RAF No 631 VGS, Sealand
	WD289	DH Chipmunk T10	RAF Gatow Station Flight, Berlin
	WD293	DH Chipmunk T10 PAX (7645M)	No 2308 Sqn ATC, Cwmbran
	WD310	DH Chipmunk T10 [905]	RAF Shawbury store
	WD318	DH Chipmunk T10 PAX (8207M)	No 145 Sqn ATC, Timperley
	WD325	DH Chipmunk T10 [N]	AAC BFWF, Middle Wallop
	WD331	DH Chipmunk T10 [A]	RAF FSS, Swinderby
	WD356	DH Chipmunk T10 (7625M)	Lincoln Field Vintage & HAC, Bushey
	WD363	DH Chipmunk T10 (G-BCIH)	Privately owned, Stansted
	WD373	DH Chipmunk T10 [12]	RAF No 2 AEF, Hurn
	WD374	DH Chipmunk T10 [903]	RN Flying Grading Flt, Plymouth
	WD390	DH Chipmunk T10 [84]	RAF No 9 AEF, Finningley
	WD413	Avro Anson C 21 (G-BFIR/ 7881M)	Privately owned, Booker
	WD480	HP Hastings C2	RAE Farnborough Fire Section
	WD496	HP Hastings C2	A&AEE Boscombe Down Fire Section
	WD499	HP Hastings C2	RAF Honington Fire Section
	WD646	Gloster Meteor TT20 (8189M) [R]	No 2030 Sqn ATC, Sheldon
	WD686	Gloster Meteor NF11	Imperial War Museum, Duxford

Serial	Type (alternative identity)	Owner, Operator or Location	Notes
WD790	Gloster Meteor NF11 (8743M) nose only	No 405 Sqn ATC, Darlington	
WD833	Fairey Firefly AS6 [910/NW]	Privately owned, Bruntingthorpe	
WD889	Fairey Firefly AS6	North East Aircraft Museum, Usworth	
WD931	EE Canberra B2 nose only	No 425 Sqn ATC, Aldridge, W Midlands	
WD935	EE Canberra B2 (8440M)	RAF St Athan Historic Aircraft Collection	
WD948	EE Canberra B2 (8530M) [R]	CTE, RAF Manston	
WD955	EE Canberra T17 [EM]	RAF No 360 Sqn, Wyton	
WE113	EE Canberra B2 [BJ]	RAF No 231 OCU, Wyton	
WE139	EE Canberra PR3 (8369M)	RAF Museum, Hendon	
WE146	EE Canberra PR3	RAE Llanbedr Fire Section	
WE168	EE Canberra PR3 (8049M)	RAF Manston, on display	
WE173	EE Canberra PR3 (8740M)	RAF Coltishall, Fire Section	
WE188	EE Canberra T4	BAe Samlesbury, stored	
WE192	EE Canberra T4 [92]	BAe Samlesbury, stored	
WE569	Auster T7 (G-ASAJ)	Privately owned, Oakington	
WE600	Auster T7 (mod) (7602M)	RAF St Athan Historic Aircraft Collection	
WE925	Gloster Meteor F8	Wales Aircraft Museum, Cardiff	
WE982	Slingsby Prefect TXI (8781M)	RAF Museum, Hendon	
WE990	Slingsby Prefect TXI (BGA 2583)	RAFGSA Swanton Morley	
WF122	Sea Prince T1 (A2673) [575/CU]	Cornwall Aero Park, Helston	
WF125	Sea Prince T1 (A2674) [576/CU]	RN Fire School, Predannack	
WF128	Sea Prince T1 (8611M)	Norfolk & Suffolk Aviation Museum, Flixton	
WF137	Sea Prince C1 [999/CU]	Second World War Aircraft Preservation Society, Lasham	
WF219	Hawker Sea Hawk F1 (A2439)	FAA Museum, RNAS Yeovilton	
WF225	Hawker Sea Hawk F1 (A2645) [CU]	RNAS Culdrose, at main gate	
WF259	Hawker Sea Hawk F2 (A2483) [171/A]	Royal Scottish Museum of Flight, East Fortune	
WF299	Hawker Sea Hawk FB3 (A2662/A2509/8164M)	Cornwall Aero Park, Helston	
WF369	Vickers Varsity T1 [F]	Newark Air Museum, Winthorpe	
WF372	Vickers Varsity T1 [T]	Privately owned, Sibson	
WF376	Vickers Varsity T1	Bristol Airport Fire Section	
WF379	Vickers Varsity T1	RAE West Freugh, Fire Section	
WF408	Vickers Varsity T1 (8395M)	RAF Cosford Aerospace Museum	
WF410	Vickers Varsity T1 [F]	Brunel Technical College, Lulsgate	
WF413	Vickers Varsity T1 [V]	CTE, RAF Manston	
WF425	Vickers Varsity T1	Imperial War Museum, Duxford	
WF643	Gloster Meteor F8 [X]	Norfolk & Suffolk Aviation Museum, Flixton	
WF784	Gloster Meteor T7 (7895M)	RAF Quedgeley, at main gate	
WF791	Gloster Meteor T7	RAF CFS, Scampton	
WF825	Gloster Meteor T7 (8359M) [Z]	No 2491 Sqn ATC, RAF Lyneham	
WF877	Gloster Meteor T7	Torbay Aircraft Museum, Paignton	
WF890	EE Canberra T17 [EJ]	RAF No 360 Sqn, Wyton	
WF911	EE Canberra B2 nose only	Pennine Aviation Museum, Bacup	
WF916	EE Canberra T17 [EL]	RAF No 360 Sqn, Wyton	
WF922	EE Canberra PR3	Midland Air Museum, Coventry	
WG303	DH Chipmunk T10 PAX (8208M)	RAFGSA, Bicester	
WG307	DH Chipmunk 22 (G-BCYJ)	Privately owned, Lossiemouth	
WG308	DH Chipmunk T10	RAF No 7 AEF, Newton	
WG316	DH Chipmunk 22 (G-BCAH)	Privately owned, Cranfield	
WG321	DH Chipmunk T10 [G]	AAC BFWF, Middle Wallop	
WG323	DH Chipmunk T10 [F]	AAC BFWF, Middle Wallop	
WG348	DH Chipmunk 22 (G-BBMV)	Privately owned, Booker	
WG350	DH Chipmunk 22 (G-BCYE)	Privately owned, Biggin Hill	
WG403	DH Chipmunk T10 [O]	AAC BFWF, Middle Wallop	

Notes	Serial	Type (alternative identity)	Owner, Operator or Location
	WG407	DH Chipmunk T10 [81]	RAF No 9 AEF, Finningley
	WG418	DH Chipmunk T10 PAX (8209M/G-ATDY)	RAF No 10 AEF, Woodvale
	WG419	DH Chipmunk T10 PAX (8206M)	RAF Finningley
	WG422	DH Chipmunk 22 (G-BFAX/ 8394M)	Privately owned, Sibson
	WG430	DH Chipmunk T10 [I]	RAF No 1 AEF, Manston
	WG432	DH Chipmunk T10 [L]	AAC BFWF, Middle Wallop
	WG458	DH Chipmunk T10	RAF Shawbury store
	WG463	DH Chipmunk T10 PAX (8363M)	No 188 Sqn ATC, Ipswich
	WG464	DH Chipmunk T10 PAX (8364M)	No 131 Sqn ATC, Newcastle
	WG465	DH Chipmunk 22 (G-BCEY)	Privately owned, Debden
	WG466	DH Chipmunk T10	AAC store, RAF Shawbury
	WG469	DH Chipmunk T10	RAF No 7 AEF, Newton
	WG471	DH Chipmunk T10 PAX (8210M)	RAF No 11 AEF, Leeming
	WG477	DH Chipmunk T10 PAX (8362M)	No 281 Sqn ATC, Birkdale
	WG478	DH Chipmunk T10 [J]	RAF Shawbury store
	WG479	DH Chipmunk T10 [K]	RAF FSS, Swinderby
	WG480	DH Chipmunk T10 [K]	RAF Shawbury store
	WG486	DH Chipmunk T10	AAC store, RAF Shawbury
	WG496	Slingsby Sedbergh TXI	RAF Halton Glider Flight
	WG497	Slingsby Sedbergh TXI	RAF store, Syerston
	WG498	Slingsby Sedbergh TXI	RAF Cranwell Glider Flight
	WG499	Slingsby Sedbergh TXI	RAF store, Syerston
	WG655	Hawker Sea Fury T20 [910/GN]	RN Historic Flight, RNAS Yeovilton
	WG718	WS51 Dragonfly HR5 (A2531) [934/-]	Wales Aircraft Museum, Cardiff
	WG719	WS51 Dragonfly HR5 (G-BRMA) [902]	British Rotorcraft Museum, Weston-super-Mare
	WG724	WS51 Dragonfly HR5 [932]	North East Aircraft Museum
	WG751	WS51 Dragonfly HR5	Privately owned, Ramsgreave, Lancs
	WG752	WS51 Dragonfly HR5 [901]	Alleyn's School CCF, Dulwich
	WG760	English Electric P1A (7755M)	RAF Binbrook
	WG763	English Electric P1A (7816M)	Manchester Air & Space Museum
	WG768	Short SB5 (8005M)	RAF Cosford Aerospace Museum
	WG774	BAC 221	Science Museum, RNAS Yeovilton
	WG777	Fairey FD2 (7986M)	RAF Cosford Aerospace Museum
	WG789	EE Canberra B2	MoD(PE) RAE Bedford
	WH132	Gloster Meteor T7 (7906M) [J]	No 276 Sqn ATC, Chelmsford
	WH166	Gloster Meteor T7 (8052M)	RAF Digby, at main gate
	WH291	Gloster Meteor F8	Second World War Aircraft Preservation Society, Lasham
	WH301	Gloster Meteor F8 (7930M) [T]	RAF Museum, Hendon
	WH364	Gloster Meteor F8 (8169M)	RAF Kemble, at main gate
	WH453	Gloster Meteor D16 [L]	MoD(PE) RAE Llanbedr
	WH589	Hawker Sea Fury (G-AGHB)	Privately owned, Cranfield
	WH646	EE Canberra T17 [EG]	RAF No 360 Sqn, Wyton
	WH657	EE Canberra B2	RFD Ltd, Godalming
	WH664	EE Canberra T17 [EH]	RAF No 360 Sqn, Wyton
	WH665	EE Canberra T17 (8763M) [J]	RAF No 2 SoTT, Cosford
	WH670	EE Canberra B2 [CB]	RAF No 100 Sqn, Wyton
	WH699	EE Canberra B2T (8755M) (really WJ637)	RAFC Cranwell, Trenchard Hall on display
	WH703	EE Canberra B2 (8490M) [S]	RAF Abingdon, BDRF
	WH718	EE Canberra TT18 [CW]	RAF No 100 Sqn, Wyton
	WH725	EE Canberra B2	Imperial War Museum, Duxford
	WH734	EE Canberra TT2	Flight Refuelling Ltd, Hurn
	WH740	EE Canberra T17 (8762M) [K]	RAF No 2 SoTT, Cosford
	WH773	EE Canberra PR7 (8696M)	No 2331 Sqn ATC, RAF Wyton
	WH774	EE Canberra PR7	MoD(PE) RAE Farnborough, stored
	WH775	EE Canberra PR7 (8628M)	RAF St Athan, stored

Serial	Type (alternative identity)	Owner, Operator or Location	Notes
WH779	EE Canberra PR7 [CK]	RAF No 100 Sqn, Wyton	
WH780	EE Canberra T22 [853]	RN FRADU, Yeovilton	
WH791	EE Canberra PR7 (8187M)	RAF Cottesmore, at main gate	
WH794	EE Canberra PR7 (8652M)	RAF Catterick, BDRF	
WH796	EE Canberra PR7 (nose only)	Bomber County Museum, Cleethorpes	
WH797	EE Canberra T22 [851]	RN FRADU, Yeovilton	
WH798	EE Canberra PR7	Wales Aircraft Museum, Cardiff	
WH801	EE Canberra T22 [850]	RN FRADU, Yeovilton	
WH803	EE Canberra T22 [856]	RN FRADU, Yeovilton	
WH840	EE Canberra T4 (8350M)	RAF Locking, at main gate	
WH844	EE Canberra T4	MoD(PE) RAE Farnborough, stored	
WH846	EE Canberra T4	BAe Samlesbury, stored	
WH848	EE Canberra T4 [BD]	RAF No 231 OCU, Wyton	
WH849	EE Canberra T4 [BE]	RAF No 231 OCU, Wyton	
WH850	EE Canberra T4	BAe Samlesbury, stored	
WH854	EE Canberra B2 nose only	Martin Baker Aircraft, Chalgrove	
WH856	EE Canberra TT18 (8742M) [849]	RAF Abingdon, AS&RU	
WH863	EE Canberra T17 (8693M)	RAF Marham, BDRT	
WH869	EE Canberra B2 (8515M)	RAF Abingdon, BDRF	
WH872	EE Canberra T17 [W]	RAE Bedford Fire Section	
WH876	EE Canberra D14	MoD(PE) A&AEE Boscombe Down	
WH887	EE Canberra TT18 [847]	RN FRADU, Yeovilton	
WH902	EE Canberra T17 [EK]	RAF No 360 Sqn, Wyton	
WH903	EE Canberra B2 (8584M) nose only	RAF Exhibition Flight, Abingdon	
WH904	EE Canberra T19 [04]	Marshalls, Cambridge in store	
WH911	EE Canberra E15	Wales Aircraft Museum, Cardiff	
WH914	EE Canberra B2 (G-29-373) [U]	BAe Samlesbury, stored	
WH919	EE Canberra B2	RAF St Athan, stored	
WH946	EE Canberra B6 (Mod) (8185M)	Bomber County Aviation Museum, Cleethorpes	
WH952	EE Canberra B6	MoD(PE) RAE Bedford, for ground instruction	
WH953	EE Canberra B6	MoD(PE) RAE Bedford	
WH957	EE Canberra E15 [CX]	RAF St Athan, stored	
WH960	EE Canberra B15 (8344M) [A]	RAF No 2 SoTT, Cosford	
WH964	EE Canberra E15 [V]	RAF St Athan, stored	
WH972	EE Canberra E15 [CM]	RAF No 100 Sqn, Wyton	
WH981	EE Canberra E15 [CN]	RAF No 100 Sqn, Wyton	
WH983	EE Canberra E15 [CP]	RAF No 100 Sqn, Wyton	
WH984	EE Canberra B15 (8101M) [E]	RAF No 2 SoTT, Cosford	
WH991	WS51 Dragonfly HR5	Lincolnshire Aviation Museum, Tattershall	
WJ231	Hawker Sea Fury FB11 [115/0]	FAA Museum, RNAS Yeovilton	
WJ288	Hawker Sea Fury FB11 (G-SALY) [029]	Privately owned, Lympne	
WJ306	Slingsby Sedbergh TXI	RAF No 621 VGS, Weston-super-Mare	
WJ329	Handley Page Hastings C2	RAF Leeming Fire Section	
WJ349	Percival Sea Prince C2	No 11 Sqn ATC, Weybridge	
WJ350	Percival Sea Prince C2	Guernsey Airport Fire Section	
WJ358	Auster AOP6 (G-ARYD)	Museum of Army Flying, Middle Wallop	
WJ565	EE Canberra T17 [C]	RAF St Athan, stored	
WJ567	EE Canberra B2 [CC]	RAF No 100 Sqn, Wyton	
WJ573	EE Canberra B2 (7656M)	RAF Museum Store, Henlow	
WJ574	EE Canberra TT18 [844]	RN FRADU, Yeovilton	
WJ576	EE Canberra T17	Wales Aircraft Museum, Cardiff	
WJ581	EE Canberra T17	Wales Aircraft Museum, Cardiff	
WJ603	EE Canberra B2 (8664M) [G]	RAF Wattisham, BDRT	
WJ607	EE Canberra T17 [EB]	RAF No 360 Sqn, Wyton	
WJ611	EE Canberra B2 (8451M)	Aldergrove Fire Section	
WJ614	EE Canberra TT18 [846]	RN FRADU, Yeovilton	
WJ627	EE Canberra B2	RAE Bedford Fire Section	
WJ629	EE Canberra TT18 (8747M) [845]	RAF Chivenor, BDRT	
WJ630	EE Canberra T17 [ED]	RAF No 360 Sqn, Wyton	

Notes	Serial	Type (alternative identity)	Owner, Operator or Location
	WJ633	EE Canberra T17 [EF]	RAF No 360 Sqn, Wyton
	WJ636	EE Canberra TT18 [842]	RN FRADU, Yeovilton
	WJ639	EE Canberra TT18 [39]	BAe Samlesbury, stored
	WJ640	EE Canberra B2 (8722M) [L]	RAF No 2 SoTT, Cosford
	WJ676	EE Canberra B2 (7796M)	Princess Alexandra RAF Hospital Wroughton
	WJ678	EE Canberra B2 [CF]	RAF No 100 Sqn, Wyton
	WJ680	EE Canberra TT18 [CT]	RAF No 100 Sqn, Wyton
	WJ681	EE Canberra B2T (8735M)	RAF Brawdy Fire Section
	WJ682	EE Canberra TT18 [CU]	RAF No 100 Sqn, Wyton
	WJ715	EE Canberra TT18 [CV]	RAF No 100 Sqn, Wyton
	WJ717	EE Canberra TT18 [841]	RN FRADU, Yeovilton
	WJ721	EE Canberra TT18 [21]	BAe Samlesbury, stored
	WJ722	EE Canberra B2	Privately owned, Macclesfield
	WJ731	EE Canberra B2 [BK]	RAF No 231 OCU, Wyton
	WJ756	EE Canberra E15 [CL]	RAF No 100 Sqn, Wyton
	WJ775	EE Canberra B6 (8581M) [Z]	CSDE RAF, Swanton Morley
	WJ817	EE Canberra PR7 (8695M)	RAF Wyton, BDRT
	WJ821	EE Canberra PR7 (8668M)	Bassingbourn, on display
	WJ825	EE Canberra PR7 (8697M)	RAF Honington, BDRT
	WJ861	EE Canberra T4 [BF]	RAF No 231 OCU, Wyton
	WJ865	EE Canberra T4	RAE Apprentice School, Farnborough
	WJ866	EE Canberra T4 [BL]	RAF No 231 OCU, Wyton
	WJ867	EE Canberra T4 (8643M)	RAF Abingdon
	WJ870	EE Canberra T4 (8683M)	RAF St Mawgan, BDRF
	WJ872	EE Canberra T4 (8492M) (nose only)	No 2408 Sqn ATC, Hornchurch
	WJ874	EE Canberra T4 [858]	RN FRADU, Yeovilton
	WJ876	EE Canberra T4 nose only	RAF Exhibition Flight, Abingdon
	WJ877	EE Canberra T4 [BG]	RAF No 231 OCU, Wyton
	WJ879	EE Canberra T4 [BH]	RAF No 231 OCU, Wyton
	WJ880	EE Canberra T4 (8491M) [39] nose only	Privately owned, Kilmarnock
	WJ893	Vickers Varsity T1	RAE Aberporth Fire Section
	WJ898	Vickers Varsity T1 [N]	Aldergrove Fire Section
	WJ902	Vickers Varsity T1 [C]	RAF Wittering Fire Section
	WJ903	Vickers Varsity T1 [C]	Dumfries & Galloway Aviation Museum Tinwald Downs
	WJ907	Vickers Varsity T1 [G]	Norwich Airport Fire Section
	WJ916	Vickers Varsity T1	RAF Lyneham Fire Section
	WJ944	Vickers Varsity T1 [Y]	Wales Aircraft Museum, Cardiff
	WJ945	Vickers Varsity T1 (G-BEDV) [21]	Duxford Aviation Society
	WJ975	EE Canberra T19 [S]	Bomber County Aviation Museum, Cleethorpes
	WJ977	EE Canberra T17 (8761M) [R]	RAF Wyton
	WJ981	EE Canberra T17 [EN]	RAF No 360 Sqn, Wyton
	WJ986	EE Canberra T17 [EP]	RAF No 360 Sqn, Wyton
	WJ992	EE Canberra T4	MoD(PE) RAE Bedford
	WK102	EE Canberra T17 [EQ] (8780M)	RAF No 2 SoTT, Cosford
	WK111	EE Canberra T17 [EA]	RAF No 360 Sqn, Wyton
	WK118	EE Canberra TT18 [CQ]	RAF No 100 Sqn, Wyton
	WK122	EE Canberra TT18 [22]	BAe Samlesbury, stored
	WK123	EE Canberra TT18 [840]	RN FRADU, Yeovilton
	WK124	EE Canberra TT18 [CR]	RAF No 100 Sqn, Wyton
	WK126	EE Canberra TT18 [843]	RN FRADU, Yeovilton
	WK127	EE Canberra TT18 [CS]	RAF No 100 Sqn, Wyton
	WK128	EE Canberra B2	Flight Refuelling Ltd, Hurn
	WK142	EE Canberra TT18 [848]	RN FRADU, Yeovilton
	WK143	EE Canberra B2	Flight Refuelling Ltd, Hurn
	WK144	EE Canberra B2 (8689M) [W]	RAF St Athan, fire section
	WK145	EE Canberra B2	RAE Llanbedr Fire Section
	WK146	EE Canberra B2 nose only	RAF Exhibition Flt, Abingdon
	WK162	EE Canberra B2 [CA]	RAF No 100 Sqn, Wyton
	WK163	EE Canberra B6	MoD(PE) RAE Bedford
	WK198	VS Swift F4 (7428M)	North East Aircraft Museum, Usworth

Serial	Type (alternative identity)	Owner, Operator or Location	Notes
WK275	VS Swift F4	Privately owned, Upper Hill, nr Leominster	
WK277	VS Swift FR5 (7719M) [N]	Newark Air Museum, Winthorpe	
WK281	VS Swift FR5 (7712M) [S]	RAF St Athan Historic Aircraft Collection	
WK511	DH Chipmunk T10 [905]	RN store, RAF Shawbury	
WK512	DH Chipmunk T10 [A]	AAC BFWF, Middle Wallop	
WK517	DH Chipmunk T10 [84]	RAF No 11 AEF, Leeming	
WK518	DH Chipmunk T10	RAF Battle of Britain Flight, Coningsby	
WK549	DH Chipmunk T10 [Y]	Privately owned, Currock Hill	
WK550	DH Chipmunk T10 [J]	RAF FSS, Swinderby	
WK554	DH Chipmunk T10	RAF store, Shawbury	
WK559	DH Chipmunk T10 [M]	AAC BFWF, Middle Wallop	
WK562	DH Chipmunk T10 [T]	RAF No 3 AEF, Filton	
WK570	DH Chipmunk T10 PAX (8211M)	RAF No 358 Sqn ATC, Hurn	
WK572	DH Chipmunk T10 [X]	RAF No 3 AEF, Filton	
WK574	DH Chipmunk T10 [738/VL]	RNAS Yeovilton Station Flight	
WK575	DH Chipmunk T10 PAX [F]	No 301 Sqn ATC, Bury St Edmunds	
WK576	DH Chipmunk T10 PAX (8357M)	No 1206 Sqn ATC, Lichfield	
WK585	DH Chipmunk T10	RAF No 12 AEF, Turnhouse	
WK586	DH Chipmunk T10	RAF Shawbury store	
WK587	DH Chipmunk T10 PAX (8212M)	St Ignatius Coll, Enfield	
WK589	DH Chipmunk T10 [C]	RAF No 6 AEF, Abingdon	
WK590	DH Chipmunk T10 [82]	RAF No 9 AEF, Finningley	
WK608	DH Chipmunk T10 [906]	RN Flying Grading Flt, Plymouth	
WK609	DH Chipmunk T10 [L]	RAF No 3 AEF, Filton	
WK613	DH Chipmunk T10 [P]	Pennine Aviation Museum, Bacup	
WK620	DH Chipmunk T10 [T]	AAC BFWF, Middle Wallop	
WK624	DH Chipmunk T10 [12]	RAF No 10 AEF, Woodvale	
WK626	DH Chipmunk T10 PAX (8213M)	Privately owned, White Waltham	
WK630	DH Chipmunk T10 [11]	RAF No 2 AEF, Hurn	
WK633	DH Chipmunk T10 [B]	RAF FSS, Swinderby	
WK634	DH Chipmunk T10 [902]	RN Flying Grading Flt, Plymouth	
WK635	DH Chipmunk T10	RNAS Yeovilton, Station Flight	
WK638	DH Chipmunk T10 [83]	RAF No 9 AEF, Finningley	
WK639	DH Chipmunk T10 [10]	RAF No 10 AEF, Woodvale	
WK640	DH Chipmunk T10 [C]	RAF FSS, Swinderby	
WK642	DH Chipmunk T10	RAF No 4 AEF, Exeter	
WK643	DH Chipmunk T10 [G]	RAF FSS, Swinderby	
WK654	Gloster Meteor F8 (8092M) [X]	RAF Neatishead, at main gate	
WK714	Gloster Meteor F8 (really WK914) [K]	RAeS Medway Branch, Rochester	
WK800	Gloster Meteor D16 [Z]	MoD(PE) RAE Llanbedr	
WK935	Gloster Meteor Prone Pilot (7869M)	RAF Cosford Aerospace Museum	
WK968	Gloster Meteor F8 (8053M) [A]	RAF Odiham, at main gate	
WK991	Gloster Meteor F8 (7825M)	Imperial War Museum, Duxford	
WL168	Gloster Meteor F8 (7750M) [A]	RAF St Athan Historic Aircraft Collection	
WL181	Gloster Meteor F8	North East Aircraft Museum, Usworth	
WL332	Gloster Meteor T7	Wales Aircraft Museum, Cardiff	
WL345	Gloster Meteor T7	Privately owned, Hastings	
WL349	Gloster Meteor T7 [Z]	Staverton Airport, on display	
WL360	Gloster Meteor T7 (7920M) [G]	RAF Locking, at main gate	
WL375	Gloster Meteor T7	Dumfries & Galloway Aviation Museum, Tinwald Downs	
WL405	Gloster Meteor T7	North East Aircraft Museum, Usworth	
WL419	Gloster Meteor T7	Martin Baker Aircraft, Chalgrove	
WL505	DH Vampire FB9 (7705M)	RAF St Athan Historic Aircraft Collection	

Notes	Serial	Type (alternative identity)	Owner, Operator or Location
	WL626	Vickers Varsity T1 (G-BHDD) [P]	East Midlands Historic Aircraft Group
	WL627	Vickers Varsity T1 (8488M) [D]	RAF Newton Fire Section
	WL628	Vickers Varsity T1 [X]	RAF Wattisham Fire Section
	WL635	Vickers Varsity T1	RAF Machrihanish Police School
	WL678	Vickers Varsity T1 [C]	Leeds-Bradford Airport Fire Section
	WL679	Vickers Varsity T1	MoD(PE) RAE Farnborough
	WL732	BP Sea Balliol T21	RAF Cosford Aerospace Museum
	WL738	Avro Shackleton MR2C (8567M)	RAF Lossiemouth, at main gate
	WL741	Avro Shackleton AEW2 (8692M)	CTE, RAF Manston
	WL747	Avro Shackleton AEW2	RAF No 8 Sqn, Lossiemouth
	WL754	Avro Shackleton AEW2 (8665M) [54]	RAF Valley, fire section
	WL756	Avro Shackleton AEW2	RAF No 8 Sqn, Lossiemouth
	WL757	Avro Shackleton AEW2	RAF No 8 Sqn, Lossiemouth
	WL790	Avro Shackleton AEW2	RAF No 8 Sqn, Lossiemouth
	WL795	Avro Shackleton AEW2 (8753M)	RAF St Mawgan, on display
	WL798	Avro Shackleton MR2C (8114M) [Z]	RAF No 2 SoTT, Cosford
	WL801	Avro Shackleton MR2C (8629M) [01]	RAF No 2 SoTT, Cosford
	WL925	Slingsby Cadet TX3 (really WV925)	Air Cadet Recruiting Team, Cosford
	WM145	AW Meteor NF11 (nose only)	N. Yorks Recovery Group, Chop Gate
	WM167	AW Meteor TT20 (G-LOSM) [M]	Brencham Historic Collection, Hurn
	WM224	AW Meteor TT20 (8177M) [X]	Privately owned, North Weald
	WM292	AW Meteor TT20 [841]	Wales Aircraft Museum, Cardiff
	WM366	AW Meteor NF13 (4X-FNA)	Second World War Aircraft Preservation Society, store
	WM571	DH Sea Venom FAW 21 [742/VL]	Wessex Aviation Society, Wimborne
	WM913	Hawker Sea Hawk FB5 (A2510/8162M) [616]	Newark Air Museum, Winthorpe
	WM961	Hawker Sea Hawk FB5 [J] (A2517)	Torbay Aircraft Museum, Paignton
	WM969	Hawker Sea Hawk FB5 (A2530)	Imperial War Museum, Duxford
	WM983	Hawker Sea Hawk FB5 (A2511)	Chilton Cantelo House School, Somerset
	WM993	Hawker Sea Hawk FB5 (A2522)	RN HMS Royal Arthur, Corsham
	WM994	Hawker Sea Hawk FB5 (A2503/G-SEAH)	Brencham Historic Collection, Hurn
	WN108	Hawker Sea Hawk FB5 [033]	Shorts Apprentice School, Belfast
	WN464	Fairey Gannet AS6 (A2540)	Cornwall Aero Park, Helston
	WN493	WS51 Dragonfly HR5	FAA Museum, RNAS Yeovilton
	WN499	WS51 Dragonfly HR5 [Y]	Torbay Aircraft Museum, Paignton
	WN516	BP Balliol T2	North East Aircraft Museum
	WN901	Hawker Hunter F2 (7543M)	RAF Newton Fire Section
	WN904	Hawker Hunter F2 (7544M) [3]	Imperial War Museum, Duxford
	WN907	Hawker Hunter F2 (7416M)	Staravia, Ascot
	WP180	Hawker Hunter F5 (8473M) [K] (really WP190)	RAF Stanbridge, at main gate
	WP185	Hawker Hunter F5 (7583M)	RAF Museum, Hendon
	WP270	EoN Eton TX1 (8598M)	Manchester Air & Space Museum
	WP271	EoN Eton TX1	Stored Keevil
	WP314	Percival Sea Prince T1 (8634M) [579/CU]	RAF Police School, Syerston
	WP320	Percival Sea Prince T1 [573/CU]	RAF Leuchars Fire Section

Serial	Type (alternative Identity)	Owner, Operator or Location	Notes
WP321	Percival Sea Prince T1 (G-BRFC) [750/CU]	Privately owned, Bourn	
WP503	WS51 Dragonfly HR3 [901]	Bomber County Aviation Museum, Cleethorpes	
WP515	EE Canberra B2	RAF No 100 Sqn, Wyton	
WP772	DH Chipmunk T10 [Q]	AAC BFWF, Middle Wallop	
WP776	DH Chipmunk T10 [817]	RNAS Culdrose Station Flight	
WP784	DH Chipmunk T10 PAX	Privately owned, RAF Abingdon	
WP786	DH Chipmunk T10 [D]	RAF FSS, Swinderby	
WP788	DH Chipmunk 22 (G-BCHL)	Privately owned, Sleap	
WP790	DH Chipmunk 22 (G-BBNC) [T]	Mosquito Aircraft Museum, London Colney	
WP795	DH Chipmunk T10 [901]	RN Flying Grading Flt, Plymouth	
WP801	DH Chipmunk T10 [911]	RN Flying Grading Flt, Plymouth	
WP803	DH Chipmunk T10	RAF Shawbury store	
WP805	DH Chipmunk T10 [D]	RAF No 6 AEF, Abingdon	
WP808	DH Chipmunk 22 (G-BDEU)	Privately owned, Sibson	
WP809	DH Chipmunk T10 [912]	RN, Shawbury store	
WP833	DH Chipmunk T10	RAF No 4 AEF, Exeter	
WP837	DH Chipmunk T10 [L]	RAF No 5 AEF, Cambridge	
WP839	DH Chipmunk T10 [A]	RAF No 8 AEF, Shawbury	
WP840	DH Chipmunk T10 [09]	RAF No 2 AEF, Hurn	
WP843	DH Chipmunk 22 (G-BDBP)	Privately owned, Tollerton	
WP844	DH Chipmunk T10	RAF store, Shawbury	
WP845	DH Chipmunk T10 PAX	No 1329 Sqn ATC, Stroud	
WP851	DH Chipmunk 22 (G-BDET)	Privately owned, Stapleford	
WP855	DH Chipmunk T10 [3]	RAF No 1 AEF, Manston	
WP856	DH Chipmunk T10 [904]	RN Flying Grading Flt, Plymouth	
WP857	DH Chipmunk 22 (G-BDRJ) [24]	Privately owned, Felthorpe	
WP859	DH Chipmunk T10 [E]	RAF No 8 AEF, Shawbury	
WP860	DH Chipmunk T10	RAF No 12 AEF, Turnhouse	
WP863	DH Chipmunk T10 PAX (8360M)	No 1304 Sqn, ATC, Chippenham	
WP869	DH Chipmunk T10 PAX (8215M)	RAF No 8 AEF, Shawbury	
WP871	DH Chipmunk T10	RAF Shawbury store	
WP872	DH Chipmunk T10	AAC, Shawbury store	
WP896	DH Chipmunk T10 [11]	RAF No 10 AEF, Woodvale	
WP900	DH Chipmunk T10 [13]	RAF No 10 AEF, Woodvale	
WP901	DH Chipmunk T10 [B]	RAF No 6 AEF, Abingdon	
WP904	DH Chipmunk T10 [909]	RN Flying Grading Flt, Plymouth	
WP906	DH Chipmunk T10 [816]	RNAS Culdrose Station Flight	
WP912	DH Chipmunk T10 (8467M)	RAF Cosford Aerospace Museum	
WP914	DH Chipmunk T10 [E]	RAF No 6 AEF, Abingdon	
WP920	DH Chipmunk T10 [10]	RAF No 2 AEF, Hurn	
WP925	DH Chipmunk T10 [C]	AAC BFWF, Middle Wallop	
WP927	DH Chipmunk T10 PAX (8216M/G-ATJK)	No 1430 Sqn ATC, RAF Woodvale	
WP928	DH Chipmunk T10 [D]	AAC BFWF, Middle Wallop	
WP929	DH Chipmunk T10 [F]	RAF No 8 AEF, Shawbury	
WP930	DH Chipmunk T10 [J]	AAC BFWF, Middle Wallop	
WP962	DH Chipmunk T10 [V]	RAF No 3 AEF, Filton	
WP964	DH Chipmunk T10	AAC Middle Wallop	
WP967	DH Chipmunk T10	RAF No 12 AEF, Turnhouse	
WP970	DH Chipmunk T10 [T]	RAF No 5 AEF, Cambridge	
WP972	DH Chipmunk T10 PAX (8667M)	CSDE RAF Swanton Morley	
WP974	DH Chipmunk T10 [N]	RAF No 3 AEF, Filton	
WP977	DH Chipmunk 22 (G-BHRD)	Privately owned, Oxford	
WP978	DH Chipmunk T10 PAX	RAF No 2 AEF, Hurn	
WP979	DH Chipmunk T10	CSDE RAF Swanton Morley	
WP980	DH Chipmunk T10 [E]	RAF FSS, Swinderby	
WP981	DH Chipmunk T10	AAC Shawbury store	
WP983	DH Chipmunk T10 [B]	AAC BFWF, Middle Wallop	
WP984	DH Chipmunk T10	RAF No 7 AEF, Newton	
WR539	DH Venom FB4 (8399M) [F]	Wales Aircraft Museum, Cardiff	
WR960	Avro Shackleton AEW2 (8772M)	Manchester Air & Space Museum	

Notes	Serial	Type (alternative identity)	Owner, Operator or Location
	WR963	Avro Shackleton AEW2	RAF No 8 Sqn, Lossiemouth
	WR965	Avro Shackleton AEW2	RAF No 8 Sqn, Lossiemouth
	WR967	Avro Shackleton MR2C (8398M)	RAF Lossiemouth, as a simulator
	WR971	Avro Shackleton MR3 (8119M) [Q]	RAF No 2 SoTT, Cosford
	WR974	Avro Shackleton MR3 (8117M) [K]	RAF Cosford Aerospace Museum
	WR977	Avro Shackleton MR3 (8186M) [B]	Newark Air Museum, Winthorpe
	WR981	Avro Shackleton MR3 (8120M)	RAF Topcliffe Fire Section
	WR982	Avro Shackleton MR3 (8106M) [J]	RAF No 2 SoTT, Cosford
	WR985	Avro Shackleton MR3 (8103M) [H]	RAF No 2 SoTT, Cosford
	WS103	Gloster Meteor T7 [709/VL]	FAA Museum store, Wroughton
	WS692	Gloster Meteor NF12 (7605M)	Newark Air Museum, Winthorpe
	WS726	Gloster Meteor NF14 (7960M) [G]	No 1855 Sqn ATC, Royton
	WS739	Gloster Meteor NF14 (7961M)	Newark Air Museum, Winthorpe
	WS760	Gloster Meteor NF14 (7964M)	Lincoln Field Vintage & HAC, Bushey
	WS774	Gloster Meteor NF14 (7959M)	RAF Hospital Ely, at main gate
	WS776	Gloster Meteor NF14 (7716M) [K]	RAF North Luffenham, at main gate
	WS792	Gloster Meteor NF14 (7965M) [K]	RAF Carlisle, at main gate
	WS807	Gloster Meteor NF14 (7973M) [N]	RAF Watton, at main gate
	WS832	Gloster Meteor NF14 [W]	Solway Aviation Society, Carlisle
	WS838	Gloster Meteor NF14	RAF Cosford Aerospace Museum
	WS840	Gloster Meteor NF14 (7969M)	Aldergrove Fire Section
	WS843	Gloster Meteor NF14 (7937M) [Y]	RAF St Athan Historic Aircraft Collection
	WS844	Gloster Meteor NF14 (7967M) [JCF] really WS788	RAF Leeming, at main gate
	WT121	Douglas Skyraider AEW1 [415/CU]	FAA Museum, RNAS Yeovilton
	WT301	EE Canberra B6 (Mod) [W]	Defence School, Chattenden
	WT305	EE Canberra B6 (8511M) [X]	RAF Wyton, at main gate
	WT308	EE Canberra B(I)6	MoD(PE) RAE Farnborough
	WT309	EE Canberra B(I)6	MoD(PE) A&AEE Boscombe Down
	WT327	EE Canberra B(I)8	MoD(PE) RAE Bedford
	WT333	EE Canberra B(I)8	MoD(PE) RAE Bedford
	WT339	EE Canberra B(I)8 (8198M)	RAF College Cranwell Fire Section
	WT346	EE Canberra B(I)8 (8197M)	RAF Cosford Aerospace Museum
	WT478	EE Canberra T4 [BA]	RAF No 231 OCU, Wyton
	WT480	EE Canberra T4	RAF No 231 OCU, Wyton
	WT483	EE Canberra T4	BAe Samlesbury store
	WT486	EE Canberra T4 (8102M)	Aldergrove Fire Section
	WT488	EE Canberra T4	BAe Samlesbury store
	WT507	EE Canberra PR7 (8548M) [44] nose only	No 384 Sqn ATC, Mansfield
	WT509	EE Canberra PR7 [CG]	RAF No 100 Sqn, Wyton
	WT510	EE Canberra T22 [854]	RN FRADU, Yeovilton
	WT518	EE Canberra PR7 (8691M)	Wales Aircraft Museum, Cardiff
	WT519	EE Canberra PR7 [CH]	RAF No 100 Sqn, Wyton
	WT520	EE Canberra PR7 (8184M) [20]	RAF Swinderby, on display
	WT525	EE Canberra T22 [855]	RN FRADU, Yeovilton
	WT532	EE Canberra PR7 (8728M)	MoD(PE) RAE Bedford
	WT534	EE Canberra PR7 (8549M) [43] nose only	No 489 Sqn ATC, Solihull
	WT535	EE Canberra T22 [852]	RN FRADU, Yeovilton
	WT536	EE Canberra PR7 (8063M) [F]	RAF No 2 SoTT, Cosford
	WT537	EE Canberra PR7	BAe Samlesbury store
	WT538	EE Canberra PR7 [CJ]	RAF No 100 Sqn, Wyton
	WT555	Hawker Hunter F1 (7499M)	RAF Cosford Aerospace Museum

Serial	Type (alternative identity)	Owner, Operator or Location	Notes
WT569	Hawker Hunter F1 (7491M)	No 2117 Sqn ATC, Kenfig Hill, Mid-Glamorgan	
WT612	Hawker Hunter F1 (7496M)	RAF Henlow	
WT619	Hawker Hunter F1 (7525M)	Manchester Air & Space Museum	
WT651	Hawker Hunter F1 (7532M) [C]	RAF Lawford Heath, Warwicks, on display	
WT660	Hawker Hunter F1 (7421M) [C]	RAF Carlisle, at main gate	
WT680	Hawker Hunter F1 (7533M) [Z]	No 1429 Sqn ATC at RAE Aberporth	
WT684	Hawker Hunter F1 (7422M)	RAF Brize Norton Fire Section	
WT694	Hawker Hunter F1 (7510M) [Y]	RAF Newton, at main gate	
WT711	Hawker Hunter GA11 [837/VL]	RN store, RAF Shawbury	
WT722	Hawker Hunter T8C [878/VL]	RN FRADU, Yeovilton	
WT723	Hawker Hunter GA11 [866/VL]	RN FRADU, Yeovilton	
WT744	Hawker Hunter GA11 [868/VL]	RN FRADU, Yeovilton	
WT745	Hawker Hunter T8C	RN store, RAF Shawbury	
WT746	Hawker Hunter F4 (7770M) [A]	RAF No 1 SoTT, Halton	
WT799	Hawker Hunter T8C [879/-]	RN store, RAF Shawbury	
WT804	Hawker Hunter GA11 [831/VL]	RN store, RAF Shawbury	
WT806	Hawker Hunter GA11 [838/VL]	RN FRADU, Yeovilton	
WT809	Hawker Hunter GA11 [867/VL]	RN store, RAF Shawbury	
WT867	Slingsby Cadet TX3	RAF store, Syerston	
WT868	Slingsby Cadet TX3	RAF No 643 VGS, Scampton	
WT869	Slingsby Cadet TX3	RAF No 618 VGS, West Malling	
WT870	Slingsby Cadet TX3	RAF store, Syerston	
WT871	Slingsby Cadet TX3	RAF No 622 VGS, Upavon	
WT877	Slingsby Cadet TX3	RAF No 621 VGS, Weston-super-Mare	
WT898	Slingsby Cadet TX3	RAF No 662 VGS, Arbroath	
WT899	Slingsby Cadet TX3	RAF No 661 VGS, Kirknewton	
WT900	Slingsby Cadet TX3 [S]	RAF No 663 VGS, Kinloss	
WT901	Slingsby Cadet TX3	RAF store, Syerston	
WT902	Slingsby Cadet TX3	RAF No 622 VGS, Upavon	
WT903	Slingsby Cadet TX3	RAF No 661 VGS, Kirknewton	
WT904	Slingsby Cadet TX3	RAF store, Syerston	
WT905	Slingsby Cadet TX3	RAF No 4 MGSP, Dishforth	
WT906	Slingsby Cadet TX3	RAF No 4 MGSP, Dishforth	
WT908	Slingsby Cadet TX3	RAF No 662 VGS, Arbroath	
WT909	Slingsby Cadet TX3	RAF store, Syerston	
WT910	Slingsby Cadet TX3	RAF No 617 VGS, Manston	
WT911	Slingsby Cadet TX3	RAF store, Syerston	
WT913	Slingsby Cadet TX3	RAF No 614 VGS, Wethersfield	
WT914	Slingsby Cadet TX3 [C]	RAF Syerston, stored	
WT915	Slingsby Cadet TX3	RAF No 661 VGS, Kirknewton	
WT917	Slingsby Cadet TX3	RAF No 614 VGS, Wethersfield	
WT918	Slingsby Cadet TX3	RAF No 643 VGS, Scampton	
WT919	Slingsby Cadet TX3	RAF No 661 VGS, Kirknewton	
WT933	Bristol Sycamore 3 (G-ALSW/7709M)	Newark Air Museum, Winthorpe	
WV106	Douglas Skyraider AEW1 [427/C]	Cornwall Aero Park, Helston	
WV198	S55 Whirlwind HAR21 (G-BJWY/A2576) [K]	Privately owned, Heysham, Lancs	
WV256	Hawker Hunter GA11 [862/VL]	RN FRADU, Yeovilton	
WV267	Hawker Hunter GA11 [836/VL]	RN FRADU, Yeovilton	
WV276	Hawker Hunter F4 (7847M)	RAF No 1 SoTT, Halton	
WV318	Hawker Hunter T7B [ZS]	RAF No 208 Sqn, Lossiemouth	
WV322	Hawker Hunter T8B [ZC]	RAF No 237 OCU, Honington	
WV363	Hawker Hunter T8 [872/VL]	RN FRADU, Yeovilton	
WV372	Hawker Hunter T7	RAF No 237 OCU, Honington	
WV381	Hawker Hunter GA11 [732]	UKAEA, Culham, Oxon	
WV382	Hawker Hunter GA11 [830/VL]	RN store, RAF Shawbury	
WV383	Hawker Hunter T7	MoD(PE) RAE Farnborough	
WV396	Hawker Hunter T8C [877/VL]	RN FRADU, Yeovilton	
WV483	Percival Provost T1 (7693M) [N-E]	Privately owned, Blackbushe	

27

Notes	Serial	Type (alternative identity)	Owner, Operator or Location
	WV493	Percival Provost T1 (G-BDYG/7696M) [29]	Royal Scottish Museum of Flight, East Fortune
	WV495	Percival Provost T1 (7697M) [P-C]	Chiltern Historical Aircraft Preservation Group, Booker
	WV499	Percival Provost T1 (7698M) [P-G]	RAF St Athan Historic Aircraft Collection
	WV544	Percival Provost T1 (7700M)	AAC Netheravon Fire Section
	WV562	Percival Provost T1 (7606M) [P-C]	RAF Cosford Aerospace Museum
	WV605	Percival Provost T1 [O-V]	Norfolk & Suffolk Aviation Museum, Flixton
	WV606	Percival Provost T1 (7622M) [P-B]	Newark Air Museum, Winthorpe
	WV679	Percival Provost T1 (7615M) [O-J]	Torbay Aircraft Museum, Paignton
	WV686	Percival Provost T1 (7621M) (G-BLFT) [O-P]	Privately owned, Blackbushe
	WV701	Percival Pembroke C1	RAF No 60 Sqn, Wildenrath
	WV703	Percival Pembroke C1 (8108M/ G-IIIM)	Privately owned, Tattershall Thorpe
	WV705	Percival Pembroke C1	Marine Aircraft Preservation Group, Wimborne
	WV740	Percival Pembroke C1	RAF No 60 Sqn, Wildenrath
	WV746	Percival Pembroke C1	RAF No 60 Sqn, Wildenrath
	WV753	Percival Pembroke C1 (8113M)	Wales Aircraft Museum, Cardiff
	WV781	Bristol Sycamore HR12 (G-ALTD/7839M)	RAF SAREW, Finningley, for display
	WV783	Bristol Sycamore HR12 (G-ALSP/7841M)	RAF Museum Store, Henlow
	WV787	EE Canberra B2/8 (8799M)	RAF Abingdon, BDRF
	WV795	Hawker Sea Hawk FGA6 (A2661/8151M)	Privately owned, Peasedown St John, Avon
	WV797	Hawker Sea Hawk FGA4 (A2637/8155M)	Air Service Training, Perth
	WV798	Hawker Sea Hawk FGA6 (A2557) [028/CU]	Second World War Aircraft Preservation Society, Lasham
	WV826	Hawker Sea Hawk FGA6 (A2532) [147/CU]	Wales Aircraft Museum, Cardiff
	WV843	Hawker Sea Hawk FGA4 nose only	Torbay Aircraft Museum, Paignton
	WV856	Hawker Sea Hawk FGA6 [163]	FAA Museum, RNAS Yeovilton
	WV903	Hawker Sea Hawk FGA6 (A2632/8153M) [128/C] [SAH-8]	RNAS Culdrose, SAH
	WV908	Hawker Sea Hawk FGA6 (A2660/8154M) [188/A]	RN Historic Flight, RNAS Yeovilton
	WV911	Hawker Sea Hawk FGA4 (A2526) [115/C]	RN AES, Lee-on-Solent
	WW138	DH Sea Venom FAW21 [229/O]	FAA Museum, RNAS Yeovilton
	WW145	DH Sea Venom FAW21 [680/LM]	Royal Scottish Museum of Flight, East Fortune
	WW217	DH Sea Venom FAW22 [736]	Newark Air Museum, Winthorpe
	WW388	Percival Provost T1 (7616M)	Privately owned, Llanelli
	WW397	Percival Provost T1 (8060M/ G-BKHP) [N-E]	Privately owned, RAF Lyneham
	WW421	Percival Provost T1 (7688M)	Lincolnshire Aviation Museum, Tattershall
	WW442	Percival Provost T1 (7618M)	Privately owned, St Merryn
	WW444	Percival Provost T1 [D]	Privately owned, Coventry
	WW453	Percival Provost T1 [B-P]	Air Service Training, Perth
	WW654	Hawker Hunter GA11 [833/VL]	RN FRADU, Yeovilton
	WX788	DH Venom NF3	Wales Aircraft Museum, Cardiff
	WX853	DH Venom NF3 (7443M)	Mosquito Aircraft Museum, London Colney
	WX905	DH Venom NF3 (7458M)	RAF Museum Store, Henlow

Serial	Type (alternative identity)	Owner, Operator or Location	Notes
WZ415	DH Vampire T11 [72]	Lincoln Field Vintage & HAC, Bushey	
WZ416	DH Vampire T11	Lincoln Field Vintage & HAC, Bushey	
WZ425	DH Vampire T11	Wales Aircraft Museum, Cardiff	
WZ450	DH Vampire T11 [23]	No 2371 Sqn ATC, Tile Cross	
WZ464	DH Vampire T11 (N62430) [40]	LFV&HAC, Bushey, Herts	
WZ476	DH Vampire T11	Mosquito Aircraft Museum, London Colney	
WZ507	DH Vampire T11 (G-VTII)	Privately owned, Cranfield	
WZ514	DH Vampire T11	Privately owned, Irby Hall, Merseyside	
WZ515	DH Vampire T11 [60]	Skyfame Collection, Duxford	
WZ518	DH Vampire T11	North East Aviation Museum, Usworth	
WZ544	DH Vampire T11 (pod only) (7652M)	MoD, Spitalgate	
WZ549	DH Vampire T11 (8118M) [F]	Lincolnshire Aviation Museum, Tattershall	
WZ550	DH Vampire T11 (7902M) [R]	Chiltern Historical Aircraft Preservation Group, Booker	
WZ553	DH Vampire T11 [40]	Bruntingthorpe Aviation Collection, Loughborough	
WZ557	DH Vampire T11	N Yorks Recovery Group, Chop Gate	
WZ576	DH Vampire T11 (8174M)	No 2192 Sqn ATC, Appleby	
WZ581	DH Vampire T11 [77]	Privately owned, Ruislip	
WZ584	DH Vampire T11 [U]	St Albans College of FE	
WZ589	DH Vampire T11 [19]	Lashenden Air Warfare Museum, Headcorn	
WZ590	DH Vampire T11 [19]	Imperial War Museum, Duxford	
WZ608	DH Vampire T11 [56] (nose only)	British Aviation Heritage, Bruntingthorpe	
WZ616	DH Vampire T11 [60]	Lincoln Field Vintage & HAC, Bushey	
WZ662	Auster AOP9 (G-BKVK)	The Old Training Plane Co, Shobdon	
WZ672	Auster AOP9 (G-BDER)	Privately owned, Sibson	
WZ706	Auster AOP9 (7851M)	Royal Military College of Science, Shrivenham	
W7711	Auster 9/Beagle E3 (G-AVHT)	Privately owned, Middle Wallop	
WZ721	Auster AOP9	Museum of Army Flying, Middle Wallop	
WZ724	Auster AOP9 (7432M/WZ670)	AAC Middle Wallop, at main gate	
WZ736	Avro 707A (7868M)	Manchester Air & Space Museum	
WZ744	Avro 707C (7932M)	RAF Cosford Aerospace Museum	
WZ753	Slingsby Grasshopper TX1	Emanuel School CCF, London SW11	
WZ754	Slingsby Grasshopper TX1	Strathallan School CCF, Fordangenny, nr Perth	
WZ755	Slingsby Grasshopper TX1	King's School CCF, Bruton, Somerset	
WZ756	Slingsby Grasshopper TX1	RAF No 2 MGSP, Locking	
WZ757	Slingsby Grasshopper TX1	RAF No 2 MGSP, Locking	
WZ758	Slingsby Grasshopper TX1	King's School CCF, Grantham, Lincs	
WZ760	Slingsby Grasshopper TX1	RAF No 2 MGSP, Locking	
WZ761	Slingsby Grasshopper TX1	RAF No 1 MGSP, Halton	
WZ762	Slingsby Grasshopper TX1	RAF No 3 MGSP, Cosford	
WZ764	Slingsby Grasshopper TX1	RAF No 1 MGSP, Halton	
WZ765	Slingsby Grasshopper TX1	Radley College CCF, Abingdon	
WZ767	Slingsby Grasshopper TX1	RAF No 1 MGSP, Halton	
WZ768	Slingsby Grasshopper TX1	Warwick School CCF	
WZ769	Slingsby Grasshopper TX1	RAF No 2 MGSP, Locking	
WZ772	Slingsby Grasshopper TX1	RAF No 1 MGSP, Halton	
WZ773	Slingsby Grasshopper TX1	Edinburgh Academy CCF, Lothian	
WZ778	Slingsby Grasshopper TX1	RAF No 4 MGSP, Dishforth	
WZ779	Slingsby Grasshopper TX1	Ratcliffe College CCF, Syston, Leics	
WZ780	Slingsby Grasshopper TX1	Clifton College CCF, Bristol	
WZ781	Slingsby Grasshopper TX1	RAF No 4 MGSP, Dishforth	
WZ782	Slingsby Grasshopper TX1	Charterhouse School CCF, Godalming	
WZ784	Slingsby Grasshopper TX1	RAF No 4 MGSP, Dishforth	
WZ785	Slingsby Grasshopper TX1	Wellingborough School CCF, Northants	
WZ787	Slingsby Grasshopper TX1	RAF No 4 MGSP, Dishforth	
WZ789	Slingsby Grasshopper TX1	RAF No 3 MGSP, Cosford	
WZ791	Slingsby Grasshopper TX1	Royal Grammar School CCF, High Wycombe	
WZ792	Slingsby Grasshopper TX1	Barnard Castle School, CCF	
WZ793	Slingsby Grasshopper TX1	Lord Wandsworth College CCF, Basingstoke	

Notes	Serial	Type (alternative identity)	Owner, Operator or Location
	WZ794	Slingsby Grasshopper TX1	Kings School CCF, Canterbury, Kent
	WZ795	Slingsby Grasshopper TX1	RAF No 1 MGSP, Halton
	WZ796	Slingsby Grasshopper TX1	Eastbourne College CCF, East Sussex
	WZ797	Slingsby Grasshopper TX1	Canford School CCF, Dorset
	WZ798	Slingsby Grasshopper TX1	RAF No 2 MGSP, Locking
	WZ816	Slingsby Grasshopper TX1	RAF No 2 MGSP, Locking
	WZ817	Slingsby Grasshopper TX1	RAF No 4 MGSP, Dishforth
	WZ818	Slingsby Grasshopper TX1	Oakham School CCF, Leics
	WZ819	Slingsby Grasshopper TX1	RAF No 4 MGSP, Dishforth
	WZ820	Slingsby Grasshopper TX1	Whitgift School CCF, Croydon
	WZ822	Slingsby Grasshopper TX1	RAF No 1 MGSP, Halton
	WZ824	Slingsby Grasshopper TX1	St Bees School CCF, Cumbria
	WZ825	Slingsby Grasshopper TX1	Bradfield College CCF, Reading, Berks
	WZ826	Slingsby Grasshopper TX1	Dulwich College CCF, London
	WZ827	Slingsby Grasshopper TX1	RAF ACCGS, Syerston
	WZ828	Slingsby Grasshopper TX1	Heles School CCF, Exeter, Devon
	WZ829	Slingsby Grasshopper TX1	Launceston College CCF, Cornwall
	WZ831	Slingsby Grasshopper TX1	Oratory School CCF, Reading
	WZ845	DH Chipmunk T10 [2]	RAF No 1 AEF, Manston
	WZ847	DH Chipmunk T10 [F]	RAF No 6 AEF, Abingdon
	WZ849	DH Chipmunk T10 PAX (8439M)	No 1404 Sqn ATC, Chatham
	WZ856	DH Chipmunk T10	RAF No 7 AEF, Newton
	WZ862	DH Chipmunk T10	RAF Gatow Station Flight, Berlin
	WZ866	DH Chipmunk T10 PAX (8217M)	No 498 Sqn ATC, Wishaw
	WZ868	DH Chipmunk 22 (G-BCIW)	Privately owned, Duxford
	WZ869	DH Chipmunk T10 PAX (8019M) [R]	No 391 Sqn ATC, Handforth
	WZ872	DH Chipmunk T10 [E]	RAF No 5 AEF, Cambridge
	WZ877	DH Chipmunk T10 [G]	RAF No 6 AEF, Abingdon
	WZ878	DH Chipmunk T10 [86]	RAF No 11 AEF, Leeming
	WZ879	DH Chipmunk T10 [85]	RAF No 11 AEF, Leeming
	WZ882	DH Chipmunk T10 [K]	AAC BFWF, Middle Wallop
	WZ884	DH Chipmunk T10 [P]	AAC BFWF, Middle Wallop
	XA109	DH Sea Vampire T22	Royal Scottish Museum of Flight, East Fortune
	XA129	DH Sea Vampire T22	FAA Museum, RNAS Yeovilton
	XA225	Slingsby Grasshopper TX1	Churchers College CCF, Petersfield
	XA226	Slingsby Grasshopper TX1	RAF No 1 MGSP, Halton
	XA228	Slingsby Grasshopper TX1	Glenalmond Trinity College CCF, Tayside
	XA229	Slingsby Grasshopper TX1	RAF No 3 MGSP, Cosford
	XA230	Slingsby Grasshopper TX1	Uppingham School CCF, Leics
	XA231	Slingsby Grasshopper TX1	Kimbolton School CCF, Cambs
	XA233	Slingsby Grasshopper TX1	RAF No 1 MGSP, Halton
	XA236	Slingsby Grasshopper TX1	RAF No 1 MGSP, Halton
	XA237	Slingsby Grasshopper TX1	Queen Victoria School CCF, Dunblane
	XA239	Slingsby Grasshopper TX1	Perse School CCF, Cambridge
	XA240	Slingsby Grasshopper TX1	Radley College CCF, Abingdon
	XA241	Slingsby Grasshopper TX1	Trinity School CCF, Croydon
	XA243	Slingsby Grasshopper TX1	Bournemouth School CCF, Dorset
	XA244	Slingsby Grasshopper TX1	RAF No 3 MGSP, Cosford
	XA282	Slingsby Cadet TX3	RAF
	XA284	Slingsby Cadet TX3	RAF Syerston, store
	XA286	Slingsby Cadet TX3	RAF No 615 VGS, Kenley
	XA288	Slingsby Cadet TX3	RAF No 636 VGS, Swansea
	XA289	Slingsby Cadet TX3	RAF store, Syerston
	XA290	Slingsby Cadet TX3	RAF No 661 VGS, Kirknewton
	XA292	Slingsby Cadet TX3	RAF No 615 VGS, Kenley
	XA293	Slingsby Cadet TX3	RAF store, Syerston
	XA295	Slingsby Cadet TX3	RAF store, Syerston
	XA302	Slingsby Cadet TX3	RAF store, Syerston
	XA308	Slingsby Cadet TX3	RAF No 621 VGS, Weston-super-Mare
	XA309	Slingsby Cadet TX3	RAF No 614 VGS, Wethersfield
	XA310	Slingsby Cadet TX3	RAF store, Syerston
	XA311	Slingsby Cadet TX3	RAF store, Syerston
	XA454	Fairey Gannet COD4	RNAS Yeovilton Fire Section

Serial	Type (alternative identity)	Owner, Operator or Location	Notes
XA459	Fairey Gannet ECM6 (A2608) [E/-]	Wales Aircraft Museum, Cardiff	
XA460	Fairey Gannet ECM6 [768/BY]	Kelsterton College of Technology, Connah's Quay	
XA466	Fairey Gannet COD4 [777/LM]	FAA Museum, RNAS Yeovilton	
XA508	Fairey Gannet T2 (A2472) [627/GN]	Midland Air Museum, Coventry	
XA536	EE Canberra T19 (8605M)	RAF Abingdon Fire Section	
XA549	Gloster Javelin FAW1 (7717M) [E]	RAF Museum Store, Swinderby	
XA553	Gloster Javelin FAW1 (7470M)	RAF Stanmore Park, on display	
XA564	Gloster Javelin FAW1 (7464M)	RAF Cosford Aerospace Museum	
XA634	Gloster Javelin FAW4 (7641M) [L]	RAF Leeming, at main gate	
XA699	Gloster Javelin FAW9 (7809M)	Midland Air Museum, Coventry	
XA801	Gloster Javelin FAW2 (7739M)	RAF Stafford, at main gate	
XA847	English Electric P1B (8371M)	RAF Museum, Hendon	
XA862	Westland Whirlwind HAR1 (A2542/G-AMJT)	Midland Air Museum, Coventry	
XA864	Westland Whirlwind HAR1	FAA Museum, RNAS Yeovilton	
XA866	Westland Whirlwind HAR1 (A2550) [448]	Donnington Park, on display	
XA868	Westland Whirlwind HAR1 (A2551)	Privately owned, Horsham	
XA870	Westland Whirlwind HAR1 (A2543)	Cornwall Aero Park, Helston	
XA876	Slingsby Sky I	RAFGSA, Syerston	
XA880	DH Devon C2	MoD(PE) RAE Llanbedr	
XA893	Avro Vulcan B1 (8591M) nose only	RAF Exhibition Flight, Abingdon	
XA900	Avro Vulcan B1 (7896M)	RAF Cosford Aerospace Museum	
XA917	HP Victor B1 (7827M) nose only	RAF Marham, ground instruction	
XA932	HP Victor K1 (8517M)	RAF Museum, on display Marham	
XB259	Blackburn Beverley C1 (G-AOAI)	Museum of Army Transport, Beverley	
XB261	Blackburn Beverley C1	Southend Airport Hotel	
XB288	Blackburn Beverley C1	Privately owned, Worminghall, Bucks	
XB446	Grumman Avenger ECM6B [992/C]	FAA Museum, RNAS Yeovilton	
XB480	Hiller HT1 (A2577) [537]	FAA Museum, RNAS Yeovilton	
XB833	NA Sabre 4	Privately owned, Duxford	
XD145	SARO SR53	RAF Cosford Aerospace Museum	
XD163	Westland Whirlwind HAR10 (8645M) [X]	British Rotorcraft Museum, Wroughton	
XD165	Westland Whirlwind HAR10 (8673M)	RAF No 1 SoTT, Halton	
XD182	Westland Whirlwind HAR10 (8612M)	RAF Odiham Fire Section	
XD186	Westland Whirlwind HAR10 (8730M)	RAF Chivenor, on display	
XD220	VS Scimitar F1	FAA Museum store, RNAY Wroughton	
XD317	VS Scimitar F1 [112/R]	FAA Museum, RNAS Yeovilton	
XD332	VS Scimitar F1 (A2574) [612]	Cornwall Aero Park, Helston	
XD375	DH Vampire T11 (7887M)	City of Norwich Aviation Museum	
XD377	DH Vampire T11 (8203M)	RAF Cosford Aerospace Museum	
XD382	DH Vampire T11 (8033M)	RAF Shawbury, at main gate	
XD425	DH Vampire T11 [16]	Dumfries & Galloway Aviation Museum, Tinwald Downs	
XD429	DH Vampire T11 (7604M) [28] (really XD542)	RAF Cranwell, at main gate	
XD434	DH Vampire T11 [25]	Manchester University, Barton	
XD435	DH Vampire T11 [26]	No 480 Sqn ATC, Kenilworth, Warwicks	
XD445	DH Vampire T11 [51]	Bomber County Aviation Museum, Cleethorpes	
XD447	DH Vampire T11 [33]	Lincolnshire Aviation Museum, Tattershall	

Notes	Serial	Type (alternative identity)	Owner, Operator or Location
	XD452	DH Vampire T11 (7990M) [66]	Mosquito Aircraft Museum, London Colney
	XD453	DH Vampire T11 (7890M)	No 1010 Sqn ATC, Old Sarum
	XD459	DH Vampire T11 [63]	Lincoln Field Vintage & HAC, Bushey
	XD463	DH Vampire T11 (8023M)	No 1360 Sqn ATC, Stapleford, Notts
	XD506	DH Vampire T11 (7983M) [E]	RAF Swinderby, on display
	XD515	DH Vampire T11 (7998M)	Newark Air Museum, Winthorpe
	XD527	DH Vampire T11 [46]	RAF Manston Fire Section
	XD528	DH Vampire T11 (8159M)	No 2415 Sqn ATC, Penkridge, Staffs
	XD534	DH Vampire T11 [41]	Military Aircraft Preservation Group, Manchester
	XD535	DH Vampire T11	WR Tuscon Technical College, Fulwood, Lancs
	XD536	DH Vampire T11 (7734M)	No 2287 Sqn ATC, Reading
	XD547	DH Vampire T11 [Z]	Strathallan Aircraft Collection
	XD593	DH Vampire T11 [50]	Newark Air Museum, Winthorpe
	XD596	DH Vampire T11 (7939M) [V2]	No 424 Sqn ATC, Testwood, Hants
	XD599	DH Vampire T11 [A]	Hunter One Collection, Hurn
	XD601	DH Vampire T11 (7878M) [32]	Lincoln Field Vintage & HAC, Bushey
	XD602	DH Vampire T11 (7737M)	No 495 Sqn ATC, Wylde Green, W Midlands
	XD613	DH Vampire T11 (8122M) [M]	RAF Cosford, on parade ground
	XD616	DH Vampire T11 [56]	No 1239 Sqn ATC, Hoddesdon, Herts
	XD622	DH Vampire T11 (8160M)	No 2214 Sqn, ATC, Usworth
	XD624	DH Vampire T11 [O]	Macclesfield Technical College
	XD626	DH Vampire T11 [Q]	Midland Air Museum, Coventry
	XD674	Hunting Jet Provost T1 (7570M) [T]	RAF St Athan Historic Aircraft Collection
	XD818	Vickers Valiant B(K)1 (7894M)	Bomber Command Museum, Hendon
	XD826	Vickers Valiant B(K)I (7872M) (nose only)	No 1289 Sqn ATC, Stratford-on-Avon
	XD875	Vickers Valiant B(K)I (nose only)	No 163 Sqn ATC, Coventry
	XE317	Bristol Sycamore HR14 (G-AMWO) [S-N]	Newark Air Museum, Winthorpe
	XE327	Hawker Sea Hawk FGA6 (A2556) [644/LH]	RN Llangennech, Dyfed, on display
	XE339	Hawker Sea Hawk FGA6 (8156M/A2635) [149/E] [SAH-7]	RNAS Culdrose, SAH
	XE340	Hawker Sea Hawk FGA6 [131/Z]	Strathallan Aircraft Collection
	XE364	Hawker Sea Hawk FGA6 (really XE489) (G-JETH) [485-J]	Brencham Historic Collection, Hurn
	XE368	Hawker Sea Hawk FGA6 (A2534) [200/J]	Cornwall Aero Park, Helston
	XE369	Hawker Sea Hawk FGA6 (A2580/8158M/A2633)	RNAS Lee-on-Solent, BDRF
	XE587	Hawker Hunter F6 [7]	MoD(PE) RAE Farnborough
	XE597	Hawker Hunter FGA9 [F]	RAF Brawdy
	XE601	Hawker Hunter FGA9	MoD(PE) ETPS Boscombe Down
	XE606	Hawker Hunter F6A [11]	RAF Brawdy
	XE624	Hawker Hunter FGA9 [G]	RAF Brawdy
	XE627	Hawker Hunter F6A [10]	RAF Brawdy
	XE643	Hawker Hunter FGA9 (8586M) nose only	RAF Exhibition Flight, Abingdon
	XE650	Hawker Hunter FGA9 (G-9-449)	Privately owned, Macclesfield
	XE653	Hawker Hunter F6A (8829M) [D]	RAF No 2 SoTT, Cosford
	XE656	Hawker Hunter F6 (8678M) [35]	RAF No 1 SoTT, Halton
	XE665	Hawker Hunter T8C [876]	RN FRADU, Yeovilton
	XE668	Hawker Hunter GA11 [832/VL]	RN FRADU, Yeovilton

Serial	Type (alternative identity)	Owner, Operator or Location	Notes
XE670	Hawker Hunter F4 (8585M) nose only	RAF Exhibition Flight, Abingdon	
XE673	Hawker Hunter GA11 [680] (tail from XE689)	RN store, RAF Shawbury	
XE677	Hawker Hunter F4	Loughborough University of Technology	
XE682	Hawker Hunter GA11 [833/VL]	RN store, RAF Shawbury	
XE685	Hawker Hunter GA11 [861/VL]	RN FRADU, Yeovilton	
XE689	Hawker Hunter GA11 [864/VL]	RN FRADU, Yeovilton	
XE707	Hawker Hunter GA11 [865/VL]	RN FRADU, Yeovilton	
XE712	Hawker Hunter T7 [708]	RN store, RAF Shawbury	
XE785	Slingsby Cadet TX3	RAF No 663 VGS, Kinloss	
XE786	Slingsby Cadet TX3	RAF No 4 MGSP, Dishforth	
XE789	Slingsby Cadet TX3	RAF No 662 VGS, Arbroath	
XE790	Slingsby Cadet TX3	RAF No 614 VGS, Wethersfield	
XE791	Slingsby Cadet TX3	RAF store, Syerston	
XE793	Slingsby Cadet TX3 (8666M)	RAF St Athan	
XE794	Slingsby Cadet TX3	RAF No 4 MGSP, Dishforth	
XE795	Slingsby Cadet TX3	RAF No 643 VGS, Scampton	
XE798	Slingsby Cadet TX3 [E]	RAF store, Syerston	
XE799	Slingsby Cadet TX3	RAF store, Syerston	
XE800	Slingsby Cadet TX3	RAF No 622 VGS, Upavon	
XE801	Slingsby Cadet TX3	RAF No 617 VGS, Manston	
XE802	Slingsby Cadet TX3	RAF Syerston store	
XE806	Slingsby Cadet TX3	RAF St Athan	
XE807	Slingsby Cadet TX3	RAF No 615 VGS, Kenley	
XE808	Slingsby Cadet TX3	RAF No 4 MGSP, Dishforth	
XE810	Slingsby Cadet TX3	RAF store, Syerston	
XE812	Slingsby Cadet TX3	RAF store, Syerston	
XE849	DH Vampire T11 (7928M) [V3]	No 936 Sqn ATC, Ware, Herts	
XE852	DH Vampire T11 [60]	BAe Apprentice School, Hawarden	
XE855	DH Vampire T11	Midland Air Museum, Coventry	
XE856	DH Vampire T11	Second World War Aircraft Preservation Society, Lasham	
XE860	DH Vampire T11 [69]	Privately owned, Keevil	
XE872	DH Vampire T11 [62]	Midland Air Museum, Coventry	
XE874	DH Vampire T11 (8582M) [61]	RAF Valley	
XE897	DH Vampire T11 (really XD403)	Strathallan Aircraft Collection	
XE920	DH Vampire T11 (8196M) [D]	RAF Museum Store, Henlow	
XE921	DH Vampire T11 [64]	Privately owned, Keevil	
XE928	DH Vampire T11 [76]	Privately owned, Keevil	
XE935	DH Vampire T11 [30]	Nene Valley Aviation Society, Sibson	
XE946	DH Vampire T11 (7473M) nose only	RAF Museum store, Cardington	
XE950	DH Vampire T11 (8175M)	Gordon School CCF, Chobham	
XE956	DH Vampire T11 [N]	St Albans College of FE	
XE979	DH Vampire T11 [54]	Privately owned, Stonehouse, Glos	
XE982	DH Vampire T11 (7564M)	No 124 Sqn ATC, Hereford	
XE995	DH Vampire T11 [53]	Torbay Aircraft Museum, Paignton	
XE998	DH Vampire T11 [36]	No 723 Sqn ATC Wigan	
XF113	VS Swift F7 (nose only)	Privately owned, Peasedown St John, Avon	
XF114	VS Swift F7	Kelsterton College of Technology, Connah's Quay	
XF274	Gloster Meteor T7	RAE/AIU on display, Farnborough	
XF289	Hawker Hunter T8C [875/VL]	RN FRADU, Yeovilton	
XF300	Hawker Hunter GA11 [860/VL]	RN FRADU, Yeovilton	
XF301	Hawker Hunter GA11 [834/VL]	RN FRADU, Yeovilton	
XF310	Hawker Hunter T8C [876/VL]	RN FRADU, Yeovilton	
XF319	Hawker Hunter F4 (7849M) [B]	RAF No 1 SoTT, Halton	
XF321	Hawker Hunter T7	MoD(PE) RAE Bedford	
XF357	Hawker Hunter T8C [877/VL]	RN FRADU, Yeovilton	
XF358	Hawker Hunter T8C [870/VL]	RN FRADU, Yeovilton	
XF368	Hawker Hunter GA11 [863/VL]	RN FRADU, Yeovilton	
XF375	Hawker Hunter F6 (8736M) [05]	RAFC Cranwell, Engineering Wing	

Notes	Serial	Type (alternative identity)	Owner, Operator or Location
	XF383	Hawker Hunter F6 (8706M) [V]	RAF Wittering, BDRF
	XF383	Hawker Hunter F51 (really E-409) [71]	Wales Aircraft Museum, Cardiff
	XF386	Hawker Hunter F6 (8707M) [75]	RAF Coltishall, BDRF
	XF418	Hawker Hunter F6A [16]	RAF Brawdy
	XF419	Hawker Hunter FGA9 [C]	RAF Brawdy
	XF431	Hawker Hunter FGA9 [O]	RAF store, St Athan
	XF435	Hawker Hunter FGA9 [52]	RAF store, St Athan
	XF445	Hawker Hunter FGA9 (8715M) [T] (really XG264)	RAF Brawdy, BDRT
	XF509	Hawker Hunter F6 (8708M) [73]	RAF Chivenor, at main gate
	XF515	Hawker Hunter F6A (8830M) [C]	No 2 SoTT, Cosford
	XF516	Hawker Hunter F6A (8685M) [19]	RAFC Cranwell, Engineering Wing
	XF526	Hawker Hunter F6 (8679M) [78] [E]	RAF No 1 SoTT, Halton
	XF527	Hawker Hunter F6 (8680M) [70]	RAF No 1 SoTT, Halton
	XF545	Percival Provost T1 (7957M) [O-K]	RAF Linton-on-Ouse, at main gate
	XF597	Percival Provost T1 (G-BKFW) [G]	Privately owned, Oakington
	XF603	Percival Provost T1 [H]	Rolls-Royce Tech Coll, Filton
	XF690	Percival Provost T1 (G-BGKA/ 8041M)	Leicester Aircraft Preservation Group, RAF Newton
	XF708	Avro Shackleton MR3 [C]	Imperial War Museum, Duxford
	XF730	Avro Shackleton MR3 [F]	RAF Kinloss Fire Section
	XF785	Bristol 173 (G-ALBN/7648M)	RAF Museum Store, Henlow
	XF799	Percival Pembroke C1	RAF No 60 Sqn, Wildenrath
	XF836	Percival Provost T1 (8043M/ G-AWRY)	Privately owned, Thruxton
	XF844	Percival Provost T1 [30]	RAE Farnborough Apprentice School
	XF877	Percival Provost T1 (G-AWVF) [JX]	Privately owned, Bourn
	XF898	Percival Provost T1 [Z]	Chiltern Historical Aircraft Preservation Group, Booker
	XF914	Percival Provost T1	Lincoln Field Vintage & HAC, Cranfield
	XF926	Bristol 188 (8368M)	RAF Cosford Aerospace Museum
	XF967	Hawker Hunter T8C [XC]	RAF No 237 OCU, Lossiemouth
	XF974	Hawker Hunter F4 (7949M) [C]	RAF No 1 SoTT, Halton
	XF985	Hawker Hunter T8C [873/VL]	RN FRADU, Yeovilton
	XF990	Hawker Hunter F6 (8007M) nose only	RAF FF&SS, Catterick
	XF994	Hawker Hunter T8C [874/VL]	RN FRADU, Yeovilton
	XF995	Hawker Hunter T8B [XF]	RAF No 12 Sqn, Lossiemouth
	XG151	Hawker Hunter FGA9 (8798M)	RAF Lossiemouth, BDRT
	XG152	Hawker Hunter F6A [20]	RAF Brawdy
	XG154	Hawker Hunter FGA9 [54]	RAF store, St Athan
	XG158	Hawker Hunter F6A (8686M) [21]	RAE Farnborough Apprentice School
	XG160	Hawker Hunter F6A [B] (8831M)	RAF No 2 SoTT, Cosford
	XG164	Hawker Hunter F6 (8681M) [31]	RAF No 1 SoTT, Halton
	XG172	Hawker Hunter F6A [A] (8832M)	RAF No 2 SoTT, Cosford
	XG194	Hawker Hunter FGA9 [55] (8839M)	RAF No 2 SoTT, Cosford
	XG196	Hawker Hunter F6A (8702M) [25]	RAF Bracknell, on gate
	XG209	Hawker Hunter F6 (8709M) [69]	RAF No 1 SoTT, Halton
	XG210	Hawker Hunter F6	BAe, Hatfield/Dunsfold

Serial	Type (alternative identity)	Owner, Operator or Location	Notes
XG225	Hawker Hunter F6A (8713M) [S]	RAF No 2 SoTT, Cosford	
XG226	Hawker Hunter F6A (8800M) [28]	RAF FF&SS, Catterick	
XG228	Hawker Hunter FGA9 [56]	RAF store, St Athan	
XG252	Hawker Hunter FGA9 (8840M) [U]	RAF No 2 SoTT, Cosford	
XG254	Hawker Hunter FGA9 [57]	RAF store, St Athan	
XG274	Hawker Hunter F6 (8710M) [71]	RAF No 1 SoTT, Halton	
XG290	Hawker Hunter F6 (8711M) [74]	RAF No 1 SoTT, Halton	
XG327	EE Lightning F1 (8188M)	RAF Manston, Fire Section	
XG329	EE Lightning F1 (8050M)	RAFC Cranwell, Engineering Wing	
XG337	EE Lightning F1 (8056M) [M]	RAF Cosford Aerospace Museum	
XG452	Westland Belvedere HC1 (G-BRMB/7997M)	British Rotorcraft Museum, Weston-super-Mare	
XG454	Westland Belvedere HC1 (8366M)	Manchester Air & Space Museum	
XG474	Westland Belvedere HC1 (8367M) [O]	RAF Museum, Hendon	
XG496	DH Devon C2 (G-ANDX) [K]	MoD(PE) RAE Farnborough	
XG502	Bristol Sycamore HR14	Museum of Army Flying, Middle Wallop	
XG504	Bristol Sycamore HR14	Privately owned, Dunblane	
XG506	Bristol Sycamore HR14 (7852M)	Bomber County Aviation Museum, Cleethorpes	
XG518	Bristol Sycamore HR14 (8009M) [S-E]	North East Aircraft Museum, Usworth	
XG540	Bristol Sycamore HR14 (7899M/8345M) [Y-S]	RAF Shawbury at main gate	
XG544	Bristol Sycamore HR14	Torbay Aircraft Museum, Paignton	
XG547	Bristol Sycamore HR14 (G-HAPR/8010M) [S-T]	British Rotorcraft Museum, Weston-super-Mare	
XG573	WS55 Whirlwind HAR3	CDE, Porton Down, Wilts	
XG574	WS55 Whirlwind HAR3 (A2575) [752/PO]	FAA Museum store, Wroughton	
XG577	WS55 Whirlwind HAR3 (A2571)	Imperial War Museum, Duxford	
XG592	WS55 Whirlwind HAS7 [54]	Wales Aircraft Museum, Cardiff	
XG594	WS55 Whirlwind HAS7 [517/PO]	Strathallan Aircraft Collection	
XG596	WS55 Whirlwind HAS7 (A2651) [66]	British Rotorcraft Museum, Weston-super-Mare	
XG613	DH Sea Venom FAW21	Imperial War Museum, Duxford	
XG629	DH Sea Venom FAW22	Torbay Aircraft Museum, Paignton	
XG680	DH Sea Venom FAW22 [735/VL]	North East Aircraft Museum, Usworth	
XG691	DH Sea Venom FAW22 [737/VL]	Cornwall Aero Park, Helston	
XG730	DH Sea Venom FAW22 [499/A]	Mosquito Aircraft Museum, London Colney	
XG734	DH Sea Venom FAW22 [669/LM]	Castlereagh College, NI	
XG737	DH Sea Venom FAW22 [438/BY]	Wales Aircraft Museum, Cardiff	
XG743	DH Sea Vampire T22 [789-BY]	Imperial War Museum, Duxford	
XG797	Fairey Gannet ECM6 [766/BY]	Imperial War Museum, Duxford	
XG831	Fairey Gannet ECM6 (A2539) [396]	Cornwall Aero Park, Helston	
XG882	Fairey Gannet T5 (8754M) [771/LM]	RAF Lossiemouth on display	
XG883	Fairey Gannet T5 [773/BY]	Wales Aircraft Museum, Cardiff	
XG888	Fairey Gannet T5	RNAS Culdrose, stored	
XG900	Short SC1	Science Museum store, Hayes	
XG905	Short SC1	Ulster Folk & Transport Museum, County Down	

Notes	Serial	Type (alternative identity)	Owner, Operator or Location
	XH124	Blackburn Beverley C1 (8025M)	RAF Museum, Hendon
	XH132	Short SC9 Canberra	MoD(PE) RS&RE Bedford
	XH135	EE Canberra PR9	RAF No 1 PRU, Wyton
	XH136	EE Canberra PR9 (8782M)	RAF No 2 SoTT, Cosford
	XH165	EE Canberra PR9 [AK]	RAF No 1 PRU, Wyton
	XH169	EE Canberra PR9 [AQ]	RAF No 1 PRU, Wyton
	XH170	EE Canberra PR9 (8739M)	RAF Wyton, on gate
	XH171	EE Canberra PR9 (8746M)	RAF No 2 SoTT, Cosford
	XH174	EE Canberra PR9	RAF No 1 PRU, Wyton
	XH175	EE Canberra PR9 [AP]	RAF No 1 PRU, Wyton
	XH228	EE Canberra B(I)8 [B]	RAF FF&SS Catterick
	XH278	DH Vampire T11 (8595M/ 7866M)	No 2482 Sqn ATC, RAF Henlow
	XH304	DH Vampire T11	RAF Vintage Pair CFS, Scampton
	XH312	DH Vampire T11 [18]	Privately owned, Chester
	XH313	DH Vampire T11 [E]	St Albans College of FE
	XH318	DH Vampire T11 (7761M) [64]	No 424 Sqn ATC, Calmore, Hants
	XH328	DH Vampire T11 [66]	Lincoln Field Vintage & HAC, Cranfield
	XH329	DH Vampire T11 [70]	Privately owned, Keevil
	XH330	DH Vampire T11 [40]	Lincoln Field Vintage & HAC, Bushey
	XH537	Avro Vulcan B2 MRR (8749M)	RAF Abingdon, on display
	XH539	Avro Vulcan B2	RAF Waddington, rescue training
	XH554	Avro Vulcan B2 (8694M)	RAF FF&SS Catterick
	XH558	Avro Vulcan B2	RAF Marham Fire Section
	XH560	Avro Vulcan K2	RAF No 50 Sqn, Waddington
	XH561	Avro Vulcan K2 (8809M)	RAF FF&SS, Catterick
	XH562	Avro Vulcan K2 (8758M)	RAF FF&SS, Catterick
	XH563	Avro Vulcan B2 MRR (8744M)	RAF Scampton, preserved
	XH567	EE Canberra B6(mod)	MoD(PE) RAE Bedford
	XH568	EE Canberra B6(mod)	MoD(PE) RAE Bedford
	XH583	EE Canberra T4 (G-27-374)	BAe Samlesbury, stored
	XH590	HP Victor K1A	RAF Manston, CTE
	XH592	HP Victor B1A (8429M) [L]	RAF No 2 SoTT, Cosford
	XH593	HP Victor B1A (8428M) [T]	RAF Aerospace Museum, Cosford
	XH616	HP Victor K1A	RAF Manston, CTE
	XH648	HP Victor K1A	Imperial War Museum, Duxford
	XH669	HP Victor K2	RAF No 57 Sqn, Marham
	XH670	HP Victor SR2 nose only	Lincolnshire Aviation Museum, Tattershall
	XH671	HP Victor K2	RAF No 55 Sqn, Marham
	XH672	HP Victor K2	RAF No 57 Sqn, Marham
	XH673	HP Victor K2	RAF No 57 Sqn, Marham
	XH675	HP Victor K2	RAF No 55 Sqn, Marham
	XH764	Gloster Javelin FAW9 (7972M)	RAF Manston on display
	XH767	Gloster Javelin FAW9 (7955M)	No 187 Sqn ATC, Worcester
	XH837	Gloster Javelin FAW7 (8032M) nose only	No 114 Sqn ATC, West Ruislip
	XH892	Gloster Javelin FAW9 (7982M) [B]	Norfolk & Suffolk Aviation Museum, Flixton
	XH897	Gloster Javelin FAW9	Imperial War Museum, Duxford
	XH903	Gloster Javelin FAW9 (7938M)	RAF Innsworth, at main gate
	XH980	Gloster Javelin FAW9 (7867M) [A]	RAF West Raynham, at main gate
	XH992	Gloster Javelin FAW9 (7829M) [P]	Newark Air Museum, Winthorpe
	XJ314	RR Thrust Measuring Rig	Science Museum, Strathallan
	XJ319	DH Sea Devon C20 (G-AMXP)	RNAS Culdrose Station Flight
	XJ324	DH Sea Devon C20 (G-AMXZ)	RNAS Culdrose Station Flight
	XJ348	DH Sea Devon C20 (G-AMXX/ G-NAVY)	Privately owned, Shoreham
	XJ380	Bristol Sycamore HR14 (8628M)	RAF Finningley, for display
	XJ389	Fairey Jet Gyrodyne (G-AJJP)	RAF Cosford, Aerospace Museum

Serial	Type (alternative identity)	Owner, Operator or Location	Notes
XJ393	WS55 Whirlwind HAR3 (A2538)	Torbay Aircraft Museum, Paignton	
XJ402	WS55 Whirlwind HAR3 (A2572) [61]	FAA Museum store, RNAS Yeovilton	
XJ407	WS55 Whirlwind HAR10 (G-BKHB)	Privately owned, Tattershall Thorpe	
XJ409	WS55 Whirlwind HAR10	Wales Aircraft Museum, Cardiff	
XJ411	WS55 Whirlwind HAR10 [Z]	RAE Farnborough Fire Section	
XJ430	WS55 Whirlwind HAR10	CTE, RAF Manston	
XJ435	WS55 Whirlwind HAR10 (8671M) [V]	RAF No 1 SoTT, Halton	
XJ445	WS55 Whirlwind HAR5	CDE, Porton Down, Wilts	
XJ476	DH Sea Vixen FAW1 (nose section)	Southampton Hall of Aviation	
XJ481	DH Sea Vixen FAW1 [VL]	FAA Museum, RNAS Yeovilton	
XJ482	DH Sea Vixen FAW1 (A2598) [713/VL]	Norfolk & Suffolk Aviation Museum, Flixton	
XJ524	DH Sea Vixen FAW (TT) 2 (8804M) [E]	RAF FF&SS, Catterick	
XJ526	DH Sea Vixen FAW2 (8145M) [38]	RAF FF&SS, Catterick	
XJ560	DH Sea Vixen FAW2 (8142M) [242]	MoD(PE) RAE Bedford	
XJ565	DH Sea Vixen FAW2 [127/E]	Mosquito Aircraft Museum, London Colney	
XJ571	DH Sea Vixen FAW2 (8140M) [133/E]	RAF No 2 SoTT, Cosford	
XJ572	DH Sea Vixen FAW2 (8803M)	RAF FF&SS, Catterick	
XJ575	DH Sea Vixen FAW2 (A2611) [-/VL] [SAH-13]	Cornwall Aero Park, Helston	
XJ579	DH Sea Vixen FAW2	MoD(PE) RAE Farnborough, stored	
XJ580	DH Sea Vixen FAW2 [131/E]	Christchurch Memorial Group	
XJ582	DH Sea Vixen FAW2 (8130M) [702]	RAF Cottesmore Fire Section	
XJ584	DH Sea Vixen FAW2 (A2621) [SAH-16]	Cornwall Aero Park, Helston	
XJ604	DH Sea Vixen FAW2 (8222M) [755/VL]	RAF No 1 SoTT, Halton	
XJ607	DH Sea Vixen FAW2 (8171M) [701]	RAF No 2 SoTT, Cosford	
XJ608	DH Sea Vixen FAW2 (8802M)	EOD, North Luffenham, ground instr	
XJ609	DH Sea Vixen FAW2 (8172M) painted 8171M [702/VL]	RAF Abingdon BDRF	
XJ634	Hawker Hunter F6A (8684M) [29]	RAFC Cranwell, Engineering Wing	
XJ639	Hawker Hunter F6A (8687M) [31]	RAFC Cranwell, Engineering Wing	
XJ676	Hawker Hunter F6A [32]	RAF Brawdy	
XJ683	Hawker Hunter FGA9	RAF Brawdy	
XJ695	Hawker Hunter FGA9 (8677M/8738M) [J]	RAF Manston Fire School	
XJ723	WS55 Whirlwind HAR10	OPITB, Montrose	
XJ726	WS55 Whirlwind HAR10 [Q]	Nene Valley Aviation Society, Sibson	
XJ727	WS55 Whirlwind HAR10 (8661M) [L]	RAF No 1 SoTT, Halton	
XJ729	WS55 Whirlwind HAR10 (8732M)	RAF Finningley, for display	
XJ763	WS55 Whirlwind HAR10 (G-BKHA)	Privately owned, Biggin Hill	
XJ772	DH Vampire T11 [H]	Brooklands Technical College	
XJ782	Avro Vulcan B2 MRR (8766M)	RAF Finningley on display	
XJ823	Avro Vulcan B2	Privately owned, Carlisle Airport	
XJ824	Avro Vulcan B2	Imperial War Museum, Duxford	
XJ825	Avro Vulcan K2 (8810M)	RAF Waddington BDRT	
XJ917	Bristol Sycamore HR14 [S-H]	Cornwall Aero Park, Helston	
XJ918	Bristol Sycamore HR14 (8190M)	Cosford Aerospace Museum	

Notes	Serial	Type (alternative identity)	Owner, Operator or Location
	XK149	Hawker Hunter F6A (8714M) [34]	RAFC Cranwell, Engineering Wing
	XK412	Auster AOP9	Privately owned, Wooton Basset
	XK416	Auster AOP9 (G-AYUA/ 7855M)	Lincoln Field Vintage & HAC, Bushey
	XK417	Auster AOP9 (G-AVXY)	Privately owned, Leicester
	XK418	Auster AOP9 (7976M)	Second World War Aircraft Preservation Society, Lasham
	XK421	Auster AOP9 (8365M)	Cotswold Aircraft Restoration Group, RAF Innsworth
	XK482	Saro Skeeter AOP12 (7840M/ G-BJWC) [C]	Privately owned, Carnforth
	XK488	Blackburn Buccaneer S1	FAA Museum, RNAS Yeovilton
	XK526	Blackburn Buccaneer S2 (8648M)	RAF Honington, at main gate
	XK527	Blackburn Buccaneer S2D (8818M)	MoD(PE) BAe Brough
	XK530	Blackburn Buccaneer S2	Nene Valley Aviation Society, RAE Bedford
	XK531	Blackburn Buccaneer S1 (8403M)	Defence School, Winterbourne Gunner
	XK532	Blackburn Buccaneer S1 (A2581) [632/LM]	RAF Lossiemouth, on display
	XK590	DH Vampire T11 [V]	Wellesbourne Aviation Group
	XK623	DH Vampire T11 [56] (G-VAMP)	Hunter One Collection, Hurn
	XK624	DH Vampire T11 [32]	Norfolk & Suffolk Aviation Museum, Flixton
	XK625	DH Vampire T11 [12]	Privately owned, North Weald
	XK627	DH Vampire T11	Pennine Aviation Museum, Bacup
	XK632	DH Vampire T11 [67]	Lincoln Field Vintage & HAC, Bushey
	XK637	DH Vampire T11 [56]	No 1855 Sqn ATC, Royton, Manchester
	XK655	DH Comet 2R (G-AMXA)	Strathallan Aircraft Collection
	XK659	DH Comet 2 nose only	Privately owned, Elland, W. Yorks
	XK695	DH Comet 2R (G-AMXH)	Imperial War Museum, Duxford
	XK697	DH Comet 2R (G-AMXJ) [D]	Air Scouts, RAF Wyton
	XK699	DH Comet C2 (G-AMXM/ 7971M)	RAF Museum Store, Henlow
	XK724	Folland Gnat F1 (7715M)	RAFC Cranwell, Engineering Wing
	XK740	Folland Gnat F1 (8396M)	RAF Cosford Aerospace Museum
	XK741	Folland Gnat F1	Midland Air Museum, Coventry
	XK776	ML Utility I	Museum of Army Flying, Middle Wallop
	XK788	Slingsby Grasshopper TX1	Sevenoaks School CCF, RAF West Malling
	XK789	Slingsby Grasshopper TX1	RAF No 3 MGSP, Cosford
	XK790	Slingsby Grasshopper TX1	RAF No 1 MGSP, Halton
	XK819	Slingsby Grasshopper TX1	Malvern College CCF, Great Malvern
	XK820	Slingsby Grasshopper TX1	RAF No 2 MGSP, Locking
	XK822	Slingsby Grasshopper TX1	Kings College School CCF, Wimbledon
	XK824	Slingsby Grasshopper TX1	Wycliffe School CCF, Stonehouse, Glos
	XK884	Percival Pembroke C1	RAF No 60 Sqn, Wildenrath
	XK885	Percival Pembroke C1 (8452M)	RAF St Athan
	XK895	DH Sea Devon C20	RNAS Culdrose Station Flight
	XK906	WS55 Whirlwind HAS7	AAC Netheravon Fire Section
	XK907	WS55 Whirlwind HAS7 [9]	Midland Air Museum, Coventry
	XK911	WS55 Whirlwind HAS7 (A2603) [519/PO]	RN store, Wroughton
	XK912	WS55 Whirlwind HAS7 [60/CU]	Privately owned, Crudwell, Wilts
	XK936	WS55 Whirlwind HAS7 [62]	Imperial War Museum, Duxford
	XK943	WS55 Whirlwind HAS7 (A2653/8796M) [57]	RAF Abingdon, BDRF
	XK944	WS55 Whirlwind HAS7 (A2607)	Brunel Technical College, Bristol
	XK968	WS55 Whirlwind HAR10 (8445M) [E]	RAF Manston, on display

Serial	Type (alternative identity)	Owner, Operator or Location	Notes
XK969	WS55 Whirlwind HAR10 (8646M)	RAF Odiham, BDRT	
XK988	WS55 Whirlwind HAR10 (A2646) [D]	Museum of Army Flying, Middle Wallop	
XL158	HP Victor K2	RAF No 57 Sqn, Marham	
XL160	HP Victor K2	RAF No 57 Sqn, Marham	
XL161	HP Victor K2	RAF No 55 Sqn, Marham	
XL162	HP Victor K2	RAF No 55 Sqn, Marham	
XL163	HP Victor K2	RAF No 55 Sqn, Marham	
XL164	HP Victor K2	RAF No 57 Sqn, Marham	
XL188	HP Victor K2	RAF No 55 Sqn, Marham	
XL189	HP Victor K2	RAF No 57 Sqn, Marham	
XL190	HP Victor K2	RAF No 55 Sqn, Marham	
XL191	HP Victor K2	RAF No 55 Sqn, Marham	
XL192	HP Victor K2	RAF No 57 Sqn, Marham	
XL231	HP Victor K2	RAF No 232 OCU, Marham	
XL233	HP Victor K2	RAF No 55 Sqn, Marham	
XL318	Avro Vulcan B2 (8733M)	Bomber Command Museum, Hendon	
XL319	Avro Vulcan B2	North East Aircraft Museum, Usworth	
XL321	Avro Vulcan B2 (8759M)	RAF FF&SS Catterick	
XL360	Avro Vulcan B2	Midland Air Museum, Coventry	
XL386	Avro Vulcan B2 (8760M)	RAF Manston Fire Section	
XL388	Avro Vulcan B2 (8750M)	RAF Honington Fire Section	
XL391	Avro Vulcan B2	Privately owned, Blackpool	
XL392	Avro Vulcan B2 (8745M)	RAF Valley Fire Section	
XL426	Avro Vulcan B2	RAF No 50 Sqn, Waddington	
XL427	Avro Vulcan B2 (8756M)	RAF Machrihanish Fire Section	
XL445	Avro Vulcan K2 (8811M)	RAF Lyneham, BDRT	
XL449	Fairey Gannet AEW3 [LM]	Wales Aircraft Museum, Cardiff	
XL450	Fairey Gannet AEW3 (8601M)	British Aviation Heritage, Bruntingthorpe	
XL471	Fairey Gannet AEW3 [043/R]	MoD(PE) RAE Farnborough	
XL472	Fairey Gannet AEW3 [044/R]	A&AEE Boscombe Down, derelict	
XL497	Fairey Gannet AEW3 [041/R]	HMS Gannet, Prestwick, at gate	
XL500	Fairey Gannet AEW3 (A2701) [LM]	RN Historic Flt, RNAS Culdrose	
XL502	Fairey Gannet AEW3 (8610M)	RAF Leuchars BDRF	
XL503	Fairey Gannet AEW3 [070/E]	FAA Museum, RNAS Yeovilton	
XL511	HP Victor K2	RAF No 55 Sqn, Marham	
XL512	HP Victor K2	RAF No 57 Sqn, Marham	
XL563	Hawker Hunter T7	MoD(PE) RAE/IAM Farnborough	
XL564	Hawker Hunter T7 [4]	MoD(PE) ETPS Boscombe Down	
XL565	Hawker Hunter T7	RAE Farnborough	
XL566	Hawker Hunter T7 [86]	RAF Shawbury store	
XL567	Hawker Hunter T7 (8723M) [84]	RAF Chivenor Fire Section	
XL568	Hawker Hunter T7B [ZF]	RAF No 12 Sqn, Lossiemouth	
XL569	Hawker Hunter T7 (8833M) [80]	RAF TMTS, Scampton	
XL572	Hawker Hunter T7 (8834M) [83]	RAF TMTS, Scampton	
XL573	Hawker Hunter T7 [WC]	RAF No 237 OCU, Lossiemouth	
XL576	Hawker Hunter T7 (8835M) [81]	RAF TMTS, Scampton	
XL577	Hawker Hunter T7 (8676M) [01]	RAFC Cranwell, Engineering Wing	
XL578	Hawker Hunter T7 [77]	RAF store, St Athan	
XL580	Hawker Hunter T8M [719/VL]	RN, No 899 Sqn, Yeovilton	
XL583	Hawker Hunter T7 [84]	RAF Brawdy Dog Pound	
XL584	Hawker Hunter T8C [877/VL]	RN FRADU, Yeovilton	
XL586	Hawker Hunter T7 [85]	MoD(PE)/BAe, Warton	
XL587	Hawker Hunter T7 (8807M)	RAF TMTS, Scampton	
XL591	Hawker Hunter T7 [VC]	RAF No 237 OCU, Lossiemouth	
XL592	Hawker Hunter T7 (8836M) [82]	RAF TMTS, Scampton	
XL595	Hawker Hunter T7 [78]	RAF store, St Athan	
XL598	Hawker Hunter T8C [880/VL]	RN FRADU, Yeovilton	
XL600	Hawker Hunter T7 [Y]	RAF TMTS, Scampton	
XL601	Hawker Hunter T7	RAF No 237 OCU, Lossiemouth	
XL602	Hawker Hunter T8M	MoD(PE) BAe Dunsfold	
XL603	Hawker Hunter T8M [720]	RN No 899 Sqn, Yeovilton	

Notes	Serial	Type (alternative identity)	Owner, Operator or Location
	XL609	Hawker Hunter T7 [YF]	RAF No 12 Sqn, Lossiemouth
	XL612	Hawker Hunter T7 [2]	MoD(PE) ETPS Boscombe Down
	XL613	Hawker Hunter T7 [UC]	RAF No 237 OCU, Lossiemouth
	XL614	Hawker Hunter T7B [YC]	RAF No 237 OCU, Lossiemouth
	XL616	Hawker Hunter T7 [YS]	RAF No 208 Sqn, Lossiemouth
	XL617	Hawker Hunter T7 (8837M) [89]	RAF TMTS, Scampton
	XL618	Hawker Hunter T7 [05]	RAF Shawbury store
	XL621	Hawker Hunter T7	RAF No 237 OCU, Lossiemouth
	XL623	Hawker Hunter T7 (8770M) [90]	RAF No 2 SoTT, Cosford
	XL629	EE Lightning T4	A&AEE Boscombe Down, at main gate
	XL703	SAL Pioneer CC1 (8034M)	Manchester Air & Space Museum
	XL714	DH Tiger Moth (G-AOGR)	Privately owned, Shipdham
	XL717	DH Tiger Moth (G-AOXG) [LM]	FAA Museum, RNAS Yeovilton
	XL728	Westland Wessex HAS1	MoD(PE) RAE Farnborough
	XL735	Saro Skeeter AOP12	No 1404 Sqn ATC, Manston
	XL738	Saro Skeeter AOP12 (7860M)	Southampton Hall of Aviation
	XL762	Saro Skeeter AOP12 (8017M)	Royal Scottish Museum of Flight, East Fortune
	XL763	Saro Skeeter AOP12	Southall Technical College
	XL764	Saro Skeeter AOP12 (7940M)	Newark Air Museum, Winthorpe
	XL765	Saro Skeeter AOP12	Midland Air Museum, Coventry
	XL770	Saro Skeeter AOP12 (8046M)	Royal Military College of Science, Shrivenham
	XL809	Saro Skeeter AOP12 (PH-HOF)	The Old Training Plane Co, Shobdon
	XL811	Saro Skeeter AOP12 [157]	The Aircraft Collection, Warmington
	XL812	Saro Skeeter AOP12 (G-SARO)	Privately owned, Dalcross
	XL813	Saro Skeeter AOP12	Museum of Army Flying, Middle Wallop
	XL814	Saro Skeeter AOP12	AAC Historic Aircraft Flight, Middle Wallop
	XL824	Bristol Sycamore HR14 (8021M)	Manchester Air & Space Museum
	XL829	Bristol Sycamore HR14	Bristol Industrial Museum
	XL836	WS55 Whirlwind HAS7 (A2642) [65/FL]	RN Predannack Fire Section
	XL839	WS55 Whirlwind HAR9 (A2665) [588/CU]	RNAS Lee-on-Solent Fire Section
	XL840	WS55 Whirlwind HAS7 [56]	Nene Valley Aviation Society, Sibson
	XL846	WS55 Whirlwind HAS7 (A2625) [85]	RNAS Yeovilton, fire section
	XL847	WS55 Whirlwind HAS7 (A2626) [83]	AAC, BDRF Middle Wallop
	XL853	WS55 Whirlwind HAS7 (A2630)	Museum of Army Flying, Andover store
	XL875	WS55 Whirlwind HAR9	Air Service Training, Perth
	XL880	WS55 Whirlwind HAR9 (A2714) [433/ED]	RNAS AES Lee-on-Solent
	XL898	WS55 Whirlwind HAR9 (8654M) [30/ED]	Boscombe Down, Fire Section
	XL899	WS55 Whirlwind HAR9 [587/CU]	RN Predannack Fire Section
	XL929	Percival Pembroke C1	RAF No 60 Sqn, Wildenrath
	XL954	Percival Pembroke C1	RAF No 60 Sqn, Wildenrath
	XL993	SAL Twin Pioneer CC1 (8388M)	RAF Cosford Aerospace Museum
	XM135	BAC Lightning F1 [135]	Imperial War Museum, Duxford
	XM139	BAC Lightning F1 (8411M) [F]	RAF Wattisham
	XM144	BAC Lightning F1 (8417M) [J]	RAF Leuchars, at main gate
	XM147	BAC Lightning F1 (8412M) [J]	RAF Wattisham
	XM169	BAC Lightning F1A (8422M) [W]	RAF Leuchars
	XM172	BAC Lightning F1A (8427M) [B]	RAF Coltishall, at main gate
	XM173	BAC Lightning F1A (8414M) [A]	RAF Bentley Priory, at main gate

Serial	Type (alternative identity)	Owner, Operator or Location	Notes
XM178	BAC Lightning F1A (8418M) [Y]	RAF Leuchars	
XM181	BAC Lightning F1A (8415M)	RAF Binbrook	
XM183	BAC Lightning F1A (8416M)	RAF Binbrook	
XM191	BAC Lightning F1A (8590M) nose only	RAF Exhibition Flight, Abingdon	
XM192	BAC Lightning F1A (8413M) [K]	RAF Wattisham, at main gate	
XM223	DH Devon C2 [J]	MoD(PE) RAE Farnborough	
XM275	EE Canberra B(I)8	RAF Wattisham Fire Section	
XM296	DH Heron C4	RN FONAC, RNAS Yeovilton	
XM300	Westland Wessex HAS1	Wales Aircraft Museum, Cardiff	
XM326	Westland Wessex HAS1 [515]	RNAS Portland Fire Section	
XM327	Westland Wessex HAS3 [410/KE]	RN store, Wroughton	
XM328	Westland Wessex HAS3 [06/AN]	RN store, Wroughton	
XM329	Westland Wessex HAS1 (A2609) [533/PO]	RN AES Lee-on-Solent	
XM330	Westland Wessex HAS1	MoD(PE) RAE Farnborough	
XM331	Westland Wessex HAS3 [653/PO]	RNAS Lee-on-Solent Fire Section	
XM349	Hunting Jet Provost T3A [H]	RAF CFS, Scampton	
XM350	Hunting Jet Provost T3A [89]	RAF No 7 FTS, Church Fenton	
XM351	Hunting Jet Provost T3 (8078M) [05]	RAF No 2 SoTT, Cosford	
XM352	Hunting Jet Provost T3A [92]	RAF No 7 FTS, Church Fenton	
XM355	Hunting Jet Provost T3 (8229M) [G]	RAF No 1 SoTT, Halton	
XM357	Hunting Jet Provost T3A [45]	RAF No 1 FTS, Linton-on-Ouse	
XM358	Hunting Jet Provost T3A [53]	RAF No 1 FTS, Linton-on-Ouse	
XM362	Hunting Jet Provost T3 (8230M) [S]	RAF No 1 SoTT, Halton	
XM365	Hunting Jet Provost T3A [37]	RAF No 1 FTS, Linton-on-Ouse	
XM367	Hunting Jet Provost T3 (8083M) [04]	RAF No 2 SoTT, Cosford	
XM369	Hunting Jet Provost T3 (8084M) [07]	RAF No 1 SoTT, Halton	
XM370	Hunting Jet Provost T3A [93]	RAF No 7 FTS, Church Fenton	
XM371	Hunting Jet Provost T3A [K]	RAF CFS, Scampton	
XM372	Hunting Jet Provost T3A [55]	RAF No 1 FTS, Linton-on-Ouse	
XM374	Hunting Jet Provost T3A [83]	RAF No 7 FTS, Church Fenton	
XM375	Hunting Jet Provost T3 (8231M) [B]	RAF No 1 SoTT, Halton	
XM376	Hunting Jet Provost T3A [97]	RAF No 7 FTS, Church Fenton	
XM378	Hunting Jet Provost T3A	RAF St Athan, hack	
XM381	Hunting Jet Provost T3 (8232M) [O]	RAF No 1 SoTT, Halton	
XM383	Hunting Jet Provost T3A [90]	RAF No 7 FTS, Church Fenton	
XM386	Hunting Jet Provost T3 (8076M) [08]	RAF No 1 SoTT, Halton	
XM387	Hunting Jet Provost T3A [I]	RAF CFS, Scampton	
XM401	Hunting Jet Provost T3A [17]	RAF No 1 FTS, Linton-on-Ouse	
XM402	Hunting Jet Provost T3 (8055AM) [J]	RAF No 1 SoTT, Halton	
XM403	Hunting Jet Provost T3A [A]	RAF CFS, Scampton	
XM404	Hunting Jet Provost T3 (8055BM) [24]	RAF No 1 SoTT, Halton	
XM405	Hunting Jet Provost T3A [42]	RAF No 1 FTS, Linton-on-Ouse	
XM408	Hunting Jet Provost T3 (8233M) [P]	RAF No 1 SoTT, Halton	
XM409	Hunting Jet Provost T3 (8082M) [A]	RAF No 1 SoTT, Halton	
XM410	Hunting Jet Provost T3 (8054AM) [C]	RAF No 1 SoTT, Halton	
XM411	Hunting Jet Provost T3 (8434M) [L]	RAF No 1 SoTT, Halton	
XM412	Hunting Jet Provost T3A [41]	RAF No 1 FTS, Linton-on-Ouse	
XM414	Hunting Jet Provost T3A [101]	RAF No 7 FTS, Church Fenton	

Notes	Serial	Type (alternative identity)	Owner, Operator or Location
	XM415	Hunting Jet Provost T3 (nose only)	No 424 Sqn ATC, Southampton
	XM417	Hunting Jet Provost T3 (8054BM) [D]	RAF No 1 SoTT, Halton
	XM419	Hunting Jet Provost T3A [102]	RAF No 7 FTS, Church Fenton
	XM424	Hunting Jet Provost T3A [30]	RAF No 1 FTS, Linton-on-Ouse
	XM425	Hunting Jet Provost T3A [88]	RAF No 7 FTS, Church Fenton
	XM426	Hunting Jet Provost T3 nose only	No 1151 Sqn ATC, Wallsend-on-Tyne
	XM455	Hunting Jet Provost T3A [F]	RAF CFS, Scampton
	XM458	Hunting Jet Provost T3A [B]	RAF CFS, Scampton
	XM459	Hunting Jet Provost T3A [20]	RAF Shawbury store
	XM461	Hunting Jet Provost T3A [11]	RAF No 1 FTS, Linton-on-Ouse
	XM463	Hunting Jet Provost T3A [38]	RAF No 1 FTS, Linton-on-Ouse
	XM464	Hunting Jet Provost T3A [23]	RAF No 1 FTS, Linton-on-Ouse
	XM465	Hunting Jet Provost T3A [85]	RAF No 7 FTS, Church Fenton
	XM466	Hunting Jet Provost T3A [31]	RAF No 1 FTS, Linton-on-Ouse
	XM467	Hunting Jet Provost T3 (8085M) [06]	RAF No 1 SoTT, Halton
	XM468	Hunting Jet Provost T3 (8081M) [B]	RAF No 1 SoTT, Halton
	XM470	Hunting Jet Provost T3A	RAF Shawbury store
	XM471	Hunting Jet Provost T3A [10]	RAF No 1 FTS, Linton-on-Ouse
	XM472	Hunting Jet Provost T3A [22]	RAF No 1 FTS, Linton-on-Ouse
	XM473	Hunting Jet Provost T3A [19]	RAF No 1 FTS, Linton-on-Ouse
	XM474	Hunting Jet Provost T3 (8121M)	Shrewsbury School CCF
	XM475	Hunting Jet Provost T3A [96]	RAF No 7 FTS, Church Fenton
	XM478	Hunting Jet Provost T3A [33]	RAF No 1 FTS, Linton-on-Ouse
	XM479	Hunting Jet Provost T3A [54]	RAF No 1 FTS, Linton-on-Ouse
	XM480	Hunting Jet Provost T3 (8080M) [02]	RAF No 1 SoTT, Halton
	XM529	Saro Skeeter AOP12 (7979M/ G-BDNS)	Privately owned, Handforth
	XM553	Saro Skeeter AOP12 (G-AWSV)	Privately owned, Middle Wallop
	XM555	Saro Skeeter AOP12 (8027M)	RAF Cosford Aerospace Museum
	XM556	Saro Skeeter AOP12 (G-HELI/7870M) [V]	British Rotorcraft Museum, Weston-super-Mare
	XM561	Saro Skeeter AOP12 (7980M)	Lincolnshire Aviation Museum, Tattershall
	XM564	Saro Skeeter AOP12	Royal Armoured Corps, Bovington
	XM569	Avro Vulcan B2	Wales Aircraft Museum, Cardiff
	XM575	Avro Vulcan B2 (G-BLMC)	Privately owned, EMA
	XM594	Avro Vulcan B2	Newark Air Museum, Winthorpe
	XM597	Avro Vulcan B2	Royal Scottish Museum of Flight, East Fortune
	XM598	Avro Vulcan B2 (8778M)	RAF Cosford Aerospace Museum
	XM602	Avro Vulcan B2 (8771M)	RAF St Athan, preserved
	XM603	Avro Vulcan B2	BAe Woodford
	XM607	Avro Vulcan B2 (8779M)	RAF Waddington, on display
	XM612	Avro Vulcan B2	City of Norwich Aviation Museum
	XM652	Avro Vulcan B2	Sheffield Leisure Centre
	XM655	Avro Vulcan B2 (G-VULC)	Privately owned, Wellesbourne Mountford
	XM656	Avro Vulcan B2 (8757M)	RAF Cottesmore Fire Section
	XM657	Avro Vulcan B2 (8734M)	RAF Manston Fire School
	XM660	WS55 Whirlwind HAS7 [78]	North East Air Museum, Usworth
	XM665	WS55 Whirlwind HAS7	Booker Aircraft Museum
	XM667	WS55 Whirlwind HAS7 (A2629) [556/CU]	RNAS Lee-on-Solent, BDRF
	XM685	WS55 Whirlwind HAS7 (G-AYZJ) [518/PO]	Newark Air Museum, Winthorpe
	XM693	HS Gnat T1 (7891M)	BAe, Hamble
	XM694	HS Gnat T1	RAE Bedford Apprentice School
	XM697	HS Gnat T1	No 1349 Sqn ATC, Woking
	XM698	HS Gnat T1 (8090M/8497M)	RAF Cosford Aerospace Museum
	XM706	HS Gnat T1 (8572M) [12]	RAF No 1 SoTT, Halton
	XM708	HS Gnat T1 (8573M) [18] [72]	RAF No 1 SoTT, Halton

Serial	Type (alternative identity)	Owner, Operator or Location	Notes
XM709	HS Gnat T1 (8617M) [67]	RAF No 1 SoTT, Halton	
XM715	HP Victor K2	RAF No 55 Sqn, Marham	
XM717	HP Victor K2	RAF No 55 Sqn, Marham	
XM832	Westland Wessex HAS1	RN NASU, Yeovilton	
XM833	Westland Wessex HAS3	Second World War Aircraft Preservation Society, Lasham	
XM836	Westland Wessex HAS3 [651/PO]	RN store, Wroughton	
XM838	Westland Wessex HAS3 [405/LN]	RN AES, Lee-on-Solent	
XM843	Westland Wessex HAS1 (A2693) [527/CU]	RN AES, Lee-on-Solent	
XM845	Westland Wessex HAS1 (A2682) [530/PO]	RNAS Lee-on-Solent, BDRF	
XM868	Westland Wessex HAS1 (A2711) [517/PO]	RN AES Lee-on-Solent	
XM870	Westland Wessex HAS3 [652/PO]	RN AES, Lee-on-Solent	
XM874	Westland Wessex HAS1 (A2689) [521/PO]	RNAS Culdrose, SAH	
XM916	Westland Wessex HAS3 [666/PO]	Fire Section, Wroughton	
XM917	Westland Wessex HAS1 (A2692) [528/CU]	RN AES Lee-on-Solent	
XM919	Westland Wessex HAS3 [55]	RNAS Yeovilton Fire Section	
XM923	Westland Wessex HAS3	RNAY Fleetlands	
XM926	Westland Wessex HAS1	MoD(PE) RAE Farnborough	
XM927	Westland Wessex HAS3 (8814M) [660/PO]	RAF Shawbury, BDRT	
XM969	BAC Lightning T4 (8592M)	RAF Binbrook Fire Section	
XM987	BAC Lightning T4	RAF Coningsby, BDRF	
XM997	BAC Lightning T4	RAF FF&SS, Catterick	
XN126	WS55 Whirlwind HAR10 (8655M) [S]	RAF No 1 SoTT, Halton	
XN132	Sud Alouette AH2	AAC Cyprus	
XN137	Hunting Jet Provost T3 [95] nose only	No 95 Sqn ATC, Crewe, Cheshire	
XN148	Slingsby Sedbergh TX1	RAF ACCGS, Syerston	
XN150	Slingsby Sedbergh TX1	RAF No 636 VGS, Swansea	
XN151	Slingsby Sedbergh TX1	RAF store, Syerston	
XN155	Slingsby Sedbergh TX1	RAF No 617 VGS, Manston	
XN156	Slingsby Sedbergh TX1	RAF store, Syerston	
XN157	Slingsby Sedbergh TX1	RAF No 631 VGS, Sealand	
XN185	Slingsby Sedbergh TX1	RAF No 4 MGSP, Dishforth	
XN186	Slingsby Sedbergh TX1	RAF No 618 VGS, West Malling	
XN187	Slingsby Sedbergh TX1	RAF No 662 VGS, Arbroath	
XN198	Slingsby Cadet TX3	RAF No 663 VGS, Kinloss	
XN238	Slingsby Cadet TX3	RAF St Athan	
XN239	Slingsby Cadet TX3	RAF store, Syerston	
XN240	Slingsby Cadet TX3	RAF No 621 VGS, Weston-super-Mare	
XN241	Slingsby Cadet TX3	RAF No 4 MGSP, Dishforth	
XN243	Slingsby Cadet TX3	RAF No 622 VGS, Upavon	
XN244	Slingsby Cadet TX3	RAF No 626 VGS, Predannack	
XN246	Slingsby Cadet TX3	RAF No 617 VGS, Manston	
XN252	Slingsby Cadet TX3	RAF No 661 VGS, Kirknewton	
XN253	Slingsby Cadet TX3 [L]	RAF Syerston stored	
XN258	WS55 Whirlwind HAR9 [589/CU]	Cornwall Aero Park, Helston	
XN261	WS55 Whirlwind HAS7 (A2652) [61]	RNAS Lee-on-Solent, dumped	
XN263	WS55 Whirlwind HAS7	Royal Military College of Science, Shrivenham	
XN264	WS55 Whirlwind HAS7 [53]	Privately owned, Swindon	
XN297	WS Whirlwind HAR9 (really XN311) (A2643)	RNAY Fleetlands Apprentice Training School	
XN298	WS55 Whirlwind HAR9 [810/LS]	Linwood School, Winton, nr Bournemouth	
XN299	WS55 Whirlwind HAS7 [758]	Torbay Aircraft Museum, Paignton	

43

Notes	Serial	Type (alternative identity)	Owner, Operator or Location
	XN302	WS55 Whirlwind HAS7 (A2654) [LS]	RNAS Lee-on-Solent Fire Section
	XN304	WS55 Whirlwind HAS7 [64]	Norfolk & Suffolk Aviation Museum, Flixton
	XN306	WS55 Whirlwind HAR9 [434/ED]	RNAS Portland Fire Section
	XN308	WS55 Whirlwind HAS7 (A2605) [510/PO]	RNAS Lee-on-Solent, BDRF
	XN309	WS55 Whirlwind HAR9 (A2663) [590/CU]	Second World War Aircraft Preservation Society, Lasham
	XN314	WS55 Whirlwind HAS7 (A2614)	RNAS Lee-on-Solent, BDRF
	XN332	Saro P531 (G-APNV/A2579) [759]	FAA Museum, RNAS Yeovilton
	XN334	Saro P531 (A2525)	British Rotorcraft Museum, at Yeovilton
	XN341	Saro Skeeter AOP12 (8022M)	RAF St Athan Historic Aircraft Collection
	XN344	Saro Skeeter AOP12 (8018M)	Science Museum, South Kensington
	XN351	Saro Skeeter AOP12 (G-BKSC)	Privately owned, Shobdon
	XN359	WS55 Whirlwind HAR9 (A2712) [434/ED]	RNAS Lee-on-Solent, BDRF
	XN380	WS55 Whirlwind HAS7 [67]	Lashenden Air Warfare Museum, Headcorn
	XN382	WS55 Whirlwind HAS7	Museum of Army Flying, Andover store
	XN385	WS55 Whirlwind HAS7	RN Historic Flight, stored Wroughton
	XN386	WS55 Whirlwind HAR9 [435/ED] (A2713)	RN store, Wroughton
	XN387	WS55 Whirlwind HAR9 (8564M)	RAF Odiham, BDRF
	XN435	Auster AOP9 (G-BGBU)	Privately owned, Egham
	XN437	Auster AOP9 (G-AXWA)	Privately owned, Biggin Hill
	XN441	Auster AOP9 (G-BGKT)	Privately owned, Reymerston Hall
	XN453	DH Comet 2e	RAE Farnborough Fire Section
	XN458	Hunting Jet Provost T3 (8234M) [H]	RAF No 1 SoTT, Halton
	XN459	Hunting Jet Provost T3A [20]	RAF No 1 FTS, Linton-on-Ouse
	XN461	Hunting Jet Provost T3A [28]	RAF No 1 FTS, Linton-on-Ouse
	XN462	Hunting Jet Provost T3A [87]	RAF No 7 FTS, Church Fenton
	XN466	Hunting Jet Provost T3A [29]	RAF No 1 FTS, Linton-on-Ouse
	XN467	Hunting Jet Provost T4 (8559M) [F]	RAF No 1 SoTT, Halton
	XN470	Hunting Jet Provost T3A	RAF No 1 FTS, Linton-on-Ouse
	XN471	Hunting Jet Provost T3A [24]	RAF No 1 FTS, Linton-on-Ouse
	XN472	Hunting Jet Provost T3A [32]	RAF No 1 FTS, Linton-on-Ouse
	XN492	Hunting Jet Provost T3 (8079M) [08]	RAF No 2 SoTT, Cosford
	XN493	Hunting Jet Provost T3 nose only	RAF Exhibition Flt, Abingdon
	XN494	Hunting Jet Provost T3A [43]	RAF No 1 FTS, Linton-on-Ouse
	XN495	Hunting Jet Provost T3A [102] (8786M)	RAF Abingdon, BDRF
	XN497	Hunting Jet Provost T3A [52]	RAF No 1 FTS, Linton-on-Ouse
	XN498	Hunting Jet Provost T3A [16]	RAF No 1 FTS, Linton-on-Ouse
	XN499	Hunting Jet Provost T3A [L]	RAF CFS, Scampton
	XN500	Hunting Jet Provost T3A [80]	RAF No 7 FTS, Church Fenton
	XN501	Hunting Jet Provost T3A [G]	RAF CFS, Scampton
	XN502	Hunting Jet Provost T3A [D]	RAF CFS, Scampton
	XN503	Hunting Jet Provost T3 nose only	RAF Exhibition Flt, Abingdon
	XN505	Hunting Jet Provost T3A [25]	RAF No 1 FTS, Linton-on-Ouse
	XN506	Hunting Jet Provost T3A [81]	RAF No 7 FTS, Church Fenton
	XN508	Hunting Jet Provost T3A [98]	RAF No 7 FTS, Church Fenton
	XN509	Hunting Jet Provost T3A [50]	RAF No 1 FTS, Linton-on-Ouse
	XN510	Hunting Jet Provost T3A [40]	RAF No 1 FTS, Linton-on-Ouse
	XN511	Hunting Jet Provost T3 [21] (nose only)	No 117 Sqn ATC, Blackpool Airport
	XN512	Hunting Jet Provost T3 (8435M) [E]	RAF No 1 SoTT, Halton

Serial	Type (alternative identity)	Owner, Operator or Location	Notes
XN547	Hunting Jet Provost T3A [48]	RAF No 1 FTS, Linton-on-Ouse	
XN548	Hunting Jet Provost T3A [103]	RAF No 7 FTS, Church Fenton	
XN549	Hunting Jet Provost T3 (8235M) [R]	RAF No 1 SoTT, Halton	
XN550	Hunting Jet Provost T3 [40] nose only	No 730 Sqn ATC, Truro	
XN551	Hunting Jet Provost T3A [100]	RAF No 7 FTS, Church Fenton	
XN552	Hunting Jet Provost T3A [86]	RAF No 7 FTS, Church Fenton	
XN553	Hunting Jet Provost T3A [34]	RAF No 1 FTS, Linton-on-Ouse	
XN554	Hunting Jet Provost T3 (8436M) [K]	RAF No 1 SoTT, Halton	
XN574	Hunting Jet Provost T3A [21]	RAF No 1 FTS, Linton-on-Ouse	
XN577	Hunting Jet Provost T3A [18]	RAF No 1 FTS, Linton-on-Ouse	
XN579	Hunting Jet Provost T3A [14]	RAF No 1 FTS, Linton-on-Ouse	
XN581	Hunting Jet Provost T3A [C]	RAF CFS, Scampton	
XN582	Hunting Jet Provost T3A [95]	RAF No 7 FTS, Church Fenton	
XN584	Hunting Jet Provost T3A [E]	RAF CFS, Scampton	
XN585	Hunting Jet Provost T3A [12]	RAF Linton-on-Ouse, Fire Section	
XN586	Hunting Jet Provost T3A [91]	RAF No 7 FTS, Church Fenton	
XN589	Hunting Jet Provost T3A [46]	RAF No 1 FTS, Linton-on-Ouse	
XN593	Hunting Jet Provost T3A [27]	RAF No 1 FTS, Linton-on-Ouse	
XN594	Hunting Jet Provost T3 (8077M) [09]	RAF No 2 SoTT, Cosford	
XN595	Hunting Jet Provost T3A [82]	RAF No 7 FTS, Church Fenton	
XN602	Hunting Jet Provost T3 (8088M)	RAF Manston Fire Section	
XN605	Hunting Jet Provost T3A [J]	RAF CFS, Scampton	
XN606	Hunting Jet Provost T3A [36]	RAF No 1 FTS, Linton-on-Ouse	
XN629	Hunting Jet Provost T3A [39]	RAF No 1 FTS, Linton-on-Ouse	
XN632	Hunting Jet Provost T3 (8352M)	RAF St Athan, CTTS	
XN634	Hunting Jet Provost T3A [94]	RAF No 7 FTS, Church Fenton	
XN636	Hunting Jet Provost T3A [15]	RAF No 1 FTS, Linton-on-Ouse	
XN637	Hunting Jet Provost T3 (G-BKOU)	Privately owned, Bushey	
XN640	Hunting Jet Provost T3A [99]	RAF No 7 FTS, Church Fenton	
XN641	Hunting Jet Provost T3A [47]	RAF store, Shawbury	
XN643	Hunting Jet Provost T3A (8704M) [26]	RAF Abingdon, BDRF	
XN647	DH Sea Vixen FAW2 (A2610)	Cornwall Aero Park, Helston	
XN649	DH Sea Vixen FAW2 [126]	MoD(PE) RAE Farnborough store	
XN650	DH Sea Vixen FAW2 (A2639)	Wales Aircraft Museum, Cardiff	
XN652	DH Sea Vixen D3 (8817M)	RAF FF&SS, Catterick	
XN653	DH Sea Vixen FAW2	MoD(PE) RAE Farnborough store	
XN685	DH Sea Vixen FAW2 (8173M)	RAF No 2 SoTT, Cosford	
XN688	DH Sea Vixen FAW2 (8141M)	MoD(PE) RAE Farnborough, fire section	
XN691	DH Sea Vixen FAW2 (8143M) [N]	RAF No 2 SoTT, Cosford	
XN692	DH Sea Vixen FAW2 (A2624) [SAH-17] [254/H]	RNAS Culdrose, SAH	
XN694	DH Sea Vixen FAW2	Flight Refuelling Ltd, Hurn	
XN696	DH Sea Vixen FAW2 [751]	Privately owned, Suffolk	
XN699	DH Sea Vixen FAW2 (8224M) [752]	RAF No 1 SoTT, Halton	
XN700	DH Sea Vixen FAW2 (8138M)	MoD(PE) RAE Farnborough, store	
XN705	DH Sea Vixen FAW2 (8225M)	MoD(PE) RAE Farnborough, store	
XN706	DH Sea Vixen FAW2 (A2613) [127/E]	MoD(PE) RAE Farnborough, store	
XN707	DH Sea Vixen FAW2 (8144M)	MoD(PE) RAE Farnborough, store	
XN714	Hunting H126	RAF Cosford Aerospace Museum	
XN728	BAC Lightning F2A (8546M) [V]	Privately owned, Balderton, Notts	
XN734	BAC Lightning F2 (8346M/ G-27-239)	BAe Warton	
XN769	BAC Lightning F2 (8402M) [Z]	London ATCC, West Drayton	

Notes	Serial	Type (alternative identity)	Owner, Operator or Location
	XN774 [F]	BAC Lightning F2A (8551M)	RAF Coningsby
	XN776	BAC Lightning F2A [B] (8535M)	Royal Scottish Museum of Flight, East Fortune
	XN781 [B]	BAC Lightning F2A (8538M)	RAF Leuchars
	XN816	AW Argosy E1 (8489M) [G]	RAF No 2 SoTT, Cosford
	XN817	AW Argosy C1	MoD(PE) West Freugh
	XN819	AW Argosy C1 (8205M)	RAF Finningley Fire Section
	XN855	AW Argosy E1 (8556M)	CTE, RAF Manston
	XN923	HS Buccaneer S1	MoD(PE) A&AEE Boscombe Down
	XN925	HS Buccaneer S1 (8087M/ A2602)	RAF FF&SS Catterick
	XN928	HS Buccaneer S1 (8179M)	Wales Aircraft Museum, Cardiff
	XN930	HS Buccaneer S1 (8180M) [632/LM]	RAF Honington, fire section
	XN934	HS Buccaneer S1 (A2600) [631/LS]	RNAS Culdrose Fire Section
	XN953	HS Buccaneer S1 (A2655/ 8182M) [SAH-23]	RNAS Culdrose, SAH
	XN957	HS Buccaneer S1 [630/LM]	FAA Museum, RNAS Yeovilton
	XN962	HS Buccaneer S1 (8183M) nose only	RAF Exhibition Flight, Abingdon
	XN964	HS Buccaneer S1 [613/LM]	Privately owned, Bruntingthorpe
	XN965	HS Buccaneer S1 [636]	MoD(PE) RAE Farnborough store
	XN967	HS Buccaneer S1 (A2627) [103-E]	Cornwall Aero Park, Helston
	XN974	HS Buccaneer S2A	MoD(PE)/BAe Warton
	XN976	HS Buccaneer S2B [NF]	RAF No 12 Sqn, Lossiemouth
	XN977	HS Buccaneer 92B	RAF Shawbury, store
	XN981	HS Buccaneer S2B [FS]	RAF No 208 Sqn, Lossiemouth
	XN982	HS Buccaneer S2A	MoD(PE)/BAe, Brough
	XN983	HS Buccaneer S2B [PF]	RAF No 12 Sqn, Lossiemouth
	XP000	DHC Beaver AL1 (7735M) really XP812	Warbirds of GB, Blackbushe
	XP105	Westland Wessex HAS3 (A2698) [403/CU]	RNAS Lee-on-Solent Fire Section
	XP110	Westland Wessex HAS3 [55/PO]	RN store, Wroughton
	XP116	Westland Wessex HAS3 (A2618) [520]	RN AES Lee-on-Solent
	XP117	Westland Wessex HAS1 (A2681) [521/PO]	RNAS Culdrose, SAH
	XP118	Westland Wessex HAS3 [664/PO]	RN, Predannack Fire Section
	XP137	Westland Wessex HAS3 [665/PO]	RN AES, Lee-on-Solent
	XP139	Westland Wessex HAS3	RN Predannack Fire Section
	XP140	Westland Wessex HAS3 (8806M) [654/PO]	RAF Chilmark, BDRT
	XP142	Westland Wessex HAS3	FAA Museum, RNAS Yeovilton
	XP143	Westland Wessex HAS3 [50]	RN AES Lee-on-Solent
	XP149	Westland Wessex HAS1 (A2669) [574/CU]	RN AES Lee-on-Solent
	XP150	Westland Wessex HAS3 [406-AN]	RN AES Lee-on-Solent
	XP151	Westland Wessex HAS1 (A2684) [047/R]	RN AES Lee-on-Solent
	XP157	Westland Wessex HAS1 (A2680)	RN AES Lee-on-Solent
	XP158	Westland Wessex HAS1 (A2688) [522/CU]	RNAS Culdrose, SAH
	XP159	Westland Wessex HAS1 [047/R]	No 2407 Sqn ATC, Fleet, Hants
	XP160	Westland Wessex HAS1 (A2650) [521/CU] [SAH-24]	RNAS Culdrose, SAH
	XP165	Westland Scout AH1	British Rotorcraft Museum, Weston-super-Mare

Serial	Type (alternative identity)	Owner, Operator or Location	Notes
XP166	Westland Scout AH1 (G-APVL)	MoD(PE) RAE Farnborough, in store	
XP189	Westland Scout AH1 (G-ARGI)	MoD(PE) RAE Farnborough	
XP190	Westland Scout AH1	Army Apprentice College, Arborfield	
XP191	Westland Scout AH1	Royal Military College of Science, Shrivenham	
XP226	Fairey Gannet AEW3 (A2667) [073/E]	Newark Air Museum, Winthorpe	
XP241	Auster AOP9	Tagmore Nurseries, Rabley Heath, Herts	
XP242	Auster AOP9	Museum of Army Flying Middle Wallop	
XP244	Auster AOP9 (7864M)	Army Apprentice College, Arborfield	
XP248	Auster AOP9 (7822M)	No 2293 Sqn ATC, Marlborough	
XP279	Auster AOP9 (G-BWKK)	Privately owned, Breighton	
XP280	Auster AOP9	Leicester Museum of Technology	
XP281	Auster AOP9	Imperial War Museum, Duxford	
XP282	Auster AOP9 (G-BGTC)	Privately owned, Swanton Morley	
XP283	Auster AOP9 (7859M)	Privately owned, Shoreham	
XP286	Auster AOP9 (8044M)	Privately owned, Thruxton	
XP299	WS55 Whirlwind HAR10 (8726M)	RAF Cosford Aerospace Museum	
XP328	WS55 Whirlwind HAR10 (G-BKHC)	Privately owned, Tattershall Thorpe	
XP330	WS55 Whirlwind HAR10	CAA Fire School, Teesside Airport	
XP333	WS55 Whirlwind HAR10 (8650M) [G]	RAF Odiham, Fire Section	
XP338	WS55 Whirlwind HAR10 (8647M) [N]	RAF No 2 SoTT, Cosford	
XP339	WS55 Whirlwind HAR10	Bomber County Aviation Museum, Cleethorpes	
XP341	WS55 Whirlwind HAR10 (8340M) [E]	RAFC Cranwell, Fire Section	
XP344	WS55 Whirlwind HAR10 (8764M) [X]	RAFC Cranwell, Engineering Wing	
XP350	WS55 Whirlwind HAR10	Cornwall Aero Park, Helston	
XP351	WS55 Whirlwind HAR10 (8672M) [Z]	RAF Shawbury, BDRF	
XP352	WS55 Whirlwind HAR10 (8701M)	RAF Abingdon, BDRF	
XP353	WS55 Whirlwind HAR10 (8720M)	RAF FF&SS, Catterick	
XP354	WS55 Whirlwind HAR10 (8721M)	RAF No 1 SoTT, Halton	
XP355	WS55 Whirlwind HAR10 (8463M/G-BEBC) [A]	City of Norwich Aviation Museum	
XP356	WS55 Whirlwind HAR10	RAE Farnborough Fire Section	
XP357	WS55 Whirlwind HAR10 (8499M)	RAF Manston Fire Section	
XP359	WS55 Whirlwind HAR10 (8447M)	RAF Exhibition Flight, Abingdon	
XP360	WS55 Whirlwind HAR10 [V]	Second World War Aircraft Preservation Society, Lasham	
XP361	WS55 Whirlwind HAR10 (8731M)	RAF Boulmer, on display	
XP393	WS55 Whirlwind HAR10 [U]	RAE Farnborough, Fire Section	
XP394	WS55 Whirlwind HAR10 [C]	RAF Manston, Fire Section	
XP395	WS55 Whirlwind HAR10 (8674M)	RAF No 1 SoTT, Halton	
XP399	WS55 Whirlwind HAR10	Privately owned, Tor View Garage, Glastonbury, Som	
XP400	WS55 Whirlwind HAR10 (8444M) [N]	RAF Manston, Fire Section	
XP404	WS55 Whirlwind HAR10 (8682M)	RAF Finningley	
XP405	WS55 Whirlwind HAR10 (8656M) [Y]	RAF No 1 SoTT, Halton	
XP409	AW Argosy C1 (8221M)	Defence School, Winterbourne Gunner	
XP411	AW Argosy C1 (8442M) [C]	RAF No 2 SoTT, Cosford	
XP439	AW Argosy E1 (8558M)	RAF Lossiemouth Fire Section	
XP442	AW Argosy C1 (8454M) [10]	RAF No 1 SoTT, Halton	
XP444	AW Argosy C1 (8455M) [D]	RAF No 2 SoTT, Cosford	

Notes	Serial	Type (alternative identity)	Owner, Operator or Location
	XP454	Slingsby Grasshopper TX1	Kimbolton School CCF, Cambs
	XP455	Slingsby Grasshopper TX1	RAF No 1 MGSP, Halton
	XP458	Slingsby Grasshopper TX1	RAF No 1 MGSP, Halton
	XP459	Slingsby Grasshopper TX1	Woodbridge School CCF, Suffolk
	XP462	Slingsby Grasshopper TX1	Felsted School CCF, Essex
	XP463	Slingsby Grasshopper TX1	William Parker School CCF, East Sussex
	XP464	Slingsby Grasshopper TX1	Sherborne School CCF, Dorset
	XP487	Slingsby Grasshopper TX1	Brentwood School, Essex
	XP488	Slingsby Grasshopper TX1	RAF No 1 MGSP, Halton
	XP490	Slingsby Grasshopper TX1	RAF ACCGS, Syerston
	XP492	Slingsby Grasshopper TX1	King's College CCF, Taunton
	XP493	Slingsby Grasshopper TX1	RAF ACCGS, Syerston
	XP494	Slingsby Grasshopper TX1	Stamford School, Lincs
	XP502	HS Gnat T1 (8576M) [02]	RAF St Athan
	XP503	HS Gnat T1 (8568M) [08]	RAF No 1 SoTT, Halton
	XP504	HS Gnat T1 (8618M) [68] [04]	RAF No 1 SoTT, Halton
	XP505	HS Gnat T1 [05]	Science Museum, South Kensington
	XP511	HS Gnat T1 (8619M) [65]	RAF No 1 SoTT, Halton
	XP513	HS Gnat T1 [13]	MoD(PE) A&AEE Boscombe Down
	XP514	HS Gnat T1 (8635M)	RAF No 2 SoTT, Cosford
	XP515	HS Gnat T1 (8614M) [59]	RAF Wattisham, BDRF
	XP516	HS Gnat T1 (8580M) [16]	MoD(PE) RAE Farnborough
	XP530	HS Gnat T1 (8606M) [60]	RAF No 1 SoTT, Halton
	XP531	HS Gnat T1	RAF Coltishall, BDRF
	XP532	HS Gnat T1 (8577M/8615M) [32]	MoD(PE) RAE Farnborough
	XP533	HS Gnat T1 (8632M) [33] [74]	RAF No 1 SoTT, Halton
	XP534	HS Gnat T1 (8620M) [64]	RAF No 1 SoTT, Halton
	XP535	HS Gnat T1 (A2679) [SAH-1]	RNAS Culdrose, SAH
	XP538	HS Gnat T1 (8607M) [61]	RAF No 1 SoTT, Halton
	XP540	HS Gnat T1 (8608M) [62]	RAF No 1 SoTT, Halton
	XP541	HS Gnat T1 (8616M) [41]	RAF Abingdon, BDRF
	XP542	HS Gnat T1 (8575M) [42]	RAF St Athan, CTTS
	XP547	Hunting Jet Provost T4 [03]	RAF No 1 TWU, Brawdy
	XP556	Hunting Jet Provost T4 [B]	RAF CATCS, Shawbury
	XP557	Hunting Jet Provost T4 (8494M) [65]	RAF No 1 SoTT, Halton
	XP558	Hunting Jet Provost T4 (8627M/A2628) [20]	RAF St Athan
	XP563	Hunting Jet Provost T4 [C]	RAF CATCS, Shawbury
	XP564	Hunting Jet Provost T4 [04]	RAF Brawdy Dog Pound
	XP567	Hunting Jet Provost T4 (8510M) [23]	RAF No 1 SoTT, Halton
	XP573	Hunting Jet Provost T4 (8236M) [19]	RAF No 1 SoTT, Halton
	XP583	Hunting Jet Provost T4 (8400M) [12]	CTE, RAF Manston
	XP585	Hunting Jet Provost T4 (8407M) [24]	RAF No 1 SoTT, Halton
	XP627	Hunting Jet Provost T4	North East Aircraft Museum, Usworth
	XP629	Hunting Jet Provost T4 [P]	RAF CATCS, Shawbury
	XP638	Hunting Jet Provost T4 [A]	RAF CATCS, Shawbury
	XP640	Hunting Jet Provost T4 (8501M) [E]	RAF No 1 SoTT, Halton
	XP672	Hunting Jet Provost T4 (8458M) [C]	RAF No 1 SoTT, Halton
	XP677	Hunting Jet Provost T4 (8587M) nose only	RAF Exhibition Flight, Abingdon
	XP680	Hunting Jet Provost T4 (8460M)	RAF St Athan
	XP686	Hunting Jet Provost T4 (8401M/8502M) [B]	RAF No 1 SoTT, Halton
	XP688	Hunting Jet Provost T4 [E]	RAF CATCS, Shawbury
	XP693	BAC Lightning F6 [M]	MoD(PE) BAe Warton
	XP694	BAC Lightning F3 [BO]	RAF No 11 Sqn, Binbrook
	XP695	BAC Lightning F3 (8808M)	RAF Binbrook, BDRF
	XP701	BAC Lightning F3 [DB]	RAF LTF, Binbrook
	XP702	BAC Lightning F3	RAF Binbrook, store
	XP706	BAC Lightning F3 [DD]	RAF LTF, Binbrook
	XP707	BAC Lightning F3	RAF Binbrook, store

Serial	Type (alternative identity)	Owner, Operator or Location	Notes
XP741	BAC Lightning F3 [DD]	RAF Binbrook, store	
XP745	BAC Lightning F3 (8453M) [H]	RAF Boulmer, at main gate	
XP748	BAC Lightning F3 (8446M) [M]	RAF Binbrook, at main gate	
XP749	BAC Lightning F3 [BK2]	RAF LTF, Binbrook	
XP750	BAC Lightning F3 [DE]	RAF LTF, Binbrook	
XP751	BAC Lightning F3 [AQ]	RAF No 5 Sqn, Binbrook	
XP761	BAC Lightning F3 (8438M) [N]	RAF Binbrook Fire Section	
XP764	BAC Lightning F3 [AR]	RAF No 5 Sqn, Binbrook	
XP769	DHC Beaver AL1	AAC, Aldergrove	
XP771	DHC Beaver AL1	AAC, Aldergrove	
XP772	DHC Beaver AL1	Museum of Army Transport, Beverley	
XP774	DHC Beaver AL1	AAC, Shawbury store	
XP775	DHC Beaver AL1	AAC, Shawbury store	
XP778	DHC Beaver AL1	AAC Beaver Training Flt, Middle Wallop	
XP779	DHC Beaver AL1	AAC, Shawbury store	
XP780	DHC Beaver AL1	AAC, Shawbury store	
XP804	DHC Beaver AL1	AAC, Shawbury store	
XP806	DHC Beaver AL1	Army Apprentice College, Arborfield	
XP808	DHC Beaver AL1	AAC, Shawbury store	
XP810	DHC Beaver AL1	AAC, Shawbury store	
XP814	DHC Beaver AL1	AAC, Shawbury store	
XP816	DHC Beaver AL1	Museum of Army Flying, Middle Wallop	
XP817	DHC Beaver AL1	AAC, Middle Wallop	
XP818	DHC Beaver AL1	AAC, Shawbury store	
XP820	DHC Beaver AL1	AAC Beaver Training Flt, Middle Wallop	
XP821	DHC Beaver AL1	Museum of Army Flying, Middle Wallop	
XP822	DHC Beaver AL1	AAC, Shawbury store	
XP823	DHC Beaver AL1	AAC, Shawbury store	
XP825	DHC Beaver AL1	AAC, Aldergrove	
XP826	DHC Beaver AL1 [L]	AAC No 29 Flt, Alberta, Canada	
XP827	DHC Beaver AL1	AAC, Shawbury store	
XP831	Hawker P1127 (8406M)	RAF Museum, Hendon	
XP841	Handley Page HP115	FAA Museum, RNAS Yeovilton	
XP846	Westland Scout AH1 [Y]	AAC No 660 Sqn, Sek Kong	
XP847	Westland Scout AH1	Museum of Army Flying, Middle Wallop	
XP848	Westland Scout AH1	AAC AETW, Middle Wallop	
XP849	Westland Scout AH1	MoD(PE) ETPS Boscombe Down	
XP850	Westland Scout AH1	AAC store, Wroughton	
XP852	Westland Scout AH1	AAC store, Wroughton	
XP853	Westland Scout AH1	AAC AETW, Middle Wallop	
XP854	Westland Scout AH1 (7898M/TAD043)	AAC AETW, Middle Wallop	
XP855	Westland Scout AH1	AAC store, Wroughton	
XP856	Westland Scout AH1	AAC AETW, Middle Wallop	
XP857	Westland Scout AH1	AAC Middle Wallop, BDRF	
XP883	Westland Scout AH1	AAC, UK	
XP884	Westland Scout AH1	AAC AETW, Middle Wallop	
XP885	Westland Scout AH1 [Y]	AAC ATS, Middle Wallop	
XP886	Westland Scout AH1	AAC store, Wroughton	
XP887	Westland Scout AH1 [C]	AAC No 660 Sqn, Sek Kong	
XP888	Westland Scout AH1	AAC AETW, Middle Wallop	
XP891	Westland Scout AH1 [Z]	AAC No 658 Sqn, Netheravon	
XP893	Westland Scout AH1 [S]	AAC store, Wroughton	
XP894	Westland Scout AH1 [D]	AAC No 660 Sqn, Sek Kong	
XP897	Westland Scout AH1	AAC store, Wroughton	
XP898	Westland Scout AH1	AAC store, Wroughton	
XP899	Westland Scout AH1 [D]	Army Apprentice College, Arborfield	
XP900	Westland Scout AH1 [Z]	AAC ATS, Middle Wallop	
XP902	Westland Scout AH1 [T]	AAC store, Wroughton	
XP903	Westland Scout AH1	AAC store, Wroughton	
XP905	Westland Scout AH1	AAC AETW, Middle Wallop	
XP906	Westland Scout AH1 [F]	AAC store, Wroughton	
XP907	Westland Scout AH1	AAC, No 657 Sqn, Oakington	
XP909	Westland Scout AH1	AAC store, Wroughton	
XP910	Westland Scout AH1	AAC store, Wroughton	
XP915	DH Comet 3B (G-ANLO)	BAe Woodford	

Notes	Serial	Type (alternative identity)	Owner, Operator or Location
	XP919	DH Sea Vixen FAW2 (8163M) [706/VL]	City of Norwich Aviation Museum
	XP920	DH Sea Vixen FAW2	MoD(PE) RAE Farnborough, stored
	XP921	DH Sea Vixen FAW2 (8226M) [753/VL]	RAF No 1 SoTT, Halton
	XP924	DH Sea Vixen D3	Flight Refuelling Ltd, Hurn
	XP925	DH Sea Vixen FAW2 [752]	MoD(PE) RAE Farnborough, stored
	XP956	DH Sea Vixen FAW2	MoD(PE) RAE Farnborough, stored
	XP967	Sud Alouette AH2	AAC, Cyprus
	XP976	Hawker Kestrel FGA1	RAF Wittering Fire Section
	XP980	Hawker Kestrel FGA1 (A2700)	RNAS Culdrose, SAH
	XP984	Hawker Kestrel FGA1 (A2658)	RNEC Manadon, for instruction
	XR107	AW Argosy T2 (8441M) [B]	RAF No 2 SoTT, Cosford
	XR137	AW Argosy E1	RAF Northolt Fire Section
	XR140	AW Argosy E1 (8579M) [56]	RAF No 1 SoTT, Halton
	XR220	BAC TSR2 (7933M)	RAF Cosford Aerospace Museum
	XR222	BAC TSR2	Imperial War Museum, Duxford
	XR232	Sud Alouette AH2 (F-WEIP)	AAC Cyprus
	XR240	Auster AOP9 (G-BDFH)	Privately owned, Booker
	XR241	Auster AOP9 (G-AXRR)	Privately owned, Duxford
	XR243	Auster AOP9 (8057M)	RAF St Athan, Historic Aircraft Collection
	XR244	Auster AOP9	AAC Historic Aircraft Flight, Middle Wallop
	XR246	Auster AOP9 (7862M/G-AZBU)	Privately owned, Reymerston Hall
	XR267	Auster AOP9 (G-BJXR)	Cotswold Aircraft Restoration Group, RAF Innsworth
	XR269	Auster AOP9 (G-BDXY)	Privately owned, Leicester
	XR271	Auster AOP9	Museum of Artillery, Woolwich
	XR376	Sud Alouette AH2	AAC, Cyprus
	XR378	Sud Alouette AH2	AAC, Cyprus
	XR379	Sud Alouette AH2	AAC, Cyprus
	XR382	Sud Alouette AH2	AAC, Cyprus
	XR385	Sud Alouette AH2	AAC, Cyprus
	XR386	Sud Alouette AH2	AAC, Cyprus
	XR436	Saro P531/2	Museum of Army Flying, stored Middle Wallop
	XR441	DH Sea Heron C1 (G-AORG)	RNAS Yeovilton, Station Flight
	XR442	DH Sea Heron C1 (G-AORH)	RNAS Yeovilton, Station Flight
	XR443	DH Sea Heron C1 (G-ARKU)	RNAS Yeovilton, Station Flight
	XR445	DH Sea Heron C1 (G-ARKW)	RNAS Yeovilton, Station Flight
	XR455	WS55 Whirlwind HAR10 (8219M) [J]	CTE, RAF Manston
	XR458	WS55 Whirlwind HAR10 (8662M) [H]	RAF No 1 SoTT, Halton
	XR478	WS55 Whirlwind HAR10 [P]	Defence School, Winterbourne Gunner
	XR479	WS55 Whirlwind HAR10 [A]	RAE Farnborough, Fire Section
	XR481	WS55 Whirlwind HAR10	RAF store, Wroughton
	XR482	WS55 Whirlwind HAR10 [G]	Defence School, Winterbourne Gunner
	XR483	WS55 Whirlwind HAR10	RAF store, Wroughton
	XR485	WS55 Whirlwind HAR10 [Q]	Norfolk & Suffolk Aviation Museum, Flixton
	XR486	WS55 Whirlwind HCC12 (8727M)	RAF St Athan Historic Aircraft Collection
	XR493	Westland Scout AH1 (G-APVM/8040M)	MoD(PE) Farnborough
	XR497	Westland Wessex HC2	RAF No 22 Sqn SAR
	XR498	Westland Wessex HC2 [X]	RAF No 72 Sqn, Aldergrove
	XR499	Westland Wessex HC2 [W]	RAF No 72 Sqn, Aldergrove
	XR501	Westland Wessex HC2	RAF No 22 Sqn SAR
	XR502	Westland Wessex HC2 [Z]	RAF No 72 Sqn, Aldergrove
	XR503	Westland Wessex HC2	MoD(PE) RAE Bedford
	XR504	Westland Wessex HC2	RAF No 22 Sqn SAR

Note:

No 22 Sqn SAR and the SAREW are based at Finningley:
A Flt — Chivenor; B Flt — Leuchars; C Flt and SARTF — Valley; D Flt — Leconfield; E Flt — Manston; F Flt — Coltishall

Serial	Type (alternative identity)	Owner, Operator or Location	Notes
XR505	Westland Wessex HC2 [WA]	RAF No 2 FTS, Shawbury	
XR506	Westland Wessex HC2	RAF No 72 Sqn, Aldergrove	
XR507	Westland Wessex HC2	RAF No 22 Sqn SAR	
XR508	Westland Wessex HC2 [D]	RAF No 28 Sqn, Sek Kong	
XR509	Westland Wessex HC2 (8752M)	RAF Benson, for crash rescue training	
XR511	Westland Wessex HC2 [L]	RAF No 72 Sqn, Aldergrove	
XR515	Westland Wessex HC2 [B]	RAF No 28 Sqn, Sek Kong	
XR516	Westland Wessex HC2 [WB]	RAF No 2 FTS, Shawbury	
XR517	Westland Wessex HC2 [N]	RAF No 72 Sqn, Aldergrove	
XR518	Westland Wessex HC2	RAF No 22 Sqn SAR	
XR519	Westland Wessex HC2 [WC]	RAF No 2 FTS, Shawbury	
XR520	Westland Wessex HC2	RAF No 22 Sqn SAR	
XR521	Westland Wessex HC2 [WD]	RAF No 2 FTS, Shawbury	
XR522	Westland Wessex HC2 [I]	RAF No 28 Sqn, Hong Kong	
XR523	Westland Wessex HC2 [M]	RAF No 72 Sqn, Aldergrove	
XR524	Westland Wessex HC2	RAF No 22 Sqn SAR	
XR525	Westland Wessex HC2 [G]	RAF No 72 Sqn, Aldergrove	
XR526	Westland Wessex HC2 (8147M)	Westlands, Sherborne	
XR527	Westland Wessex HC2 [C]	RAF No 28 Sqn, Sek Kong	
XR528	Westland Wessex HC2 [A]	RAF No 28 Sqn, Sek Kong	
XR529	Westland Wessex HC2 [E]	RAF No 72 Sqn, Aldergrove	
XR534	HS Gnat T1 (8578M) [65]	RAF Valley	
XR535	HS Gnat T1 (8569M) [05]	RAF No 1 SoTT, Halton	
XR537	HS Gnat T1 (8642M)	RAF No 2 SoTT, Cosford	
XR538	HS Gnat T1 (8621M) [69]	RAF No 1 SoTT, Halton	
XR540	HS Gnat T1 (8636M/A2708) [SAH-5]	RNAS Culdrose, SAH	
XR541	HS Gnat T1 (8602M)	RAF St Athan, CTTS	
XR569	HS Gnat T1 (8560M) [08]	RAF No 1 SoTT, Halton	
XR571	HS Gnat T1 (8493M) [23]	RAF Red Arrows Scampton on display	
XR572	HS Gnat T1 (A2676) [SAH-3]	RNAS Culdrose, SAH	
XR574	HS Gnat T1 (8631M) [24] [72]	RAF No 1 SoTT, Halton	
XR588	Westland Wessex HC2	RAF No 22 Sqn SAR	
XR595	Westland Scout AH1	AAC store, Wroughton	
XR597	Westland Scout AH1	AAC Exhibition Unit, Middle Wallop	
XR600	Westland Scout AH1 [B]	AAC store, Wroughton	
XR601	Westland Scout AH1	Army Apprentice College, Arborfield	
XR602	Westland Scout AH1	AAC No 659 Sqn, Detmold	
XR603	Westland Scout AH1 [A]	AAC, UK	
XR604	Westland Scout AH1	AAC Middle Wallop, BDRF	
XR627	Westland Scout AH1	AAC No 657 Sqn, Oakington	
XR629	Westland Scout AH1	AAC store, Wroughton	
XR630	Westland Scout AH1	AAC No 658 Sqn, Netheravon	
XR632	Westland Scout AH1	AAC store, Wroughton	
XR635	Westland Scout AH1	AAC AETW, Middle Wallop	
XR637	Westland Scout AH1	AAC No 658 Sqn, Netheravon	
XR639	Westland Scout AH1 [X]	AAC store, Wroughton	
XR643	Hunting Jet Provost T4 (8516M) [26]	RAF No 1 SoTT, Halton	
XR650	Hunting Jet Provost T4 (8459M) [28]	RAF No 1 SoTT, Halton	
XR651	Hunting Jet Provost T4 (8431M) [A]	RAF No 1 SoTT, Halton	
XR653	Hunting Jet Provost T4 [H]	RAF CATCS, Shawbury	
XR654	Hunting Jet Provost T4 [34]	Aircraft Radio Museum, Coventry	
XR658	Hunting Jet Provost T4 (8192M)	RAF Exhibition Flight, Abingdon	
XR662	Hunting Jet Provost T4 (8410M) [25]	RAF No 1 SoTT, Halton	
XR669	Hunting Jet Provost T4 (8062M) [02] nose only	RAF No 1 SoTT, Halton	
XR670	Hunting Jet Provost T4 (8498M) [64]	RAF No 1 SoTT, Halton	
XR672	Hunting Jet Provost T4 (8495M) [C] [73]	RAF No 1 SoTT, Halton	
XR673	Hunting Jet Provost T4 [L]	RAF CATCS, Shawbury	
XR674	Hunting Jet Provost T4 [D]	RAF CATCS, Shawbury	
XR679	Hunting Jet Provost T4 [04]	RAF No 1 TWU, Brawdy	

Notes	Serial	Type (alternative identity)	Owner, Operator or Location
	XR681	Hunting Jet Provost T4 (8588M) nose only	RAF Exhibition Flight, Abingdon
	XR700	Hunting Jet Provost T4 (8589M) nose only	RAF Exhibition Flight, Abingdon
	XR701	Hunting Jet Provost T4 [K]	RAF CATCS, Shawbury
	XR704	Hunting Jet Provost T4 (8506M) [30]	RAF No 1 SoTT, Halton
	XR713	EE Lightning F3 [AR]	RAF store, Binbrook
	XR716	EE Lightning F3 [AS]	RAF No 5 Sqn, Binbrook
	XR717	EE Lightning F3	A&AEE, Boscombe Down Fire Section
	XR718	EE Lightning F3 [BK1]	RAF LTF, Binbrook
	XR720	EE Lightning F3 [DA]	RAF LTF, Binbrook
	XR724	EE Lightning F6 [BC]	RAF No 11 Sqn, Binbrook
	XR725	EE Lightning F6	RAF store, Binbrook
	XR726	EE Lightning F6	RAF store, Binbrook
	XR727	EE Lightning F6 [AB]	RAF No 5 Sqn, Binbrook
	XR728	EE Lightning F6	RAF store, Binbrook
	XR747	EE Lightning F6	RAF No 11 Sqn, Binbrook
	XR749	EE Lightning F3 [BM]	RAF No 11 Sqn, Binbrook
	XR751	EE Lightning F3 [DC]	RAF LTF, Binbrook
	XR752	EE Lightning F6 [BL]	RAF No 11 Sqn, Binbrook
	XR753	EE Lightning F6	RAF No 5 Sqn, Binbrook
	XR754	EE Lightning F6 [AE]	RAF No 5 Sqn, Binbrook
	XR755	EE Lightning F6 [BF]	RAF No 11 Sqn, Binbrook
	XR756	EE Lightning F6 [BB]	RAF No 11 Sqn, Binbrook
	XR757	EE Lightning F6 [AL]	RAF No 5 Sqn, Binbrook
	XR758	EE Lightning F6 [AH]	RAF No 5 Sqn, Binbrook
	XR759	EE Lightning F6 [AG]	RAF store, Binbrook
	XR760	EE Lightning F6 [BD]	RAF store, Binbrook
	XR763	EE Lightning F6 [AE]	RAF store, Binbrook
	XR769	EE Lightning F6 [BG]	RAF No 11 Sqn, Binbrook
	XR770	EE Lightning F6 [AA]	RAF No 5 Sqn, Binbrook
	XR771	EE Lightning F6 [BA]	RAF No 11 Sqn, Binbrook
	XR772	EE Lightning F6 [AD]	RAF No 5 Sqn, Binbrook
	XR773	EE Lightning F6 [BD]	RAF No 11 Sqn, Binbrook
	XR777	Westland Scout AH1 (really XT625)	St George's Barracks, Sutton Coldfield
	XR806	BAC VC10 C1	RAF No 10 Sqn, Brize Norton
	XR807	BAC VC10 C1	RAF No 10 Sqn, Brize Norton
	XR808	BAC VC10 C1	RAF No 10 Sqn, Brize Norton
	XR810	BAC VC10 C1	RAF No 10 Sqn, Brize Norton
	XR951	HS Gnat T1 (8603M) [26]	RAF No 1 SoTT, Halton
	XR953	HS Gnat T1 (8609M) [63]	RAF No 1 SoTT, Halton
	XR954	HS Gnat T1 (8570M) [30]	RAF No 1 SoTT, Halton
	XR955	HS Gnat T1 (A2678) [SAH-2]	RNAS Culdrose, SAH
	XR977	HS Gnat T1 (8640M)	RAF Cosford Aerospace Museum
	XR980	HS Gnat T1 (8622M) [70]	RAF No 1 SoTT, Halton
	XR984	HS Gnat T1 (8571M) [52]	RAF No 1 SoTT, Halton
	XR987	HS Gnat T1 (8641M) [10]	RAF No 2 SoTT, Cosford
	XR991	HS Gnat T1 (8637M/A2709)	RNAS Culdrose, SAH
	XR993	HS Gnat T1 (A2677) [SAH-4]	RNAS Culdrose, SAH
	XR998	HS Gnat T1 (8623M) [71]	RAF No 1 SoTT, Halton
	XS100	HS Gnat T1 (8561M) [57]	RAF No 1 SoTT, Halton
	XS101	HS Gnat T1 (8638M) (G-GNAT)	Privately owned, Cranfield
	XS102	HS Gnat T1 (8624M) [66]	RAF No 1 SoTT, Halton
	XS104	HS Gnat T1 (8604M) [44]	RAF No 2 SoTT, Cosford
	XS105	HS Gnat T1 (8625M) [35]	RAF No 2 SoTT, Cosford
	XS107	HS Gnat T1 (8639M)	RAF No 2 SoTT, Cosford
	XS109	HS Gnat T1 (8626M) [63] [75]	RAF No 1 SoTT, Halton
	XS110	HS Gnat T1 (8562M) [20]	RAF No 1 SoTT, Halton
	XS119	Westland Wessex HAS3 [655/PO]	RN AES Lee-on-Solent
	XS120	Westland Wessex HAS1 (8653M) [520/CU]	RAF Abingdon Fire Section
	XS122	Westland Wessex HAS3 (A2707) [655/PO]	RNEC Manadon, for instruction

Serial	Type (alternative identity)	Owner, Operator or Location	Notes
XS125	Westland Wessex HAS1 (A2648) [517/PO]	RN AES Lee-on-Solent	
XS127	Westland Wessex HAS3	RNAS Predannack Fire Section	
XS128	Westland Wessex HAS1 (A2670) [437/PO]	RN AES Lee-on-Solent	
XS149	Westland Wessex HAS3 [661/GL]	RN store, Wroughton	
XS150	Westland Wessex HAS1	RN AES Lee-on-Solent	
XS153	Westland Wessex HAS3 [662/PO]	RN AES Lee-on-Solent	
XS175	Hunting Jet Provost T4	WR Tuscon Technical College, Fulwood, Lancs	
XS176	Hunting Jet Provost T4 (8514M) [N]	RAF No 1 SoTT, Halton	
XS177	Hunting Jet Provost T4 [N]	RAF CATCS, Shawbury	
XS178	Hunting Jet Provost T4 [05]	RAF No 1 TWU, Brawdy	
XS179	Hunting Jet Provost T4 (8237M) [20]	RAF No 1 SoTT, Halton	
XS180	Hunting Jet Provost T4 (8238M) [21]	RAF No 1 SoTT, Halton	
XS181	Hunting Jet Provost T4 [F]	RAF CATCS, Shawbury	
XS186	Hunting Jet Provost T4 (8408M) [M]	RAF No 1 SoTT, Halton	
XS209	Hunting Jet Provost T4 (8409M) [29]	RAF No 1 SoTT, Halton	
XS210	Hunting Jet Provost T4 (8239M) [22]	RAF No 1 SoTT, Halton	
XS215	Hunting Jet Provost T4 (8507M) [17]	RAF No 1 SoTT, Halton	
XS216	Hunting Jet Provost T4 [Q]	RAF Finningley, for rescue training	
XS217	Hunting Jet Provost T4 [O]	RAF CATCS, Shawbury	
XS218	Hunting Jet Provost T4 (8508M) [18]	RAF No 1 SoTT, Halton	
XS219	Hunting Jet Provost T4 [00]	RAF No 1 TWU, Brawdy	
XS230	BAC Jet Provost T5	MoD(PE) A&AEE/ETPS Boscombe Down	
XS231	BAC Jet Provost T5 (G-ATAJ)	RAF Shawbury store	
XS235	HS Comet 4C	MoD(PE) A&AEE Boscombe Down	
XS241	Westland Wessex HU5	MoD(PE) RAE Farnborough	
XS416	EE Lightning T5 [AT]	RAF No 5 Sqn, Binbrook	
XS417	EE Lightning T5 [DZ]	RAF LTF, Binbrook	
XS418	EE Lightning T5 (8531M)	RAF Binbrook	
XS419	EE Lightning T5 [DV]	RAF LTF, Binbrook	
XS420	EE Lightning T5	RAF store, Binbrook	
XS422	EE Lightning T5	MoD(PE) ETPS Boscombe Down	
XS423	EE Lightning T5 (8532M)	RAF Binbrook	
XS449	EE Lightning T5 (8533M)	RAF Binbrook	
XS450	EE Lightning T5 (8534M) [X]	RAF Binbrook	
XS451	EE Lightning T5 (8503M)	RAF Newton, for ground instruction	
XS452	EE Lightning T5	RAF store, Binbrook	
XS454	EE Lightning T5 (8535M) [Y]	RAF Binbrook fire section	
XS456	EE Lightning T5 [DT]	RAF LTF, Binbrook	
XS457	EE Lightning T5	RAF Binbrook	
XS458	EE Lightning T5 [BT]	RAF No 11 Sqn, Binbrook	
XS459	EE Lightning T5 [DW]	RAF LTF, Binbrook	
XS463	Westland Wasp HAS1 (A2647) [601/RO]	British Rotorcraft Museum, at RNAY Fleetlands	
XS479	Westland Wessex HU5 [XF] (8819M)	RAF JATE, Brize Norton	
XS481	Westland Wessex HU5	RN store, Wroughton	
XS482	Westland Wessex HU5 [A-D]	MoD(PE) A&AEE Boscombe Down	
XS483	Westland Wessex HU5 [T]	RN No 845 Sqn, Yeovilton	
XS484	Westland Wessex HU5 [821/CU]	RN No 771 Sqn, Culdrose	
XS485	Westland Wessex HU5C	RAF No 84 Sqn, Akrotiri	
XS486	Westland Wessex HU5 [ZH]	RN No 771 Sqn, Culdrose	
XS488	Westland Wessex HU5 [XK]	RN store, Wroughton	
XS489	Westland Wessex HU5 [P]	RN No 845 Sqn, Yeovilton	
XS491	Westland Wessex HU5 [XM]	RN store, Wroughton	

Notes	Serial	Type (alternative identity)	Owner, Operator or Location
	XS492	Westland Wessex HU5 [623/PO]	RN No 772 Sqn, Portland
	XS493	Westland Wessex HU5 [VE]	RNAY Fleetlands
	XS496	Westland Wessex HU5 [625/PO]	RN No 772 Sqn, Portland
	XS498	Westland Wessex HU5C	RNAY, Fleetlands
	XS506	Westland Wessex HU5 [XE]	RN store, Wroughton
	XS507	Westland Wessex HU5 [RN]	RN Presentation Team, Yeovilton
	XS508	Westland Wessex HU5 [ZP]	RN No 707 Sqn, Yeovilton
	XS509	Westland Wessex HU5 (A2597)	MoD(PE) ETPS Boscombe Down
	XS510	Westland Wessex HU5 [626]	RN No 772 Sqn, Portland
	XS511	Westland Wessex HU5	RN NASU, Yeovilton
	XS513	Westland Wessex HU5 [E]	RN No 845 Sqn, Yeovilton
	XS514	Westland Wessex HU5 [L]	RN No 845 Sqn, Yeovilton
	XS515	Westland Wessex HU5 [N]	RN No 845 Sqn, Yeovilton
	XS516	Westland Wessex HU5 [Q]	RN No 845 Sqn Yeovilton
	XS517	Westland Wessex HU5 [ZC]	RNAY Fleetlands
	XS518	Westland Wessex HU5C	MoD(PE) A&AEE Boscombe Down
	XS520	Westland Wessex HU5 [F]	RN No 845 Sqn, Yeovilton
	XS521	Westland Wessex HU5 [B]	RN No 845 Sqn, Ascension Is
	XS522	Westland Wessex HU5 [ZL]	RN No 707 Sqn, Yeovilton
	XS523	Westland Wessex HU5 [824/CU]	RN No 771 Sqn, Culdrose
	XS527	Westland Wasp HAS1	RN No 829 Sqn, Portland
	XS528	Westland Wasp HAS1 [423]	RN store, Wroughton
	XS529	Westland Wasp HAS1 [461]	RN No 829 Sqn, Portland
	XS532	Westland Wasp HAS1 [457]	RN store, Wroughton
	XS535	Westland Wasp HAS1 [500]	RN store, Wroughton
	XS537	Westland Wasp HAS1 (A2672) [582]	RNAS Portland, for instruction
	XS538	Westland Wasp HAS1 [451]	RN No 829 Sqn, Portland
	XS539	Westland Wasp HAS1 [435]	RN No 829 Sqn, Portland
	XS541	Westland Wasp HAS1 [602]	RN No 829 Sqn, Portland
	XS545	Westland Wasp HAS1 (A2702) [635]	RN AES Lee-on-Solent
	XS562	Westland Wasp HAS1 [611]	RN No 829 Sqn, Portland
	XS565	Westland Wasp HAS1 [445]	MoD(PE) RAE Farnborough
	XS566	Westland Wasp HAS1 [607]	RN No 829 Sqn, Portland
	XS567	Westland Wasp HAS1	RN No 829 Sqn, Portland
	XS568	Westland Wasp HAS1 [441]	RNAY Fleetlands Apprentice School
	XS569	Westland Wasp HAS1	RNAY Fleetlands Apprentice School
	XS570	Westland Wasp HAS1 (A2699) [AP]	RN AES Lee-on-Solent
	XS572	Westland Wasp HAS1 [414]	RN store, Wroughton
	XS576	DH Sea Vixen FAW2 [125/E]	Imperial War Museum, Duxford
	XS577	DH Sea Vixen D3	Flight Refuelling Ltd, Hurn
	XS580	DH Sea Vixen FAW2 [755]	MoD(PE) RAE Farnborough, store
	XS587	DH Sea Vixen FAW(TT)2 (8828M)	RAF No 2 SoTT, Cosford
	XS590	DH Sea Vixen FAW2 [131/E]	FAA Museum, RNAS Yeovilton
	XS595	HS Andover C1 [A]	RAF Brize Norton Fire Section
	XS596	HS Andover C1	RAF No 115 Sqn, Benson
	XS597	HS Andover C1	RAF No 32 Sqn, Northolt
	XS598	HS Andover C1 [E]	RAF Brize Norton for instruction
	XS603	HS Andover E3	RAF No 115 Sqn, Benson
	XS605	HS Andover E3	RAF No 115 Sqn, Benson
	XS606	HS Andover C1	MoD(PE) A&AEE/ETPS Boscombe Down
	XS607	HS Andover C1	MoD(PE) RAE West Freugh
	XS610	HS Andover E3	RAF No 115 Sqn, Benson
	XS637	HS Andover C1	RAF CinC AFNORTH, Oslo
	XS639	HS Andover E3A	RAF No 115 Sqn, Benson
	XS640	HS Andover E3	RAF No 115 Sqn, Benson
	XS641	HS Andover E3A	RAF No 115 Sqn, Benson
	XS642	HS Andover C1 [C] (8785M)	RAF Benson Fire Section
	XS643	HS Andover E3A	RAF No 115 Sqn, Benson
	XS644	HS Andover C1 (Mod)	RAF EWAU, Wyton
	XS646	HS Andover C1	MoD(PE) RAE Farnborough
	XS647	HS Andover C1	British Aerospace, Woodford

erial	Type (alternative identity)	Owner, Operator or Location	Notes
S650	Slingsby Swallow TX1 (8801M)	RAF St Athan Historic Aircraft Collection	
S651	Slingsby Swallow TX1	RAF store Syerston	
S652	Slingsby Swallow TX1 (BGA 1107)	RAF No 662 VGS, Arbroath	
S674	Westland Wessex HC2 [R]	RAF No 72 Sqn, Aldergrove	
S675	Westland Wessex HC2	RAF No 22 Sqn, SAR	
S676	Westland Wessex HC2 [WJ]	RAF No 2 FTS, Shawbury	
S677	Westland Wessex HC2 [WK]	RAF No 2 FTS, Shawbury	
S679	Westland Wessex HC2 [WG]	RAF No 2 FTS, Shawbury	
S695	HS Kestrel FGA1 (A2619) [SAH-6]	RNAS Culdrose, SAH	
S709	HS Dominie T1 [M]	RAF No 6 FTS, Finningley	
S710	HS Dominie T1 [O]	RAF No 6 FTS, Finningley	
S711	HS Dominie T1 [L]	RAF No 6 FTS, Finningley	
S712	HS Dominie T1 [A]	RAF No 6 FTS, Finningley	
S713	HS Dominie T1 [C]	RAF No 6 FTS, Finningley	
S714	HS Dominie T1 [P]	RAF No 6 FTS, Finningley	
S726	HS Dominie T1 [T]	RAF No 6 FTS, Finningley	
S727	HS Dominie T1 [D]	RAF No 6 FTS, Finningley	
S728	HS Dominie T1 [E]	RAF No 6 FTS, Finningley	
S729	HS Dominie T1 [G]	RAF No 6 FTS, Finningley	
S730	HS Dominie T1 [H]	RAF No 6 FTS, Finningley	
S731	HS Dominie T1 [J]	RAF No 6 FTS, Finningley	
S732	HS Dominie T1 [B]	RAF No 6 FTS, Finningley	
S733	HS Dominie T1 [Q]	RAF No 6 FTS, Finningley	
S734	HS Dominie T1 [N]	RAF No 6 FTS, Finningley	
S735	HS Dominie T1 [R]	RAF No 6 FTS, Finningley	
S736	HS Dominie T1 [S]	RAF No 6 FTS, Finningley	
S737	HS Dominie T1 [K]	RAF No 6 FTS, Finningley	
S738	HS Dominie T1 [U]	RAF No 6 FTS, Finningley	
S739	HS Dominie T1 [F]	RAF No 6 FTS, Finningley	
XS743	Beagle Basset CC1	MoD(PE) FTPS Boscombe Down	
XS705	Beagle Basset CC1	MoD(PE) A&AEE/ETPS Boscombe Down	
XS770	Beagle Basset CC1	MoD(PE) A&AEE Boscombe Down	
XS789	HS Andover CC2	RAF Queen's Flight, Benson	
XS790	HS Andover CC2	RAF Queen's Flight, Benson	
XS791	HS Andover CC2	RAF No 32 Sqn, Northolt	
XS792	HS Andover CC2	RAF No 32 Sqn, Northolt	
XS793	HS Andover CC2	RAF Queen's Flight, Benson	
XS794	HS Andover CC2	RAF No 32 Sqn, Northolt	
XS859	Slingsby Swallow TX1	RAF ACCGS, Syerston	
XS862	Westland Wessex HAS3 [650/PO]	RN AES Lee-on-Solent	
XS863	Westland Wessex HAS1	Imperial War Museum, Duxford	
XS865	Westland Wessex HAS1 (A2694) [529/CU]	RN AES Lee-on-Solent	
XS866	Westland Wessex HAS1 (A2705) [520/CU]	RN AES Lee-on-Solent	
XS867	Westland Wessex HAS1 (A2671)	RN Fire Section Lee-on-Solent	
XS868	Westland Wessex HAS1 (A2691/A2706)	RNAY Fleetlands, on gate	
XS869	Westland Wessex HAS1 (A2649) [508/PO]	RN Air Medical School, Seafield Park, rescue training	
XS870	Westland Wessex HAS1 (A2697) [-/PO]	RN AES Lee-on-Solent	
XS871	Westland Wessex HAS1 (8457M) [AI]	RAF Odiham, Fire Section	
XS872	Westland Wessex HAS1 (A2666) [572/CU]	RNAY Fleetlands Apprentice School	
XS873	Westland Wessex HAS1 (A2686) [525/CU]	RN AES Lee-on-Solent	
XS876	Westland Wessex HAS1 (A2695) [523/CU]	RN AES Lee-on-Solent	
XS877	Westland Wessex HAS1 (A2687) [516/PO]	RNAS Culdrose, SAH	
XS878	Westland Wessex HAS1 (A2683)	RN AES Lee-on-Solent	

Notes	Serial	Type (alternative identity)	Owner, Operator or Location
	XS881	Westland Wessex HAS1 (A2675) [046/CU]	Scottish Aircraft Collection Trust, Perth
	XS882	Westland Wessex HAS1 (A2696) [524/CU]	RN AES Lee-on-Solent
	XS885	Westland Wessex HAS1 (A2668) [512/PO]	RNAS Culdrose, SAH
	XS886	Westland Wessex HAS1 (A2685) [527/CU]	RN AES Lee-on-Solent
	XS887	Westland Wessex HAS1 (A2690) [514/PO]	RNAS Culdrose, SAH
	XS888	Westland Wessex HAS1 [521]	RN Exhibition Unit, Fleetlands
	XS895	EE Lightning F6 [DF]	RAF LTF, Binbrook
	XS897	EE Lightning F6	RAF store, Binbrook
	XS898	EE Lightning F6 [AK]	RAF No 5 Sqn, Binbrook
	XS899	EE Lightning F6 [AJ]	RAF No 5 Sqn, Binbrook
	XS901	EE Lightning F6 [BH]	RAF No 11 Sqn, Binbrook
	XS903	EE Lightning F6 [AM]	RAF No 5 Sqn, Binbrook
	XS904	EE Lightning F6 [BM]	RAF No 11 Sqn, Binbrook
	XS919	EE Lightning F6 [BN]	RAF No 11 Sqn, Binbrook
	XS921	EE Lightning F6	RAF No 5 Sqn, Binbrook
	XS922	EE Lightning F6 [AG]	RAF No 11 Sqn, Binbrook
	XS923	EE Lightning F6	RAF No 11 Sqn, Binbrook
	XS925	EE Lightning F6 [BA]	RAF No 11 Sqn, Binbrook
	XS927	EE Lightning F6	RAF No 11 Sqn, Binbrook
	XS928	EE Lightning F6 [BJ]	RAF No 11 Sqn, Binbrook
	XS929	EE Lightning F6 [BC]	RAF store, Binbrook
	XS932	EE Lightning F6 [AC]	RAF No 5 Sqn, Binbrook
	XS933	EE Lightning F6 [BE]	RAF No 11 Sqn, Binbrook
	XS935	EE Lightning F6	RAF store, Binbrook
	XS936	EE Lightning F6	RAF store, Binbrook
	XT108	Agusta-Bell Sioux AH1 [U]	Museum of Army Flying, Middle Wallop
	XT131	Agusta-Bell Sioux AH1 [B]	AAC Historic Aircraft Flight, Middle Wallop
	XT133	Agusta-Bell Sioux AH1 (7923M)	Royal Engineers' Museum, Chatham
	XT140	Agusta-Bell Sioux AH1	Air Service Training, Perth
	XT141	Agusta-Bell Sioux AH1 (8509M)	RAF AMS, Brize Norton
	XT150	Agusta-Bell Sioux AH1 (7883M) [R]	Wessex Aviation Society, Wimborne
	XT151	Westland Sioux AH1	Royal Military College of Science, Shrivenham
	XT175	Westland Sioux AH1 (TAD175)	CSE Oxford for ground instruction
	XT176	Westland Sioux AH1 [C]	RM 3CBAS, RNAS Yeovilton
	XT190	Westland Sioux AH1	Museum of Army Flying, Middle Wallop
	XT199	Westland Sioux AH1 [C]	Privately owned, Fairoaks
	XT200	Westland Sioux AH1 [F]	Newark Air Museum, Winthorpe
	XT236	Westland Sioux AH1	Museum of Army Flying, Middle Wallop
	XT242	Westland Sioux AH1	Wessex Aviation Society, Wimborne
	XT248	Westland Sioux AH1 (G-BKNF)	Privately owned, Panshanger
	XT255	Westland Wessex HAS3 (8751M)	RAF No 14 MU, Carlisle
	XT256	Westland Wessex HAS3 (A2615)	RN AES Lee-on-Solent
	XT257	Westland Wessex HAS3 (8719M)	RAF No 1 SoTT, Halton
	XT270	HS Buccaneer S2B [C]	RAF Shawbury store
	XT271	HS Buccaneer S2A [C]	RAF store, St Athan
	XT272	HS Buccaneer S2	MoD(PE), RAE Bedford
	XT273	HS Buccaneer S2A [D]	RAF store, St Athan
	XT274	HS Buccaneer S2A [E]	RAF store, St Athan
	XT275	HS Buccaneer S2B [B]	RAF Shawbury store
	XT276	HS Buccaneer S2B [S]	RAF Shawbury store
	XT277	HS Buccaneer S2A	RAF No 2 SoTT, Cosford
	XT279	HS Buccaneer S2B [C]	RAF No 16 Sqn, Laarbruch
	XT280	HS Buccaneer S2B [NS]	RAF No 208 Sqn, Lossiemouth

Serial	Type (alternative identity)	Owner, Operator or Location	Notes
XT281	HS Buccaneer S2B (8705M) [ET]	RAF Lossiemouth, ground instruction	
XT283	HS Buccaneer S2A [GC]	RAF No 237 OCU, Lossiemouth	
XT284	HS Buccaneer S2A [H]	RAF store, St Athan	
XT286	HS Buccaneer S2B [W]	RAF store, St Athan	
XT287	HS Buccaneer S2B [F]	RAF No 16 Sqn, Laarbruch	
XT288	HS Buccaneer S2B	MoD(PE) BAe, Scampton	
XT415	Westland Wasp HAS1 [476]	RN No 829 Sqn, Portland	
XT416	Westland Wasp HAS1 [442]	RNAY Fleetlands	
XT420	Westland Wasp HAS1 [604]	RN No 829 Sqn, Portland	
XT421	Westland Wasp HAS1 [433]	RN No 829 Sqn, Portland	
XT422	Westland Wasp HAS1 [326]	RN store, Wroughton	
XT423	Westland Wasp HAS1 [434]	RN No 829 Sqn, Portland	
XT426	Westland Wasp HAS1 [455]	RN No 829 Sqn, Portland	
XT427	Westland Wasp HAS1 [606]	FAA Museum, RNAS Yeovilton	
XT428	Westland Wasp HAS1 [475]	RN store, Wroughton	
XT429	Westland Wasp HAS1 [445]	RN No 829 Sqn, Portland	
XT430	Westland Wasp HAS1 [444]	RN store, Wroughton	
XT431	Westland Wasp HAS1	RN No 829 Sqn, Portland	
XT432	Westland Wasp HAS1 [415]	RN No 829 Sqn, Portland	
XT434	Westland Wasp HAS1 [600]	RN No 829 Sqn, Portland	
XT437	Westland Wasp HAS1 [426]	RN No 829 Sqn, Portland	
XT439	Westland Wasp HAS1 [605]	RN No 829 Sqn, Portland	
XT441	Westland Wasp HAS1 (A2703) [337]	RN Wroughton Fire Section	
XT443	Westland Wasp HAS1 [422]	RN No 829 Sqn, Portland	
XT449	Westland Wessex HU5 [C]	RN No 845 Sqn, Yeovilton	
XT450	Westland Wessex HU5 [V]	RN Predannack Fire Section	
XT451	Westland Wessex HU5 [XN]	RN store, Wroughton	
XT453	Westland Wessex HU5 [A]	RN No 845 Sqn, Yeovilton	
XT455	Westland Wessex HU5 [U]	RN No 845 Sqn, Yeovilton	
XT456	Westland Wessex HU5 [XZ]	RN store, Wroughton	
XT458	Westland Wessex HU5 [622/PO]	RN No 772 Sqn, Portland	
XT460	Westland Wessex HU5 [K]	RN No 845 Sqn, Yeovilton	
XT461	Westland Wessex HU5 [W]	RN No 845 Sqn, Yeovilton	
XT463	Westland Wessex HU5C	RAF No 608 Flt, Topcliffe	
XT466	Westland Wessex HU5 [XV]	RN store, Wroughton	
XT467	Westland Wessex HU5	RN store, Wroughton	
XT468	Westland Wessex HU5 [D]	RNAY Fleetlands	
XT469	Westland Wessex HU5 [XN]	RN store, Wroughton	
XT470	Westland Wessex HU5 [A]	AAC Netheravon, fire section	
XT471	Westland Wessex HU5 [ZK]	RN No 707 Sqn, Yeovilton	
XT472	Westland Wessex HU5 [XC]	RAF, No 47 Parachute Regiment, Lyneham	
XT474	Westland Wessex HU5 [820/CU]	RN NASU, Yeovilton	
XT475	Westland Wessex HU5 [627]	RN No 772 Sqn, Portland	
XT479	Westland Wessex HU5C	RAF, RNAY Fleetlands	
XT480	Westland Wessex HU5 [XQ]	RN store, Wroughton	
XT481	Westland Wessex HU5 [XF]	RN store, Wroughton	
XT482	Westland Wessex HU5 [ZM]	RN No 707 Sqn, Yeovilton	
XT484	Westland Wessex HU5 [H]	RN No 845 Sqn, Yeovilton	
XT485	Westland Wessex HU5 [621/PO]	RN No 772 Sqn, Portland	
XT486	Westland Wessex HU5 [XR]	RN store, Wroughton	
XT487	Westland Wessex HU5 (A2723) [815/LS]	RN AES, Lee-on-Solent	
XT548	Westland Sioux AH1 [D]	Army Apprentice College, Arborfield	
XT550	Westland Sioux AH1 [D]	Museum of Army Flying Middle Wallop	
XT567	Westland Sioux AH1	Privately owned, Fairoaks	
XT575	Vickers Viscount (OE-LAG)	MoD(PE) RS&RE Bedford	
XT595	McD Phantom FG1 (8550M) nose only	RAF Exhibition Flight, Abingdon	
XT596	McD Phantom FG1	MoD(PE)/BAe, Scampton	
XT597	McD Phantom FG1	MoD(PE) A&AEE Boscombe Down	

Notes	Serial	Type (alternative identity)	Owner, Operator or Location
	XT601	Westland Wessex HC2	RAF No 22 Sqn SAR
	XT602	Westland Wessex HC2	RAF No 22 Sqn SAR
	XT603	Westland Wessex HC2 [WF]	RAF No 2 FTS, Shawbury
	XT604	Westland Wessex HC2	RAF No 22 Sqn SAR
	XT605	Westland Wessex HC2 [E]	RAF No 28 Sqn, Sek Kong
	XT606	Westland Wessex HC2	RAF No 84 Sqn, Cyprus
	XT607	Westland Wessex HC2 [P]	RAF No 72 Sqn, Aldergrove
	XT614	Westland Scout AH1 [G]	AAC No 660 Sqn, Sek Kong
	XT616	Westland Scout AH1 [W]	AAC store, Wroughton
	XT617	Westland Scout AH1	AAC store, Wroughton
	XT618	Westland Scout AH1 [K]	AAC No 660 Sqn, Sek Kong
	XT620	Westland Scout AH1 [B]	AAC store, Wroughton
	XT621	Westland Scout AH1	AAC No 655 Sqn, Aldergrove
	XT623	Westland Scout AH1	AAC No 655 Sqn, Aldergrove
	XT624	Westland Scout AH1 [W]	AAC, ATS Middle Wallop
	XT626	Westland Scout AH1	AAC No 656 Sqn, Netheravon
	XT627	Westland Scout AH1	AAC No 660 Sqn, Brunei
	XT628	Westland Scout AH1 [J]	AAC No 660 Sqn, Sek Kong
	XT630	Westland Scout AH1 [F]	AAC No 655 Sqn, Aldergrove
	XT631	Westland Scout AH1 [D]	MoD(PE) A&AEE Boscombe Down
	XT632	Westland Scout AH1	AAC No 657 Sqn, Oakington
	XT633	Westland Scout AH1	AAC store, Wroughton
	XT634	Westland Scout AH1	AAC store, Wroughton
	XT636	Westland Scout AH1 [X]	AAC, ATS Middle Wallop
	XT637	Westland Scout AH1	AAC No 658 Sqn, Netheravon
	XT638	Westland Scout AH1	AAC No 651 Sqn, Hildesheim
	XT639	Westland Scout AH1 [Y]	AAC store, Wroughton
	XT640	Westland Scout AH1	AAC AETW, Middle Wallop
	XT642	Westland Scout AH1 [A]	AAC No 656 Sqn, Netheravon
	XT643	Westland Scout AH1 [B]	AAC No 660 Sqn, Sek Kong
	XT644	Westland Scout AH1	AAC store, Wroughton
	XT645	Westland Scout AH1	AAC No 656 Sqn, Netheravon
	XT646	Westland Scout AH1	AAC store, Wroughton
	XT648	Westland Scout AH1	AAC store, Wroughton
	XT649	Westland Scout AH1	AAC store, Wroughton
	XT653	Slingsby Swallow TX1	RAF St Athan
	XT657	BHC SR.N6 Winchester 5	British Hovercraft Corpn
	XT661	Vickers Viscount (9G-AAV)	MoD(PE) RS&RE Bedford
	XT667	Westland Wessex HC2 [F]	RAF No 28 Sqn, Sek Kong
	XT668	Westland Wessex HC2 [S]	RAF No 72 Sqn, Aldergrove
	XT669	Westland Wessex HC2 [T]	RAF No 72 Sqn, Aldergrove
	XT670	Westland Wessex HC2	RAF No 22 Sqn SAR
	XT671	Westland Wessex HC2 [D]	RAF No 72 Sqn, Aldergrove
	XT672	Westland Wessex HC2 [WE]	RAF No 2 FTS, Shawbury
	XT673	Westland Wessex HC2 [G]	RAF No 28 Sqn, Sek Kong
	XT674	Westland Wessex HC2	RAF No 22 Sqn SAR
	XT675	Westland Wessex HC2 [J]	RAF No 28 Sqn, Sek Kong
	XT676	Westland Wessex HC2 [I]	RAF No 72 Sqn, Aldergrove
	XT678	Westland Wessex HC2 [S]	RAF No 28 Sqn, Sek Kong
	XT680	Westland Wessex HC2	RAF No 22 Sqn SAR
	XT681	Westland Wessex HC2 [U]	RAF No 72 Sqn, Aldergrove
	XT752	Fairey Gannet T5 [-/LM] (G-APYO/WN365)	RNAS Culdrose, store
	XT755	Westland Wessex HU5 [V]	RN No 845 Sqn, Yeovilton
	XT756	Westland Wessex HU5 [ZJ]	RN No 707 Sqn, Yeovilton
	XT757	Westland Wessex HU5 [XH] (A2722)	RN AES, Lee-on-Solent
	XT759	Westland Wessex HU5 [XY]	RN store, Wroughton
	XT760	Westland Wessex HU5	RNAY Fleetlands
	XT761	Westland Wessex HU5 [P]	RN NASU, Yeovilton
	XT762	Westland Wessex HU5	MoD(PE) RS&RE Bedford
	XT764	Westland Wessex HU5 [G]	RN No 845 Sqn, D Flt, Ascension Is
	XT765	Westland Wessex HU5 [J]	RN No 845 Sqn, Yeovilton
	XT766	Westland Wessex HU5 [822/CU]	RN No 771 Sqn, Culdrose
	XT767	Westland Wessex HU5 [624/PO]	RN No 772 Sqn, Portland
	XT768	Westland Wessex HU5	Westlands, Yeovil
	XT769	Westland Wessex HU5 [823/CU]	RN No 771 Sqn, Culdrose

Serial	Type (alternative identity)	Owner, Operator or Location	Notes
XT770	Westland Wessex HU5 [P]	RN No 845 Sqn, Yeovilton	
XT771	Westland Wessex HU5 [620]	RN No 772 Sqn, Portland	
XT772	Westland Wessex HU5 (8805M)	RAF Valley SAR, instructional use	
XT773	Westland Wessex HU5	RN NASU Yeovilton	
XT778	Westland Wasp HAS1 [430]	RN No 829 Sqn, Portland	
XT779	Westland Wasp HAS1 [322]	RN No 829 Sqn, Portland	
XT780	Westland Wasp HAS1 [636]	RNAY Fleetlands Apprentice School	
XT782	Westland Wasp HAS1 [324]	RN No 829 Sqn, Portland	
XT783	Westland Wasp HAS1 [470]	RN No 829 Sqn, Portland	
XT784	Westland Wasp HAS1 [446]	RN No 829 Sqn, Portland	
XT785	Westland Wasp HAS1 [462]	RN No 829 Sqn, Portland	
XT786	Westland Wasp HAS1 [441]	RN No 829 Sqn, Portland	
XT788	Westland Wasp HAS1 [442]	RN store, Wroughton	
XT790	Westland Wasp HAS1 [603]	RN No 829 Sqn, Portland	
XT791	Westland Wasp HAS1 [421]	RN No 829 Sqn, Portland	
XT793	Westland Wasp HAS1 [440]	RN No 829 Sqn, Portland	
XT795	Westland Wasp HAS1	RN No 829 Sqn, Portland	
XT803	Westland Sioux AH1 [Y]	Privately owned, Panshanger	
XT827	Westland Sioux AH1 [D]	Army Apprentice College, Arborfield	
XT847	Westland Sioux AH1	Privately owned, Fairoaks	
XT852	McD Phantom FGR2	MoD(PE) BAe, Scampton	
XT853	McD Phantom FGR2	MoD(PE) BAe, Scampton	
XT857	McD Phantom FG1 [C]	RAF No 111 Sqn, Leuchars	
XT858	McD Phantom FG1	MoD(PE) BAe Brough (structures test)	
XT859	McD Phantom FG1 [K]	RAF No 111 Sqn, Leuchars	
XT860	McD Phantom FG1 [L]	RAF No 43 Sqn, Leuchars	
XT861	McD Phantom FG1 [C]	RAF No 43 Sqn, Leuchars	
XT863	McD Phantom FG1 [G]	RAF No 111 Sqn, Leuchars	
XT864	McD Phantom FG1 [J]	RAF No 111 Sqn, Leuchars	
XT865	McD Phantom FG1 [U]	RAF No 111 Sqn, Leuchars	
XT867	McD Phantom FG1 [H]	RAF No 111 Sqn, Leuchars	
XT870	McD Phantom FG1 [S]	RAF No 111 Sqn, Leuchars	
XT872	McD Phantom FG1 [T]	RAF No 111 Sqn, Leuchars	
XT873	McD Phantom FG1 [A]	RAF No 111 Sqn, Leuchars	
XT874	McD Phantom FG1 [E]	RAF No 111 Sqn, Leuchars	
XT875	McD Phantom FG1 [K]	RAF No 43 Sqn, Leuchars	
XT891	McD Phantom FGR2 [Z]	RAF No 228 OCU, Coningsby	
XT892	McD Phantom FGR2 [V]	RAF No 228 OCU, Coningsby	
XT893	McD Phantom FGR2 [Q]	MoD(PE), BAe Brough	
XT894	McD Phantom FGR2 [P]	MoD(PE), BAe Brough	
XT895	McD Phantom FGR2 [H]	RAF No 228 OCU, Coningsby	
XT896	McD Phantom FGR2 [Y]	RAF No 228 OCU, Coningsby	
XT897	McD Phantom FGR2 [M]	RAF No 228 OCU, Coningsby	
XT898	McD Phantom FGR2 [E]	RAF No 228 OCU, Coningsby	
XT899	McD Phantom FGR2 [K]	RAF No 19 Sqn, Wildenrath	
XT900	McD Phantom FGR2 [O]	MoD(PE), BAe Brough	
XT901	McD Phantom FGR2 [Y]	RAF No 56 Sqn, Wattisham	
XT902	McD Phantom FGR2 [M]	RAF No 29 Sqn, Coningsby	
XT903	McD Phantom FGR2 [R]	RAF No 228 OCU, Coningbsy	
XT905	McD Phantom FGR2 [U]	RAF No 228 OCU, Coningsby	
XT906	McD Phantom FGR2 [X]	RAF No 56 Sqn, Wattisham	
XT907	McD Phantom FGR2 [T]	RAF No 228 OCU, Coningsby	
XT908	McD Phantom FGR2 [T]	RAF No 92 Sqn, Wildenrath	
XT909	McD Phantom FGR2 [N]	RAF No 29 Sqn, Coningsby	
XT910	McD Phantom FGR2 [J]	RAF No 228 OCU, Coningsby	
XT911	McD Phantom FGR2 [K]	RAF St Athan	
XT914	McD Phantom FGR2 [N]	RAF No 228 OCU, Coningsby	
XV101	BAC VC10 C1	RAF No 10 Sqn, Brize Norton	
XV102	BAC VC10 C1	RAF No 10 Sqn, Brize Norton	
XV103	BAC VC10 C1	RAF No 10 Sqn, Brize Norton	
XV104	BAC VC10 C1	RAF No 10 Sqn, Brize Norton	
XV105	BAC VC10 C1	RAF No 10 Sqn, Brize Norton	
XV106	BAC VC10 C1	RAF No 10 Sqn, Brize Norton	
XV107	BAC VC10 C1	RAF No 10 Sqn, Brize Norton	
XV108	BAC VC10 C1	RAF No 10 Sqn, Brize Norton	
XV109	BAC VC10 C1	RAF No 10 Sqn, Brize Norton	

Notes	Serial	Type (alternative identity)	Owner, Operator or Location
	XV118	Westland Scout AH1	AAC store, Wroughton
	XV119	Westland Scout AH1	AAC store, Wroughton
	XV121	Westland Scout AH1	AAC No 658 Sqn, Netheravon
	XV122	Westland Scout AH1 [A]	AAC No 660 Sqn, Sek Kong
	XV123	Westland Scout AH1	AAC store, Wroughton
	XV124	Westland Scout AH1	AAC store, Wroughton
	XV125	Westland Scout AH1	RAF Manston Fire School
	XV126	Westland Scout AH1	AAC store, Wroughton
	XV127	Westland Scout AH1	AAC store, Wroughton
	XV128	Westland Scout AH1	AAC D&TS, Middle Wallop
	XV129	Westland Scout AH1	AAC store, Wroughton
	XV130	Westland Scout AH1	AAC store, Wroughton
	XV131	Westland Scout AH1 [X]	AAC No 660 Sqn, Brunei
	XV134	Westland Scout AH1	AAC No 658 Sqn, Netheravon
	XV135	Westland Scout AH1	AAC store, Wroughton
	XV136	Westland Scout AH1	AAC store, Wroughton
	XV137	Westland Scout AH1 [Z]	AAC No 658 Sqn, Netheravon
	XV138	Westland Scout AH1	AAC No 658 Sqn, Netheravon
	XV139	Westland Scout AH1	AAC store, Wroughton
	XV140	Westland Scout AH1	AAC No 656 Sqn, Netheravon
	XV141	Westland Scout AH1	Army Apprentice College, Arborfield
	XV147	HS Nimrod MR1 (Mod)	MoD(PE) RAE Farnborough
	XV148	HS Nimrod MR1 (Mod)	MoD(PE) BAe Woodford
	XV152	HS Buccaneer S2A (8776M) [A]	RAF CSDE, Swanton Morley
	XV154	HS Buccaneer S2A	RAF No 12 Sqn, Lossiemouth
	XV155	HS Buccaneer S2A (8716M)	BAe Brough
	XV156	HS Buccaneer S2A (8773M)	RAF St Athan, for instructional use
	XV157	HS Buccaneer S2B	RAF Shawbury store
	XV161	HS Buccaneer S2B [AF]	RAF No 12 Sqn, Lossiemouth
	XV163	HS Buccaneer S2A	RAF No 208 Sqn, Lossiemouth
	XV165	HS Buccaneer S2B [BF]	RAF No 12 Sqn, Lossiemouth
	XV168	HS Buccaneer S2B [CF]	RAF No 12 Sqn, Lossiemouth
	XV176	Lockheed Hercules C3	RAF Lyneham Transport Wing
	XV177	Lockheed Hercules C3	RAF Lyneham Transport Wing
	XV178	Lockheed Hercules C1	RAF Lyneham Transport Wing
	XV179	Lockheed Hercules C1P	RAF Lyneham Transport Wing
	XV181	Lockheed Hercules C1	RAF Lyneham Transport Wing
	XV182	Lockheed Hercules C1	RAF Lyneham Transport Wing
	XV183	Lockheed Hercules C3	RAF Lyneham Transport Wing
	XV184	Lockheed Hercules C3	RAF Lyneham Transport Wing
	XV185	Lockheed Hercules C1P	RAF Lyneham Transport Wing
	XV186	Lockheed Hercules C1	RAF Lyneham Transport Wing
	XV187	Lockheed Hercules C1P	RAF Lyneham Transport Wing
	XV188	Lockheed Hercules C3	RAF Lyneham Transport Wing
	XV189	Lockheed Hercules C3	RAF Lyneham Transport Wing
	XV190	Lockheed Hercules C3	RAF Lyneham Transport Wing
	XV191	Lockheed Hercules C1P	RAF Lyneham Transport Wing
	XV192	Lockheed Hercules C1K	RAF Lyneham Transport Wing/ 1312 Flt, Stanley
	XV193	Lockheed Hercules C3	RAF Lyneham Transport Wing
	XV195	Lockheed Hercules C1P	RAF Lyneham Transport Wing
	XV196	Lockheed Hercules C1P	RAF Lyneham Transport Wing
	XV197	Lockheed Hercules C3	RAF Lyneham Transport Wing
	XV199	Lockheed Hercules C3	RAF Lyneham Transport Wing
	XV200	Lockheed Hercules C1P	RAF Lyneham Transport Wing
	XV201	Lockheed Hercules C1K	RAF Lyneham Transport Wing/ 1312 Flt, Stanley
	XV202	Lockheed Hercules C3	RAF Lyneham Transport Wing
	XV203	Lockheed Hercules C1K	RAF Lyneham Transport Wing/ 1312 Flt, Stanley
	XV204	Lockheed Hercules C1K	RAF Lyneham Transport Wing/ 1312 Flt, Stanley
	XV205	Lockheed Hercules C1P	RAF Lyneham Transport Wing
	XV206	Lockheed Hercules C1P	RAF Lyneham Transport Wing
	XV207	Lockheed Hercules C3	RAF Lyneham Transport Wing
	XV208	Lockheed Hercules W2	MoD(PE) RAE Farnborough
	XV209	Lockheed Hercules C1	RAF Lyneham Transport Wing
	XV210	Lockheed Hercules C1P	RAF Lyneham Transport Wing
	XV211	Lockheed Hercules C1P	RAF Lyneham Transport Wing

XL584 Hawker Hunter T8C; RN FRADU, Yeovilton. *APM*

XR718 EE Lightning F3; RAF LTF, Binbrook. *PRM*

XV292 Lockheed Hercules C1P; RAF Lyneham Transport Wing. *PRM*

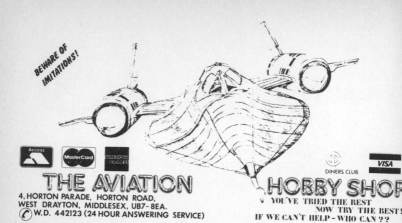

Serial	Type (alternative identity)	Owner, Operator or Location	Notes
XV212	Lockheed Hercules C3	RAF Lyneham Transport Wing	
XV213	Lockheed Hercules C1K	RAF Lyneham Transport Wing/ 1312 Flt, Stanley	
XV214	Lockheed Hercules C3	RAF Lyneham Transport Wing	
XV215	Lockheed Hercules C1	RAF Lyneham Transport Wing	
XV217	Lockheed Hercules C3	RAF Lyneham Transport Wing	
XV218	Lockheed Hercules C1P	RAF Lyneham Transport Wing	
XV219	Lockheed Hercules C3	RAF Lyneham Transport Wing	
XV220	Lockheed Hercules C3	RAF Lyneham Transport Wing	
XV221	Lockheed Hercules C3	RAF Lyneham Transport Wing	
XV222	Lockheed Hercules C3	RAF Lyneham Transport Wing	
XV223	Lockheed Hercules C3	MoD(PE) A&AEE, Boscombe Down	
XV226	HS Nimrod MR1	RAF No 42 Sqn, St Mawgan	
XV227	HS Nimrod MR2P	RAF Kinloss MR Wing	
XV228	HS Nimrod MR2P	RAF Kinloss MR Wing	
XV229	HS Nimrod MR2	RAF Kinloss MR Wing	
XV230	HS Nimrod MR2P	RAF Kinloss MR Wing	
XV231	HS Nimrod MR2	RAF Kinloss MR Wing	
XV232	HS Nimrod MR2P	RAF Kinloss MR Wing	
XV233	HS Nimrod MR2	RAF No 42 Sqn, St Mawgan	
XV234	HS Nimrod MR2P	RAF Kinloss MR Wing	
XV235	HS Nimrod MR2	RAF No 236 OCU, St Mawgan	
XV236	HS Nimrod MR2P	RAF Kinloss MR Wing	
XV237	HS Nimrod MR2P	RAF Kinloss MR Wing	
XV238	HS Nimrod MR2P	RAF Kinloss MR Wing	
XV239	HS Nimrod MR2P	RAF Kinloss MR Wing	
XV240	HS Nimrod MR2	RAF Kinloss MR Wing	
XV241	HS Nimrod MR2	RAF Kinloss MR Wing	
XV242	HS Nimrod MR2	RAF Kinloss MR Wing	
XV243	HS Nimrod MR2P	RAF Kinloss MR Wing	
XV244	HS Nimrod MR2	MoD(PE), BAe Woodford	
XV245	HS Nimrod MR2	RAF No 42 Sqn, St Mawgan	
XV246	HS Nimrod MR2	RAF No 42 Sqn, St Mawgan	
XV247	HS Nimrod MR2P	RAF Kinloss MR Wing	
XV248	HS Nimrod MR2P	RAF Kinloss MR Wing	
XV249	HS Nimrod MR2	MoD(PE), BAe Woodford	
XV250	HS Nimrod MR2	RAF Kinloss MR Wing	
XV251	HS Nimrod MR2	RAF Kinloss MR Wing	
XV252	HS Nimrod MR2	RAF Kinloss MR Wing	
XV253	HS Nimrod MR2P	RAF Kinloss MR Wing	
XV254	HS Nimrod MR2P	RAF Kinloss MR Wing	
XV255	HS Nimrod MR2P	RAF Kinloss MR Wing	
XV257	HS Nimrod MR2	RAF No 236 OCU, St Mawgan	
XV258	HS Nimrod MR2	RAF No 42 Sqn, St Mawgan	
XV259	BAe Nimrod AEW3	MoD(PE), BAe Woodford	
XV260	HS Nimrod MR2P	RAF Kinloss MR Wing	
XV261	BAe Nimrod AEW3	MoD(PE), BAe Woodford	
XV262	BAe Nimrod AEW3	MoD(PE), BAe Woodford	
XV263	BAe Nimrod AEW3	MoD(PE), BAe Woodford	
XV268	DHC Beaver AL1	AAC store, RAF Shawbury	
XV269	DHC Beaver AL1 (8011M)	AAC AETW, Middle Wallop	
XV270	DHC Beaver AL1	AAC, Aldergrove	
XV271	DHC Beaver AL1	AAC, Aldergrove	
XV272	DHC Beaver AL1	AAC, Aldergrove	
XV277	HS Harrier GR1	MoD(PE) Rolls-Royce, Filton	
XV278	HS Harrier GR1 [B]	MoD(PE) RAE Farnborough	
XV281	HS Harrier GR1 [B]	MoD(PE) RAE Farnborough	
XV290	Lockheed Hercules C3	RAF Lyneham Transport Wing	
XV291	Lockheed Hercules C1P	RAF Lyneham Transport Wing	
XV292	Lockheed Hercules C1P	RAF Lyneham Transport Wing	
XV293	Lockheed Hercules C1	RAF Lyneham Transport Wing	
XV294	Lockheed Hercules C3	RAF Lyneham Transport Wing	
XV295	Lockheed Hercules C1	RAF Lyneham Transport Wing	
XV296	Lockheed Hercules C1K	RAF Lyneham Transport Wing/ 1312 Flt, Stanley	
XV297	Lockheed Hercules C1	RAF Lyneham Transport Wing	
XV298	Lockheed Hercules C1P	RAF Lyneham Transport Wing	
XV299	Lockheed Hercules C1	RAF Lyneham Transport Wing	
XV300	Lockheed Hercules C1P	RAF Lyneham Transport Wing	
XV301	Lockheed Hercules C3	RAF Lyneham Transport Wing	

Notes	Serial	Type (alternative identity)	Owner, Operator or Location
	XV302	Lockheed Hercules C1	RAF Lyneham Transport Wing
	XV303	Lockheed Hercules C3	RAF Lyneham Transport Wing
	XV304	Lockheed Hercules C3	RAF Lyneham Transport Wing
	XV305	Lockheed Hercules C3	RAF Lyneham Transport Wing
	XV306	Lockheed Hercules C1	RAF Lyneham Transport Wing
	XV307	Lockheed Hercules C3	RAF Lyneham Transport Wing
	XV328	EE Lightning T5 [DU]	RAF LTF, Binbrook
	XV332	HS Buccaneer S2B [RS]	RAF No 208 Sqn, Lossiemouth
	XV333	HS Buccaneer S2B [DF]	RAF No 12 Sqn, Lossiemouth
	XV334	HS Buccaneer S2B [D]	RAF Shawbury store
	XV336	HS Buccaneer S2A	RAF Shawbury store
	XV337	HS Buccaneer S2C	MoD(PE) A&AEE Boscombe Down
	XV341	HS Buccaneer S2B	MoD(PE), BAe Scampton
	XV342	HS Buccaneer S2B [T]	RAF No 16 Sqn, Laarbruch
	XV344	HS Buccaneer S2C	MoD(PE) RAE Farnborough
	XV349	HS Buccaneer S2B	RAF Shawbury store
	XV350	HS Buccaneer S2B	MoD(PE), BAe Scampton
	XV352	HS Buccaneer S2B [TS]	RAF No 208 Sqn, Lossiemouth
	XV353	HS Buccaneer S2B [LS]	RAF No 208 Sqn, Lossiemouth
	XV355	HS Buccaneer S2A [AC]	RAF No 237 OCU, Lossiemouth
	XV356	HS Buccaneer S2A [B]	RAF Shawbury store
	XV359	HS Buccaneer S2C [VS]	RAF No 208 Sqn, Lossiemouth
	XV361	HS Buccaneer S2C [FF]	RAF No 12 Sqn, Lossiemouth
	XV370	Sikorsky SH-3D (G-ATYU)	MoD(PE) ETPS Boscombe Down
	XV371	Westland Sea King HAS1	MoD(PE) RAE Farnborough
	XV372	Westland Sea King HAS1	Westland Helicopters, Yeovil
	XV373	Westland Sea King HAS1	MoD(PE) A&AEE Boscombe Down
	XV393	McD Phantom FGR2 [A]	MoD(PE) BAe Brough
	XV394	McD Phantom FGR2	RAF No 228 OCU, Coningsby
	XV396	McD Phantom FGR2	RAF Coningsby
	XV398	McD Phantom FGR2 [I]	RAF No 228 OCU, Coningsby
	XV399	McD Phantom FGR2 [L]	RAF No 56 Sqn, Wattisham
	XV400	McD Phantom FGR2 [F]	RAF No 19 Sqn, Wildenrath
	XV401	McD Phantom FGR2 [L]	RAF No 29 Sqn, Coningsby
	XV402	McD Phantom FGR2 [A]	RAF No 23 Sqn, Stanley
	XV404	McD Phantom FGR2 [E]	RAF No 29 Sqn, Coningsby
	XV406	McD Phantom FGR2 [K]	RAF No 228 OCU, Coningsby
	XV407	McD Phantom FGR2 [X]	RAF St Athan
	XV408	McD Phantom FGR2 [P]	RAF No 29 Sqn, Coningsby
	XV409	McD Phantom FGR2 [A]	RAF No 29 Sqn, Coningsby
	XV410	McD Phantom FGR2 [E]	RAF No 56 Sqn, Wattisham
	XV411	McD Phantom FGR2 [M]	RAF No 19 Sqn, Wildenrath
	XV412	McD Phantom FGR2 [S]	RAF No 29 Sqn, Coningsby
	XV415	McD Phantom FGR2 [O]	RAF No 92 Sqn, Wildenrath
	XV419	McD Phantom FGR2 [G]	RAF No 23 Sqn, Stanley
	XV420	McD Phantom FGR2 [B]	RAF No 23 Sqn, Stanley
	XV421	McD Phantom FGR2 [B]	RAF No 228 OCU, Coningsby
	XV422	McD Phantom FGR2 [J]	MoD(PE)/BAe, Brough
	XV423	McD Phantom FGR2 [D]	RAF No 23 Sqn, Stanley
	XV424	McD Phantom FGR2 [G]	RAF No 228 OCU, Coningsby
	XV425	McD Phantom FGR2 [D]	RAF No 56 Sqn, Wattisham
	XV426	McD Phantom FGR2 [Q]	RAF No 23 Sqn, Stanley
	XV428	McD Phantom FGR2 [I]	RAF No 56 Sqn, Wattisham
	XV429	McD Phantom FGR2 [K]	RAF No 29 Sqn, Coningsby
	XV430	McD Phantom FGR2 [C]	RAF No 19 Sqn, Wildenrath
	XV432	McD Phantom FGR2 [T]	RAF No 29 Sqn, Coningsby
	XV433	McD Phantom FGR2 [I]	RAF No 29 Sqn, Coningsby
	XV434	McD Phantom FGR2 [J]	RAF No 29 Sqn, Coningsby
	XV435	McD Phantom FGR2 [P]	RAF No 228 OCU, Coningsby
	XV437	McD Phantom FGR2 [B]	RAF No 19 Sqn, Wildenrath
	XV438	McD Phantom FGR2 [Y]	RAF No 29 Sqn, Coningsby
	XV439	McD Phantom FGR2 [D]	MoD(PE), BAe Brough
	XV442	McD Phantom FGR2 [R]	RAF No 29 Sqn, Coningsby
	XV460	McD Phantom FGR2 [W]	RAF No 92 Sqn, Wildenrath
	XV461	McD Phantom FGR2 [G]	RAF No 56 Sqn, Wattisham
	XV462	McD Phantom FGR2 [U]	RAF No 92 Sqn, Wildenrath
	XV464	McD Phantom FGR2 [U]	RAF No 23 Sqn, Stanley
	XV465	McD Phantom FGR2 [Z]	RAF No 92 Sqn, Wildenrath
	XV466	McD Phantom FGR2 [E]	RAF No 23 Sqn, Stanley
	XV467	McD Phantom FGR2 [Q]	RAF No 92 Sqn, Wildenrath

Serial	Type (alternative identity)	Owner, Operator or Location	Notes
XV468	McD Phantom FGR2 [P]	RAF No 92 Sqn, Wildenrath	
XV469	McD Phantom FGR2 [T]	RAF No 56 Sqn, Wattisham	
XV470	McD Phantom FGR2 [G]	RAF No 19 Sqn, Wildenrath	
XV471	McD Phantom FGR2	RAF No 92 Sqn, Wildenrath	
XV472	McD Phantom FGR2 [E]	RAF No 19 Sqn, Wildenrath	
XV473	McD Phantom FGR2 [L]	RAF No 228 OCU, Coningsby	
XV474	McD Phantom FGR2 [P]	RAF No 23 Sqn, Stanley	
XV476	McD Phantom FGR2 [L]	RAF No 19 Sqn, Wildenrath	
XV478	McD Phantom FGR2 [Q]	RAF No 56 Sqn, Wattisham	
XV480	McD Phantom FGR2 [X]	RAF No 92 Sqn, Wildenrath	
XV481	McD Phantom FGR2 [H]	RAF No 19 Sqn, Wildenrath	
XV482	McD Phantom FGR2 [C]	RAF No 56 Sqn, Wattisham	
XV485	McD Phantom FGR2 [W]	RAF No 29 Sqn, Coningsby	
XV486	McD Phantom FGR2 [D]	RAF No 228 OCU, Coningsby	
XV487	McD Phantom FGR2 [Q]	RAF No 29 Sqn, Coningsby	
XV488	McD Phantom FGR2 [J]	RAF No 56 Sqn, Wattisham	
XV489	McD Phantom FGR2 [A]	RAF No 56 Sqn, Wattisham	
XV490	McD Phantom FGR2 [S]	RAF No 56 Sqn, Wattisham	
XV492	McD Phantom FGR2 [U]	RAF No 56 Sqn, Wattisham	
XV494	McD Phantom FGR2 [M]	RAF No 56 Sqn, Wattisham	
XV495	McD Phantom FGR2 [N]	RAF No 23 Sqn, Stanley	
XV496	McD Phantom FGR2 [L]	RAF No 19 Sqn, Wildenrath	
XV497	McD Phantom FGR2 [A]	RAF No 19 Sqn, Wildenrath	
XV498	McD Phantom FGR2 [R]	RAF No 92 Sqn, Wildenrath	
XV499	McD Phantom FGR2 [F]	RAF No 228 OCU, Coningsby	
XV500	McD Phantom FGR2 [J]	RAF No 56 Sqn, Wattisham	
XV501	McD Phantom FGR2 [B]	RAF No 56 Sqn, Wattisham	
XV555	HS Harrier GR1 (8566M) (really XV279)	RAF Wittering, for instructional use	
XV567	McD Phantom FG1 [I]	RAF No 43 Sqn, Leuchars	
XV568	McD Phantom FG1 [T]	RAF No 43 Sqn, Leuchars	
XV569	McD Phantom FG1 [Q]	RAF No 111 Sqn, Leuchars	
XV570	McD Phantom FG1 [N]	RAF No 111 Sqn, Leuchars	
XV571	McD Phantom FG1 [A]	RAF No 43 Sqn, Leuchars	
XV572	McD Phantom FG1 [N]	RAF No 43 Sqn, Leuchars	
XV573	McD Phantom FG1 [D]	RAF No 111 Sqn, Leuchars	
XV574	McD Phantom FG1 [Z]	RAF No 111 Sqn, Leuchars	
XV575	McD Phantom FG1 [S]	RAF No 43 Sqn, Leuchars	
XV576	McD Phantom FG1 [D]	RAF No 43 Sqn, Leuchars	
XV577	McD Phantom FG1 [M]	RAF No 43 Sqn, Leuchars	
XV579	McD Phantom FG1 [R]	RAF No 43 Sqn, Leuchars	
XV581	McD Phantom FG1 [E]	RAF No 43 Sqn, Leuchars	
XV582	McD Phantom FG1 [F]	RAF No 43 Sqn, Leuchars	
XV583	McD Phantom FG1 [B]	RAF No 111 Sqn, Leuchars	
XV584	McD Phantom FG1 [F]	RAF No 111 Sqn, Leuchars	
XV585	McD Phantom FG1 [P]	RAF No 43 Sqn, Leuchars	
XV586	McD Phantom FG1 [J]	RAF No 43 Sqn, Leuchars	
XV587	McD Phantom FG1 [G]	RAF No 43 Sqn, Leuchars	
XV590	McD Phantom FG1 [X]	RAF No 43 Sqn, Leuchars	
XV591	McD Phantom FG1 [M]	RAF No 111 Sqn, Leuchars	
XV592	McD Phantom FG1 [L]	RAF No 111 Sqn, Leuchars	
XV615	BHC SR.N6 Winchester 2	RN, Hong Kong	
XV623	Westland Wasp HAS1 [601]	RN No 829 Sqn, Portland	
XV624	Westland Wasp HAS1 [456/YM]	RN No 829 Sqn, Portland	
XV625	Westland Wasp HAS1 [471/PB]	RNEC Manadon, for instruction	
XV626	Westland Wasp HAS1 [323]	RN No 829 Sqn, Portland	
XV629	Westland Wasp HAS1	AAC AETW, Middle Wallop	
XV631	Westland Wasp HAS1 [617]	MoD(PE), RAE Farnborough	
XV632	Westland Wasp HAS1 [610]	RN No 829 Sqn, Portland	
XV634	Westland Wasp HAS1 [423]	RN No 829 Sqn, Portland	
XV636	Westland Wasp HAS1 [606]	RN No 829 Sqn, Portland	
XV638	Westland Wasp HAS1 [A430] (8826M)	RAF AMS, Brize Norton	
XV639	Westland Wasp HAS1 [612]	RN No 829 Sqn, Portland	
XV642	Westland Sea King HAS2A	MoD(PE) Westlands, Yeovil	
XV643	Westland Sea King HAS5 [705/PW]	RNAY Fleetlands	

Notes	Serial	Type (alternative identity)	Owner, Operator or Location
	XV644	Westland Sea King HAS1 (A2664) [64]	RN AES Lee-on-Solent
	XV647	Westland Sea King HAS5 [265]	RN No 814 Sqn, Culdrose
	XV648	Westland Sea King HAS2A [587]	RN No 706 Sqn, Culdrose
	XV649	Westland Sea King HAS5 [585]	RNAY Fleetlands
	XV650	Westland Sea King AEW2 [364]	RN No 849 Sqn, Culdrose
	XV651	Westland Sea King HAS5 [531]	RN No 826 Sqn, Culdrose
	XV652	Westland Sea King HAS5 [532]	RN No 826 Sqn, Culdrose
	XV653	Westland Sea King HAS5 [509]	RN No 810 Sqn, Culdrose
	XV654	Westland Sea King HAS2A [588]	RN No 706 Sqn, Culdrose
	XV655	Westland Sea King HAS5 [534]	RN No 826 Sqn, Culdrose
	XV656	Westland Sea King AEW2	RN No 849 Sqn, Culdrose
	XV657	Westland Sea King HAS2A [589]	RN NASU, Culdrose
	XV659	Westland Sea King HAS2A [705]	RN No 819 Sqn, Prestwick
	XV660	Westland Sea King HAS5 [507]	RN No 810 Sqn, Culdrose
	XV661	Westland Sea King HAS5 [502]	RN No 810 Sqn, Culdrose
	XV663	Westland Sea King HAS2A [591]	RNAY Fleetlands
	XV664	Westland Sea King HAS2A [704/PW]	RN No 819 Sqn, Prestwick
	XV665	Westland Sea King HAS5 [508]	RN NASU Culdrose
	XV666	Westland Sea King HAS2A [598]	RN No 706 Sqn, Culdrose
	XV668	Westland Sea King HAS5 [586]	RN No 706 Sqn, Culdrose
	XV669	Westland Sea King HAS1 (A2659) [410/BL]	RNAS Culdrose, Engineering Training School
	XV670	Westland Sea King HAS5 [590/CU]	RNAY Fleetlands
	XV671	Westland Sea King AEW2	RN No 849 Sqn, Culdrose
	XV672	Westland Sea King AEW2 [525]	RN No 849 Sqn, Culdrose
	XV673	Westland Sea King HAS5 [512]	RN No 810 Sqn, Culdrose
	XV674	Westland Sea King HAS2A [706/PW]	RN No 819 Sqn, Prestwick
	XV675	Westland Sea King HAS5 [274]	RN No 814 Sqn, Culdrose
	XV676	Westland Sea King HAS5 [266]	RN No 814 Sqn, Culdrose
	XV677	Westland Sea King HAS5	RNAY Fleetlands
	XV696	Westland Sea King HAS5A [503]	RN No 810 Sqn, Culdrose
	XV697	Westland Sea King AEW2	RN No 849 Sqn, Culdrose
	XV699	Westland Sea King HAS5 [272]	RN No 814 Sqn, Culdrose
	XV700	Westland Sea King HAS2A [590]	RN No 706 Sqn, Culdrose
	XV701	Westland Sea King HAS5 [589]	RNAY Fleetlands
	XV703	Westland Sea King HAS5 [271]	RN No 814 Sqn, Culdrose
	XV704	Westland Sea King AEW2 [363]	RN No 849 Sqn, Culdrose
	XV705	Westland Sea King HAS2A [596]	RN No 706 Sqn, Culdrose

Serial	Type (alternative identity)	Owner, Operator or Location	Notes
XV706	Westland Sea King HAS5	RN No 706 Sqn, Culdrose	
XV707	Westland Sea King HAS2A [707/PW]	RN No 819 Sqn, Prestwick	
XV708	Westland Sea King HAS2A [702/PW]	RN NASU, Culdrose	
XV709	Westland Sea King HAS5 [585]	RN No 706 Sqn, Culdrose	
XV710	Westland Sea King HAS2A [701/PW]	RN No 819 Sqn, Prestwick	
XV711	Westland Sea King HAS5 [011/N]	RN No 820 Sqn, Culdrose	
XV712	Westland Sea King HAS5 [270]	RN No 814 Sqn, Culdrose	
XV713	Westland Sea King HAS5 [536]	RN No 826 Sqn, Culdrose	
XV714	Westland Sea King AEW2 [354]	RN No 849 Sqn, Culdrose	
XV719	Westland Wessex HC2	RAF No 84 Sqn, Cyprus	
XV720	Westland Wessex HC2	RAF No 22 Sqn SAR	
XV721	Westland Wessex HC2	RAF No 84 Sqn, Cyprus	
XV722	Westland Wessex HC2 [WH]	RAF No 2 FTS, Shawbury	
XV723	Westland Wessex HC2 [Q]	RAF No 72 Sqn, Aldergrove	
XV724	Westland Wessex HC2	RAF No 22 Sqn SAR	
XV725	Westland Wessex HC2 [C]	RAF No 72 Sqn, Aldergrove	
XV726	Westland Wessex HC2 [J]	RAF No 72 Sqn, Aldergrove	
XV728	Westland Wessex HC2 [A]	RAF No 72 Sqn, Aldergrove	
XV729	Westland Wessex HC2	RAF No 22 Sqn SAR	
XV730	Westland Wessex HC2	RAF No 22 Sqn SAR	
XV731	Westland Wessex HC2 [Y]	RAF No 72 Sqn, Aldergrove	
XV732	Westland Wessex HCC4	RAF Queen's Flight, Benson	
XV733	Westland Wessex HCC4	RAF Queen's Flight, Benson	
XV738	HS Harrier GR3 [B]	RAF No 4 Sqn, Gutersloh	
XV740	HS Harrier GR3 [05]	RAF No 1 Sqn, Wittering	
XV741	HS Harrier GR3 [AA]	RAF No 3 Sqn, Gutersloh	
XV744	HS Harrier GR3 [D]	RAF No 233 OCU, Wittering	
XV747	HS Harrier GR3 [02]	RAF No 1 Sqn, Wittering	
XV748	HS Harrier GR3 [B]	RAF No 233 OCU, Wittering	
XV751	HS Harrier GR3 [01]	RAF No 1 Sqn, Wittering	
XV752	HS Harrier GR3	RAF Wittering	
XV753	HS Harrier GR3	RAF Wittering	
XV755	HS Harrier GR3 [M]	RAF No 233 OCU, Wittering	
XV758	HS Harrier GR3 [J]	RAF No 233 OCU, Wittering	
XV759	HS Harrier GR3 [H]	RAF No 233 OCU, Wittering	
XV760	HS Harrier GR3 [F]	RAF No 233 OCU, Wittering	
XV762	HS Harrier GR3 [09]	RAF SSF, Wittering	
XV778	HS Harrier GR3	RAF No 1 Sqn, Wittering	
XV779	HS Harrier GR3 [AP]	RAF No 3 Sqn, Gutersloh	
XV782	HS Harrier GR3	RAF No 1453 Flt, Stanley	
XV783	HS Harrier GR3 [E]	RAF No 233 OCU, Wittering	
XV784	HS Harrier GR3 [D]	RAF No 4 Sqn, Gutersloh	
XV786	HS Harrier GR3 [E]	RAF No 4 Sqn, Gutersloh	
XV789	HS Harrier GR3	RAF No 1 Sqn, Wittering	
XV790	HS Harrier GR3 [14]	RAF No 1 Sqn, Wittering	
XV793	HS Harrier GR3 [L]	RAF No 4 Sqn, Gutersloh	
XV804	HS Harrier GR3 [AD]	RAF No 3 Sqn, Gutersloh	
XV806	HS Harrier GR3 [AB]	RAF No 3 Sqn, Gutersloh	
XV808	HS Harrier GR3 [AW]	RAF No 3 Sqn, Gutersloh	
XV809	HS Harrier GR3 [AF]	RAF No 3 Sqn, Gutersloh	
XV810	HS Harrier GR3 [X]	RAF No 4 Sqn, Gutersloh	
XV814	HS Comet 4C (G-APDF)	MoD(PE) RAE Farnborough	
XV859	BHC SR.N6 Winchester 6	RN NHTU Lee-on-Solent	
XV863	HS Buccaneer S2B [CC]	RAF No 237 OCU, Lossiemouth	
XV864	HS Buccaneer S2B [KF]	RAF No 12 Sqn, Lossiemouth	
XV865	HS Buccaneer S2B [BS]	RAF No 208 Sqn, Lossiemouth	
XV866	HS Buccaneer S2B [Y]	RAF Shawbury store	
XV867	HS Buccaneer S2B [EF]	RAF No 12 Sqn, Lossiemouth	
XV868	HS Buccaneer S2B [LF]	RAF No 12 Sqn, Lossiemouth	
XV869	HS Buccaneer S2B [MF]	RAF No 12 Sqn, Lossiemouth	
XW175	HS Harrier T4	MoD(PE) RAE Bedford	

Notes	Serial	Type (alternative identity)	Owner, Operator or Location
	XW179	Westland Sioux AH1	Wessex Aviation Society, Wimborne
	XW198	Westland Puma HC1 [DL]	RAF No 230 Sqn, Gutersloh
	XW199	Westland Puma HC1 [DU]	RAF No 230 Sqn, Gutersloh
	XW200	Westland Puma HC1 [FA]	RAF No 240 OCU, Odiham
	XW201	Westland Puma HC1 [FB]	RAF No 240 OCU, Odiham
	XW202	Westland Puma HC1 [FC]	RAF No 240 OCU, Odiham
	XW204	Westland Puma HC1 [CA]	RAF No 1563 Flt, Belize
	XW206	Westland Puma HC1 [CC]	RAF No 33 Sqn, Odiham
	XW207	Westland Puma HC1 [CD]	RAF No 1563 Flt, Belize
	XW208	Westland Puma HC1 [CE]	RAF No 33 Sqn, Odiham
	XW209	Westland Puma HC1 [CF]	RAF No 1563 Flt, Belize
	XW210	Westland Puma HC1 [CG]	RAF No 33 Sqn, Odiham
	XW211	Westland Puma HC1 [CH]	RAF No 33 Sqn, Odiham
	XW212	Westland Puma HC1 [FD]	RAF No 240 OCU, Odiham
	XW213	Westland Puma HC1 [CJ]	RAF No 33 Sqn, Odiham
	XW214	Westland Puma HC1 [CK]	RAF No 33 Sqn, Odiham
	XW215	Westland Puma HC1 [DM]	RAF No 230 Sqn, Gutersloh
	XW216	Westland Puma HC1 [CL]	RAF No 33 Sqn, Odiham
	XW217	Westland Puma HC1 [DA]	RAF No 230 Sqn, Gutersloh
	XW218	Westland Puma HC1 [DT]	RAF No 230 Sqn, Gutersloh
	XW219	Westland Puma HC1 [DC]	RAF No 230 Sqn, Gutersloh
	XW220	Westland Puma HC1 [DD]	RAF No 230 Sqn, Gutersloh
	XW221	Westland Puma HC1 [DE]	RAF No 230 Sqn, Gutersloh
	XW222	Westland Puma HC1 [DF]	RAF No 230 Sqn, Gutersloh
	XW223	Westland Puma HC1 [DG]	RAF No 230 Sqn, Gutersloh
	XW224	Westland Puma HC1 [DH]	RAF No 230 Sqn, Gutersloh
	XW225	Westland Puma HC1 [FE]	RAF No 240 OCU, Odiham
	XW226	Westland Puma HC1 [DK]	RAF No 230 Sqn, Gutersloh
	XW227	Westland Puma HC1 [DN]	RAF No 230 Sqn, Gutersloh
	XW229	Westland Puma HC1 [DB]	RAF No 230 Sqn, Gutersloh
	XW231	Westland Puma HC1 [CM]	RAF No 33 Sqn, Odiham
	XW232	Westland Puma HC1 [DJ]	RAF No 230 Sqn, Gutersloh
	XW233	Westland Puma HC1 [CN]	RAF No 33 Sqn, Odiham
	XW234	Westland Puma HC1 [CO]	RAF No 33 Sqn, Odiham
	XW235	Westland Puma HC1 [CP]	RAF No 1563 Flt, Belize
	XW236	Westland Puma HC1 [CQ]	RAF No 33 Sqn, Odiham
	XW237	Westland Puma HC1 [CR]	RAF No 33 Sqn, Odiham
	XW241	Aerospatiale SA330 (F-ZJUX)	MoD(PE) RAE Bedford
	XW249	Cushioncraft CC7	Cornwall Aero Park, Helston
	XW255	BHC BH-7 Wellington	RN NHTU Lee-on-Solent
	XW265	HS Harrier T4	MoD(PE) A&AEE Boscombe Down
	XW266	HS Harrier T4A [S]	RAF No 233 OCU, Wittering
	XW267	HS Harrier T4 [T]	RAF No 233 OCU, Wittering
	XW268	HS Harrier T4A [U]	RAF No 233 OCU, Wittering
	XW269	HS Harrier T4	MoD(PE)/BAe Dunsfold
	XW270	HS Harrier T4 [12]	RAF No 1 Sqn, Wittering
	XW271	HS Harrier T4 [R]	RAF No 233 OCU, Wittering
	XW272	HS Harrier T4 (8783M)	Cranfield Institute of Technology
	XW276	Aerospatiale SA341 (F-ZWRI)	Southampton Hall of Aviation
	XW280	Westland Scout AH1	AAC store, Wroughton
	XW281	Westland Scout AH1	AAC No 658 Sqn, Netheravon
	XW282	Westland Scout AH1	AAC store, Wroughton
	XW283	Westland Scout AH1 [W]	AAC No 658 Sqn, Netheravon
	XW284	Westland Scout AH1	AAC store, Wroughton
	XW287	BAC Jet Provost T5 [P]	RAF No 6 FTS, Finningley
	XW289	BAC Jet Provost T5A [31]	RAF College, Cranwell
	XW290	BAC Jet Provost T5A [41]	RAF College, Cranwell
	XW291	BAC Jet Provost T5 [N]	RAF No 6 FTS, Finningley
	XW292	BAC Jet Provost T5A [32]	RAF College, Cranwell
	XW293	BAC Jet Provost T5 [Z]	RAF No 6 FTS, Finningley
	XW294	BAC Jet Provost T5A [45]	RAF College, Cranwell
	XW295	BAC Jet Provost T5A [67]	RAF No 1 FTS, Linton-on-Ouse
	XW296	BAC Jet Provost T5 [Q]	RAF No 6 FTS, Finningley
	XW298	BAC Jet Provost T5 [O]	RAF No 6 FTS, Finningley
	XW299	BAC Jet Provost T5A [60]	RAF No 1 FTS, Linton-on-Ouse
	XW301	BAC Jet Provost T5A [63]	RAF No 1 FTS, Linton-on-Ouse
	XW302	BAC Jet Provost T5 [T]	RAF No 6 FTS, Finningley
	XW303	BAC Jet Provost T5A [127]	RAF No 7 FTS, Church Fenton
	XW304	BAC Jet Provost T5 [X]	RAF No 6 FTS, Finningley
	XW305	BAC Jet Provost T5A [42]	RAF College, Cranwell

Serial	Type (alternative identity)	Owner, Operator or Location	Notes
XW306	BAC Jet Provost T5 [Y]	RAF No 6 FTS, Finningley	
XW307	BAC Jet Provost T5 [S]	RAF No 6 FTS, Finningley	
XW309	BAC Jet Provost T5 [V]	RAF No 6 FTS, Finningley	
XW310	BAC Jet Provost T5A [37]	RAF College, Cranwell	
XW311	BAC Jet Provost T5 [W]	RAF No 6 FTS, Finningley	
XW312	BAC Jet Provost T5A [64]	RAF No 1 FTS, Linton-on-Ouse	
XW313	BAC Jet Provost T5A [30]	RAF College, Cranwell	
XW315	BAC Jet Provost T5A [50]	RAF No 3 FTS, Scampton	
XW316	BAC Jet Provost T5A [52]	RAF No 3 FTS, Scampton	
XW317	BAC Jet Provost T5A [25]	RAF College, Cranwell	
XW318	BAC Jet Provost T5A [12]	RAF College, Cranwell	
XW319	BAC Jet Provost T5A [57]	RAF No 3 FTS, Scampton	
XW320	BAC Jet Provost T5A [71]	RAF No 1 FTS, Linton-on-Ouse	
XW321	BAC Jet Provost T5A [132]	RAF No 7 FTS, Church Fenton	
XW322	BAC Jet Provost T5A [43]	RAF College, Cranwell	
XW323	BAC Jet Provost T5A [44]	RAF College, Cranwell	
XW324	BAC Jet Provost T5 [U]	RAF No 6 FTS, Finningley	
XW325	BAC Jet Provost T5A [33]	RAF College, Cranwell	
XW326	BAC Jet Provost T5A [120]	RAF No 7 FTS, Church Fenton	
XW327	BAC Jet Provost T5A [134]	RAF No 7 FTS, Church Fenton	
XW328	BAC Jet Provost T5A [22]	RAF College, Cranwell	
XW329	BAC Jet Provost T5A [48] (8741M)	RAF Church Fenton Fire Section	
XW330	BAC Jet Provost T5A [130]	RAF No 7 FTS, Church Fenton	
XW332	BAC Jet Provost T5A [34]	RAF College, Cranwell	
XW333	BAC Jet Provost T5A [36]	RAF College, Cranwell	
XW334	BAC Jet Provost T5A [131]	RAF No 7 FTS, Church Fenton	
XW335	BAC Jet Provost T5A [27]	RAF College, Cranwell	
XW336	BAC Jet Provost T5A [6]	RAF College, Cranwell	
XW351	BAC Jet Provost T5A [74]	RAF No 1 FTS, Linton-on-Ouse	
XW352	BAC Jet Provost T5 [R]	RAF No 6 FTS, Finningley	
XW353	BAC Jet Provost T5A [51]	RAF No 3 FTS, Scampton	
XW354	BAC Jet Provost T5A [7]	RAF College, Cranwell	
XW355	BAC Jet Provost T5A [20]	RAF College, Cranwell	
XW357	BAC Jet Provost T5A [5]	RAF College, Cranwell	
XW358	BAC Jet Provost T5A [18]	RAF College, Cranwell	
XW359	BAC Jet Provost T5A [128]	RAF No 7 FTS, Church Fenton	
XW360	BAC Jet Provost T5A [129]	RAF No 7 FTS, Church Fenton	
XW361	BAC Jet Provost T5A [21]	RAF College, Cranwell	
XW362	BAC Jet Provost T5A [17]	RAF College, Cranwell	
XW363	BAC Jet Provost T5A [68]	RAF No 1 FTS, Linton-on-Ouse	
XW364	BAC Jet Provost T5A [35]	RAF College, Cranwell	
XW365	BAC Jet Provost T5A [73]	RAF No 1 FTS, Linton-on-Ouse	
XW366	BAC Jet Provost T5A [75]	RAF No 1 FTS, Linton-on-Ouse	
XW367	BAC Jet Provost T5A [26]	RAF College, Cranwell	
XW368	BAC Jet Provost T5A [55]	RAF No 3 FTS, Scampton	
XW369	BAC Jet Provost T5A [9]	RAF College, Cranwell	
XW370	BAC Jet Provost T5A [72]	RAF No 1 FTS, Linton-on-Ouse	
XW372	BAC Jet Provost T5A [121]	RAF No 7 FTS, Church Fenton	
XW373	BAC Jet Provost T5A [11]	RAF College, Cranwell	
XW374	BAC Jet Provost T5A [38]	RAF College, Cranwell	
XW375	BAC Jet Provost T5A [10]	RAF College, Cranwell	
XW404	BAC Jet Provost T5A [77]	RAF No 1 FTS, Linton-on-Ouse	
XW405	BAC Jet Provost T5A [61]	RAF No 1 FTS, Linton-on-Ouse	
XW406	BAC Jet Provost T5A [23]	RAF College, Cranwell	
XW407	BAC Jet Provost T5A [122]	RAF No 7 FTS, Church Fenton	
XW408	BAC Jet Provost T5A [24]	RAF College, Cranwell	
XW409	BAC Jet Provost T5A [123]	RAF No 7 FTS, Church Fenton	
XW410	BAC Jet Provost T5A [80]	RAF No 1 FTS, Linton-on-Ouse	
XW411	BAC Jet Provost T5A [133]	RAF No 7 FTS, Church Fenton	
XW412	BAC Jet Provost T5A [15]	RAF College, Cranwell	
XW413	BAC Jet Provost T5A [69]	RAF No 1 FTS, Linton-on-Ouse	
XW415	BAC Jet Provost T5A [53]	RAF No 3 FTS, Scampton	
XW416	BAC Jet Provost T5A [19]	RAF College, Cranwell	
XW418	BAC Jet Provost T5A [54]	RAF No 3 FTS, Scampton	
XW419	BAC Jet Provost T5A [125]	RAF No 7 FTS, Church Fenton	
XW420	BAC Jet Provost T5A [8]	RAF College, Cranwell	
XW421	BAC Jet Provost T5A [60]	RAF No 3 FTS, Scampton	
XW422	BAC Jet Provost T5A [3]	RAF College, Cranwell	
XW423	BAC Jet Provost T5A [14]	RAF College, Cranwell	

Notes	Serial	Type (alternative identity)	Owner, Operator or Location
	XW424	BAC Jet Provost T5A [62]	Privately owned, Misson, Notts
	XW425	BAC Jet Provost T5A [61]	RAF No 3 FTS, Scampton
	XW427	BAC Jet Provost T5A [56]	RAF No 3 FTS, Scampton
	XW428	BAC Jet Provost T5A [70]	RAF No 1 FTS, Linton-on-Ouse
	XW429	BAC Jet Provost T5A [28]	RAF College, Cranwell
	XW430	BAC Jet Provost T5A [58]	RAF No 3 FTS, Scampton
	XW431	BAC Jet Provost T5A [59]	RAF No 3 FTS, Scampton
	XW432	BAC Jet Provost T5A [76]	RAF No 1 FTS, Linton-on-Ouse
	XW433	BAC Jet Provost T5A [124]	RAF No 7 FTS, Church Fenton
	XW434	BAC Jet Provost T5A [126]	RAF No 7 FTS, Church Fenton
	XW435	BAC Jet Provost T5A [4]	RAF College, Cranwell
	XW436	BAC Jet Provost T5A [62]	RAF No 3 FTS, Scampton
	XW437	BAC Jet Provost T5A [1]	RAF College, Cranwell
	XW438	BAC Jet Provost T5A [2]	RAF College, Cranwell
	XW527	HS Buccaneer S2B [GF]	RAF No 12 Sqn, Lossiemouth
	XW528	HS Buccaneer S2B [C]	RAF St Athan store
	XW529	HS Buccaneer S2B	MoD(PE) A&AEE/BAe Brough
	XW530	HS Buccaneer S2B [HF]	RAF No 12 Sqn, Lossiemouth
	XW533	HS Buccaneer S2B [HC]	RAF No 237 OCU, Lossiemouth
	XW534	HS Buccaneer S2B [Z]	RAF St Athan store
	XW538	HS Buccaneer S2B (8660M) [T]	RAF Lossiemouth Fire Section
	XW540	HS Buccaneer S2B [JF]	RAF No 12 Sqn, Lossiemouth
	XW541	HS Buccaneer S2B	RAF Honington, ground instruction
	XW542	HS Buccaneer S2B [KS]	RAF No 208 Sqn, Lossiemouth
	XW543	HS Buccaneer S2B [E]	RAF No 237 OCU, Lossiemouth
	XW544	HS Buccaneer S2B	RAF No 2 SoTT, Cosford
	XW545	HS Buccaneer S2B	RAF St Athan
	XW546	HS Buccaneer S2B	RAF No 237 OCU, Lossiemouth
	XW547	HS Buccaneer S2B [JS]	RAF No 208 Sqn, Lossiemouth
	XW549	HS Buccaneer S2B	RAF St Athan store
	XW550	HS Buccaneer S2B [X]	RAF St Athan store
	XW566	SEPECAT Jaguar T2	MoD(PE) RAE Farnborough
	XW612	Westland Scout AH1 [X]	AAC No 658 Sqn, Netheravon
	XW613	Westland Scout AH1 [V]	AAC ATS, Middle Wallop
	XW614	Westland Scout AH1	AAC store, Wroughton
	XW615	Westland Scout AH1	AAC store, Wroughton
	XW616	Westland Scout AH1	AAC No 657 Sqn, Oakington
	XW626	HS Comet 4AEW (G-APDS)	MoD(PE) RAE Bedford
	XW630	HS Harrier GR3 [M]	RAF No 4 Sqn, Gutersloh
	XW635	Beagle D5/180 (G-AWSW)	RAF No 5 AEF, Teversham
	XW664	HS Nimrod R1	RAF No 51 Sqn, Wyton
	XW665	HS Nimrod R1	RAF No 51 Sqn, Wyton
	XW666	HS Nimrod R1	RAF No 51 Sqn, Wyton
	XW750	HS748 Series 107 (G-ASJT)	MoD(PE) RAE Bedford
	XW763	HS Harrier GR3 [L]	RAF No 1453 Flt, Stanley
	XW764	HS Harrier GR3 [AC]	RAF No 3 Sqn, Gutersloh
	XW768	HS Harrier GR3 [O]	RAF No 4 Sqn, Gutersloh
	XW769	HS Harrier GR3 [A]	RAF No 4 Sqn, Gutersloh
	XW788	HS125 CC1	RAF No 32 Sqn, Northolt
	XW789	HS125 CC1	RAF No 32 Sqn, Northolt
	XW790	HS125 CC1	RAF No 32 Sqn, Northolt
	XW791	HS125 CC1	RAF No 32 Sqn, Northolt
	XW795	Westland Scout AH1	AAC No 658 Sqn, Detmold
	XW796	Westland Scout AH1 [W]	AAC No 660 Sqn, Sek Kong
	XW797	Westland Scout AH1 [T]	AAC SCF, Middle Wallop
	XW798	Westland Scout AH1 [U]	AAC SCF, Middle Wallop
	XW799	Westland Scout AH1 [Y]	AAC No 658 Sqn, Netheravon
	XW836	Westland Lynx	Westlands, RNAS Yeovilton
	XW839	Westland Lynx	Rolls-Royce, Filton
	XW843	Westland Gazelle AH1	AAC No 2 Flt, Netheravon
	XW844	Westland Gazelle AH1	AAC No 661 Sqn, Hildesheim
	XW845	Westland Gazelle HT2	RN store, Wroughton
	XW846	Westland Gazelle AH1	MoD(PE) A&AEE, Westlands, Weston-super-Mare
	XW847	Westland Gazelle AH1	AAC D&TS, Middle Wallop
	XW848	Westland Gazelle AH1	AAC AETW, Middle Wallop
	XW849	Westland Gazelle AH1 [V]	RM 3 CBAS, Yeovilton
	XW851	Westland Gazelle AH1 [T]	RM 3 CBAS, Yeovilton
	XW852	Westland Gazelle HT3	RAF No 32 Sqn, Northolt

Serial	Type (alternative identity)	Owner, Operator or Location	Notes
XW853	Westland Gazelle HT2	RN store, Wroughton	
XW854	Westland Gazelle HT2 [46/CU]	RN No 705 Sqn, Culdrose	
XW855	Westland Gazelle HT3	RAF No 32 Sqn, Northolt	
XW856	Westland Gazelle HT2 [47/CU]	RN No 705 Sqn, Culdrose	
XW857	Westland Gazelle HT2 [55/CU]	RN No 705 Sqn, Culdrose	
XW858	Westland Gazelle HT3 [C]	RAF No 2 FTS, Shawbury	
XW860	Westland Gazelle HT2 [44/CU]	RN No 705 Sqn, Culdrose	
XW861	Westland Gazelle HT2 [59/CU]	RN No 705 Sqn, Culdrose	
XW862	Westland Gazelle HT3 [D]	RAF No 2 FTS, Shawbury	
XW863	Westland Gazelle HT2 [42/CU]	RN No 705 Sqn, Culdrose	
XW864	Westland Gazelle HT2 [54/CU]	RN No 705 Sqn, Culdrose	
XW865	Westland Gazelle AH1	AAC AETW, Middle Wallop	
XW866	Westland Gazelle HT3 [E]	RAF No 2 FTS, Shawbury	
XW868	Westland Gazelle HT2 [50/CU]	RN No 705 Sqn, Culdrose	
XW870	Westland Gazelle HT3 [F]	RAF No 2 FTS, Shawbury	
XW871	Westland Gazelle HT2 [49/CU]	RN store, Wroughton	
XW884	Westland Gazelle HT2 [41/CU]	RN No 705 Sqn, Culdrose	
XW885	Westland Gazelle AH1 [B]	AAC ARWS, Middle Wallop	
XW886	Westland Gazelle HT2 [48/CU]	RN No 705 Sqn, Culdrose	
XW887	Westland Gazelle HT2 [57/CU]	RN No 705 Sqn, Culdrose	
XW888	Westland Gazelle AH1 [C]	AAC ARWS, Middle Wallop	
XW889	Westland Gazelle AH1 [D]	AAC ARWS, Middle Wallop	
XW890	Westland Gazelle HT2 [53/CU]	RN No 705 Sqn, Culdrose	
XW891	Westland Gazelle HT2 [49/CU]	RN No 705 Sqn, Culdrose	
XW892	Westland Gazelle AH1	AAC No 663 Sqn, Soest	
XW893	Westland Gazelle AH1	AAC Falklands	
XW894	Westland Gazelle HT2 [52/CU]	RN No 705 Sqn, Culdrose	
XW895	Westland Gazelle HT2 [51/CU]	RN No 705 Sqn, Culdrose	
XW897	Westland Gazelle AH1	AAC No 664 Sqn, Minden	
XW898	Westland Gazelle HT3 [G]	RAF No 2 FTS, Shawbury	
XW899	Westland Gazelle AH1	AAC No 655 Sqn, Aldergrove	
XW900	Westland Gazelle AH1 (TAD-900)	AAC AETW, Middle Wallop	
XW902	Westland Gazelle HT3 [H]	RAF No 2 FTS, Shawbury	
XW903	Westland Gazelle AH1 [E]	AAC ARWS, Middle Wallop	
XW904	Westland Gazelle AH1	AAC No 664 Sqn, Minden	
XW906	Westland Gazelle HT3 [J]	RAF No 2 FTS, Shawbury	
XW907	Westland Gazelle HT2 [40/CU]	RN No 705 Sqn, Culdrose	
XW908	Westland Gazelle AH1	AAC No 655 Sqn, Ballykelly	
XW909	Westland Gazelle AH1	AAC No 663 Sqn, Soest	
XW910	Westland Gazelle HT3 [K]	RAF No 2 FTS, Shawbury	
XW911	Westland Gazelle AH1 [I]	AAC ARWS, Middle Wallop	
XW912	Westland Gazelle AH1	RM 3 CBAS, Yeovilton	
XW913	Westland Gazelle AH1	AAC No 664 Sqn, Minden	
XW916	HS Harrier GR3 [W]	RAF No 4 Sqn, Gutersloh	
XW917	HS Harrier GR3	RAF Wittering	
XW919	HS Harrier GR3 [03]	RAF No 1 Sqn, Wittering	
XW921	HS Harrier GR3 [V]	RAF No 4 Sqn, Gutersloh	
XW922	HS Harrier GR3 [K]	RAF No 233 OCU, Wittering	
XW924	HS Harrier GR3	RAF No 1 Sqn, Wittering	
XW925	HS Harrier T4 [V]	RAF No 233 OCU, Wittering	
XW927	HS Harrier T4 [S]	RAF No 4 Sqn, Gutersloh	
XW930	HS125 (G-ATPC)	MoD(PE) RAE Bedford	
XW933	HS Harrier T4 [AQ]	RAF No 3 Sqn, Gutersloh	

Notes	Serial	Type (alternative identity)	Owner, Operator or Location
	XW934	HS Harrier T4 [W]	RAF No 233 OCU, Wittering
	XW986	HS Buccaneer S2	MoD(PE) RAE Farnborough
	XW987	HS Buccaneer S2	MoD(PE) RAE West Freugh
	XW988	HS Buccaneer S2	MoD(PE) RAE Farnborough
	XX101	Cushioncraft CC7	FAA Museum, RNAS Yeovilton
	XX105	BAC 1-11/201 (G-ASJD)	MoD(PE) RAE Bedford
	XX108	SEPECAT Jaguar GR1 (G27-313)	MoD(PE) BAe Warton
	XX109	SEPECAT Jaguar GR1	MoD(PE) BAe/A&AEE Boscombe Down
	XX110	SEPECAT Jaguar GR1 [EP]	RAF No 6 Sqn, Coltishall
	XX110	SEPECAT Jaguar Replica (BAPC 169)	RAF No 1 SoTT, Halton
	XX112	SEPECAT Jaguar GR1 [EA]	RAF store, Shawbury
	XX115	SEPECAT Jaguar GR1 (JI005) (8821M)	RAF No 1 SoTT, Halton
	XX116	SEPECAT Jaguar GR1 (JI008)	BAe Warton
	XX117	SEPECAT Jaguar GR1 (JI004) [GG]	RAF No 54 Sqn, Coltishall
	XX118	SEPECAT Jaguar GR1 (JI018) (8815M)	RAF Abingdon, BDRF
	XX119	SEPECAT Jaguar GR1 [GC]	MoD(PE) ETPS Boscombe Down
	XX121	SEPECAT Jaguar GR1 [EQ]	RAF store, Shawbury
	XX139	SEPECAT Jaguar T2 [C]	RAF No 6 Sqn, Coltishall
	XX140	SEPECAT Jaguar T2 [D]	RAF No 226 OCU, Lossiemouth
	XX141	SEPECAT Jaguar T2 [E]	RAF No 226 OCU, Lossiemouth
	XX143	SEPECAT Jaguar T2 (JI002) [B]	RAF No 226 OCU, Lossiemouth
	XX144	SEPECAT Jaguar T2 [ET]	RAF No 6 Sqn, Coltishall
	XX145	SEPECAT Jaguar T2 [H]	RAF No 226 OCU, Lossiemouth
	XX146	SEPECAT Jaguar T2 [GS]	RAF No 54 Sqn, Coltishall
	XX150	SEPECAT Jaguar T2 [AX]	RAF No 14 Sqn, Bruggen
	XX154	HS Hawk T1	MoD(PE) RAE Llanbedr
	XX156	HS Hawk T1	MoD(PE) A&AEE Boscombe Down
	XX157	HS Hawk T1	RAF No 2 TWU/63 Sqn, Chivenor
	XX158	HS Hawk T1	RAF No 2 TWU/63 Sqn, Chivenor
	XX159	HS Hawk T1	RAF No 1 TWU/234 Sqn Brawdy
	XX160	HS Hawk T1	MoD(PE) RAE Llanbedr
	XX161	HS Hawk T1	RAF No 4 FTS, Valley
	XX162	HS Hawk T1 replica (BAPC 152)	RAF Exhibition Flight, Abingdon
	XX162	HS Hawk T1	RAF No 4 FTS, Valley
	XX163	HS Hawk T1	RAF No 4 FTS, Valley
	XX164	HS Hawk T1	RAF No 4 FTS, Valley
	XX165	HS Hawk T1	RAF No 4 FTS, Valley
	XX167	HS Hawk T1	RAF No 4 FTS, Valley
	XX168	HS Hawk T1	RAF No 4 FTS, Valley
	XX169	HS Hawk T1	RAF No 4 FTS, Valley
	XX170	HS Hawk T1	RAF No 4 FTS, Valley
	XX171	HS Hawk T1	RAF No 4 FTS, Valley
	XX172	HS Hawk T1	RAF No 4 FTS, Valley
	XX173	HS Hawk T1	RAF No 4 FTS, Valley
	XX174	HS Hawk T1	RAF No 4 FTS, Valley
	XX175	HS Hawk T1	RAF No 4 FTS, Valley
	XX176	HS Hawk T1	RAF No 4 FTS, Valley
	XX177	HS Hawk T1	RAF CFS, Valley
	XX178	HS Hawk T1	RAF No 4 FTS, Valley
	XX179	HS Hawk T1	RAF No 4 FTS, Valley
	XX181	HS Hawk T1	RAF CFS, Valley
	XX182	HS Hawk T1	RAF No 4 FTS, Valley
	XX183	HS Hawk T1	RAF No 4 FTS, Valley
	XX184	HS Hawk T1	RAF No 4 FTS, Valley
	XX185	HS Hawk T1	RAF No 4 FTS, Valley
	XX186	HS Hawk T1A	RAF No 2 TWU/63 Sqn, Chivenor
	XX187	HS Hawk T1 [L]	RAF No 2 TWU/151 Sqn, Chivenor
	XX188	HS Hawk T1	RAF No 1 TWU, Brawdy
	XX189	HS Hawk T1 [J]	RAF No 2 TWU/151 Sqn, Chivenor
	XX190	HS Hawk T1A	RAF No 1 TWU/234 Sqn, Brawdy
	XX191	HS Hawk T1	RAF No 1 TWU/79 Sqn, Brawdy
	XX192	HS Hawk T1	RAF No 1 TWU/234 Sqn, Brawdy

Serial	Type (alternative identity)	Owner, Operator or Location	Notes
XX193	HS Hawk T1A	RAF No 1 TWU/234 Sqn, Brawdy	
XX194	HS Hawk T1A	RAF No 1 TWU/234 Sqn, Brawdy	
XX195	HS Hawk T1	RAF No 2 TWU/63 Sqn, Chivenor	
XX196	HS Hawk T1A [N]	RAF No 2 TWU/151 Sqn, Chivenor	
XX197	HS Hawk T1A	RAF No 1 TWU/234 Sqn, Brawdy	
XX198	HS Hawk T1A	RAF No 1 TWU/79 Sqn, Brawdy	
XX199	HS Hawk T1A	RAF No 1 TWU, Brawdy	
XX200	HS Hawk T1A [O]	RAF No 2 TWU/151 Sqn, Chivenor	
XX201	HS Hawk T1A	RAF No 2 TWU/63 Sqn, Chivenor	
XX202	HS Hawk T1A [P]	RAF No 2 TWU/151 Sqn, Chivenor	
XX203	HS Hawk T1A	RAF No 2 TWU/63 Sqn, Chivenor	
XX204	HS Hawk T1A	RAF No 2 TWU/63 Sqn, Chivenor	
XX205	HS Hawk T1	RAF No 2 TWU/63 Sqn, Chivenor	
XX217	HS Hawk T1	RAF No 2 TWU/63 Sqn, Chivenor	
XX218	HS Hawk T1A	RAF No 1 TWU/234 Sqn, Brawdy	
XX219	HS Hawk T1A	RAF No 2 TWU/63 Sqn, Chivenor	
XX220	HS Hawk T1	RAF No 1 TWU/234 Sqn, Brawdy	
XX221	HS Hawk T1A	RAF No 1 TWU/79 Sqn, Brawdy	
XX222	HS Hawk T1	RAF No 1 TWU/79 Sqn, Brawdy	
XX223	HS Hawk T1	RAF CFS, Valley	
XX224	HS Hawk T1	RAF CFS, Valley	
XX225	HS Hawk T1	RAF No 4 FTS, Valley	
XX226	HS Hawk T1	RAF No 4 FTS, Valley	
XX227	HS Hawk T1	RAF Red Arrows, Scampton	
XX228	HS Hawk T1 [Q]	RAF No 2 TWU/151 Sqn, Chivenor	
XX230	HS Hawk T1 [M]	RAF No 2 TWU/151 Sqn, Chivenor	
XX231	HS Hawk T1	RAF No 4 FTS, Valley	
XX232	HS Hawk T1	RAF No 4 FTS, Valley	
XX233	HS Hawk T1	RAF No 4 FTS, Valley	
XX234	HS Hawk T1	RAF CFS, Valley	
XX235	HS Hawk T1	RAF No 4 FTS, Valley	
XX236	HS Hawk T1	RAF No 4 FTS, Valley	
XX237	HS Hawk T1	RAF No 4 FTS, Valley	
XX238	HS Hawk T1	RAF No 4 FTS, Valley	
XX239	HS Hawk T1	RAF No 4 FTS, Valley	
XX240	HS Hawk T1	RAF No 4 FTS, Valley	
XX241	HS Hawk T1	RAF No 4 FTS, Valley	
XX242	HS Hawk T1	RAF No 4 FTS, Valley	
XX243	HS Hawk T1	RAF Red Arrows, Scampton	
XX244	HS Hawk T1	RAF No 4 FTS, Valley	
XX245	HS Hawk T1	RAF No 4 FTS, Valley	
XX246	HS Hawk T1	RAF No 2 TWU/63 Sqn, Chivenor	
XX247	HS Hawk T1	RAF No 2 TWU/63 Sqn, Chivenor	
XX248	HS Hawk T1	RAF No 2 TWU/63 Sqn, Chivenor	
XX249	HS Hawk T1	RAF No 4 FTS, Valley	
XX250	HS Hawk T1	RAF CFS, Valley	
XX252	HS Hawk T1	RAF Red Arrows, Scampton	
XX253	HS Hawk T1	RAF Red Arrows, Scampton	
XX254	HS Hawk T1A	RAF No 2 TWU/63 Sqn, Chivenor	
XX255	HS Hawk T1	RAF No 2 TWU/63 Sqn, Chivenor	
XX256	HS Hawk T1	RAF No 2 TWU/63 Sqn, Chivenor	
XX258	HS Hawk T1A	RAF No 1 TWU/79 Sqn, Brawdy	
XX259	HS Hawk T1	RAF Red Arrows, Scampton	
XX260	HS Hawk T1	RAF Red Arrows, Scampton	
XX261	HS Hawk T1	RAF No 1 TWU/234 Sqn, Brawdy	
XX262	HS Hawk T1 replica (BAPC171)	RAF Exhibition Flight, Abingdon	
XX263	HS Hawk T1A	RAF No 2 TWU/63 Sqn, Chivenor	
XX264	HS Hawk T1	RAF Red Arrows, Scampton	
XX265	HS Hawk T1 [U]	RAF No 2 TWU/151 Sqn, Chivenor	
XX266	HS Hawk T1	RAF Red Arrows, Scampton	
XX278	HS Hawk T1	RAF No 2 TWU/63 Sqn, Chivenor	
XX279	HS Hawk T1A	RAF No 2 TWU/63 Sqn, Chivenor	
XX280	HS Hawk T1	RAF No 1 TWU/79 Sqn, Brawdy	
XX281	HS Hawk T1	RAF No 1 TWU/79 Sqn, Brawdy	
XX282	HS Hawk T1A	RAF No 2 TWU/63 Sqn, Chivenor	
XX283	HS Hawk T1A	RAF No 2 TWU/63 Sqn, Chivenor	
XX284	HS Hawk T1A	RAF No 2 TWU/63 Sqn, Chivenor	
XX285	HS Hawk T1 [R]	RAF No 2 TWU/151 Sqn, Chivenor	
XX286	HS Hawk T1A	RAF No 1 TWU, Brawdy	

Notes	Serial	Type (alternative identity)	Owner, Operator or Location
	XX287	HS Hawk T1A	RAF No 2 TWU/63 Sqn, Chivenor
	XX288	HS Hawk T1	RAF No 2 TWU/63 Sqn, Chivenor
	XX289	HS Hawk T1A	RAF No 2 TWU/63 Sqn, Chivenor
	XX290	HS Hawk T1	RAF No 4 FTS, Valley
	XX291	HS Hawk T1	RAF No 4 FTS, Valley
	XX292	HS Hawk T1	RAF No 4 FTS, Valley
	XX293	HS Hawk T1	RAF No 4 FTS, Valley
	XX294	HS Hawk T1	RAF No 4 FTS, Valley
	XX295	HS Hawk T1	RAF No 4 FTS, Valley
	XX296	HS Hawk T1	RAF Red Arrows, Scampton
	XX297	HS Hawk T1	RAF No 4 FTS, Valley
	XX299	HS Hawk T1	RAF No 4 FTS, Valley
	XX300	HS Hawk T1 (8827M)	RAF Chivenor, ground instruction
	XX301	HS Hawk T1A	RAF No 1 TWU/79 Sqn, Brawdy
	XX302	HS Hawk T1	RAF No 1 TWU/234 Sqn, Brawdy
	XX303	HS Hawk T1A	RAF No 1 TWU/234 Sqn, Brawdy
	XX304	HS Hawk T1	RAF Red Arrows, Scampton
	XX306	HS Hawk T1	RAF Red Arrows, Scampton
	XX307	HS Hawk T1	RAF No 4 FTS, Valley
	XX308	HS Hawk T1	RAF No 4 FTS, Valley
	XX309	HS Hawk T1	RAF No 4 FTS, Valley
	XX310	HS Hawk T1	RAF No 4 FTS, Valley
	XX311	HS Hawk T1	RAF No 4 FTS, Valley
	XX312	HS Hawk T1	RAF CFS, Valley
	XX313	HS Hawk T1	RAF No 4 FTS, Valley
	XX314	HS Hawk T1	RAF No 4 FTS, Valley
	XX315	HS Hawk T1	RAF No 1 TWU, Brawdy
	XX316	HS Hawk T1	RAF No 1 TWU/79 Sqn, Brawdy
	XX317	HS Hawk T1	RAF No 1 TWU, Brawdy
	XX318	HS Hawk T1	RAF No 1 TWU, Brawdy
	XX319	HS Hawk T1	RAF No 1 TWU, Brawdy
	XX320	HS Hawk T1 [V]	RAF No 2 TWU, Chivenor
	XX321	HS Hawk T1	RAF No 1 TWU/151 Sqn, Brawdy
	XX322	HS Hawk T1A [W]	RAF No 2 TWU/151 Sqn, Chivenor
	XX323	HS Hawk T1	RAF No 1 TWU/234 Sqn, Brawdy
	XX324	HS Hawk T1	RAF No 1 TWU/234 Sqn, Brawdy
	XX325	HS Hawk T1 [X]	RAF No 2 TWU/151 Sqn, Chivenor
	XX326	HS Hawk T1A [A]	RAF No 2 TWU/151 Sqn, Chivenor
	XX327	HS Hawk T1 [B]	RAF No 2 TWU/151 Sqn, Chivenor
	XX329	HS Hawk T1 [C]	RAF No 2 TWU/151 Sqn, Chivenor
	XX330	HS Hawk T1A [D]	RAF No 2 TWU/151 Sqn, Chivenor
	XX331	HS Hawk T1 [E]	RAF No 2 TWU/151 Sqn, Chivenor
	XX332	HS Hawk T1 [F]	RAF No 2 TWU/151 Sqn, Chivenor
	XX333	HS Hawk T1 [G]	RAF No 2 TWU/151 Sqn, Chivenor
	XX334	HS Hawk T1 [H]	RAF No 2 TWU/151 Sqn, Chivenor
	XX335	HS Hawk T1 [I]	RAF No 2 TWU/151 Sqn, Chivenor
	XX337	HS Hawk T1 [K]	RAF No 2 TWU/151 Sqn, Chivenor
	XX338	HS Hawk T1	RAF Red Arrows, Scampton
	XX339	HS Hawk T1A	RAF No 1 TWU/234 Sqn, Brawdy
	XX340	HS Hawk T1A [Z]	RAF No 2 TWU/151 Sqn, Chivenor
	XX341	HS Hawk T1 [1]	MoD(PE) ETPS Boscombe Down
	XX342	HS Hawk T1 [2]	MoD(PE) ETPS Boscombe Down
	XX343	HS Hawk T1 [3]	MoD(PE) ETPS Boscombe Down
	XX345	HS Hawk T1 [Y]	RAF No 2 TWU/151 Sqn, Chivenor
	XX346	HS Hawk T1A [T]	RAF No 2 TWU/151 Sqn, Chivenor
	XX347	HS Hawk T1	RAF No 4 FTS, Valley
	XX348	HS Hawk T1A	RAF No 1 TWU, Brawdy
	XX349	HS Hawk T1	RAF No 4 FTS, Valley
	XX350	HS Hawk T1	RAF No 1 TWU/234 Sqn, Brawdy
	XX351	HS Hawk T1A	RAF No 1 TWU/234 Sqn, Brawdy
	XX352	HS Hawk T1	RAF No 2 TWU/63 Sqn, Chivenor
	XX370	Westland Gazelle AH1 [A]	AAC ARWS, Middle Wallop
	XX371	Westland Gazelle AH1	AAC No 7 Flt, Berlin
	XX372	Westland Gazelle AH1 [B]	AAC No 658 Sqn, Netheravon
	XX373	Westland Gazelle AH1	AAC No 663 Sqn, Soest
	XX375	Westland Gazelle AH1 [C]	AAC No 658 Sqn, Netheravon
	XX376	Westland Gazelle AH1 [D]	RM 3 CBAS, Yeovilton
	XX377	Westland Gazelle AH1 [L]	RM 3 CBAS, Yeovilton
	XX378	Westland Gazelle AH1	Westlands, Yeovil, on rebuild
	XX379	Westland Gazelle AH1 [D]	AAC No 658 Sqn, Netheravon

Serial	Type (alternative identity)	Owner, Operator or Location	Notes
XX380	Westland Gazelle AH1 [A]	RM 3 CBAS, Yeovilton	
XX381	Westland Gazelle AH1	AAC No 2 Flt, Netheravon	
XX382	Westland Gazelle HT3 [M]	RAF No 2 FTS, Shawbury	
XX383	Westland Gazelle AH1 [E]	AAC No 658 Sqn, Netheravon	
XX384	Westland Gazelle AH1	AAC No 652 Sqn, Hildesheim	
XX385	Westland Gazelle AH1	AAC No 661 Sqn, Hildesheim	
XX386	Westland Gazelle AH1	AAC No 12 Flt, Wildenrath	
XX387	Westland Gazelle AH1	AAC No 661 Sqn, Hildesheim	
XX388	Westland Gazelle AH1	AAC No 652 Sqn, Hildesheim	
XX389	Westland Gazelle AH1	AAC No 652 Sqn, Hildesheim	
XX391	Westland Gazelle HT2 [56/CU]	RN No 705 Sqn, Culdrose	
XX392	Westland Gazelle AH1 [W]	AAC ARWS, Middle Wallop	
XX393	Westland Gazelle AH1	AAC No 2 Flt, Netheravon	
XX394	Westland Gazelle AH1	AAC No 2 Flt, Netheravon	
XX395	Westland Gazelle AH1	AAC No 661 Sqn, Hildesheim	
XX396	Westland Gazelle HT3 [N] (8718M)	RAF Exhibition Flight, Abingdon	
XX398	Westland Gazelle AH1	AAC No 661 Sqn, Hildesheim	
XX399	Westland Gazelle AH1 [F]	RM 3 CBAS, Yeovilton	
XX403	Westland Gazelle AH1 [Y]	AAC ARWS, Middle Wallop	
XX405	Westland Gazelle AH1	AAC No 659 Sqn, Detmold	
XX406	Westland Gazelle HT3 [P]	RAF No 2 FTS, Shawbury	
XX407	Westland Gazelle AH1	AAC No 655 Sqn, Aldergrove	
XX408	Westland Gazelle AH1	AAC No 655 Sqn, Aldergrove	
XX409	Westland Gazelle AH1	AAC No 656 Sqn, Netheravon	
XX410	Westland Gazelle HT2 [58/CU]	RN AES Lee-on-Solent	
XX411	Westland Gazelle AH1 [X] tail only	FAA Museum, RNAS Yeovilton	
XX412	Westland Gazelle AH1 [Y]	RM 3 CBAS, Yeovilton	
XX413	Westland Gazelle AH1 [Z]	RM 3 CBAS, Yeovilton	
XX414	Westland Gazelle AH1	AAC No 663 Sqn, Soest	
XX416	Westland Gazelle AH1	AAC No 663 Sqn, Soest	
XX417	Westland Gazelle AH1	AAC No 663 Sqn, Soest	
XX418	Westland Gazelle AH1	AAC No 664 Sqn, Minden	
XX419	Westland Gazelle AH1	AAC No 664 Sqn, Minden	
XX431	Westland Gazelle HT2 [43/CU]	RN No 705 Sqn, Culdrose	
XX432	Westland Gazelle AH1	AAC No 669 Sqn, Detmold	
XX433	Westland Gazelle AH1	AAC No 663 Sqn, Soest	
XX434	Westland Gazelle AH1	RAF Abingdon, BDRF	
XX435	Westland Gazelle AH1	AAC No 12 Flt, Wildenrath	
XX436	Westland Gazelle HT2 [39/CU]	RN No 705 Sqn, Culdrose	
XX437	Westland Gazelle AH1	AAC No 661 Sqn, Hildesheim	
XX438	Westland Gazelle AH1	AAC RNAY Fleetlands	
XX439	Westland Gazelle AH1	AAC No 651 Sqn, Hildesheim	
XX440	Westland Gazelle AH1 (G-BCHN)	AAC No 12 Flt, Wildenrath	
XX441	Westland Gazelle HT2 [38-CU]	RN No 705 Sqn, Culdrose	
XX442	Westland Gazelle AH1	AAC No 669 Sqn, Detmold	
XX443	Westland Gazelle AH1	AAC No 669 Sqn, Detmold	
XX444	Westland Gazelle AH1	AAC No 656 Sqn, Netheravon	
XX445	Westland Gazelle AH1	AAC No 659 Sqn, Detmold	
XX446	Westland Gazelle HT2 [CU]	RN store, Wroughton	
XX447	Westland Gazelle AH1	AAC No 669 Sqn, Detmold	
XX448	Westland Gazelle AH1	AAC No 659 Sqn, Detmold	
XX449	Westland Gazelle AH1	AAC No 669 Sqn, Detmold	
XX450	Westland Gazelle AH1 [E]	RM 3 CBAS, Yeovilton	
XX451	Westland Gazelle HT2 [58/CU]	RN No 705 Sqn, Culdrose	
XX452	Westland Gazelle AH1	AAC ARWS, Middle Wallop	
XX453	Westland Gazelle AH1	AAC No 659 Sqn, Detmold	
XX454	Westland Gazelle AH1	AAC No 659 Sqn, Detmold	
XX455	Westland Gazelle AH1	AAC No 663 Sqn, Soest	
XX456	Westland Gazelle AH1	AAC No 669 Sqn, Detmold	
XX457	Westland Gazelle AH1 [H]	AAC ARWS, Middle Wallop	
XX460	Westland Gazelle AH1	AAC No 652 Sqn, Hildesheim	
XX462	Westland Gazelle AH1	AAC No 661 Sqn, Hildesheim	

Notes	Serial	Type (alternative identity)	Owner, Operator or Location
	XX466	HS Hunter T66B/T7 [879/VL]	RN FRADU, Yeovilton
	XX467	HS Hunter T66B/T7 [86]	Air Service Training, Perth
	XX475	SA Jetstream T2 [572/CU] (N1036S)	RN No 750 Sqn, Culdrose
	XX476	SA Jetstream T2 [561/CU] (N1037S)	RN No 750 Sqn, Culdrose
	XX478	SA Jetstream T2 [564/CU] (G-AXXT)	RN No 750 Sqn, Culdrose
	XX479	SA Jetstream T2 [563/CU] (G-AXUR)	RN No 750 Sqn, Culdrose
	XX480	SA Jetstream T2 [565/CU] (G-AXXU)	RN No 750 Sqn, Culdrose
	XX481	SA Jetstream T2 [560/CU] (G-AXUP)	RN No 750 Sqn, Culdrose
	XX482	SA Jetstream T1 [J]	RAF No 6 FTS, Finningley
	XX483	SA Jetstream T2 [562/CU]	RN No 750 Sqn, Culdrose
	XX484	SA Jetstream T2 [566/CU]	RN No 750 Sqn, Culdrose
	XX485	SA Jetstream T2 [567/CU]	RN No 750 Sqn, Culdrose
	XX486	SA Jetstream T2 [569/CU]	RN No 750 Sqn, Culdrose
	XX487	SA Jetstream T2 [568/CU]	RN No 750 Sqn, Culdrose
	XX488	SA Jetstream T2 [571/CU]	RN No 750 Sqn, Culdrose
	XX489	SA Jetstream T2 [575/CU]	RN No 750 Sqn, Culdrose
	XX490	SA Jetstream T2 [570/CU]	RN No 750 Sqn, Culdrose
	XX491	SA Jetstream T1 [K]	RAF No 6 FTS, Finningley
	XX492	SA Jetstream T1 [A]	RAF No 6 FTS, Finningley
	XX493	SA Jetstream T1 [L]	RAF No 6 FTS, Finningley
	XX494	SA Jetstream T1 [B]	RAF No 6 FTS, Finningley
	XX495	SA Jetstream T1 [C]	RAF No 6 FTS, Finningley
	XX496	SA Jetstream T1 [D]	RAF No 6 FTS, Finningley
	XX497	SA Jetstream T1 [E]	RAF No 6 FTS, Finningley
	XX498	SA Jetstream T1 [F]	RAF No 6 FTS, Finningley
	XX499	SA Jetstream T1 [G]	RAF No 6 FTS, Finningley
	XX500	SA Jetstream T1 [H]	RAF No 6 FTS, Finningley
	XX507	HS125 CC2	RAF No 32 Sqn, Northolt
	XX508	HS125 CC2	RAF No 32 Sqn, Northolt
	XX513	SA Bulldog T1 [A]	RAF No 1 FTS/RNEFTS, Topcliffe
	XX514	SA Bulldog T1 [B]	RAF No 1 FTS/RNEFTS, Topcliffe
	XX515	SA Bulldog T1 [7]	RAF CFS, Scampton
	XX516	SA Bulldog T1 [C]	RAF No 1 FTS/RNEFTS Topcliffe
	XX517	SA Bulldog T1 [8]	RAF CFS, Scampton
	XX518	SA Bulldog T1 [24]	RAF Shawbury store
	XX519	SA Bulldog T1 [I]	RAF No 1 FTS/RNEFTS, Topcliffe
	XX520	SA Bulldog T1 [2]	RAF CFS, Scampton
	XX521	SA Bulldog T1 [01]	RAF, East Lowlands UAS, Turnhouse
	XX522	SA Bulldog T1 [E]	RAF No 1 FTS/RNEFTS, Topcliffe
	XX523	SA Bulldog T1 [F]	RAF No 1 FTS/RNEFTS, Topcliffe
	XX524	SA Bulldog T1 [04]	RAF, London UAS, Abingdon
	XX525	SA Bulldog T1 [03]	RAF, East Lowlands UAS, Turnhouse
	XX526	SA Bulldog T1 [C]	RAF, Oxford UAS, Abingdon
	XX527	SA Bulldog T1 [G]	RAF No 1 FTS/RNEFTS, Topcliffe
	XX528	SA Bulldog T1 [D]	RAF, Oxford UAS, Abingdon
	XX529	SA Bulldog T1 [H]	RAF No 1 FTS/RNEFTS, Topcliffe
	XX530	SA Bulldog T1 [12]	CTE, RAF Manston
	XX531	SA Bulldog T1 [4]	RAF CFS, Scampton
	XX532	SA Bulldog T1 [5]	RAF CFS, Scampton
	XX533	SA Bulldog T1 [J]	RAF No 1 FTS/RNEFTS, Topcliffe
	XX534	SA Bulldog T1 [04]	RAF, East Lowlands UAS, Turnhouse
	XX535	SA Bulldog T1 [18]	RAF Shawbury store
	XX536	SA Bulldog T1 [9]	RAF CFS, Scampton
	XX537	SA Bulldog T1 [02]	RAF, East Lowlands UAS, Turnhouse
	XX538	SA Bulldog T1 [E]	RAF Shawbury store
	XX539	SA Bulldog T1 [1]	RAF CFS, Scampton
	XX540	SA Bulldog T1 [K]	RAF No 1 FTS/RNEFTS, Topcliffe
	XX541	SA Bulldog T1 [L]	RAF No 1 FTS/RNEFTS, Topcliffe
	XX543	SA Bulldog T1 [F]	RAF, Yorkshire UAS, Finningley
	XX544	SA Bulldog T1 [01]	RAF, London UAS, Abingdon
	XX545	SA Bulldog T1 PAX [02]	RAF, East Lowlands UAS, Turnhouse
	XX546	SA Bulldog T1 [03]	RAF, London UAS, Abingdon
	XX547	SA Bulldog T1 [05]	RAF, London UAS, Abingdon
	XX548	SA Bulldog T1 [06]	RAF, London UAS, Abingdon

Serial	Type (alternative identity)	Owner, Operator or Location	Notes
XX549	SA Bulldog T1 [5]	RAF, Manchester UAS, Woodvale	
XX550	SA Bulldog T1 [8]	RAF Shawbury store	
XX551	SA Bulldog T1 [M]	RAF No 1 FTS/RNEFTS, Topcliffe	
XX552	SA Bulldog T1 [08]	RAF, London UAS, Abingdon	
XX553	SA Bulldog T1 [07]	RAF, London UAS, Abingdon	
XX554	SA Bulldog T1 [09]	RAF, London UAS, Abingdon	
XX555	SA Bulldog T1 [10]	RAF CFS, Scampton	
XX556	SA Bulldog T1 [S]	RAF, East Midlands UAS, Newton	
XX557	SA Bulldog T1 PAX	RAF Topcliffe, ground instruction	
XX558	SA Bulldog T1 [A]	RAF, Birmingham UAS, Cosford	
XX559	SA Bulldog T1 [01]	RAF, Glasgow & Strathclyde UAS, Glasgow	
XX560	SA Bulldog T1 [02]	RAF, Glasgow & Strathclyde UAS, Glasgow	
XX561	SA Bulldog T1 [A]	RAF, Aberdeen, Dundee & St Andrews UAS, Leuchars	
XX562	SA Bulldog T1 [S]	RAF, Queen's UAS, Sydenham	
XX611	SA Bulldog T1 [04]	RAF, Glasgow & Strathclyde UAS, Glasgow	
XX612	SA Bulldog T1 [05]	RAF, Wales UAS, St Athan	
XX613	SA Bulldog T1 [A]	RAF, Queen's UAS, Sydenham	
XX614	SA Bulldog T1 [1]	RAF, Manchester UAS, Woodvale	
XX615	SA Bulldog T1 [2]	RAF, Manchester UAS, Woodvale	
XX616	SA Bulldog T1 [3]	RAF, Manchester UAS, Woodvale	
XX617	SA Bulldog T1 [4]	RAF, Manchester UAS, Woodvale	
XX619	SA Bulldog T1 [B]	RAF, Yorkshire UAS, Finningley	
XX620	SA Bulldog T1 [C]	RAF, Yorkshire UAS, Finningley	
XX621	SA Bulldog T1 [D]	RAF, Yorkshire UAS, Finningley	
XX622	SA Bulldog T1 [E]	RAF, Yorkshire UAS, Finningley	
XX623	SA Bulldog T1 [M]	RAF, East Midlands UAS, Newton	
XX624	SA Bulldog T1 [G]	RAF, Yorkshire UAS, Finningley	
XX625	SA Bulldog T1 [01]	RAF, Wales UAS, St Athan	
XX626	SA Bulldog T1 [02]	RAF, Wales UAS, St Athan	
XX627	SA Bulldog T1 [03]	RAF, Wales UAS, St Athan	
XX628	SA Bulldog T1 [04]	RAF, Wales UAS, St Athan	
XX629	SA Bulldog T1 [V]	RAF, Northumbria UAS, Leeming	
XX630	SA Bulldog T1 [A]	RAF, Liverpool UAS, Woodvale	
XX631	SA Bulldog T1 [W]	RAF, Northumbria UAS, Leeming	
XX632	SA Bulldog T1 [D]	RAF, Bristol UAS, Filton	
XX633	SA Bulldog T1 [X]	RAF, Northumbria UAS, Leeming	
XX634	SA Bulldog T1 [C]	RAF, Cambridge UAS, Teversham	
XX635	SA Bulldog T1 (8767M) [S]	RAF St Athan, for ground instruction	
XX636	SA Bulldog T1 [Y]	RAF, Northumbria UAS, Leeming	
XX637	SA Bulldog T1 [Z]	RAF, Northumbria UAS, Leeming	
XX638	SA Bulldog T1 [N]	RAF No 1 FTS/RNEFTS, Topcliffe	
XX639	SA Bulldog T1 [02]	RAF, London UAS, Abingdon	
XX640	SA Bulldog T1 [U]	RAF, Queen's UAS, Sydenham	
XX653	SA Bulldog T1 [E]	RAF, Bristol UAS, Filton	
XX654	SA Bulldog T1 [A]	RAF, Bristol UAS, Filton	
XX655	SA Bulldog T1 [B]	RAF, Bristol UAS, Filton	
XX656	SA Bulldog T1 [C]	RAF, Bristol UAS, Filton	
XX657	SA Bulldog T1 [U]	RAF, Cambridge UAS, Teversham	
XX658	SA Bulldog T1 [A]	RAF, Cambridge UAS, Teversham	
XX659	SA Bulldog T1 [S]	RAF, Cambridge UAS, Teversham	
XX660	SA Bulldog T1 [A]	RAF, Oxford UAS, Abingdon	
XX661	SA Bulldog T1 [B]	RAF, Oxford UAS, Abingdon	
XX663	SA Bulldog T1 [B]	RAF, Aberdeen, Dundee & St Andrews UAS, Leuchars	
XX664	SA Bulldog T1 [05]	RAF, East Lowlands UAS, Turnhouse	
XX665	SA Bulldog T1 [E]	RAF, Aberdeen, Dundee & St Andrews UAS, Leuchars	
XX666	SA Bulldog T1 [C]	RAF, Aberdeen, Dundee & St Andrews UAS, Leuchars	
XX667	SA Bulldog T1 [D]	RAF, Aberdeen, Dundee & St Andrews UAS, Leuchars	
XX668	SA Bulldog T1 [P]	RAF No 1 FTS/RNEFTS, Topcliffe	
XX669	SA Bulldog T1 [B]	RAF, Birmingham UAS, Cosford	
XX670	SA Bulldog T1 [C]	RAF, Birmingham UAS, Cosford	
XX671	SA Bulldog T1 [D]	RAF, Birmingham UAS, Cosford	
XX672	SA Bulldog T1 [E]	RAF, Birmingham UAS, Cosford	

Notes	Serial	Type (alternative identity)	Owner, Operator or Location
	XX685	SA Bulldog T1 [L]	RAF, Liverpool UAS, Woodvale
	XX686	SA Bulldog T1 [U]	RAF, Liverpool UAS, Woodvale
	XX687	SA Bulldog T1 [A]	RAF, East Midlands UAS, Newton
	XX688	SA Bulldog T1 [S]	RAF, Liverpool UAS, Woodvale
	XX689	SA Bulldog T1 [3]	RAF CFS, Scampton
	XX690	SA Bulldog T1 [A]	RAF, Yorkshire UAS, Finningley
	XX691	SA Bulldog T1	RAF Shawbury store
	XX692	SA Bulldog T1	RAF Shawbury store
	XX693	SA Bulldog T1	RAF Shawbury store
	XX694	SA Bulldog T1 [E]	RAF, East Midlands UAS, Newton
	XX695	SA Bulldog T1 [10]	RAF, London UAS, Abingdon
	XX696	SA Bulldog T1	RAF Shawbury store
	XX697	SA Bulldog T1 [Q]	RAF, Queen's UAS, Sydenham
	XX698	SA Bulldog T1	RAF Shawbury store
	XX699	SA Bulldog T1 [Q]	RAF No 1 FTS/RNEFTS, Topcliffe
	XX700	SA Bulldog T1 [R]	RAF No 1 FTS/RNEFTS, Topcliffe
	XX701	SA Bulldog T1 [02]	RAF, Southampton UAS, Hurn
	XX702	SA Bulldog T1 [03]	RAF, Glasgow & Strathclyde UAS, Glasgow
	XX704	SA Bulldog T1 [U]	RAF, East Midlands UAS, Newton
	XX705	SA Bulldog T1 [05]	RAF, Southampton UAS, Hurn
	XX706	SA Bulldog T1 [01]	RAF, Southampton UAS, Hurn
	XX707	SA Bulldog T1 [04]	RAF, Southampton UAS, Hurn
	XX708	SA Bulldog T1 [03]	RAF, Southampton UAS, Hurn
	XX709	SA Bulldog T1 [33]	RAF Shawbury store
	XX710	SA Bulldog T1 [34]	RAF Shawbury store
	XX711	SA Bulldog T1 [E]	RAF No 13 AEF, Sydenham
	XX712	SA Bulldog T1 [D]	RAF No 1 FTS/RNEFTS, Topcliffe
	XX713	SA Bulldog T1 [6]	RAF CFS, Scampton
	XX714	SA Bulldog T1	MoD(PE) BAe Prestwick
	XX718	SEPECAT Jaguar Replica (BAPC150)	RAF Exhibition Flight, Abingdon
	XX719	SEPECAT Jaguar GR1 [GD]	RAF No 54 Sqn, Coltishall
	XX720	SEPECAT Jaguar GR1 (JI003)	BAe Warton
	XX722	SEPECAT Jaguar GR1 [EF]	RAF No 6 Sqn, Coltishall
	XX723	SEPECAT Jaguar GR1 [EQ]	RAF No 6 Sqn, Coltishall
	XX724	SEPECAT Jaguar GR1 [GH]	RAF No 54 Sqn, Coltishall
	XX725	SEPECAT Jaguar GR1 (JI010)	BAe Warton
	XX726	SEPECAT Jaguar GR1 [EB]	RAF No 6 Sqn, Coltishall
	XX727	SEPECAT Jaguar GR1 [ER]	RAF store, Shawbury
	XX728	SEPECAT Jaguar GR1 [EH] (JI009)	RAF No 6 Sqn, Coltishall
	XX729	SEPECAT Jaguar GR1 [EJ] (JI012)	RAF No 6 Sqn, Coltishall
	XX730	SEPECAT Jaguar GR1 [EC]	RAF No 6 Sqn, Coltishall
	XX731	SEPECAT Jaguar GR1 [E]	RAF No 6 Sqn, Coltishall
	XX732	SEPECAT Jaguar GR1 [ED]	RAF No 6 Sqn, Coltishall
	XX733	SEPECAT Jaguar GR1A [GL]	RAF No 54 Sqn, Coltishall
	XX734	SEPECAT Jaguar GR1 (JI014) (8816M)	MoD(PE) RAE Farnborough
	XX736	SEPECAT Jaguar GR1 (JI013)	BAe Warton
	XX737	SEPECAT Jaguar GR1 [EN] (JI015)	RAF No 6 Sqn, Coltishall
	XX738	SEPECAT Jaguar GR1 (JI016) [GJ]	RAF No 54 Sqn, Coltishall
	XX739	SEPECAT Jaguar GR1 [EE]	RAF No 6 Sqn, Coltishall
	XX740	SEPECAT Jaguar GR1 (JI017)	BAe Warton
	XX741	SEPECAT Jaguar GR1 [GM]	RAF No 54 Sqn, Coltishall
	XX743	SEPECAT Jaguar GR1 [EG]	RAF No 6 Sqn, Coltishall
	XX744	SEPECAT Jaguar GR1 [DJ]	RAF No 31 Sqn, Bruggen
	XX745	SEPECAT Jaguar GR1A [GN]	RAF No 54 Sqn, Coltishall
	XX746	SEPECAT Jaguar GR1 [AB]	RAF No 14 Sqn, Bruggen
	XX747	SEPECAT Jaguar GR1 [EK]	RAF No 6 Sqn, Coltishall
	XX748	SEPECAT Jaguar GR1 [AA]	RAF No 14 Sqn, Bruggen
	XX751	SEPECAT Jaguar GR1 [10]	RAF No 226 OCU, Lossiemouth
	XX752	SEPECAT Jaguar GR1A [GF]	RAF No 54 Sqn, Coltishall
	XX753	SEPECAT Jaguar GR1 [05]	RAF No 226 OCU, Lossiemouth
	XX754	SEPECAT Jaguar GR1 [AL]	RAF No 14 Sqn, Bruggen
	XX756	SEPECAT Jaguar GR1 [AM]	RAF No 14 Sqn, Bruggen
	XX757	SEPECAT Jaguar GR1 [CU]	RAF store, Shawbury

XW547 HS Buccaneer S2B; RAF No 208 Sqn, Lossiemouth. *PRM*

XX326/XX327 HS Hawk T1; RAF No 2 TWU/151 Sqn, Chivenor. *APM*

XX765 SEPECAT Jaguar ACT; MoD(PE)/BAe Warton. *DJM*

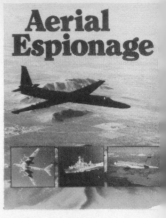

Serial	Type (alternative identity)	Owner, Operator or Location	Notes
XX761	SEPECAT Jaguar GR1 (8600M) nose only	RAF Lossiemouth for ground instruction	
XX763	SEPECAT Jaguar GR1 [24]	RAF No 226 OCU, Lossiemouth	
XX764	SEPECAT Jaguar GR1 [13]	RAF store, Shawbury	
XX765	SEPECAT Jaguar ACT	MoD(PE) BAe Warton	
XX766	SEPECAT Jaguar GR1A [GP]	RAF No 54 Sqn, Coltishall	
XX767	SEPECAT Jaguar GR1 [BD]	RAF No 17 Sqn, Bruggen	
XX818	SEPECAT Jaguar GR1 [DE]	RAF No 31 Sqn, Bruggen	
XX819	SEPECAT Jaguar GR1 [CE]	RAF store, Shawbury	
XX821	SEPECAT Jaguar GR1	RAF No 14 Sqn, Bruggen	
XX824	SEPECAT Jaguar GR1 [BH]	RAF No 17 Sqn, Bruggen	
XX824	SEPECAT Jaguar replica (BAPC 151)	RAF Exhibition Flight, Abingdon	
XX825	SEPECAT Jaguar GR1 [BN]	RAF No 17 Sqn, Bruggen	
XX826	SEPECAT Jaguar GR1 [34]	RAF No 2 Sqn, Laarbruch	
XX829	SEPECAT Jaguar T2 [GT]	RAF No 54 Sqn, Coltishall	
XX830	SEPECAT Jaguar T2 [R]	RAF No 226 OCU, Lossiemouth	
XX832	SEPECAT Jaguar T2 [S]	RAF No 226 OCU, Lossiemouth	
XX833	SEPECAT Jaguar T2 [AY]	RAF No 14 Sqn, Bruggen	
XX834	SEPECAT Jaguar T2A [37]	RAF No 2 Sqn, Laarbruch	
XX835	SEPECAT Jaguar T2 [V]	MoD(PE) RAE Farnborough	
XX836	SEPECAT Jaguar T2 [BZ]	RAF No 17 Sqn, Bruggen	
XX837	SEPECAT Jaguar T2 [Z]	RAF No 226 OCU, Lossiemouth	
XX838	SEPECAT Jaguar T2 [X]	RAF No 226 OCU, Lossiemouth	
XX839	SEPECAT Jaguar T2 [Y]	RAF No 226 OCU, Lossiemouth	
XX840	SEPECAT Jaguar T2 [T]	RAF No 226 OCU, Lossiemouth	
XX841	SEPECAT Jaguar T2 [K]	RAF No 226 OCU, Lossiemouth	
XX842	SEPECAT Jaguar T2 [T]	RAF No 41 Sqn, Coltishall	
XX843	SEPECAT Jaguar T2 [36]	RAF No 2 Sqn, Laarbruch	
XX844	SEPECAT Jaguar T2 [BY]	RAF No 17 Sqn, Bruggen	
XX845	SEPECAT Jaguar T2 [AZ]	RAF No 14 Sqn, Bruggen	
XX846	SEPECAT Jaguar T2 [A]	RAF No 226 OCU, Lossiemouth	
XX847	SEPECAT Jaguar T2	RAF store, Shawbury	
XX885	HS Buccaneer S2B [OF]	RAF No 12 Sqn, Lossiemouth	
XX886	HS Buccaneer S2B	BAe Woodford	
XX887	HS Buccaneer S2B [N]	RAF store, Shawbury	
XX888	HS Buccaneer S2B [Z]	RAF Shawbury, store	
XX889	HS Buccaneer S2B [WS]	RAF No 208 Sqn, Lossiemouth	
XX892	HS Buccaneer S2B [F]	RAF No 237 OCU, Lossiemouth	
XX893	HS Buccaneer S2B [DC]	RAF No 237 OCU, Lossiemouth	
XX894	HS Buccaneer S2B [HS]	RAF No 208 Sqn, Lossiemouth	
XX895	HS Buccaneer S2B [B]	RAF No 237 OCU, Lossiemouth	
XX896	HS Buccaneer S2B	RAF Shawbury, store	
XX897	HS Buccaneer S2B	MoD(PE) RS&RE Bedford	
XX899	HS Buccaneer S2B [JC]	RAF No 237 OCU, Lossiemouth	
XX900	HS Buccaneer S2B [MS]	RAF No 208 Sqn, Lossiemouth	
XX901	HS Buccaneer S2B [GS]	RAF No 208 Sqn, Lossiemouth	
XX914	BAC VC10 srs 1103 (G-ATDJ/ 8777M)	RAF AMS, Brize Norton	
XX919	BAC 1-11/402 (PI-C 1121)	MoD(PE) RAE Farnborough	
XX946	Panavia Tornado (P02)	MoD(PE) BAe Warton	
XX947	Panavia Tornado (P03) (8797M)	RAF Marham for ground instruction	
XX948	Panavia Tornado (P06)	MoD(PE) BAe Warton	
XX955	SEPECAT Jaguar GR1 [AN]	RAF No 14 Sqn, Bruggen	
XX956	SEPECAT Jaguar GR1 [BE]	RAF No 17 Sqn, Bruggen	
XX958	SEPECAT Jaguar GR1 [BK]	RAF No 17 Sqn, Bruggen	
XX959	SEPECAT Jaguar GR1 [CJ]	RAF store, Shawbury	
XX962	SEPECAT Jaguar GR1 [BG]	RAF No 17 Sqn, Bruggen	
XX965	SEPECAT Jaguar GR1 [GB]	RAF No 54 Sqn, Coltishall	
XX966	SEPECAT Jaguar GR1A [GK]	RAF No 54 Sqn, Coltishall	
XX967	SEPECAT Jaguar GR1 [AC]	RAF No 14 Sqn, Bruggen	
XX968	SEPECAT Jaguar GR1 [AJ]	RAF No 14 Sqn, Bruggen	
XX969	SEPECAT Jaguar GR1 [01]	RAF No 226 OCU, Lossiemouth	
XX970	SEPECAT Jaguar GR1 [BJ]	RAF No 17 Sqn, Bruggen	
XX974	SEPECAT Jaguar GR1	RAF No 17 Sqn, Bruggen	
XX975	SEPECAT Jaguar GR1 [BA]	RAF No 17 Sqn, Bruggen	
XX976	SEPECAT Jaguar GR1 [BD]	RAF No 17 Sqn, Bruggen	
XX979	SEPECAT Jaguar GR1	MoD(PE) A&AEE Boscombe Down	

Notes	Serial	Type (alternative identity)	Owner, Operator or Location
	XZ101	SEPECAT Jaguar GR1A [20]	RAF No 2 Sqn, Laarbruch
	XZ103	SEPECAT Jaguar GR1 [23]	RAF No 2 Sqn, Laarbruch
	XZ104	SEPECAT Jaguar GR1 [24]	RAF No 2 Sqn, Laarbruch
	XZ106	SEPECAT Jaguar GR1A [26]	RAF No 2 Sqn, Laarbruch
	XZ107	SEPECAT Jaguar GR1 [H]	RAF No 41 Sqn, Coltishall
	XZ108	SEPECAT Jaguar GR1A [28]	RAF No 2 Sqn, Laarbruch
	XZ109	SEPECAT Jaguar GR1A [29]	RAF No 2 Sqn, Laarbruch
	XZ111	SEPECAT Jaguar GR1 [31]	RAF No 2 Sqn, Laarbruch
	XZ112	SEPECAT Jaguar GR1 [32]	RAF No 2 Sqn, Laarbruch
	XZ113	SEPECAT Jaguar GR1 [30]	RAF No 2 Sqn, Laarbruch
	XZ114	SEPECAT Jaguar GR1 [B]	RAF No 41 Sqn, Coltishall
	XZ115	SEPECAT Jaguar GR1 [C]	RAF No 41 Sqn, Coltishall
	XZ116	SEPECAT Jaguar GR1 [D]	RAF No 41 Sqn, Coltishall
	XZ117	SEPECAT Jaguar GR1 [E]	RAF No 41 Sqn, Coltishall
	XZ118	SEPECAT Jaguar GR1 [F]	RAF No 41 Sqn, Coltishall
	XZ119	SEPECAT Jaguar GR1 [G]	RAF No 41 Sqn, Coltishall
	XZ129	HS Harrier GR3 [06]	RAF No 1 Sqn, Wittering
	XZ130	HS Harrier GR3 [AH]	RAF No 3 Sqn, Gutersloh
	XZ131	HS Harrier GR3 [M]	RAF No 4 Sqn, Gutersloh
	XZ132	HS Harrier GR3 [09]	RAF No 1 Sqn, Wittering
	XZ133	HS Harrier GR3 [10]	RAF No 1 Sqn, Wittering
	XZ136	HS Harrier GR3	MoD(PE) A&AEE Boscombe Down
	XZ138	HS Harrier GR3 [V]	RAF No 1453 Flt, Stanley
	XZ145	HS Harrier T4 [AT]	RAF No 3 Sqn, Gutersloh
	XZ146	HS Harrier T4 [Y]	RAF No 4 Sqn, Gutersloh
	XZ147	HS Harrier T4A [Z]	RAF No 233 OCU, Wittering
	XZ170	Westland Lynx AH1	MoD(PE) Westlands, Yeovil
	XZ171	Westland Lynx AH1	MoD(PE) Rolls-Royce, Filton
	XZ172	Westland Lynx AH1 [K]	AAC ARW/LCF, Middle Wallop
	XZ173	Westland Lynx AH1	AAC No 651 Sqn, Hildesheim
	XZ174	Westland Lynx AH1	AAC No 651 Sqn, Hildesheim
	XZ175	Westland Lynx AH1 [C]	AAC ARW/LCF, Middle Wallop
	XZ176	Westland Lynx AH1 [A]	AAC ATS, Middle Wallop
	XZ177	Westland Lynx AH1	AAC No 652 Sqn, Hildesheim
	XZ178	Westland Lynx AH1	AAC No 656 Sqn, Netheravon
	XZ179	Westland Lynx AH1	MoD(PE) Westlands, Yeovil
	XZ180	Westland Lynx AH1	MoD(PE) Westlands, Yeovil
	XZ181	Westland Lynx AH1	AAC No 654 Sqn, Detmold
	XZ182	Westland Lynx AH1 [N]	RM 3 CBAS, Yeovilton
	XZ183	Westland Lynx AH1	AAC No 654 Sqn, Detmold
	XZ184	Westland Lynx AH1	AAC No 654 Sqn, Detmold
	XZ185	Westland Lynx AH1	AAC No 653 Sqn, Soest
	XZ186	Westland Lynx AH1	AAC No 654 Sqn, Detmold
	XZ187	Westland Lynx AH1	AAC No 655 Sqn, Aldergrove
	XZ188	Westland Lynx AH1	AAC No 655 Sqn, Aldergrove
	XZ190	Westland Lynx AH1	AAC No 651 Sqn, Hildesheim
	XZ191	Westland Lynx AH1	AAC No 651 Sqn, Hildesheim
	XZ192	Westland Lynx AH1	AAC No 651 Sqn, Hildesheim
	XZ193	Westland Lynx AH1	AAC No 653 Sqn, Soest
	XZ194	Westland Lynx AH1	AAC No 653 Sqn, Soest
	XZ195	Westland Lynx AH1	AAC No 652 Sqn, Hildesheim
	XZ196	Westland Lynx AH1	AAC No 653 Sqn, Soest
	XZ197	Westland Lynx AH1	AAC No 653 Sqn, Soest
	XZ198	Westland Lynx AH1	AAC No 653 Sqn, Soest
	XZ199	Westland Lynx AH1	AAC No 653 Sqn, Soest
	XZ203	Westland Lynx AH1 [B]	AAC ARW/LCF, Middle Wallop
	XZ204	Westland Lynx AH1	AAC No 659 Sqn, Detmold
	XZ205	Westland Lynx AH1 [E]	AAC D&TS, Middle Wallop
	XZ206	Westland Lynx AH1	AAC No 655 Sqn, Aldergrove
	XZ207	Westland Lynx AH1	AAC No 655 Sqn, Aldergrove
	XZ208	Westland Lynx AH1	AAC No 659 Sqn, Detmold
	XZ209	Westland Lynx AH1	AAC No 659 Sqn, Detmold
	XZ210	Westland Lynx AH1	AAC No 656 Sqn, Netheravon
	XZ211	Westland Lynx AH1	AAC No 659 Sqn, Detmold
	XZ212	Westland Lynx AH1	AAC No 659 Sqn, Detmold
	XZ213	Westland Lynx AH1	AAC No 659 Sqn, Detmold
	XZ214	Westland Lynx AH1	AAC store, Wroughton
	XZ215	Westland Lynx AH1	AAC AETW, Middle Wallop
	XZ216	Westland Lynx AH1	AAC No 652 Sqn, Hildesheim
	XZ217	Westland Lynx AH1	AAC No 652 Sqn, Hildesheim

Serial	Type (alternative identity)	Owner, Operator or Location	Notes
XZ218	Westland Lynx AH1	AAC No 652 Sqn, Hildesheim	
XZ219	Westland Lynx AH1	AAC No 662 Sqn, Munster	
XZ220	Westland Lynx AH1	AAC No 654 Sqn, Detmold	
XZ221	Westland Lynx AH1	AAC No 657 Sqn, Oakington	
XZ222	Westland Lynx AH1	AAC ARW/LCF, Middle Wallop	
XZ227	Westland Lynx HAS2 [443/JP]	RN No 815 Sqn, Portland	
XZ228	Westland Lynx HAS2	RNAS Portland, ground instruction	
XZ229	Westland Lynx HAS2 [302/PO]	RNAY Fleetlands	
XZ230	Westland Lynx HAS2 [301/PO]	RN No 815 Sqn, Portland	
XZ231	Westland Lynx HAS 2 [645/PO]	RN No 702 Sqn, Portland	
XZ232	Westland Lynx HAS2 [647/PO]	RN No 702 Sqn, Portland	
XZ233	Westland Lynx HAS2 [334/SN]	RN No 815 Sqn, Portland	
XZ234	Westland Lynx HAS2 [335/CF]	RN No 815 Sqn, Portland	
XZ235	Westland Lynx HAS2	RN NASU, Yeovilton	
XZ236	Westland Lynx HAS2	MoD(PE), Westlands, Yeovil	
XZ237	Westland Lynx HAS2 [306]	RN No 815 Sqn, Portland	
XZ238	Westland Lynx HAS2 [646/PO]	RN No 702 Sqn, Portland	
XZ239	Westland Lynx HAS2 [400/GL]	RN No 815 Sqn, Portland	
XZ240	Westland Lynx HAS2	RN NASU, Yeovilton	
XZ241	Westland Lynx HAS2 [417/NM]	RN No 815 Sqn, Portland	
XZ243	Westland Lynx HAS2 [640/PO]	RN No 702 Sqn, Portland	
XZ244	Westland Lynx HAS2 [472/AM]	RN No 815 Sqn, Portland	
XZ245	Westland Lynx HAS2	RNAY Fleetlands	
XZ246	Westland Lynx HAS2 [307/PO]	RN No 815 Sqn, Portland	
XZ248	Westland Lynx HAS2 [404/FF]	RN No 815 Sqn, Portland	
XZ250	Westland Lynx HAS2 [648/PO]	RN No 702 Sqn, Portland	
XZ252	Westland Lynx HAS2 [644/PO]	RN No 702 Sqn, Portland	
XZ254	Westland Lynx HAS2 [327/AL]	RN No 815 Sqn, Portland	
XZ255	Westland Lynx HAS2 [450/SS]	RN No 815 Sqn, Portland	
XZ256	Westland Lynx HAS2 [403/BX]	RN No 815 Sqn, Portland	
XZ257	Westland Lynx HAS2	RNAY Fleetlands	
XZ280	BAe Nimrod AEW3	MoD(PE) BAe Woodford	
XZ281	BAe Nimrod AEW3	MoD(PE) BAe Woodford	
XZ282	BAe Nimrod AEW3	MoD(PE) BAe Woodford	
XZ283	HS Nimrod R1	RAF No 51 Sqn, Wyton	
XZ284	HS Nimrod MR2	RAF Kinloss, MR Wing	
XZ285	BAe Nimrod AEW3	MoD(PE) BAe Woodford	
XZ286	BAe Nimrod AEW3	MoD(PE) BAe Woodford	
XZ287	BAe Nimrod AEW3	MoD(PE) BAe Woodford	
XZ290	Westland Gazelle AH1	AAC, Falklands	
XZ291	Westland Gazelle AH1	AAC No 7 Flt, Berlin	
XZ292	Westland Gazelle AH1	AAC No 662 Sqn, Munster	
XZ294	Westland Gazelle AH1	AAC No 663 Sqn, Soest	
XZ295	Westland Gazelle AH1	AAC No 7 Flt, Berlin	
XZ296	Westland Gazelle AH1	AAC No 663 Sqn, Soest	
XZ297	Westland Gazelle AH1	AAC No 661 Sqn, Hildesheim	
XZ298	Westland Gazelle AH1	AAC No 662 Sqn, Munster	
XZ299	Westland Gazelle AH1	AAC No 657 Sqn, Oakington	
XZ300	Westland Gazelle AH1	AAC No 662 Sqn, Munster	
XZ301	Westland Gazelle AH1	AAC No 662 Sqn, Munster	
XZ302	Westland Gazelle AH1	AAC No 655 Sqn, Aldergrove	

Notes	Serial	Type (alternative identity)	Owner, Operator or Location
	XZ303	Westland Gazelle AH1	AAC No 663 Sqn, Soest
	XZ304	Westland Gazelle AH1	AAC No 7 Flt, Berlin
	XZ305	Westland Gazelle AH1	AAC No 663 Sqn, Soest
	XZ307	Westland Gazelle AH1	AAC No 663 Sqn, Soest
	XZ308	Westland Gazelle AH1 [L]	AAC ARWS, Middle Wallop
	XZ309	Westland Gazelle AH1	AAC No 664 Sqn, Minden
	XZ310	Westland Gazelle AH1	AAC No 661 Sqn, Hildesheim
	XZ311	Westland Gazelle AH1	AAC No 7 Flt, Berlin
	XZ312	Westland Gazelle AH1	AAC No 2 Flt, Netheravon
	XZ314	Westland Gazelle AH1	AAC No 656 Sqn, Netheravon
	XZ315	Westland Gazelle AH1 [P]	AAC ARWS, Middle Wallop
	XZ316	Westland Gazelle AH1 [R]	AAC ARWS, Middle Wallop
	XZ317	Westland Gazelle AH1 [Q]	AAC ARWS, Middle Wallop
	XZ318	Westland Gazelle AH1 [U]	AAC ARWS, Middle Wallop
	XZ319	Westland Gazelle AH1 [S]	AAC ARWS, Middle Wallop
	XZ320	Westland Gazelle AH1 [D]	RM 3 CBAS, Yeovilton
	XZ321	Westland Gazelle AH1	AAC No 656 Sqn, Netheravon
	XZ322	Westland Gazelle AH1 [N]	AAC ARWS, Middle Wallop
	XZ323	Westland Gazelle AH1	AAC No 655 Sqn, Aldergrove
	XZ324	Westland Gazelle AH1	AAC No 655 Sqn, Aldergrove
	XZ325	Westland Gazelle AH1	AAC No 655 Sqn, Aldergrove
	XZ326	Westland Gazelle AH1 [C]	RM 3 CBAS, Yeovilton
	XZ327	Westland Gazelle AH1	AAC No 655 Sqn, Aldergrove
	XZ328	Westland Gazelle AH1	AAC No 657 Sqn, Oakington
	XZ329	Westland Gazelle AH1 [J]	AAC ARWS, Middle Wallop
	XZ330	Westland Gazelle AH1	AAC No 657 Sqn, Oakington
	XZ331	Westland Gazelle AH1	AAC No 657 Sqn, Oakington
	XZ332	Westland Gazelle AH1 [O]	AAC ARWS, Middle Wallop
	XZ333	Westland Gazelle AH1 [A]	AAC ARWS, Middle Wallop
	XZ334	Westland Gazelle AH1	AAC No 657 Sqn, Oakington
	XZ335	Westland Gazelle AH1	AAC No 3 Flt, Topcliffe
	XZ336	Westland Gazelle AH1	AAC No 3 Flt, Topcliffe
	XZ337	Westland Gazelle AH1	AAC No 669 Sqn, Detmold
	XZ338	Westland Gazelle AH1 [X]	AAC ARWS, Middle Wallop
	XZ339	Westland Gazelle AH1	MoD(PE) A&AEE Boscombe Down
	XZ340	Westland Gazelle AH1 [T]	AAC ARWS, Middle Wallop
	XZ341	Westland Gazelle AH1	AAC D&TS, Middle Wallop
	XZ342	Westland Gazelle AH1	AAC No 661 Sqn, Hildesheim
	XZ343	Westland Gazelle AH1	Westlands, Weston-super-Mare, on rebuild
	XZ344	Westland Gazelle AH1	AAC No 656 Sqn, Netheravon
	XZ345	Westland Gazelle AH1	AAC No 3 Flt, Topcliffe
	XZ346	Westland Gazelle AH1	AAC No 3 Flt, Topcliffe
	XZ347	Westland Gazelle AH1	AAC No 3 Flt, Topcliffe
	XZ348	Westland Gazelle AH1	AAC No 2 Flt, Netheravon
	XZ349	Westland Gazelle AH1 [M]	AAC ARWS, Middle Wallop
	XZ355	SEPECAT Jaguar GR1 [J]	RAF No 41 Sqn, Coltishall
	XZ356	SEPECAT Jaguar GR1 [BP]	RAF No 17 Sqn, Bruggen
	XZ357	SEPECAT Jaguar GR1 [K]	RAF No 41 Sqn, Coltishall
	XZ358	SEPECAT Jaguar GR1 [L]	RAF No 41 Sqn, Coltishall
	XZ359	SEPECAT Jaguar GR1 [M]	RAF No 41 Sqn, Coltishall
	XZ360	SEPECAT Jaguar GR1 [N]	RAF No 41 Sqn, Coltishall
	XZ361	SEPECAT Jaguar GR1 [25]	RAF No 2 Sqn, Laarbruch
	XZ362	SEPECAT Jaguar GR1A [27]	RAF No 2 Sqn, Laarbruch
	XZ363	SEPECAT Jaguar GR1 [A]	RAF No 41 Sqn, Coltishall
	XZ364	SEPECAT Jaguar GR1 [21]	RAF No 2 Sqn, Laarbruch
	XZ365	SEPECAT Jaguar GR1A [33]	RAF No 2 Sqn, Laarbruch
	XZ366	SEPECAT Jaguar GR1A [22]	RAF No 2 Sqn, Laarbruch
	XZ367	SEPECAT Jaguar GR1 [25]	RAF No 226 OCU, Lossiemouth
	XZ368	SEPECAT Jaguar GR1 [AG]	RAF No 14 Sqn, Bruggen
	XZ369	SEPECAT Jaguar GR1 [BF]	RAF No 17 Sqn, Bruggen
	XZ370	SEPECAT Jaguar GR1 [BN]	RAF No 17 Sqn, Bruggen
	XZ371	SEPECAT Jaguar GR1 [AP]	RAF No 14 Sqn, Bruggen
	XZ372	SEPECAT Jaguar GR1 [04]	RAF No 226 OCU, Lossiemouth
	XZ373	SEPECAT Jaguar GR1 [CG]	RAF store, Shawbury
	XZ374	SEPECAT Jaguar GR1 [AD]	RAF No 14 Sqn, Bruggen
	XZ375	SEPECAT Jaguar GR1 [AK]	RAF No 14 Sqn, Bruggen
	XZ377	SEPECAT Jaguar GR1 [39]	RAF No 2 Sqn, Laarbruch
	XZ378	SEPECAT Jaguar GR1 [BB]	RAF No 17 Sqn, Bruggen
	XZ381	SEPECAT Jaguar GR1 [BL]	RAF No 17 Sqn, Bruggen

Serial	Type (alternative identity)	Owner, Operator or Location	Notes
XZ382	SEPECAT Jaguar GR1 [AE]	RAF No 14 Sqn, Bruggen	
XZ383	SEPECAT Jaguar GR1 [AF]	RAF No 14 Sqn, Bruggen	
XZ384	SEPECAT Jaguar GR1 [BC]	RAF No 17 Sqn, Bruggen	
XZ385	SEPECAT Jaguar GR1 [BE]	RAF No 17 Sqn, Bruggen	
XZ386	SEPECAT Jaguar GR1 [38]	RAF No 17 Sqn, Bruggen	
XZ387	SEPECAT Jaguar GR1	RAF No 2 Sqn, Laarbruch	
XZ388	SEPECAT Jaguar GR1 [AH]	RAF No 14 Sqn, Bruggen	
XZ389	SEPECAT Jaguar GR1 [BL]	RAF No 17 Sqn, Bruggen	
XZ390	SEPECAT Jaguar GR1A [35]	RAF No 2 Sqn, Laarbruch	
XZ391	SEPECAT Jaguar GR1 [GE]	RAF No 54 Sqn, Coltishall	
XZ392	SEPECAT Jaguar GR1 [GR]	RAF No 54 Sqn, Coltishall	
XZ394	SEPECAT Jaguar GR1 [BJ]	RAF No 17 Sqn, Bruggen	
XZ396	SEPECAT Jaguar GR1 [08]	RAF No 226 OCU, Lossiemouth	
XZ398	SEPECAT Jaguar GR1 (JI007)	BAe Warton	
XZ399	SEPECAT Jaguar GR1 [09]	RAF No 226 OCU, Lossiemouth	
XZ400	SEPECAT Jaguar GR1A [GA]	RAF No 54 Sqn, Coltishall	
XZ431	HS Buccaneer S2B [PS]	RAF No 208 Sqn, Lossiemouth	
XZ432	HS Buccaneer S2B [CS]	RAF No 208 Sqn, Lossiemouth	
XZ439	BAe Sea Harrier FRS1 [2]	MoD(PE) BAe Dunsfold	
XZ440	BAe Sea Harrier FRS1 [40]	MoD(PE) BAe Hatfield	
XZ445	BAe Harrier T4A [Q]	RAF No 233 OCU, Wittering	
XZ451	BAe Sea Harrier FRS1 [000/N]	RN No 801 Sqn, Yeovilton	
XZ455	BAe Sea Harrier FRS1 [127/L]	RN No 800 Sqn, Yeovilton	
XZ457	BAe Sea Harrier FRS1 [715]	RN No 899 Sqn, Yeovilton	
XZ458	BAe Sea Harrier FRS1 [125/L]	RN No 800 Sqn, Yeovilton	
XZ459	BAe Sea Harrier FRS1 [001/N]	RN No 801 Sqn, Yeovilton	
XZ460	BAe Sea Harrier FRS1	RNAS Yeovilton	
XZ491	BAe Sea Harrier FRS1 [711]	RN No 899 Sqn, Yeovilton	
XZ492	BAe Sea Harrier FRS1 [714]	RN No 899 Sqn, Yeovilton	
XZ493	BAe Sea Harrier FRS1	RN No 800 Sqn, Yeovilton	
XZ494	BAe Sea Harrier FRS1 [716]	RN No 899 Sqn, Yeovilton	
XZ495	BAe Sea Harrier FRS1 [003/N]	RN No 801 Sqn, Yeovilton	
XZ497	BAe Sea Harrier FRS1 [4]	MoD(PE) BAe Dunsfold	
XZ498	BAe Sea Harrier FRS1 [124/L]	RN No 800 Sqn, Yeovilton	
XZ499	BAe Sea Harrier FRS1 [002/N]	RN No 801 Sqn, Yeovilton	
XZ550	Slingsby Venture T2	RAF No 642 VGS, Linton-on-Ouse	
XZ551	Slingsby Venture T2	RAF ACCGS, Syerston	
XZ552	Slingsby Venture T2 [A]	RAF No 632 VGS, Ternhill	
XZ553	Slingsby Venture T2 [Q]	RAF ACCGS, Syerston	
XZ554	Slingsby Venture T2 [4]	RAF No 633 VGS, Cosford	
XZ555	Slingsby Venture T2 [H]	MoD(PE) Slingsby, Kirkbymoorside	
XZ556	Slingsby Venture T2 [6]	RAF No 611 VGS, Swanton Morley	
XZ557	Slingsby Venture T2 [7]	RAF No 633 VGS, Cosford	
XZ558	Slingsby Venture T2 [2]	RAF No 616 VGS, Henlow	
XZ559	Slingsby Venture T2 [3]	RAF No 616 VGS, Henlow	
XZ560	Slingsby Venture T2 [0]	RAF No 611 VGS, Swanton Morley	
XZ561	Slingsby Venture T2 [1]	RAF No 611 VGS, Swanton Morley	
XZ562	Slingsby Venture T2 [2]	RAF No 625 VGS, South Cerney	
XZ563	Slingsby Venture T2	RAF No 635 VGS, Samlesbury	
XZ564	Slingsby Venture T2	RAF No 635 VGS, Samlesbury	
XZ570	Westland Sea King HAS5	MoD(PE) A&AEE Boscombe Down/ Yeovil	
XZ571	Westland Sea King HAS5 [526]	RN No 826 Sqn, Culdrose	
XZ574	Westland Sea King HAS5 [506]	RN No 810 Sqn, Culdrose	
XZ575	Westland Sea King HAS5 [535]	RN No 826 Sqn, Culdrose	
XZ576	Westland Sea King HAS5 [411]	MoD(PE) Westlands, Yeovil	
XZ577	Westland Sea King HAS5	RN Culdrose	
XZ578	Westland Sea King HAS5 [501]	RN No 810 Sqn, Culdrose	
XZ579	Westland Sea King HAS2 [702/PW]	RN No 819 Sqn, Prestwick	
XZ580	Westland Sea King HAS5 [595]	RN No 706 Sqn, Culdrose	
XZ581	Westland Sea King HAS5 [528]	RN No 826 Sqn, Culdrose	

Notes	Serial	Type (alternative identity)	Owner, Operator or Location
	XZ582	Westland Sea King HAS2A [594/CU]	RN No 706 Sqn, Culdrose
	XZ585	Westland Sea King HAR3	RAF No 202 Sqn SAR*
	XZ586	Westland Sea King HAR3 [SB]	RAF No 202 Sqn SAR*
	XZ587	Westland Sea King HAR3	RAF No 202 Sqn SAR*
	XZ588	Westland Sea King HAR3	RAF No 202 Sqn SAR*
	XZ589	Westland Sea King HAR3	RAF No 202 Sqn SAR*
	XZ590	Westland Sea King HAR3	RAF No 202 Sqn SAR*
	XZ591	Westland Sea King HAR3 [S]	RAF No 202 Sqn SAR*
	XZ592	Westland Sea King HAR3	RAF No 202 Sqn SAR*
	XZ593	Westland Sea King HAR3	RAF No 202 Sqn SAR*
	XZ594	Westland Sea King HAR3	RAF No 202 Sqn SAR*
	XZ595	Westland Sea King HAR3	RAF No 202 Sqn SAR*
	XZ596	Westland Sea King HAR3	RAF No 202 Sqn SAR*
	XZ597	Westland Sea King HAR3 [SC]	RAF No 202 Sqn SAR*
	XZ598	Westland Sea King HAR3	RAF No 202 Sqn SAR*
	XZ599	Westland Sea King HAR3 [SA]	RAF No 202 Sqn SAR*
	XZ605	Westland Lynx AH1 [L]	RM 3 CBAS, Yeovilton
	XZ606	Westland Lynx AH1	AAC No 652 Sqn, Hildesheim
	XZ607	Westland Lynx AH1	AAC No 654 Sqn, Detmold
	XZ608	Westland Lynx AH1	AAC No 654 Sqn, Detmold
	XZ609	Westland Lynx AH1	AAC No 654 Sqn, Detmold
	XZ610	Westland Lynx AH1	AAC No 654 Sqn, Detmold
	XZ611	Westland Lynx AH1 [H]	AAC ARW/LCF, Middle Wallop
	XZ612	Westland Lynx AH1 [X]	RM 3 CBAS, Yeovilton
	XZ613	Westland Lynx AH1	AAC No 657 Sqn, Oakington
	XZ614	Westland Lynx AH1 [Y]	RM 3 CBAS, Yeovilton
	XZ615	Westland Lynx AH1	AAC No 651 Sqn, Hildesheim
	XZ616	Westland Lynx AH1	AAC No 657 Sqn, Oakington
	XZ617	Westland Lynx AH1	AAC, RNAY Fleetlands
	XZ630	Panavia Tornado	MoD(PE) A&AEE/BAe Warton
	XZ631	Panavia Tornado	MoD(PE) A&AEE Boscombe Down
	XZ640	Westland Lynx AH1 [L]	AAC ARW/LCF, Middle Wallop
	XZ641	Westland Lynx AH1	AAC No 653 Sqn, Soest
	XZ642	Westland Lynx AH1	AAC No 653 Sqn, Soest
	XZ643	Westland Lynx AH1	AAC No 653 Sqn, Soest
	XZ644	Westland Lynx AH1	AAC No 657 Sqn, Oakington
	XZ645	Westland Lynx AH1	AAC No 657 Sqn, Oakington
	XZ646	Westland Lynx AH1	AAC No 654 Sqn, Detmold
	XZ647	Westland Lynx AH1	AAC No 669 Sqn, Detmold
	XZ648	Westland Lynx AH1 [D]	AAC ARW/LCF, Middle Wallop
	XZ649	Westland Lynx AH1 [E]	AAC ARW/LCF, Middle Wallop
	XZ650	Westland Lynx AH1	AAC No 659 Sqn, Detmold
	XZ651	Westland Lynx AH1	AAC No 659 Sqn, Detmold
	XZ652	Westland Lynx AH1	AAC No 659 Sqn, Detmold
	XZ653	Westland Lynx AH1	AAC No 669 Sqn, Detmold
	XZ654	Westland Lynx AH1	AAC No 652 Sqn, Hildesheim
	XZ655	Westland Lynx AH1	AAC No 652 Sqn, Hildesheim
	XZ661	Westland Lynx AH1	AAC No 652 Sqn, Hildesheim
	XZ662	Westland Lynx AH1	AAC No 652 Sqn, Hildesheim
	XZ663	Westland Lynx AH1	AAC No 656 Sqn, Netheravon
	XZ664	Westland Lynx AH1	AAC No 655 Sqn, Aldergrove
	XZ665	Westland Lynx AH1	AAC No 655 Sqn, Aldergrove
	XZ666	Westland Lynx AH1	AAC No 655 Sqn, Aldergrove
	XZ667	Westland Lynx AH1	AAC No 653 Sqn, Soest
	XZ668	Westland Lynx AH1	AAC No 653 Sqn, Soest
	XZ669	Westland Lynx AH1	AAC No 653 Sqn, Soest
	XZ670	Westland Lynx AH1	AAC No 653 Sqn, Soest
	XZ671	Westland Lynx AH1	AAC No 652 Sqn, Hildesheim
	XZ672	Westland Lynx AH1	AAC No 669 Sqn, Detmold
	XZ673	Westland Lynx AH1	AAC No 652 Sqn, Hildesheim
	XZ674	Westland Lynx AH1	AAC No 652 Sqn, Hildesheim
	XZ675	Westland Lynx AH1	AAC No 652 Sqn, Hildesheim
	XZ676	Westland Lynx AH1	AAC No 656 Sqn, Netheravon

*No 202 Sqn and the SAREW are based at RAF Finningley with detached flights at: RAF Boulmer 'A' Flt; RAF Brawdy 'B' Flt; RAF Stanley 'C' Flt/1564 Flt; RAF Lossiemouth 'D' Flt; RNAS Culdrose the Sea King Training Flight (SKTF).

Serial	Type (alternative identity)	Owner, Operator or Location	Notes
XZ677	Westland Lynx AH1	AAC No 651 Sqn, Hildesheim	
XZ678	Westland Lynx AH1	AAC No 651 Sqn, Hildesheim	
XZ679	Westland Lynx AH1	AAC No 651 Sqn, Hildesheim	
XZ680	Westland Lynx AH1	RM 3 CBAS, Yeovilton	
XZ681	Westland Lynx AH1	AAC Middle Wallop, BDRT	
XZ689	Westland Lynx HAS2	RNAY Fleetlands	
XZ690	Westland Lynx HAS2 [330/BZ]	RN No 815 Sqn, Portland	
XZ691	Westland Lynx HAS2 [342/BT]	RN No 815 Sqn, Portland	
XZ692	Westland Lynx HAS2 [643/PO]	RN No 702 Sqn, Portland	
XZ693	Westland Lynx HAS2	RN NASU, Yeovilton	
XZ694	Westland Lynx HAS2 [344/GW]	RN No 815 Sqn, Portland	
XZ695	Westland Lynx HAS2 [466/AT]	RN No 815 Sqn, Portland	
XZ696	Westland Lynx HAS2 [642/PO]	RN No 702 Sqn, Portland	
XZ697	Westland Lynx HAS2 [341/AG]	RN No 815 Sqn, Portland	
XZ698	Westland Lynx HAS2 [424/MV]	RN No 815 Sqn, Portland	
XZ699	Westland Lynx HAS2 [300/PO]	RN No 815 Sqn, Portland	
XZ719	Westland Lynx HAS2	RN No 815 Sqn, Portland	
XZ720	Westland Lynx HAS2 [475/HM]	RN No 815 Sqn, Portland	
XZ721	Westland Lynx HAS2	RNAY Fleetlands	
XZ722	Westland Lynx HAS2	RNAY Fleetlands	
XZ723	Westland Lynx HAS2 [454/PN]	RN No 815 Sqn, Portland	
XZ724	Westland Lynx HAS2 [471/PB]	RN No 815 Sqn, Portland	
XZ725	Westland Lynx HAS2 [323/AB]	RN No 815 Sqn, Portland	
XZ726	Westland Lynx HAS2 [464/DN]	RN No 815 Sqn, Portland	
XZ727	Westland Lynx HAS2 [305]	RN No 815 Sqn, Portland	
XZ728	Westland Lynx HAS2 [332/LP]	RN No 815 Sqn, Portland	
XZ729	Westland Lynx HAS2	RN No 815 Sqn, Portland	
XZ730	Westland Lynx HAS2 [326/AW]	RN No 815 Sqn, Portland	
XZ731	Westland Lynx HAS2 [345/NC]	RN No 815 Sqn, Portland	
XZ732	Westland Lynx HAS2 [641/PO]	RN No 702 Sqn, Portland	
XZ733	Westland Lynx HAS2 [420/EX]	RN No 815 Sqn, Portland	
XZ734	Westland Lynx HAS2 [431/CY]	RN No 815 Sqn, Portland	
XZ735	Westland Lynx HAS2 [320/AZ]	RN No 815 Sqn, Portland	
XZ736	Westland Lynx HAS2 [360/MC]	RN No 815 Sqn, Portland	
XZ916	Westland Sea King HAS5 [525]	RN No 826 Sqn, Stanley	
XZ918	Westland Sea King HAS5 [020/N]	RN No 820 Sqn, Culdrose	
XZ919	Westland Sea King HAS5 [529]	RN No 826 Sqn, Stanley	
XZ920	Westland Sea King HAS5 [510]	RN No 810 Sqn, Culdrose	
XZ921	Westland Sea King HAS5 [017/N]	RN No 820 Sqn, Culdrose	
XZ922	Westland Sea King HAS5 [530]	RN No 826 Sqn, Stanley	
XZ930	Westland Gazelle HT3 [Q]	RAF No 2 FTS, Shawbury	
XZ931	Westland Gazelle HT3 [R]	RAF No 2 FTS, Shawbury	
XZ932	Westland Gazelle HT3 [S]	RAF No 2 FTS, Shawbury	
XZ933	Westland Gazelle HT3 [T]	RAF No 2 FTS, Shawbury	
XZ934	Westland Gazelle HT3 [U]	RAF No 2 FTS, Shawbury	
XZ935	Westland Gazelle HT3	RAF No 32 Sqn, Northolt	
XZ936	Westland Gazelle HT3	MoD(PE) ETPS Boscombe Down	
XZ937	Westland Gazelle HT3 [Y]	RAF No 2 FTS, Shawbury	
XZ938	Westland Gazelle HT2 [45/CU]	RN No 705 Sqn, Culdrose	
XZ939	Westland Gazelle HT3 [Z]	RAF No 2 FTS, Shawbury	
XZ940	Westland Gazelle HT3 [O]	RAF No 2 FTS, Shawbury	
XZ941	Westland Gazelle HT3 [B]	RAF No 2 FTS, Shawbury	
XZ942	Westland Gazelle HT3 [FL]	RNAY Fleetlands	
XZ964	BAe Harrier GR3 [P]	RAF No 233 OCU, Wittering	
XZ965	BAe Harrier GR3 [AM]	RAF No 3 Sqn, Gutersloh	
XZ966	BAe Harrier GR3 [C]	RAF No 1417 Flt, Belize	
XZ967	BAe Harrier GR3 [O]	RAF No 233 OCU, Wittering	
XZ968	BAe Harrier GR3 [K]	RAF No 4 Sqn, Gutersloh	
XZ969	BAe Harrier GR3 [AS]	RAF No 3 Sqn, Gutersloh	
XZ970	BAe Harrier GR3 [AR]	RAF No 3 Sqn, Gutersloh	
XZ971	BAe Harrier GR3 [N]	RAF No 233 OCU, Wittering	
XZ987	BAe Harrier GR3 [AX]	RAF No 3 Sqn, Gutersloh	
XZ989	BAe Harrier GR3	BAe Dunsfold, on rebuild	
XZ990	BAe Harrier GR3 [H]	RAF No 4 Sqn, Gutersloh	
XZ991	BAe Harrier GR3 [A]	RAF 233 OCU, Wittering	
XZ992	BAe Harrier GR3 [T]	RAF No 1453 Flt, Stanley	
XZ993	BAe Harrier GR3 [04]	RAF No 1 Sqn, Wittering	
XZ994	BAe Harrier GR3 [F]	RAF No 1417 Flt, Belize	

Notes	Serial	Type (alternative identity)	Owner, Operator or Location
	XZ995	BAe Harrier GR3 [AO]	RAF No 3 Sqn, Gutersloh
	XZ996	BAe Harrier GR3 [G]	RAF No 1417 Flt, Belize
	XZ997	BAe Harrier GR3 [O]	RAF No 1453 Flt, Stanley
	XZ998	BAe Harrier GR3 [F]	RAF No 233 OCU, Wittering
	XZ999	BAe Harrier GR3 [I]	RAF No 4 Sqn, Gutersloh
	ZA101	BAe Hawk T50 (G-HAWK)	BAe Dunsfold
	ZA105	Westland Sea King HAR3 [SD]	RAF No 202 Sqn SAR*
	ZA110	BAe Jetstream T2 [573/CU] (G-AXUO)	RN No 750 Sqn, Culdrose
	ZA111	BAe Jetstream T2 [574/CU] (G-AXFV)	RN No 750 Sqn, Culdrose
	ZA126	Westland Sea King HAS5 [012/N]	RN No 820 Sqn, Culdrose
	ZA127	Westland Sea King HAS5 [511]	RN No 810 Sqn, Culdrose
	ZA128	Westland Sea King HAS5 [014/N]	RN No 820 Sqn, Culdrose
	ZA129	Westland Sea King HAS5 [527]	RN No 826 Sqn, Culdrose
	ZA130	Westland Sea King HAS5 [353]	RN No 824 Sqn, Culdrose
	ZA131	Westland Sea King HAS5 [533]	RN No 826 Sqn, Culdrose
	ZA133	Westland Sea King HAS5 [352]	RN No 824 Sqn, Culdrose
	ZA134	Westland Sea King HAS5	RN NASU, Culdrose
	ZA135	Westland Sea King HAS5 [505]	RN No 810 Sqn, Culdrose
	ZA136	Westland Sea King HAS5 [524]	RN No 826 Sqn, Culdrose
	ZA137	Westland Sea King HAS5 [537]	RN No 826 Sqn, Culdrose
	ZA140	BAe VC10 K2 (G-ARVL) [A]	RAF No 101 Sqn, Brize Norton
	ZA141	BAe VC10 K2 (G-ARVG) [B]	RAF No 101 Sqn, Brize Norton
	ZA142	BAe VC10 K2 (G-ARVI) [C]	RAF No 101 Sqn, Brize Norton
	ZA143	BAe VC10 K2 (G-ARVK) [D]	RAF No 101 Sqn, Brize Norton
	ZA144	BAe VC10 K2 (G-ARVC) [E]	RAF No 101 Sqn, Brize Norton
	ZA147	BAe VC10 K3 (5H-MMT)	MoD(PE) A&AEE, Boscombe Down
	ZA148	BAe VC10 K3 (5Y-ADA)	MoD(PE) for RAF, Filton
	ZA149	BAe VC10 K3 (5X-UVJ)	MoD(PE) for RAF, Filton
	ZA150	BAe VC10 K3 (5H-MOG)	MoD(PE) for RAF, Filton
	ZA166	Westland Sea King HAS5 [010/N]	RN No 820 Sqn, Culdrose
	ZA167	Westland Sea King HAS5 [273]	RN No 814 Sqn, Culdrose
	ZA168	Westland Sea King HAS5 [267]	RN No 814 Sqn, Culdrose
	ZA169	Westland Sea King HAS5 [015/N]	RN No 820 Sqn, Culdrose
	ZA170	Westland Sea King HAS5 [504]	RN No 810 Sqn, Culdrose
	ZA175	BAe Sea Harrier FRS1 [710]	RN No 899 Sqn, Yeovilton
	ZA176	BAe Sea Harrier FRS1 [712]	RN No 899 Sqn, Yeovilton
	ZA190	BAe Sea Harrier FRS1 [126/L]	RN No 800 Sqn, Yeovilton
	ZA191	BAe Sea Harrier FRS1 [123/L]	RN No 800 Sqn, Yeovilton
	ZA193	BAe Sea Harrier FRS1 [004/N]	RN No 801 Sqn, Yeovilton
	ZA195	BAe Sea Harrier FRS1 [710]	RN No 899 Sqn, Yeovilton
	ZA250	BAe Harrier T52 (G-VTOL)	BAe, Dunsfold
	ZA254	Panavia Tornado F2	MoD(PE) BAe Warton
	ZA267	Panavia Tornado F2	MoD(PE) BAe Warton
	ZA283	Panavia Tornado F2	MoD(PE) A&AEE Boscombe Down
	ZA291	Westland Sea King HC4 [VB]	RN No 846 Sqn, Yeovilton
	ZA292	Westland Sea King HC4 [VH]	RN No 846 Sqn, Yeovilton
	ZA293	Westland Sea King HC4 [VK]	RN No 846 Sqn, Yeovilton
	ZA295	Westland Sea King HC4 [ZC]	RN No 707 Sqn, Yeovilton
	ZA296	Westland Sea King HC4 [VF]	RN No 846 Sqn, Yeovilton
	ZA297	Westland Sea King HC4 [VG]	RN NASU, Culdrose
	ZA298	Westland Sea King HC4 [VA] (G-BJNM)	RN No 846 Sqn, Yeovilton
	ZA299	Westland Sea King HC4 [ZD]	RN No 707 Sqn, Yeovilton

Serial	Type (alternative identity)	Owner, Operator or Location	Notes
ZA310	Westland Sea King HC4 [VS]	RN No 846 Sqn, Yeovilton	
ZA312	Westland Sea King HC4 [ZB]	RN No 707 Sqn, Yeovilton	
ZA313	Westland Sea King HC4 [VZ]	RN No 846 Sqn, Yeovilton	
ZA314	Westland Sea King HC4	MoD(PE) A&AEE, Boscombe Down	
ZA319	Panavia Tornado GR1T [B-11]	RAF TTTE, Cottesmore	
ZA320	Panavia Tornado GR1T [B-01]	RAF TTTE, Cottesmore	
ZA321	Panavia Tornado GR1 [B-58]	RAF TTTE, Cottesmore	
ZA322	Panavia Tornado GR1 [B-50]	RAF TTTE, Cottesmore	
ZA322	Panavia Tornado GR1 replica (BAPC 155) [B-50]	RAF Exhibition Flight, Abingdon	
ZA323	Panavia Tornado GR1T [B-14]	RAF TTTE, Cottesmore	
ZA324	Panavia Tornado GR1T [B-02]	RAF TTTE, Cottesmore	
ZA325	Panavia Tornado GR1T [B-03]	RAF TTTE, Cottesmore	
ZA326	Panavia Tornado GR1T	MoD(PE) RAE Bedford	
ZA327	Panavia Tornado GR1 [B-51]	RAF TTTE, Cottesmore	
ZA328	Panavia Tornado GR1	MoD(PE) A&AEE Boscombe Down	
ZA329	Panavia Tornado GR1 [B-52]	RAF TTTE, Cottesmore	
ZA330	Panavia Tornado GR1T [B-08]	MoD(PE) BAe Samlesbury, on rebuild	
ZA352	Panavia Tornado GR1T [B-04]	RAF TTTE, Cottesmore	
ZA353	Panavia Tornado GR1 [B-53]	RAF TTTE, Cottesmore	
ZA354	Panavia Tornado GR1	MoD(PE) BAe Warton	
ZA355	Panavia Tornado GR1 [B-54]	RAF TTTE, Cottesmore	
ZA356	Panavia Tornado GR1T [B-07]	RAF TTTE, Cottesmore	
ZA357	Panavia Tornado GR1T [B-05]	RAF TTTE, Cottesmore	
ZA358	Panavia Tornado GR1T [B-06]	RAF TTTE, Cottesmore	
ZA359	Panavia Tornado GR1 [B-55]	RAF TTTE, Cottesmore	
ZA360	Panavia Tornado GR1 [B-56]	RAF TTTE, Cottesmore	
ZA361	Panavia Tornado GR1 [B-57]	RAF TTTE, Cottesmore	
ZA362	Panavia Tornado GR1T [B-09]	RAF TTTE, Cottesmore	
ZA365	Panavia Tornado GR1T [14]	RAF No 27 Sqn, Marham	
ZA366	Panavia Tornado GR1T	RAF TWCU, Honington	
ZA367	Panavia Tornado GR1T [T]	RAF No 617 Sqn, Marham	
ZA368	Panavia Tornado GR1T [Y]	RAF No 9 Sqn, Honington	
ZA369	Panavia Tornado GR1	RAF TWCU, Honington	
ZA370	Panavia Tornado GR1	RAF TWCU, Honington	
ZA371	Panavia Tornado GR1	RAF TWCU, Honington	
ZA372	Panavia Tornado GR1	RAF TWCU, Honington	
ZA373	Panavia Tornado GR1	RAF TWCU, Honington	
ZA374	Panavia Tornado GR1	RAF TWCU, Honington	
ZA375	Panavia Tornado GR1	RAF TWCU, Honington	
ZA376	Panavia Tornado GR1 [E]	MoD(PE) TOEU Boscombe Down	
ZA392	Panavia Tornado GR1 [EK]	RAF No 15 Sqn, Laarbruch	
ZA393	Panavia Tornado GR1	RAF TWCU, Honington	
ZA394	Panavia Tornado GR1	RAF Marham	
ZA395	Panavia Tornado GR1 [06]	RAF No 27 Sqn, Marham	
ZA396	Panavia Tornado GR1	RAF St Athan, store	
ZA397	Panavia Tornado GR1	RAF TWCU, Honington	
ZA398	Panavia Tornado GR1	RAF TWCU, Honington	
ZA399	Panavia Tornado GR1	RAF St Athan, store	
ZA400	Panavia Tornado GR1	RAF TWCU, Honington	
ZA401	Panavia Tornado GR1	RAF TWCU, Honington	
ZA402	Panavia Tornado GR1	RAF TWCU, Honington	
ZA403	Panavia Tornado GR1	MoD(PE) for RAF	
ZA404	Panavia Tornado GR1	RAF TWCU, Honington	
ZA405	Panavia Tornado GR1	RAF TWCU, Honington	
ZA406	Panavia Tornado GR1	RAF TWCU, Honington	
ZA407	Panavia Tornado GR1	RAF TWCU, Honington	
ZA409	Panavia Tornado GR1T [EW]	RAF No 15 Sqn, Laarbruch	
ZA410	Panavia Tornado GR1T [EX]	RAF No 15 Sqn, Laarbruch	
ZA411	Panavia Tornado GR1T [GY]	RAF No 20 Sqn, Laarbruch	
ZA412	Panavia Tornado GR1T [FZ]	RAF No 16 Sqn, Laarbruch	
ZA446	Panavia Tornado GR1 [EF]	RAF No 15 Sqn, Laarbruch	
ZA447	Panavia Tornado GR1 [EA]	RAF No 15 Sqn, Laarbruch	
ZA448	Panavia Tornado GR1 [EB]	RAF No 15 Sqn, Laarbruch	
ZA449	Panavia Tornado GR1	MoD(PE) BAe Warton	
ZA450	Panavia Tornado GR1 [EC]	RAF No 15 Sqn, Laarbruch	
ZA452	Panavia Tornado GR1 [GK]	RAF No 20 Sqn, Laarbruch	
ZA453	Panavia Tornado GR1 [EG]	RAF No 15 Sqn, Laarbruch	
ZA454	Panavia Tornado GR1 [EH]	RAF No 15 Sqn, Laarbruch	
ZA455	Panavia Tornado GR1 [EJ]	RAF No 15 Sqn, Laarbruch	

Notes	Serial	Type (alternative identity)	Owner, Operator or Location
	ZA456	Panavia Tornado GR1 [GB]	RAF No 20 Sqn, Laarbruch
	ZA457	Panavia Tornado GR1	RAF No 9 Sqn, Honington
	ZA458	Panavia Tornado GR1 [FB]	RAF No 16 Sqn, Laarbruch
	ZA459	Panavia Tornado GR1 [EL]	RAF No 15 Sqn, Laarbruch
	ZA460	Panavia Tornado GR1 [FD]	RAF No 16 Sqn, Laarbruch
	ZA461	Panavia Tornado GR1 [GA]	RAF No 20 Sqn, Laarbruch
	ZA462	Panavia Tornado GR1 [EM]	RAF No 15 Sqn, Laarbruch
	ZA463	Panavia Tornado GR1 [GL]	RAF No 20 Sqn, Laarbruch
	ZA464	Panavia Tornado GR1 [GM]	RAF No 20 Sqn, Laarbruch
	ZA465	Panavia Tornado GR1 [FK]	RAF No 16 Sqn, Laarbruch
	ZA466	Panavia Tornado GR1 [FH]	RAF No 16 Sqn, Laarbruch
	ZA467	Panavia Tornado GR1 [FF]	RAF No 16 Sqn, Laarbruch
	ZA468	Panavia Tornado GR1 [FN]	RAF No 16 Sqn, Laarbruch
	ZA469	Panavia Tornado GR1 [GD]	RAF No 20 Sqn, Laarbruch
	ZA470	Panavia Tornado GR1 [FL]	RAF No 16 Sqn, Laarbruch
	ZA471	Panavia Tornado GR1 [FJ]	RAF No 16 Sqn, Laarbruch
	ZA472	Panavia Tornado GR1 [EE]	RAF No 15 Sqn, Laarbruch
	ZA473	Panavia Tornado GR1 [FM]	RAF No 16 Sqn, Laarbruch
	ZA474	Panavia Tornado GR1 [FG]	RAF No 16 Sqn, Laarbruch
	ZA475	Panavia Tornado GR1 [FC]	RAF No 16 Sqn, Laarbruch
	ZA490	Panavia Tornado GR1 [GG]	RAF No 20 Sqn, Laarbruch
	ZA491	Panavia Tornado GR1 [GC]	RAF No 20 Sqn, Laarbruch
	ZA492	Panavia Tornado GR1 [FE]	RAF No 16 Sqn, Laarbruch
	ZA493	Panavia Tornado GR1 [GH]	RAF No 20 Sqn, Laarbruch
	ZA540	Panavia Tornado GR1T [B-12]	RAF TTTE, Cottesmore
	ZA541	Panavia Tornado GR1T [S]	RAF No 617 Sqn, Marham
	ZA542	Panavia Tornado GR1 [N]	RAF No 617 Sqn, Marham
	ZA543	Panavia Tornado GR1 [T]	RAF No 9 Sqn, Honington
	ZA544	Panavia Tornado GR1T	RAF TWCU, Honington
	ZA545	Panavia Tornado GR1 [T]	MoD(PE) TOEU, Boscombe Down
	ZA546	Panavia Tornado GR1 [L]	RAF No 617 Sqn, Marham
	ZA547	Panavia Tornado GR1 [A]	RAF No 617 Sqn, Marham
	ZA548	Panavia Tornado GR1T [B-10]	RAF TTTE, Cottesmore
	ZA549	Panavia Tornado GR1T	RAF TWCU, Honington
	ZA550	Panavia Tornado GR1 [C]	RAF No 617 Sqn, Marham
	ZA551	Panavia Tornado GR1T	RAF TWCU, Honington
	ZA552	Panavia Tornado GR1T	RAF TWCU, Honington
	ZA553	Panavia Tornado GR1 [P]	RAF No 617 Sqn, Marham
	ZA554	Panavia Tornado GR1 [B]	RAF No 617 Sqn, Marham
	ZA555	Panavia Tornado GR1T	RAF TWCU, Honington
	ZA556	Panavia Tornado GR1	RAF TWCU, Honington
	ZA557	Panavia Tornado GR1 [E]	RAF No 617 Sqn, Marham
	ZA559	Panavia Tornado GR1 [U]	RAF No 9 Sqn, Honington
	ZA560	Panavia Tornado GR1 [08]	RAF No 27 Sqn, Marham
	ZA561	Panavia Tornado GR1 [J]	RAF No 617 Sqn, Marham
	ZA562	Panavia Tornado GR1T [12]	RAF No 27 Sqn, Marham
	ZA563	Panavia Tornado GR1	MoD(PE) TOEU, Boscombe Down
	ZA564	Panavia Tornado GR1 [S]	RAF No 9 Sqn, Honington
	ZA585	Panavia Tornado GR1 [05]	RAF No 27 Sqn, Marham
	ZA587	Panavia Tornado GR1 [B]	RAF No 9 Sqn, Honington
	ZA588	Panavia Tornado GR1 [C]	RAF No 9 Sqn, Honington
	ZA589	Panavia Tornado GR1 [D]	RAF No 9 Sqn, Honington
	ZA590	Panavia Tornado GR1 [E]	RAF No 9 Sqn, Honington
	ZA591	Panavia Tornado GR1 [F]	RAF No 9 Sqn, Honington
	ZA592	Panavia Tornado GR1 [G]	RAF No 9 Sqn, Honington
	ZA593	Panavia Tornado GR1 [H]	RAF No 9 Sqn, Honington
	ZA594	Panavia Tornado GR1T	RAF TWCU, Honington
	ZA595	Panavia Tornado GR1T	RAF TWCU, Honington
	ZA596	Panavia Tornado GR1 [L]	RAF No 9 Sqn, Honington
	ZA597	Panavia Tornado GR1	RAF No 9 Sqn, Honington
	ZA598	Panavia Tornado GR1T	RAF TWCU, Honington
	ZA599	Panavia Tornado GR1T	RAF TWCU, Honington
	ZA600	Panavia Tornado GR1 [07]	RAF No 27 Sqn, Marham
	ZA601	Panavia Tornado GR1 [M]	RAF No 617 Sqn, Marham
	ZA602	Panavia Tornado GR1T [B-13]	RAF TTTE, Cottesmore
	ZA604	Panavia Tornado GR1T	RAF TWCU, Honington
	ZA605	Panavia Tornado GR1 [O]	RAF No 617 Sqn, Marham
	ZA606	Panavia Tornado GR1 [09]	RAF No 27 Sqn, Marham
	ZA607	Panavia Tornado GR1 [01]	RAF No 27 Sqn, Marham
	ZA608	Panavia Tornado GR1 [Z]	RAF No 617 Sqn, Marham

Serial	Type (alternative identity)	Owner, Operator or Location	Notes
ZA609	Panavia Tornado GR1 [02]	RAF No 27 Sqn, Marham	
ZA610	Panavia Tornado GR1 [11]	RAF No 27 Sqn, Marham	
ZA611	Panavia Tornado GR1 [03]	RAF No 27 Sqn, Marham	
ZA612	Panavia Tornado GR1T	RAF TWCU, Honington	
ZA613	Panavia Tornado GR1 [04]	RAF No 27 Sqn, Marham	
ZA614	Panavia Tornado GR1 [U]	MoD(PE) TOEU, Boscombe Down	
ZA625	Slingsby Venture T2 [1]	RAF No 616 VGS, Henlow	
ZA626	Slingsby Venture T2 [C]	RAF No 632 VGS, Ternhill	
ZA627	Slingsby Venture T2 [7]	RAF No 625 VGS, South Cerney	
ZA628	Slingsby Venture T2 [B]	RAF No 632 VGS, Ternhill	
ZA629	Slingsby Venture T2 [9]	RAF No 633 VGS, Cosford	
ZA630	Slingsby Venture T2	RAF No 642 VGS, Linton-on-Ouse	
ZA631	Slingsby Venture T2 [1]	RAF No 613 VGS, Halton	
ZA632	Slingsby Venture T2 [2]	RAF No 613 VGS, Halton	
ZA633	Slingsby Venture T2 [3]	RAF No 613 VGS, Halton	
ZA634	Slingsby Venture T2	RAF No 635 VGS, Samlesbury	
ZA652	Slingsby Venture T2 [6]	RAF No 612 VGS, Benson	
ZA653	Slingsby Venture T2 [1]	RAF No 612 VGS, Benson	
ZA654	Slingsby Venture T2 [2]	RAF No 612 VGS, Benson	
ZA655	Slingsby Venture T2 [V]	RAF No 644 VGS, Syerston	
ZA656	Slingsby Venture T2 [6]	RAF No 624 VGS, Chivenor	
ZA657	Slingsby Venture T2	RAF No 644 VGS, Syerston	
ZA658	Slingsby Venture T2 [3]	RAF ACCGS/644 VGS, Syerston	
ZA659	Slingsby Venture T2	RAF No 642 VGS, Linton-on-Ouse	
ZA660	Slingsby Venture T2 [6]	RAF No 637 VGS, Little Rissington	
ZA661	Slingsby Venture T2 [3]	RAF No 637 VGS, Little Rissington	
ZA662	Slingsby Venture T2 [7]	RAF No 637 VGS, Little Rissington	
ZA663	Slingsby Venture T2 [3]	RAF No 624 VGS, Chivenor	
ZA664	Slingsby Venture T2 [4]	RAF No 624 VGS, Chivenor	
ZA665	Slingsby Venture T2	RAF ACCGS/644 VGS, Syerston	
ZA666	Slingsby Venture T2	RAF No 625 VGS, South Cerney	
ZA670	B-V Chinook HC1 [BN]	RAF No 18 Sqn, Gutersloh	
ZA671	B-V Chinook HC1	MoD(PE) A&AEE Boscombe Down	
ZA672	B-V Chinook HC1 [EX]	RAF No 7 Sqn, Odiham	
ZA673	B-V Chinook HC1 [BQ]	RAF No 18 Sqn, Gutersloh	
ZA674	B-V Chinook HC1 [BA]	RAF No 18 Sqn, Gutersloh	
ZA675	B-V Chinook HC1 [BB]	RAF No 18 Sqn, Gutersloh	
ZA676	B-V Chinook HC1 [FG]	RAF No 240 OCU, Odiham	
ZA677	B-V Chinook HC1 [BR]	RAF No 18 Sqn, Gutersloh	
ZA678	B-V Chinook HC1 [FL]	RAF No 240 OCU, Odiham	
ZA679	B-V Chinook HC1 [EV]	RAF No 7 Sqn, Odiham	
ZA680	B-V Chinook HC1 [J]	RAF No 1310 Flt, Falklands	
ZA681	B-V Chinook HC1 [ES]	RAF No 7 Sqn, Odiham	
ZA682	B-V Chinook HC1 [BY]	RAF No 18 Sqn, Gutersloh	
ZA683	B-V Chinook HC1 [FI]	RAF No 240 OCU, Odiham	
ZA684	B-V Chinook HC1 [F]	RAF No 1310 Flt, Falklands	
ZA704	B-V Chinook HC1 [BV]	RAF No 18 Sqn, Gutersloh	
ZA705	B-V Chinook HC1 [EZ]	RAF No 7 Sqn, Odiham	
ZA707	B-V Chinook HC1	RAF ASF, Odiham	
ZA708	B-V Chinook HC1 [BE]	MoD(PE) A&AEE, Boscombe Down	
ZA709	B-V Chinook HC1 [A]	RAF No 1310 Flt, Falklands	
ZA710	B-V Chinook HC1 [EY]	RAF No 7 Sqn, Odiham	
ZA711	B-V Chinook HC1 [ET]	RAF No 7 Sqn, Odiham	
ZA712	B-V Chinook HC1 [ER]	RAF No 7 Sqn, Odiham	
ZA713	B-V Chinook HC1 [EN]	RAF No 7 Sqn, Odiham	
ZA714	B-V Chinook HC1 [E]	RAF No 1310 Flt, Falklands	
ZA715	B-V Chinook HC1 [C]	RAF No 1310 Flt, Falklands	
ZA717	B-V Chinook HC1 [B]	RAF No 1310 Flt, Falklands	
ZA718	B-V Chinook HC1 [EQ]	RAF No 7 Sqn, Odiham	
ZA720	B-V Chinook HC1 [BG]	RAF No 18 Sqn, Gutersloh	
ZA721	B-V Chinook HC1 [EP]	RAF No 7 Sqn, Odiham	
ZA726	Westland Gazelle AH1	AAC No 663 Sqn, Soest	
ZA727	Westland Gazelle AH1	AAC No 661 Sqn, Hildesheim	
ZA728	Westland Gazelle AH1 [X]	RM 3 CBAS, Yeovilton	
ZA729	Westland Gazelle AH1	AAC No 652 Sqn, Hildesheim	
ZA730	Westland Gazelle AH1 [F]	RM 3 CBAS, Yeovilton	
ZA731	Westland Gazelle AH1 [C]	AAC No 29 Flt, Suffield, Canada	
ZA732	Westland Gazelle AH1 [D]	AAC No 29 Flt, Suffield, Canada	
ZA733	Westland Gazelle AH1 [E]	AAC No 29 Flt, Suffield, Canada	
ZA734	Westland Gazelle AH1	AAC No 25 Flt, Belize	

Notes	Serial	Type (alternative identity)	Owner, Operator or Location
	ZA735	Westland Gazelle AH1	AAC No 25 Flt, Belize
	ZA736	Westland Gazelle AH1 [A]	AAC No 29 Flt, Suffield, Canada
	ZA737	Westland Gazelle AH1 [V]	AAC ARWS, Middle Wallop
	ZA765	Westland Gazelle AH1	AAC No 25 Flt, Belize
	ZA766	Westland Gazelle AH1	AAC No 663 Sqn, Soest
	ZA767	Westland Gazelle AH1	AAC No 25 Flt, Belize
	ZA768	Westland Gazelle AH1 [F]	AAC ARWS, Middle Wallop
	ZA769	Westland Gazelle AH1 [K]	AAC ARWS, Middle Wallop
	ZA770	Westland Gazelle AH1 [B]	AAC No 29 Flt, Suffield, Canada
	ZA771	Westland Gazelle AH1 [Z]	AAC ARWS, Middle Wallop
	ZA772	Westland Gazelle AH1	AAC No 656 Sqn, Netheravon
	ZA773	Westland Gazelle AH1	AAC No 655 Sqn, Aldergrove
	ZA774	Westland Gazelle AH1	AAC No 655 Sqn, Aldergrove
	ZA775	Westland Gazelle AH1	AAC No 656 Sqn, Netheravon
	ZA776	Westland Gazelle AH1 [B]	RM 3 CBAS, Yeovilton
	ZA777	Westland Gazelle AH1	AAC No 661 Sqn, Hildesheim
	ZA801	Westland Gazelle HT3 [V]	RAF Abingdon, BDRF
	ZA802	Westland Gazelle HT3 [W]	RAF No 2 FTS, Shawbury
	ZA803	Westland Gazelle HT3 [X]	RAF No 2 FTS, Shawbury
	ZA804	Westland Gazelle HT3 [I]	RAF No 2 FTS, Shawbury
	ZA934	Westland Puma HC1	MoD(PE) A&AEE/ETPS, Boscombe Down
	ZA935	Westland Puma HC1 [CT]	RAF No 33 Sqn, Odiham
	ZA936	Westland Puma HC1 [CU]	RAF No 33 Sqn, Odiham
	ZA937	Westland Puma HC1 [CV]	RAF No 33 Sqn, Odiham
	ZA938	Westland Puma HC1 [CW]	RAF No 33 Sqn, Odiham
	ZA939	Westland Puma HC1 [CX]	RAF No 33 Sqn, Odiham
	ZA940	Westland Puma HC1 [CY]	RAF No 33 Sqn, Odiham
	ZA941	Westland Puma HC1	MoD(PE) RAE Farnborough
	ZA947	Douglas Dakota C3 (KG661)	MoD(PE) RAE Farnborough
	ZB500	Westland Lynx (G-LYNX)	Westlands Yeovil
	ZB506	Westland Sea King Mk 4X	MoD(PE) RAE Bedford
	ZB507	Westland Sea King Mk 4X	MoD(PE) RAE Farnborough
	ZB600	BAe Harrier T4A [R]	RAF No 4 Sqn, Gutersloh
	ZB601	BAe Harrier T4A [X]	RAF No 233 OCU, Wittering
	ZB602	BAe Harrier T4A [Y]	RAF No 233 OCU, Wittering
	ZB603	BAe Harrier T4A [AZ]	RAF No 3 Sqn, Gutersloh
	ZB604	BAe Harrier T4N [717/VL]	RN No 899 Sqn, Yeovilton
	ZB605	BAe Harrier T4N [718/VL]	RN No 899 Sqn, Yeovilton
	ZB606	BAe Harrier T4N	RN No 899 Sqn, Yeovilton
	ZB615	SEPECAT Jaguar T2	MoD(PE) IAM Farnborough
	ZB625	Westland Gazelle HT3 [N]	RAF No 2 FTS, Shawbury
	ZB626	Westland Gazelle HT3 [L]	RAF No 2 FTS, Shawbury
	ZB627	Westland Gazelle HT3 [A]	RAF No 2 FTS, Shawbury
	ZB628	Westland Gazelle HT3 [V]	RAF No 2 FTS, Shawbury
	ZB629	Westland Gazelle HT3	RAF No 32 Sqn, Northolt
	ZB646	Westland Gazelle HT2 [CU]	RN store, Wroughton
	ZB647	Westland Gazelle HT2 [CU]	RN store, Wroughton
	ZB648	Westland Gazelle HT2 [CU]	MoD(PE), RAE Farnborough
	ZB649	Westland Gazelle HT2 [CU]	RNAY Fleetlands
	ZB665	Westland Gazelle AH1	AAC store, Wroughton
	ZB666	Westland Gazelle AH1 [G]	AAC ARWS, Middle Wallop
	ZB667	Westland Gazelle AH1	AAC store, Wroughton
	ZB668	Westland Gazelle AH1	AAC store, Wroughton
	ZB669	Westland Gazelle AH1	AAC store, Wroughton
	ZB670	Westland Gazelle AH1	AAC No 655 Sqn, Aldergrove
	ZB671	Westland Gazelle AH1	AAC, RNAY Fleetlands
	ZB672	Westland Gazelle AH1	AAC, Falklands
	ZB673	Westland Gazelle AH1	AAC, Falklands
	ZB674	Westland Gazelle AH1	AAC, Falklands
	ZB675	Westland Gazelle AH1	AAC, Falklands
	ZB676	Westland Gazelle AH1	AAC No 655 Sqn, Aldergrove
	ZB677	Westland Gazelle AH1	AAC No 655 Sqn, Aldergrove
	ZB678	Westland Gazelle AH1	AAC store, Wroughton
	ZB679	Westland Gazelle AH1	AAC, RNAY Fleetlands
	ZB680	Westland Gazelle AH1	AAC No 29 Flt, Suffield, Canada
	ZB681	Westland Gazelle AH1	AAC No 655 Sqn, Aldergrove
	ZB682	Westland Gazelle AH1	AAC store, Wroughton
	ZB683	Westland Gazelle AH1	AAC store, Wroughton

Serial	Type (alternative identity)	Owner, Operator or Location	Notes
ZB684	Westland Gazelle AH1	MoD(PE) for AAC	
ZB685	Westland Gazelle AH1	MoD(PE) for AAC	
ZB686	Westland Gazelle AH1	MoD(PE) for AAC	
ZB687	Westland Gazelle AH1	MoD(PE) for AAC	
ZB688	Westland Gazelle AH1	MoD(PE) for AAC	
ZB689	Westland Gazelle AH1	MoD(PE) for AAC	
ZB690	Westland Gazelle AH1	MoD(PE) for AAC	
ZB691	Westland Gazelle AH1	MoD(PE) for AAC	
ZB692	Westland Gazelle AH1	MoD(PE) for AAC	
ZB693	Westland Gazelle AH1	MoD(PE) for AAC	
ZD230	BAC Super VC10 (G-ASGA)	RAF Abingdon, store	
ZD231	BAC Super VC10 (G-ASGB)	RAF Abingdon, store	
ZD232	BAC Super VC10 (G-ASGD) (8699M)	RAF Brize Norton, JATE	
ZD233	BAC Super VC10 (G-ASGE)	RAF Brize Norton	
ZD234	BAC Super VC10 (G-ASGF) (8700M)	RAF Brize Norton	
ZD235	BAC Super VC10 (G-ASGG)	RAF Abingdon, store	
ZD236	BAC Super VC10 (G-ASGH)	RAF Abingdon, store	
ZD237	BAC Super VC10 (G-ASGI)	RAF Abingdon, store	
ZD238	BAC Super VC10 (G-ASGJ)	RAF Abingdon, store	
ZD239	BAC Super VC10 (G-ASGK)	RAF Abingdon, store	
ZD240	BAC Super VC10 (G-ASGL)	RAF Abingdon, store	
ZD241	BAC Super VC10 (G-ASGM)	RAF Abingdon, store	
ZD242	BAC Super VC10 (G-ASGP)	RAF Abingdon, store	
ZD243	BAC Super VC10 (G-ASGR)	RAF Abingdon, store	
ZD249	Westland Lynx HAS3	MoD(PE) A&AEE Boscombe Down	
ZD250	Westland Lynx HAS3 [630/PO]	RN No 702 Sqn, Portland	
ZD251	Westland Lynx HAS3 [631/PO]	RN No 702 Sqn, Portland	
ZD252	Westland Lynx HAS3 [303]	RN No 815 Sqn, Portland	
ZD253	Westland Lynx HAS3 [304/PO]	RN No 815 Sqn, Portland	
ZD254	Westland Lynx HAS3 [632/PO]	RN No 702 Sqn, Portland	
ZD255	Westland Lynx HAS3 [479]	RN No 815 Sqn, Portland	
ZD256	Westland Lynx HAS3	RN NASU, Yeovilton	
ZD257	Westland Lynx HAS3 [346/PO]	RN No 815 Sqn, Portland	
ZD258	Westland Lynx HAS3	RN No 815 Sqn, Gibraltar	
ZD259	Westland Lynx HAS3 [333/BM]	RN No 815 Sqn, Portland	
ZD260	Westland Lynx HAS3	RN NATIU, Lee-on-Solent	
ZD261	Westland Lynx HAS3	RN store, Wroughton	
ZD262	Westland Lynx HAS3	RN store, Wroughton	
ZD263	Westland Lynx HAS3	RN store, Wroughton	
ZD264	Westland Lynx HAS3	RN store, Wroughton	
ZD265	Westland Lynx HAS3	RN NASU, Yeovilton	
ZD266	Westland Lynx HAS3	RN NASU, Yeovilton	
ZD267	Westland Lynx HAS3	MoD(PE) Westlands, Yeovil	
ZD268	Westland Lynx HAS3	RN NASU, Yeovilton	
ZD272	Westland Lynx AH1	AAC No 656 Sqn, Netheravon	
ZD273	Westland Lynx AH1	AAC No 656 Sqn, Netheravon	
ZD274	Westland Lynx AH1	AAC No 656 Sqn, Netheravon	
ZD275	Westland Lynx AH1	AAC No 657 Sqn, Oakington	
ZD276	Westland Lynx AH1	AAC No 652 Sqn, Hildesheim	
ZD277	Westland Lynx AH1	AAC store, Wroughton	
ZD278	Westland Lynx AH1	AAC store, Wroughton	
ZD279	Westland Lynx AH1	AAC store, Wroughton	
ZD280	Westland Lynx AH1	AAC store, Wroughton	
ZD281	Westland Lynx AH1	AAC No 657 Sqn, Oakington	
ZD282	Westland Lynx AH1	AAC Westlands, Yeovil	
ZD283	Westland Lynx AH1 [M]	AAC LCF, Middle Wallop	
ZD284	Westland Lynx AH1	AAC store, Wroughton	
ZD285	Westland Lynx AH5	MoD(PE) RAE Bedford	
ZD318	BAe Harrier GR5	MoD(PE) for RAF	
ZD319	BAe Harrier GR5	MoD(PE) for RAF	
ZD320	BAe Harrier GR5	MoD(PE) for RAF	
ZD476	Westland Sea King HC4 [ZA]	RN No 707 Sqn, Yeovilton	
ZD477	Westland Sea King HC4 [VC]	RN No 846 Sqn, Yeovilton	

Notes	Serial	Type (alternative identity)	Owner, Operator or Location
	ZD478	Westland Sea King HC4 [VE]	RN No 846 Sqn, Yeovilton
	ZD479	Westland Sea King HC4 [ZE]	RN No 707 Sqn, Yeovilton
	ZD480	Westland Sea King HC4 [VG]	RN No 846 Sqn, Yeovilton
	ZD485	FMA IA58 Pucara (A-515)	RAF Cosford Aerospace Museum
	ZD493	BAC VC10 (G-ARVJ)	RAF Brize Norton
	ZD565	Westland Lynx HAS3	MoD(PE) for RN
	ZD566	Westland Lynx HAS3	MoD(PE) for RN
	ZD567	Westland Lynx HAS3	MoD(PE) for RN
	ZD574	B-V Chinook HC1 [EW]	RAF No 7 Sqn, Odiham
	ZD575	B-V Chinook HC1	RAF Odiham
	ZD576	B-V Chinook HC1	RAF Odiham
	ZD578	BAe Sea Harrier FRS1	MoD(PE) for RN
	ZD579	BAe Sea Harrier FRS1	MoD(PE) for RN
	ZD580	BAe Sea Harrier FRS1	MoD(PE) for RN
	ZD581	BAe Sea Harrier FRS1	MoD(PE) for RN
	ZD582	BAe Sea Harrier FRS1	MoD(PE) for RN
	ZD607	BAe Sea Harrier FRS1	MoD(PE) for RN
	ZD608	BAe Sea Harrier FRS1	MoD(PE) for RN
	ZD609	BAe Sea Harrier FRS1	MoD(PE) for RN
	ZD610	BAe Sea Harrier FRS1	MoD(PE) for RN
	ZD611	BAe Sea Harrier FRS1	MoD(PE) for RN
	ZD612	BAe Sea Harrier FRS1	MoD(PE) for RN
	ZD613	BAe Sea Harrier FRS1	MoD(PE) for RN
	ZD614	BAe Sea Harrier FRS1	MoD(PE) for RN
	ZD615	BAe Sea Harrier FRS1	MoD(PE) for RN
	ZD620	BAe 125 CC3	RAF No 32 Sqn, Northolt
	ZD621	BAe 125 CC3	RAF No 32 Sqn, Northolt
	ZD625	Westland Sea King HC4 [ZF]	RN No 707 Sqn, Yeovilton
	ZD626	Westland Sea King HC4	RN NASU, Culdrose
	ZD627	Westland Sea King HC4	RN NASU, Culdrose
	ZD630	Westland Sea King HAS5 [013]	RN No 820 Sqn, Culdrose
	ZD631	Westland Sea King HAS5 [590]	RN No 706 Sqn, Culdrose
	ZD632	Westland Sea King HAS5 [591]	RN No 706 Sqn, Culdrose
	ZD633	Westland Sea King HAS5	RN NASU, Culdrose
	ZD634	Westland Sea King HAS5	RN NASU, Culdrose
	ZD635	Westland Sea King HAS5	RN NASU, Culdrose
	ZD636	Westland Sea King HAS5	RN NASU, Culdrose
	ZD637	Westland Sea King HAS5	RN NASU, Culdrose
	ZD643	Schleicher Vanguard TX1 (BGA2884)	RAF No 618 VGS, West Malling
	ZD644	Schleicher Vanguard TX1 (BGA2883)	RAF No 618 Sqn, West Malling
	ZD645	Schleicher Vanguard TX1 (BGA2885)	RAF No 618 Sqn, West Malling
	ZD646	Schleicher Vanguard TX1 (BGA2886)	RAF No 618 VGS, West Malling
	ZD647	Schleicher Vanguard TX1 (BGA2887)	RAF No 618 VGS, West Malling
	ZD648	Schleicher Vanguard TX1 (BGA2888)	RAF No 618 VGS, West Malling
	ZD649	Schleicher Vanguard TX1 (BGA2889)	RAF ACCGS, Syerston
	ZD650	Schleicher Vanguard TX1 (BGA2890)	RAF No 618 VGS, West Malling
	ZD651	Schleicher Vanguard TX1 (BGA2891)	RAF ACCGS, Syerston
	ZD652	Schleicher Vanguard TX1 (BGA2892)	RAF No 618 VGS, West Malling
	ZD657	Schleicher Valiant TX1 (BGA2893)	RAF ACCGS, Syerston
	ZD658	Schleicher Valiant TX1 (BGA2894)	RAF ACCGS, Syerston
	ZD659	Schleicher Valiant TX1 (BGA2895)	RAF No 618 VGS, West Malling
	ZD660	Schleicher Valiant TX1 (BGA2896)	RAF No 645 VGS, Catterick
	ZD661	Schleicher Valiant TX1 (BGA2897)	RAF ACCGS, Syerston
	ZD667	BAe Harrier GR3	MoD(PE) for RAF
	ZD668	BAe Harrier GR3	MoD(PE) for RAF

Serial	Type (alternative identity)	Owner, Operator or Location	Notes
ZD669	BAe Harrier GR3	MoD(PE) for RAF	
ZD670	BAe Harrier GR3	MoD(PE) for RAF	
ZD671	BAe Harrier T4	MoD(PE) for RAF	
ZD672	BAe Harrier T4	MoD(PE) for RAF	
ZD673	BAe Harrier T4	MoD(PE) for RAF	
ZD674	BAe Harrier T4	MoD(PE) for RAF	
ZD703	BAe 125 CC3	RAF No 32 Sqn, Northolt	
ZD704	BAe 125 CC3	RAF No 32 Sqn, Northolt	
ZD707	Panavia Tornado GR1 [DB]	RAF No 31 Sqn, Bruggen	
ZD708	Panavia Tornado GR1	RAF No Sqn,	
ZD709	Panavia Tornado GR1 [GJ]	RAF No 20 Sqn, Laarbruch	
ZD710	Panavia Tornado GR1 [DC]	RAF No 31 Sqn, Bruggen	
ZD711	Panavia Tornado GR1T [DY]	RAF No 31 Sqn, Bruggen	
ZD712	Panavia Tornado GR1T [DZ]	RAF No 31 Sqn, Bruggen	
ZD713	Panavia Tornado GR1T	RAF No Sqn,	
ZD714	Panavia Tornado GR1	RAF No Sqn,	
ZD715	Panavia Tornado GR1T [GF]	RAF No 20 Sqn, Laarbruch	
ZD716	Panavia Tornado GR1	RAF No Sqn,	
ZD717	Panavia Tornado GR1	RAF No Sqn,	
ZD718	Panavia Tornado GR1 [GE]	RAF No 20 Sqn, Laarbruch	
ZD719	Panavia Tornado GR1 [DD]	RAF No 31 Sqn, Bruggen	
ZD720	Panavia Tornado GR1 [DF]	RAF No 31 Sqn, Bruggen	
ZD738	Panavia Tornado GR1	MoD(PE) RAE Bedford	
ZD739	Panavia Tornado GR1 [DE]	RAF No 31 Sqn, Bruggen	
ZD740	Panavia Tornado GR1 [DA]	RAF No 31 Sqn, Bruggen	
ZD741	Panavia Tornado GR1T [GT]	RAF No 20 Sqn, Laarbruch	
ZD742	Panavia Tornado GR1T [CY]	RAF No 17 Sqn, Bruggen	
ZD743	Panavia Tornado GR1T [CZ]	RAF No 17 Sqn, Bruggen	
ZD744	Panavia Tornado GR1	RAF No Sqn,	
ZD745	Panavia Tornado GR1 [DH]	RAF No 31 Sqn, Bruggen	
ZD746	Panavia Tornado GR1 [DJ]	RAF No 31 Sqn, Bruggen	
ZD747	Panavia Tornado GR1	RAF No 31 Sqn, Bruggen	
ZD748	Panavia Tornado GR1 [DG]	RAF No 31 Sqn, Bruggen	
ZD749	Panavia Tornado GR1	RAF No Sqn,	
ZD788	Panavia Tornado GR1	MoD(PE) for RAF	
ZD789	Panavia Tornado GR1	MoD(PE) for RAF	
ZD790	Panavia Tornado GR1	MoD(PE) for RAF	
ZD791	Panavia Tornado GR1	MoD(PE) for RAF	
ZD792	Panavia Tornado GR1	MoD(PE) for RAF	
ZD793	Panavia Tornado GR1	RAF No 17 Sqn, Bruggen	
ZD808	Panavia Tornado GR1	MoD(PE) for RAF	
ZD809	Panavia Tornado GR1	MoD(PE) for RAF	
ZD810	Panavia Tornado GR1	MoD(PE) for RAF	
ZD811	Panavia Tornado GR1	MoD(PE) for RAF	
ZD812	Panavia Tornado GR1T	MoD(PE) for RAF	
ZD842	Panavia Tornado GR1T	MoD(PE) for RAF	
ZD843	Panavia Tornado GR1	MoD(PE) for RAF	
ZD844	Panavia Tornado GR1	MoD(PE) for RAF	
ZD845	Panavia Tornado GR1	MoD(PE) for RAF	
ZD846	Panavia Tornado GR1	MoD(PE) for RAF	
ZD847	Panavia Tornado GR1	MoD(PE) for RAF	
ZD848	Panavia Tornado GR1	MoD(PE) for RAF	
ZD849	Panavia Tornado GR1	MoD(PE) for RAF	
ZD850	Panavia Tornado GR1	MoD(PE) for RAF	
ZD851	Panavia Tornado GR1	MoD(PE) for RAF	
ZD890	Panavia Tornado GR1	MoD(PE) for RAF	
ZD891	Panavia Tornado GR1	MoD(PE) for RAF	
ZD892	Panavia Tornado GR1	MoD(PE) for RAF	
ZD893	Panavia Tornado GR1	MoD(PE) for RAF	
ZD894	Panavia Tornado GR1	MoD(PE) for RAF	
ZD895	Panavia Tornado GR1	MoD(PE) for RAF	
ZD899	Panavia Tornado F2T	MoD(PE) A&AEE Boscombe Down	
ZD900	Panavia Tornado F2T	MoD(PE) A&AEE Boscombe Down	
ZD901	Panavia Tornado F2T [AA]	RAF No 229 OCU, Coningsby	
ZD902	Panavia Tornado F2T [AC]	RAF No 229 OCU, Coningsby	
ZD903	Panavia Tornado F2T [AB]	RAF No 229 OCU, Coningsby	
ZD904	Panavia Tornado F2T [AD]	RAF No 229 OCU, Coningsby	
ZD905	Panavia Tornado F2	MoD(PE) for RAF	
ZD906	Panavia Tornado F2	MoD(PE) for RAF	
ZD932	Panavia Tornado F2	MoD(PE) for RAF	

Notes	Serial	Type (alternative identity)	Owner, Operator or Location
	ZD933	Panavia Tornado F2	MoD(PE) for RAF
	ZD934	Panavia Tornado F2T	MoD(PE) for RAF
	ZD935	Panavia Tornado F2T	MoD(PE) for RAF
	ZD936	Panavia Tornado F2	MoD(PE) for RAF
	ZD937	Panavia Tornado F2	MoD(PE) for RAF
	ZD938	Panavia Tornado F2	MoD(PE) for RAF
	ZD939	Panavia Tornado F2	MoD(PE) for RAF
	ZD940	Panavia Tornado F2	MoD(PE) for RAF
	ZD941	Panavia Tornado F2	MoD(PE) for RAF
	ZD948	Lockheed TriStar C1 (G-BFCA)	RAF No 216 Sqn, Brize Norton
	ZD949	Lockheed TriStar C1 (G-BFCB)	RAF No 216 Sqn, Brize Norton
	ZD950	Lockheed TriStar C1 (G-BFCC)	RAF No 216 Sqn, Brize Norton
	ZD951	Lockheed TriStar C1 (G-BFCD)	RAF No 216 Sqn, Brize Norton
	ZD952	Lockheed TriStar C1 (G-BFCE)	RAF No 216 Sqn, Brize Norton
	ZD953	Lockheed TriStar C1 (G-BFCF)	RAF No 216 Sqn, Brize Norton
	ZD974	Schleicher Janus C (BGA2875)	RAF ACCGS, Syerston
	ZD975	Schleicher Janus C (BGA2876)	RAF ACCGS, Syerston
	ZE350	McD Phantom F3 [T]	RAF No 74 Sqn, Wattisham
	ZE351	McD Phantom F3 [I]	RAF No 74 Sqn, Wattisham
	ZE352	McD Phantom F3 [G]	RAF No 74 Sqn, Wattisham
	ZE353	McD Phantom F3 [E]	RAF No 74 Sqn, Wattisham
	ZE354	McD Phantom F3 [R]	RAF No 74 Sqn, Wattisham
	ZE355	McD Phantom F3 [S]	RAF No 74 Sqn, Wattisham
	ZE356	McD Phantom F3 [Q]	RAF No 74 Sqn, Wattisham
	ZE357	McD Phantom F3 [N]	RAF No 74 Sqn, Wattisham
	ZE358	McD Phantom F3	RAF No 74 Sqn, Wattisham
	ZE359	McD Phantom F3 [J]	RAF No 74 Sqn, Wattisham
	ZE360	McD Phantom F3	RAF No 74 Sqn, Wattisham
	ZE361	McD Phantom F3 [P]	RAF No 74 Sqn, Wattisham
	ZE362	McD Phantom F3 [V]	RAF No 74 Sqn, Wattisham
	ZE363	McD Phantom F3	RAF No 74 Sqn, Wattisham
	ZE364	McD Phantom F3 [Z]	RAF No 74 Sqn, Wattisham
	ZE368	Westland Sea King HAR3	MoD(PE) for RAF
	ZE369	Westland Sea King HAR3	MoD(PE) for RAF
	ZE370	Westland Sea King HAR3	MoD(PE) for RAF
	ZE375	Westland Lynx AH5	MoD(PE) for AAC
	ZE376	Westland Lynx AH5	MoD(PE) for AAC
	ZE377	Westland Lynx AH5	MoD(PE) for AAC
	ZE378	Westland Lynx AH5	MoD(PE) for AAC
	ZE379	Westland Lynx AH5	MoD(PE) for AAC
	ZE380	Westland Lynx AH5	MoD(PE) for AAC
	ZE381	Westland Lynx AH5	MoD(PE) for AAC
	ZE382	Westland Lynx AH5	MoD(PE) for AAC
	ZE383	Westland Lynx AH5	MoD(PE) for AAC
	ZE395	BAe 125 CC3	RAF No 32 Sqn, Northolt
	ZE396	BAe 125 CC3	RAF No 32 Sqn, Northolt
	ZE410	Agusta A109A (AE-334)	AAC No 658 Sqn, Netheravon
	ZE411	Agusta A109A (AE-331)	AAC No 658 Sqn, Netheravon
	ZE412	Agusta A109A	AAC No 658 Sqn, Netheravon
	ZE413	Agusta A109A	AAC No 658 Sqn, Netheravon
	ZE432	BAC 1-11/479 (DQ-FBV)	MoD(PE) A&AEE/ETPS Boscombe Down
	ZE433	BAC 1-11/479 (DQ-FBQ)	MoD(PE) RAE Bedford
	ZE438	BAe Jetstream T3	RN No 750 Sqn, Culdrose
	ZE439	BAe Jetstream T3	RN No 750 Sqn, Culdrose
	ZE440	BAe Jetstream T3	RN No 750 Sqn, Culdrose
	ZE441	BAe Jetstream T3	RN No 750 Sqn, Culdrose
	ZE477	Westland Lynx 3	Westlands, Yeovil
	ZE495	Grob Viking TX1 (BGA3000)	RAF No 631 VGS, Sealand
	ZE496	Grob Viking TX1 (BGA3001)	RAF No 631 VGS, Sealand
	ZE497	Grob Viking TX1 (BGA3002)	RAF No 622 VGS, Upavon
	ZE498	Grob Viking TX1 (BGA3003)	RAF ACCGS, Syerston
	ZE499	Grob Viking TX1 (BGA3004)	RAF No 631 VGS, Sealand
	ZE500	Grob Viking TX1 (BGA3005)	RAF ACCGS, Syerston
	ZE501	Grob Viking TX1 (BGA3006)	RAF No 645 VGS, Catterick
	ZE502	Grob Viking TX1 (BGA3007)	RAF No 645 VGS, Catterick
	ZE503	Grob Viking TX1 (BGA3008)	RAF ACCGS, Syerston
	ZE504	Grob Viking TX1 (BGA3009)	RAF No 645 VGS, Catterick
	ZE520	Grob Viking TX1 (BGA3010)	RAF No 645 VGS, Catterick
	ZE521	Grob Viking TX1 (BGA3011)	RAF
	ZE522	Grob Viking TX1 (BGA3012)	RAF

Serial	Type (alternative identity)	Owner, Operator or Location	Notes
ZE523	Grob Viking TX1 (BGA3013)	RAF	
ZE524	Grob Viking TX1 (BGA3014)	RAF	
ZE525	Grob Viking TX1 (BGA3015)	RAF	
ZE526	Grob Viking TX1 (BGA3016)	RAF	
ZE527	Grob Viking TX1 (BGA3017)	RAF	
ZE528	Grob Viking TX1 (BGA3018)	RAF	
ZE529	Grob Viking TX1 (BGA3019)	RAF No 631 VGS, Sealand	
ZE530	Grob Viking TX1 (BGA3020)	RAF ACCGS, Syerston	
ZE531	Grob Viking TX1 (BGA3021)	RAF No 645 VGS, Catterick	
ZE532	Grob Viking TX1 (BGA3022)	RAF ACCGS, Syerston	
ZE533	Grob Viking TX1 (BGA3023)	RAF	
ZE534	Grob Viking TX1 (BGA3024)	RAF	
ZE650	Grob Viking TX1 (BGA3025)	RAF	
ZE551	Grob Viking TX1 (BGA3026)	RAF	
ZE552	Grob Viking TX1 (BGA3027)	RAF	
ZE553	Grob Viking TX1 (BGA3028)	RAF	
ZE554	Grob Viking TX1 (BGA3029)	RAF	
ZE555	Grob Viking TX1 (BGA3030)	RAF	
ZE556	Grob Viking TX1 (BGA3031)	RAF	
ZE557	Grob Viking TX1 (BGA3032)	RAF	
ZE558	Grob Viking TX1 (BGA3033)	RAF	
ZE559	Grob Viking TX1 (BGA3034)	RAF	
ZE660	Grob Viking TX1 (BGA3035)	RAF	
ZE561	Grob Viking TX1 (BGA3036)	RAF	
ZE562	Grob Viking TX1 (BGA3037)	RAF	
ZE563	Grob Viking TX1 (BGA3038)	RAF	
ZE564	Grob Viking TX1 (BGA3039)	RAF	
ZE584	Grob Viking TX1 (BGA3040)	RAF	
ZE585	Grob Viking TX1 (BGA3041)	RAF	
ZE586	Grob Viking TX1 (BGA3042)	RAF	
ZE587	Grob Viking TX1 (BGA3043)	RAF	
ZE588	Grob Viking TX1 (BGA3044)	RAF	
ZE589	Grob Viking TX1 (BGA3045)	RAF	
ZE590	Grob Viking TX1 (BGA3046)	RAF	
ZE591	Grob Viking TX1 (BGA3047)	RAF	
ZE592	Grob Viking TX1 (BGA3048)	RAF	
ZE593	Grob Viking TX1 (BGA3049)	RAF	
ZE594	Grob Viking TX1 (BGA3050)	RAF	
ZE595	Grob Viking TX1 (BGA3051)	RAF	
ZE600	Grob Viking TX1 (BGA3052)	RAF	
ZE601	Grob Viking TX1 (BGA3053)	RAF	
ZE602	Grob Viking TX1 (BGA3054)	RAF	
ZE603	Grob Viking TX1 (BGA3055)	RAF	
ZE604	Grob Viking TX1 (BGA3056)	RAF	
ZE605	Grob Viking TX1 (BGA3057)	RAF	
ZE606	Grob Viking TX1 (BGA3058)	RAF	
ZE607	Grob Viking TX1 (BGA3059)	RAF	
ZE608	Grob Viking TX1 (BGA3060)	RAF	
ZE609	Grob Viking TX1 (BGA3061)	RAF	
ZE610	Grob Viking TX1 (BGA3062)	RAF	
ZE611	Grob Viking TX1 (BGA3063)	RAF	
ZE612	Grob Viking TX1 (BGA3064)	RAF	
ZE613	Grob Viking TX1 (BGA3065)	RAF	
ZE614	Grob Viking TX1 (BGA3066)	RAF	
ZE625	Grob Viking TX1 (BGA3067)	RAF	
ZE626	Grob Viking TX1 (BGA3068)	RAF	
ZE627	Grob Viking TX1 (BGA3069)	RAF	
ZE628	Grob Viking TX1 (BGA3070)	RAF	
ZE629	Grob Viking TX1 (BGA3071)	RAF	
ZE630	Grob Viking TX1 (BGA3072)	RAF	
ZE631	Grob Viking TX1 (BGA3073)	RAF	
ZE632	Grob Viking TX1 (BGA3074)	RAF	
ZE633	Grob Viking TX1 (BGA3075)	RAF	
ZE634	Grob Viking TX1 (BGA3076)	RAF	
ZE635	Grob Viking TX1 (BGA3077)	RAF	
ZE636	Grob Viking TX1 (BGA3078)	RAF	
ZE637	Grob Viking TX1 (BGA3079)	RAF	
ZE650	Grob Viking TX1 (BGA3080)	RAF	
ZE651	Grob Viking TX1 (BGA3081)	RAF	
ZE652	Grob Viking TX1 (BGA3082)	RAF	

Notes	Serial	Type (alternative identity)	Owner, Operator or Location
	ZE653	Grob Viking TX1 (BGA3083)	RAF
	ZE654	Grob Viking TX1 (BGA3084)	RAF
	ZE655	Grob Viking TX1 (BGA3085)	RAF
	ZE656	Grob Viking TX1 (BGA3086)	RAF
	ZE657	Grob Viking TX1 (BGA3087)	RAF
	ZE658	Grob Viking TX1 (BGA3088)	RAF
	ZE659	Grob Viking TX1 (BGA3089)	RAF
	ZE677	Grob Viking TX1 (BGA3090)	RAF
	ZE678	Grob Viking TX1 (BGA3091)	RAF
	ZE679	Grob Viking TX1 (BGA3092)	RAF
	ZE680	Grob Viking TX1 (BGA3093)	RAF
	ZE681	Grob Viking TX1 (BGA3094)	RAF
	ZE682	Grob Viking TX1 (BGA3095)	RAF
	ZE683	Grob Viking TX1 (BGA3096)	RAF
	ZE684	Grob Viking TX1 (BGA3097)	RAF
	ZE685	Grob Viking TX1 (BGA3098)	RAF
	ZE686	Grob Viking TX1 (BGA3099)	RAF
	ZE704	Lockheed TriStar (N508PA)	RAF No 216 Sqn, Brize Norton
	ZE705	Lockheed TriStar (N509PA)	RAF No 216 Sqn, Brize Norton

ZA111 BAe Jetstream T2; RN No 750 Sqn, Culdrose. *APM*

ZE477 Westland Lynx 3; Westland Helicopters, Yeovil. *PRM*

Deletions

The following serials of British aircraft which were shown in the fifth edition of *Military Aircraft Markings* have been deleted from the 1985 edition. The reason for the deletion has been given wherever possible.

Serial	Type (alternative identity)	Owner, Operator or Location	Notes
N5903	Gloster Gladiator II	Re-serialled N2276	
P3308	Hawker Hurricane IIB	To Canada as C-GCWH	
R7524	Percival Proctor 1	Written off France 9 June 1984	
LA607	Hawker Tempest II	To USA as N607LA	
MC280	NA Harvard IIB	Re-serialled EX280	
RS709	DH Mosquito B35	Returned to US owners	
WJ728	EE Canberra B2	Broken up March 1984	
WJ897	Vickers Varsity TX1	Written off 19 August 1984	
XA456	Fairey Gannet AS4	Burnt at Predannack	
XA903	Avro Vulcan B1	Scrapped September 1984	
XA923	HP Victor B1	Scrapped September 1984	
XA939	HP Victor B(K)1A	Burnt at Catterick	
XE390	Hawker Sea Hawk FGA6	To Canada	
XF416	Hawker Hunter FGA9	To Zimbabwe AF	
XF511	Hawker Hunter FGA9	To Zimbabwe AF	
XF519	Hawker Hunter FGA9	To Zimbabwe AF	
XG155	Hawker Hunter FGA9	To Zimbabwe AF	
XG207	Hawker Hunter FGA9	To Zimbabwe AF	
XH166	EE Canberra PR9	To Chilean AF as 341	
XH167	EE Canberra PR9	To Chilean AF as 342	
XH588	HP Victor K1A	Burnt October 1983	
XJ724	WS55 Whirlwind HAR10	Burnt Catterick	
XK862	Percival Pembroke C1	Burnt St Athan	
XK896	DH Sea Devon C20	Written off	
XK940	WS55 Whirlwind HAS7	Registration G-AYXT carried	
XM453	Hunting Jet Provost T3A	Written off 21 November 1983	
XN473	Hunting Jet Provost T3A	Written off 15 August 1984	
XN657	DH Sea Vixen D3	Scrapped Llanbedr	
XN658	DH Sea Vixen FAW2	Scrapped Farnborough	
XN697	DH Sea Vixen FAW2	Scrapped Hurn	
XR761	EE Lightning F6	Written off 7 November 1984	
XS416	EE Lightning T5	Written off 19 July 1984	
XS920	EE Lightning F6	Written off 13 July 1984	
XT435	Westland Wasp HAS1	To RNZN as NZ3907	
XT459	Westland Wessex HU5	Written off 7 December 1983	
XT781	Westland Wasp HAS1	To RNZN as NZ3908	
XT794	Westland Wasp HAS1	Written off 13 April 1984	
XV354	HS Buccaneer S2A	Broken up	
XV622	Westland Wasp HAS1	To RNZN	
XX180	HS Hawk T1	Written off 7 November 1984	
XX251	HS Hawk T1	Written off 21 March 1984	
XX257	HS Hawk T1	Written off 31 August 1984	
XX298	HS Hawk T1	Written off 29 October 1984	
XX367	Bristol Britannia	To 9Q-CHY	
XX750	SEPECAT Jaguar GR1	Written off 7 February 1984	
XX915	SEPECAT Jaguar T2	Written off 17 January 1984	
XZ135	HS Harrier GR3	Written off 3 June 1984	
XZ393	SEPECAT Jaguar GR1A	Written off 12 July 1984	
XZ395	SEPECAT Jaguar GR1	Written off 22 August 1984	
XZ430	HS Buccaneer S2B	Written off 20 May 1984	
XZ496	BAe Sea Harrier FRS1	Written off 16 March 1984	
ZA408	Panavia Tornado GR1	Written off 12 July 1984	
ZA451	Panavia Tornado GR1	Written off 6 February 1984	
ZA494	Panavia Tornado GR1	Written off 18 July 1984	
ZA603	Panavia Tornado GR1	Written off 8 November 1984	
ZD696	BAe 146 C1	To Dan Air as G-SCHH	

1746M/K4972	7532M/WT651	7817M/TX214	7969M/WS840	8085M/XM467
4354M/BL614	7533M/WT680	7822M/XP248	7971M/XK699	8087M/XN925
5377M/EP120	7543M/WN901	7825M/WK991	7972M/XH764	8088M/XN602
5405M/LF738	7544M/WN904	7827M/XA917	7973M/WS807	8090M/XM698
5466M/LF751	7564M/XE982	7829M/XH992	7976M/XK418	8092M/WK654
5690M/MK356	7570M/XD674	7839M/WV781	7979M/XM529	8101M/WH984
5713M/BM597	7582M/WP190	7840M/XK482	7980M/XM561	8102M/WT486
5758M/DG202	7583M/WP185	7841M/WV783	7982M/XH892	8103M/WR985
6372M/EE549	7602M/WE600	7847M/WV276	7983M/XD506	8106M/WR982
6490M/LA255	7604M/XD542	7849M/XF319	7986M/WG777	8108M/WV703
6709M/TE356	7605M/WS692	7850M/XA923	7990M/XD452	8113M/WV753
6850M/TE184	7606M/WV562	7851M/WZ706	7997M/XG452	8114M/WL798
6944M/RW386	7607M/TJ138	7852M/XG506	7998M/XD515	8117M/WR974
6947M/RW388	7615M/WV679	7855M/XK416	8005M/WG768	8118M/WZ549
6948M/DE673	7616M/WW388	7859M/XP283	8007M/XH837	8119M/WR971
6960M/MT847	7618M/WW442	7860M/XL738	8009M/XG518	8120M/WR981
7000M/TE392	7621M/WV686	7862M/XR246	8010M/XG547	8121M/XM474
7001M/TE356	7622M/WV606	7863M/WZ679	8011M/XV269	8122M/XD613
7008M/EE549	7625M/WD356	7864M/XP244	8012M/VS562	8128M/WH775
7014M/N6720	7630M/VZ304	7865M/TX226	8017M/XL762	8129M/WH779
7015M/NL985	7641M/XA634	7866M/XH278	8018M/XN344	8138M/XN700
7060M/VF301	7645M/WD293	7867M/XH980	8019M/WZ869	8139M/XJ582
7090M/EE531	7646M/VX461	7868M/WZ736	8021M/XL824	8140M/XJ571
7118M/LA198	7648M/XF785	7869M/WK935	8022M/XN341	8141M/XN688
7119M/LA226	7656M/WJ573	7870M/XM556	8023M/XD463	8142M/XJ560
7150M/PK683	7663M/XA571	7878M/WD601	8025M/XH124	8143M/XN691
7151M/VT229	7688M/WW421	7881M/WD413	8027M/XM555	8144M/XN707
7154M/WB188	7693M/WV483	7883M/XT150	8033M/XD382	8145M/XJ526
7174M/VX272	7696M/WV493	7887M/XD375	8034M/XL703	8147M/XR526
7175M/VV106	7697M/WV495	7890M/XD453	8040M/XR493	8151M/WV795
7200M/VT812	7698M/WV499	7891M/XM693	8041M/XF690	8153M/WV903
7241M/TE311	7700M/WV544	7894M/XD818	8043M/XF836	8154M/WV908
7243M/TE462	7704M/TW936	7895M/WF784	8044M/XP286	8155M/WV797
7244M/TB382	7705M/WL505	7896M/XA900	8046M/XL770	8156M/XE339
7245M/RW382	7706M/WB584	7898M/XP854	8049M/WE168	8157M/XE390
7246M/TD248	7709M/WT933	7899M/XG540	8050M/XG329	8158M/XE369
7256M/TB752	7711M/PS915	7900M/WA576	8052M/WH166	8159M/XD528
7257M/TB252	7712M/WK281	7902M/WZ550	8053M/WK968	8160M/XD622
7288M/PK724	7715M/XK724	7906M/WH132	8054AM/XM410	8162M/WM913
7293M/RW393	7716M/WS776	7917M/WA591	8054BM/XM417	8163M/XP919
7323M/VV217	7717M/XA549	7920M/WL360	8055AM/XM402	8164M/WF299
7325M/R5868	7718M/WA577	7923M/XT133	8055BM/XM404	8169M/WH364
7362M/475081	7719M/WK277	7928M/XE849	8056M/XG337	8171M/XJ607
7416M/WN907	7729M/WB758	7930M/WH301	8057M/XR243	8172M/XJ609
7421M/WT660	7734M/XD536	7931M/RD253	8060M/WW397	8173M/XN685
7422M/WT684	7735M/XP812	7932M/WZ744	8062M/XR669	8174M/WZ576
7428M/WK198	7737M/XD602	7933M/XR220	8063M/WT536	8175M/XE950
7432M/WZ724	7739M/XA801	7937M/WS843	8070M/EP120	8177M/WM224
7443M/WX853	7750M/WL168	7938M/XH903	8071M/TE476	8179M/XN928
7451M/TE476	7755M/WG760	7939M/XD596	8072M/PK624	8180M/XN930
7458M/WX905	7758M/PM651	7940M/XL764	8075M/RW382	8182M/XN953
7464M/XA564	7759M/PK664	7949M/XF974	8076M/XM386	8183M/XN962
7470M/XA553	7761M/XH318	7955M/XH767	8077M/XN594	8184M/WT520
7473M/XE946	7770M/WT746	7957M/XF545	8078M/XM351	8186M/WR977
7491M/WT569	7796M/WJ676	7959M/WS774	8079M/XN492	8187M/WH791
7496M/WT612	7805M/TW117	7960M/WS726	8080M/XM480	8188M/XG327
7499M/WT555	7806M/TA639	7961M/WS739	8081M/XM468	8189M/WD646
7510M/WT694	7809M/XA699	7964M/WS760	8082M/XM409	8190M/XJ918
7525M/WT619	7814M/XD511	7965M/WS792	8083M/XM367	8192M/XR658
7530M/WT648	7816M/WG763	7967M/WS788	8084M/XM369	8194M/XK862

8196M/XE920	8388M/XL993	8499M/XP357	8607M/XP538	8685M/XF516
8197M/WT346	8389M/VX573	8501M/XP640	8608M/XP540	8686M/XG158
8198M/WT339	8390M/SL542	8502M/XP686	8609M/XR953	8687M/XJ639
8203M/XD377	8391M/SL574	8503M/XS451	8610M/XL502	8689M/WK144
8205M/XN819	8392M/SL674	8506M/XR704	8611M/WF128	8691M/WT518
8206M/WG419	8394M/WG422	8507M/XS215	8612M/XD182	8692M/WL741
8207M/WD318	8395M/WF408	8508M/XS218	8613M/XJ724	8693M/WH863
8208M/WG303	8396M/XK740	8509M/XT141	8614M/XP515	8694M/XH554
8209M/WG418	8398M/WR967	8510M/XP567	8615M/XP532	8695M/WJ817
8210M/WG471	8399M/WR539	8511M/WT305	8616M/XP541	8696M/WH773
8211M/WK570	8400M/XP583	8512M/VP973	8617M/XM709	8697M/WJ825
8212M/WK587	8401M/XP686	8514M/XS176	8618M/XP504	8699M/ZD232
8213M/WK626	8402M/XN769	8515M/WH869	8619M/XP511	8700M/ZD234
8215M/WP869	8403M/XK531	8516M/XR643	8620M/XP534	8701M/XP352
8216M/WP927	8405M/TG536	8517M/XA932	8621M/XR538	8702M/XG196
8217M/WZ866	8406M/XP831	8530M/WD948	8622M/XR980	8703M/VW453
8218M/WB645	8407M/XP585	8531M/XS418	8623M/XR998	8704M/XN643
8219M/XR455	8408M/XS186	8532M/XS423	8624M/XS102	8705M/XT281
8221M/XP409	8409M/XS209	8533M/XS449	8625M/XS105	8706M/XF383
8222M/XJ604	8410M/XR662	8534M/XS450	8626M/XS109	8707M/XF386
8224M/XN699	8411M/XM139	8535M/XS454	8627M/XP558	8708M/XF509
8225M/XN705	8412M/XM147	8538M/XN781	8628M/XJ380	8709M/XG209
8226M/XP921	8413M/XM192	8546M/XN728	8629M/WL801	8710M/XG274
8229M/XM355	8414M/XM173	8548M/WT507	8631M/XR574	8711M/XG290
8230M/XM362	8415M/XM181	8549M/WT534	8632M/XP533	8712M/XF439
8231M/XM375	8416M/XM183	8550M/XT595	8634M/WP314	8713M/XG225
8232M/XM381	8417M/XM144	8551M/XN774	8635M/XP514	8714M/XK149
8233M/XM408	8418M/XM178	8554M/TG511	8636M/XR540	8715M/XG264
8234M/XN458	8422M/XM169	8556M/XN855	8637M/XR991	8716M/XV155
8235M/XN534	8427M/XM172	8558M/XP439	8638M/XS101	8718M/XX396
8236M/XP573	8428M/XH593	8559M/XN467	8639M/XS107	8719M/XT257
8237M/XS179	8429M/XH592	8560M/XR569	8640M/XR977	8720M/XP353
8238M/XS180	8431M/XR661	8561M/XS100	8641M/XR987	8721M/XP354
8239M/XS210	8434M/XM411	8562M/XS110	8642M/XR537	8722M/WJ640
8340M/XP341	8435M/XN512	8564M/XN387	8643M/WJ867	8723M/XL567
8344M/WH960	8436M/XN554	8565M/E-408	8645M/XD163	8726M/XP299
8345M/XG540	8438M/XP761	8566M/XV279	8646M/XK969	8727M/XR486
8346M/XN734	8439M/WZ849	8567M/WL738	8647M/XP338	8728M/WT532
8350M/WH840	8440M/WD935	8568M/XP503	8648M/XK526	8729M/WJ815
8352M/XN632	8441M/XR107	8569M/XR535	8650M/XP333	8730M/XD186
8355M/KN645	8442M/XP411	8570M/XR954	8651M/XP532	8731M/XP361
KG374	8444M/XP400	8571M/XR984	8652M/WH794	8732M/XJ729
8357M/WK576	8445M/XK968	8572M/XM706	8653M/XS120	8733M/XL318
8359M/WF825	8446M/XP748	8573M/XM708	8654M/XL898	8734M/XM657
8360M/WP863	8447M/XP359	8575M/XP542	8655M/XN126	8735M/WJ681
8361M/WB670	8451M/WJ611	8576M/XP502	8656M/XP405	8736M/XF375
8362M/WG477	8452M/XK885	8577M/XP532	8657M/VZ634	8738M/XJ695
8363M/WG463	8453M/XP745	8578M/XR534	8659M/XV340	8739M/XH170
8364M/WG464	8454M/XP442	8579M/XR140	8660M/XW538	8740M/WE173
8365M/XK421	8455M/XP444	8580M/XP516	8661M/XJ727	8741M/XW329
8366M/XG454	8457M/XS871	8581M/WJ775	8662M/XR458	8742M/WH856
8367M/XG474	8458M/XP672	8582M/XE874	8664M/WJ603	8743M/WD790
8368M/XF926	8459M/XR650	8584M/WH903	8665M/WL754	8744M/XH563
8369M/WE139	8460M/XP680	8585M/XE670	8666M/XE793	8745M/XL392
8370M/N1671	8462M/XX477	8586M/XE643	8667M/XP972	8746M/XH171
8371M/XA847	8463M/XP355	8587M/XP677	8668M/WJ821	8747M/WJ629
8372M/K8042	8465M/W1048	8588M/XR681	8670M/XL384	8749M/XH537
8373M/P2617	8466M/L-866	8589M/XR700	8671M/XJ435	8750M/XL388
8375M/NX611	8467M/WP912	8590M/XM191	8672M/XP351	8751M/XT255
8376M/RF398	8473M/WP190	8591M/XA893	8673M/XD165	8752M/XR509
8377M/R9125	8488M/WL627	8592M/XM969	8674M/XP395	8753M/WL795
8378M/T9707	8489M/XN816	8595M/XH278	8676M/XL577	8754M/XG882
8379M/DG590	8490M/WH703	8598M/WP270	8677M/XJ695	8755M/WJ637
8380M/Z7197	8491M/WJ880	8600M/XX761	8678M/XE656	8756M/XL427
8382M/VR930	8492M/WJ872	8601M/XL450	8679M/XF526	8757M/XM656
8383M/K9942	8493M/XR571	8602M/XR541	8680M/XF527	8758M/XH562
8384M/X4590	8494M/XP557	8603M/XR951	8681M/XG164	8759M/XL321
8385M/N5912	8495M/XR672	8604M/XS104	8682M/XP404	8760M/XL386
8386M/NV778	8497M/XM698	8605M/XA536	8683M/WJ870	8761M/WJ977
8387M/T6296	8498M/XR670	8606M/XP530	8684M/XJ634	8762M/WH740

8763M/WH665	8778M/XM598	8800M/XG226	8815M/XX118	8829M/XE653
8764M/XP344	8779M/XM607	8801M/XS650	8816M/XX734	8830M/XF515
8766M/XJ782	8780M/WK102	8802M/XJ608	8817M/XN652	8831M/XG160
8767M/XX635	8781M/WE982	8803M/XJ572	8818M/XK527	8832M/XG172
8768M/A-522	8782M/XH136	8804M/XJ524	8819M/XS479	8833M/XL569
8769M/A-528	8783M/XW272	8805M/XT772	8820M/VP952	8834M/XL572
8770M/XL623	8784M/VP976	8806M/XP140	8821M/XX115	8835M/XL576
8771M/XM602	8785M/XS642	8807M/XL587	8822M/VP957	8836M/XL592
8772M/WR960	8786M/XN495	8808M/XP695	8823M/VP965	8837M/XL617
8773M/XV156	8795M/VP958	8809M/XH561	8824M/VP971	8838M/34037
8774M/XV338	8796M/XK943	8810M/XJ825	8825M/WB530	8839M/XG194
8775M/XV354	8797M/XX947	8811M/XL445	8826M/XV638	8840M/XG252
8776M/XV152	8798M/XG151	8813M/VT260	8827M/XX300	
8777M/XX914	8799M/WV787	8814M/XM927	8828M/XS587	

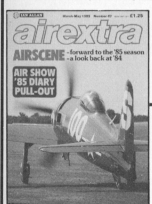

RN engineering 'A' airframe number cross-reference for serials listed in Military Aircraft Markings

A646/SX300	A2557/WV798	A2625/XL846	A2664/XV644	A2695/XS876
A680/DE373	A2571/XG577	A2626/XL847	A2665/XL839	A2696/XS882
A2001/W5984	A2572/XJ402	A2627/XN967	A2666/XS872	A2697/XS870
A2055/SX336	A2574/XD332	A2628/XP558	A2667/XP226	A2698/XP105
A2123/NL750	A2575/XG574	A2629/XM667	A2668/XS885	A2699/XS570
A2126/BB731	A2576/WV198	A2630/XL853	A2669/XP149	A2700/XP980
A2127/DE373	A2577/XB480	A2632/WV903	A2670/XS128	A2701/XL500
A2439/WF219	A2579/XN332	A2633/XE369	A2671/XS867	A2702/XS545
A2459/XA523	A2580/XE369	A2635/XE339	A2672/XS537	A2703/XT441
A2472/XA508	A2581/XK532	A2636/XE390	A2673/WF122	A2705/XS866
A2483/WF259	A2597/XS509	A2637/WV797	A2674/WF125	A2706/XS868
A2503/WM994	A2598/XJ482	A2639/XN650	A2675/XS881	A2707/XS122
A2509/WF299	A2600/XN934	A2642/XL836	A2676/XR572	A2708/XR540
A2510/WM913	A2602/XN925	A2643/XN311	A2677/XR993	A2709/XR991
A2511/WM983	A2603/XK911	A2645/WF225	A2678/XR955	A2710/
A2517/WM961	A2605/XN308	A2646/XK988	A2679/XP535	A2711/XM868
A2522/WM993	A2607/XK944	A2647/XS463	A2680/XP157	A2712/XN359
A2525/XN334	A2608/XA459	A2648/XS125	A2681/XP117	A2713/XN386
A2526/WV911	A2609/XM329	A2649/XS869	A2682/XM845	A2714/XL880
A2530/WM969	A2610/XN647	A2650/XP160	A2683/XS878	A2715
A2531/WG718	A2611/XJ575	A2651/XG596	A2684/XP151	A2716
A2532/WV826	A2613/XN706	A2652/XN261	A2685/XS886	A2717
A2534/XLJ68	A2614/XN314	A2653/XK913	A2686/XS873	A2718
A2538/XJ393	A2615/XT256	A2654/XN302	A2687/XS877	A2719
A2539/XG831	A2616/XN651	A2655/XN953	A2688/XP158	A2720
A2540/WN464	A2618/XP116	A2658/XP984	A2689/XM874	A2721
A2542/XA862	A2619/XS695	A2659/XV669	A2690/XS887	A2722/XT757
A2543/XA870	A2621/XJ584	A2660/WV908	A2691/XS868	A2723/XT487
A2550/XA866	A2622/XJ602	A2661/WV795	A2692/XM917	
A2551/XA868	A2623/XN697	A2662/WF299	A2693/XM843	
A2556/XE327	A2624/XN692	A2663/XN309	A2694/XS865	

RN Landing Platform and Shore Station Code-letters

Tail code	Name and Pennant Number	Type/task	Tail code	Name and Pennant Number	Type/task
AB	HMS Ambuscade (F172)	Type 21	HE	HMS Herald (A138)	Hecla
AC	HMS Achilles (F12)	Leander	HL	HMS Hecla (A133)	Hecla
AE	HMS Ariadne (F72)	Leander	HM	HMS Hermione (F58)	Leander
AG	HMS Avenger (F185)	Type 21	HT	HMS Hecate (A137)	Hecla
AJ	HMS Ajax (F114)	Leander	ID	HMS Intrepid (L11)	Assault
AL	HMS Alacrity (F174)	Type 21	JO	HMS Juno (F52)	Leander
AM	HMS Andromeda (F57)	Leander	JP	HMS Jupiter (F60)	Leander
AN	HMS Antrim (D18)	County	L	HMS Illustrious (R06)	Carrier
AP	HMS Apollo (F70)	Leander	LC	HMS Leeds Castle (P258)	Fishery protection
AR	HMS Arethusa (F38)	Leander			
AT	HMS Argonaut (F56)	Leander	LD	HMS Londonderry (F108)	Type 12
AU	HMS Aurora (F10)	Leander	LE	HMS Leander (F109)	Leander
AV	HMS Active (F171)	Type 21	LN	RFA Sir Lancelot (L3029)	Landing ship
AW	HMS Arrow (F173)	Type 21	LP	HMS Liverpool (D92)	Type 42
AZ	HMS Amazon (F169)	Type 21	LS	RNAS Lee-on-Solent (HMS Daedalus)	
BA	HMS Beaver (F93)	Type 22			
BD	RFA Sir Bedivere (L3004)	Landing ship	LT	HMS Lowestoft (F103)	Type 12
BE	RFA Blue Rover (A270)	Fleet tanker	LY	HMS Lyness (A339)	Support ship
BK	HMS Berwick (F115)	Type 12	MC	HMS Manchester (D95)	Type 42
BM	HMS Birmingham (D86)	Type 42	MV	HMS Minerva (F45)	Leander
BS	HMS Bristol (D23)	Type 82	N	HMS Invincible (R05)	Carrier
BT	HMS Brilliant (F90)	Type 22	NA	HMS Naiad (F39)	Leander
BV	HMS Black Rover (A273)	Fleet tanker	NC	HMS Newcastle (D87)	Type 42
BW	HMS Broadsword (F88)	Type 22	NF	HMS Norfolk (D21)	County
BX	HMS Battleaxe (F89)	Type 22	NM	HMS Nottingham (D91)	Type 42
BZ	HMS Brazen (F91)	Type 22	OD	RFA Olmeda (A124)	Fleet tanker
CF	HMS Cardiff (D108)	Type 42	ON	RFA Olna (A123)	Fleet tanker
CP	HMS Cleopatra (F28)	Leander	OW	RFA Olwen (A122)	Fleet tanker
CU	RNAS Culdrose (HMS Seahawk)		PB	HMS Phoebe (F42)	Leander
			PL	HMS Plymouth (F126)	Type 12
CY	HMS Charybdis (F75)	Leander	PN	HMS Penelope (F127)	Leander
DC	HMS Dumbarton Castle (P268)	Fishery protection	PO	RNAS Portland (HMS Osprey)	
DM	HMS Diomede (F16)	Leander	PV	RFA Sir Percivale (L3036)	Landing ship
DN	HMS Danae (F47)	Leander	PW	Prestwick Airport (HMS Gannet)	
ED	HMS Endurance (A171)	Ice Patrol			
EU	HMS Euryalus (F15)	Leander	R	HMS Ark Royal (R06)	Carrier
EX	HMS Exeter (D89)	Type 42	RG	RFA Regent (A486)	Support ship
FA	RFA Fort Austin (A386)	Support ship	RL	HMS Rhyl (F129)	Type 12
FF	HMS Fife (D20)	County	RO	HMS Rothesay (F107)	Type 12
FG	RFA Fort Grange (A385)	Support ship	RS	RFA Resource (A480)	Support ship
FL	RNAY Fleetlands		SC	HMS Scylla (F71)	Leander
FM	HMS Falmouth (F113)	Type 12	SN	HMS Southampton (D90)	Type 42
FS	HMS Fearless (L10)	Assault	SS	HMS Sirius (F40)	Leander
GA	HMS Galatea (F18)	Leander	ST	RFA Stromness (A344)	Support ship
GL	HMS Glamorgan (D19)	County	TB	RFA Tarbatness (A345)	Support ship
GN	RFA Green Rover (A268)	Fleet tanker	TP	RFA Tidepool (A76)	Fleet tanker
GR	RFA Sir Geraint (L3027)	Landing ship	TS	RFA Tidespring (A75)	Fleet tanker
GV	RFA Gold Rover (A271)	Fleet tanker	VL	RNAS Yeovilton (HMS Heron)	
GW	HMS Glasgow (D88)	Type 42			
GY	RFA Grey Rover (A269)	Fleet tanker	WU	RNAY Wroughton	
H	HMS Hermes (R12)	Carrier	XB	HMS Boxer (F92)	Type 22
HD	HMS Hydra (A144)	Hecla	YM	HMS Yarmouth (F101)	Type 12

Irish Army Air Corps Military Aircraft Markings

Serial	Type (alternative identity)	Owner, Operator or Location	Notes
34	Miles Magister	Engineering Wing, Baldonnel	
141	Avro Anson	Irish Aviation Museum, Dublin	
164	DH Chipmunk	Engineering Wing, Baldonnel (stored)	
165	DH Chipmunk	Engineering Wing, Baldonnel	
166	DH Chipmunk	Engineering Wing, Baldonnel	
167	DH Chipmunk	Engineering Wing, Baldonnel	
168	DH Chipmunk	Training Wing, Gormanston	
172	DH Chipmunk	Engineering Wing, Baldonnel	
173	DH Chipmunk	Basic Flying Training Wing, Gormanston	
176	DH Dove	Civil Defence, Phoenix Park	
181	Percival Provost T1	Fire Section, Baldonnel	
183	Percival Provost T1	Apprentice School, Baldonnel	
184	Percival Provost T1	Apprentice School, Baldonnel	
187	DH Vampire T11	Fire Section, Baldonnel	
191	DH Vampire T11	Irish Aviation Museum, Dublin	
192	DH Vampire T11	Bolton Street Technical College, Dublin	
195	Sud Alouette III	Engineering Wing, Baldonnel	
196	Sud Alouette III	No 1 Support Wing, Baldonnel	
197	Sud Alouette III	No 1 Support Wing, Baldonnel	
198	DH Vampire T11 (XE977)	On display, Casement	
199	DH Chipmunk	Training Wing, Gormanston	
202	Sud Alouette III	No 1 Support Wing, Baldonnel	
203	Cessna FR172H	No 2 Support Wing, Gormanston	
204	Cessna FR172H	Fire Section, Baldonnel	
205	Cessna FR172H	No 2 Support Wing, Gormanston	
206	Cessna FR172H	No 2 Support Wing, Gormanston	
207	Cessna FR172H	No 2 Support Wing, Gormanston	
208	Cessna FR172H	No 2 Support Wing, Gormanston	
209	Cessna FR172H	No 2 Support Wing, Gormanston	
210	Cessna FR172H	No 2 Support Wing, Gormanston	
211	Sud Alouette III	No 1 Support Wing, Baldonnel	
212	Sud Alouette III	No 1 Support Wing, Baldonnel	
213	Sud Alouette III	No 1 Support Wing, Baldonnel	
214	Sud Alouette III	No 1 Support Wing, Baldonnel	
215	Fouga Super Magister	No 1 Support Wing, Baldonnel	
216	Fouga Super Magister	No 1 Support Wing, Baldonnel	
217	Fouga Super Magister	No 1 Support Wing, Baldonnel	
218	Fouga Super Magister	No 1 Support Wing, Baldonnel	
219	Fouga Super Magister	No 1 Support Wing, Baldonnel	
220	Fouga Super Magister	No 1 Support Wing, Baldonnel	
221	Fouga Super Magister [3-KE]	Engineering Wing, Baldonnel	
222	SIAI SF-260W Warrior	Training Wing, Baldonnel	
223	SIAI SF-260W Warrior	Training Wing, Baldonnel	
225	SIAI SF-260W Warrior	Training Wing, Baldonnel	
226	SIAI SF-260W Warrior	Training Wing, Baldonnel	
227	SIAI SF-260W Warrior	Training Wing, Baldonnel	
228	SIAI SF-260W Warrior	Training Wing, Baldonnel	
229	SIAI SF-260W Warrior	Training Wing, Baldonnel	
230	SIAI SF-260W Warrior	Training Wing, Baldonnel	
231	SIAI SF-260W Warrior	Training Wing, Baldonnel	
232	Beech King Air 200 (EI-BCY)	Maritime Squadron, Baldonnel	
233	SIAI SF-260MC	Engineering Wing, Baldonnel (stored)	
234	Beech King Air 200 (EI-BFJ)	Maritime Squadron, Baldonnel	
235	SIAI SF-260W Warrior	Training Wing, Baldonnel	
237	Aerospatiale Gazelle	Advanced Flying Training School, Baldonnel	
238	HS125/700B	Transport Squadron, Baldonnel	
240	Beech King Air 200	Transport Squadron, Baldonnel	
241	Aerospatiale Gazelle	Advanced Flying Training School, Baldonnel	
243	Cessna FR172P	No 2 Support Wing, Gormanston	

Overseas Military Aircraft Markings

Aircraft included in this section are a selection of those likely to be seen visiting UK civil and military airfields on transport flights, exchange visits, exercises and for air shows. It is not a comprehensive list of *all* aircraft operated by the air arms concerned.

Serial	Serial	Serial
AUSTRALIA	**AUSTRIA**	AT09
Royal Australian Air Force	**Oesterreichische**	AT10
Boeing 707-338C	**Luftstreitkrafte**	AT11
A20-623	Saab 105ÖE	AT12
A20-624	(yellow)	AT13
A20-627	1101/A	AT14
A20-629	1102/B	AT15
Lockheed	1104/D	AT16
C-130H Hercules	1105/E	AT17
A97-001	1106/F	AT18
A97-002	1107/G	AT19
A97-003	1108/H	AT20
A97-004	1109/I	AT21
A97-005	1110/J	AT22
A97-006	Saab 105ÖE	AT23
A97-007	(green)	AT24
A97-008	1111/A	AT25
A97-009	1112/B	AT26
A97-010	1114/D	AT27
A97-011	1116/F	AT28
A97-012	1117/G	AT29
Lockheed	1119/I	AT30
C130E Hercules	1120/J	AT31
A97-159	Saab 105ÖE (red)	AT32
A97-160	1122/B	AT33
A97-167	1123/C	**Dassault Mirage**
A97-168	1124/D	**5BA**
A97-171	1125/E	BA01
A97-172	1126/F	BA03
A97-177	1127/G	BA04
A97-178	1128/H	BA05
A97-180	1129/I	BA08
A97-187	1130/J	BA10
A97-189	Saab 105ÖE (blue)	BA11
A97-190	1131/A	BA13
Lockheed	1132/B	BA15
P-3B Orion	1133/C	BA16
A9-291	1134/D	BA17
A9-292	1135/E	BA18
A9-293	1136/F	BA19
A9-294	1137/G	BA20
A9-295	1139/I	BA21
A9-296	1140/J	BA22
A9-297	**Short SC7**	BA23
A9-298	**Skyvan 3M**	BA26
A9-300	5S-TA	BA27
A9-605	5S-TB	BA30
Lockheed		BA31
P-3C Orion		BA33
A9-751	**BELGIUM**	BA35
A9-752	**Force Aerienne Belge/**	BA37
A9-753	**Belgische Luchtmacht**	BA39
A9-754	**D-BD Alpha Jet**	BA42
A9-755	AT01	BA43
A9-756	AT02	BA44
A9-757	AT03	BA45
A9-758	AT05	BA46
A9-759	AT06	BA48
A9-760	AT08	BA50

Serial	Serial	Serial
BA51	**Dassault**	FA70
BA52	**Mystere 20**	FA71
BA53	CM01	FA72
BA54	CM02	FA73
BA56	**Hawker-Siddeley**	FA74
BA57	**HS748 srs 2A**	FA75
BA59	CS01	FA76
BA60	CS02	FA77
BA62	CS03	FA78
BA63	**General Dynamics**	FA79
Dassault Mirage	**F-16A**	FA80
5BD	FA01	FA81
BD01	FA02	FA82
BD03	FA03	FA83
BD04	FA04	FA84
BD05	FA05	FA85
BD06	FA06	FA86
BD07	FA09	FA87
BD09	FA10	FA88
BD10	FA12	FA89
BD11	FA15	FA90
BD12	FA16	FA91
BD13	FA17	FA92
BD14	FA18	FA93
BD15	FA19	FA94
Dassault Mirage	FA20	FA95
5BR	FA21	FA96
BR03	FA22	**General Dynamics**
BR04	FA23	**F-16B**
BR07	FA24	FB01
BR09	FA25	FB02
BR10	FA27	FB03
BR12	FA28	FB04
BR13	FA30	FB05
BR14	FA31	FB06
BR15	FA32	FB07
BR17	FA33	FB08
BR19	FA34	FB09
BR20	FA36	FB10
BR21	FA37	FB11
BR22	FA38	FB12
BR23	FA39	FB13
BR24	FA40	FB14
BR25	FA42	FB15
BR26	FA43	FB17
BR27	FA44	FB18
Boeing 727-29C	FA45	FB19
CB01	FA46	FB20
CB02	FA47	**Westland Sea**
Swearingen	FA48	**King Mk48**
Merlin IIIA	FA49	RS01
CF01	FA50	RS02
CF02	FA51	RS03
CF04	FA52	RS04
CF05	FA53	RS05
CF06	FA54	**Siai Marchetti**
Lockheed	FA55	**SF.26OMB**
C-130H Hercules	FA56	ST03
CH01	FA57	ST04
CH02	FA58	ST07
CH03	FA60	ST09
CH04	FA61	ST11
CH05	FA62	ST12
CH06	FA63	ST14
CH07	FA64	ST15
CH08	FA65	ST16
CH09	FA66	ST17
CH10	FA67	ST18
CH11	FA68	ST19
CH12	FA69	ST20

Overseas Serials

Serial	Serial	Serial
ST21	104639*	104806*
ST22	104640	104807
ST23	104641	104808*
ST24	104642*	104810*
ST25	104643	104815*
ST26	104644	104821
ST27	104645	104823
ST29	104646	104824*
ST30	104648*	104826*
ST31	104650*	104827
ST32	104652	104828
ST33	104658*	104829
ST34	104661*	104830
ST35	**Canadair**	104834
ST36	**Starfighter**	104837*
	104701	104838
Belgische Landmacht	104702	104839*
Britten-Norman	104704	104840
BN-2A Islander	104705	104841*
B01/LA	104709	104842*
B02/LB	104710	104843*
B03/LC	104711*	104845*
B04/LD	104713*	104847*
B05/LE	104714	104848*
B06/LF	104716*	104854
B07/LG	104718	104857
B08/LH	104720	104861
B09/LI	104721	104862*
B10/LJ	104722	104864
B11/LK	104723	104865*
B12/LL	104731	104866*
	104732	104869*
Belgische Zeemacht	104733*	104873*
Sud Alouette III	104735*	104877
M1 (OT-ZPA)	104737*	104883*
M2 (OT-ZPB)	104739*	104891*
M3 (OT-ZPC)	104743*	104892
	104744	104893*
BRAZIL	104747*	104895
Forca Aerea Brazileira	104750*	104899*
Lockheed	104751	**DHC CC-115**
C-130E Hercules	104753	**Buffalo**
C-130 2451	104754	115451
C-130 2454	104756*	115452
C-130 2455	104760	115453
C-130 2456	104761*	115454
C-130 2457	104763	115455
C-130 2458	104768	115456
C-130 2459	104769	115457
C-130 2460	104770*	115458
Lockheed	104772	115459
KC-130H Hercules	104773*	115460
C-130 2461	104774	115461
C-130 2462	104775	115463
Lockheed	104776*	115464
C-130H Hercules	104780*	115465
C-130 2463	104781	**Lockheed**
C-130 2464	104783	**C-130E Hercules**
C-130 2465	104784*	130305
	104785*	130306
CANADA	104786*	130307
Canadian Armed Forces	104787*	130308
1st CAG, Sollingen	104788*	130309
West Germany*	104789	130310
Canadair CF104D	104790*	130311
Starfighter	104792	130313
104631	104795*	130314
104634	104796*	130315
104636*	104799*	130316
104638*	104804	130317

Serial	Serial	Serial
130318	140113	AT158
130319	140114	AT160
130320	140115	**Lockheed**
130321	140116	**C-130H Hercules**
130322	140117	B678
130323	140118	B679
130324	**Canadair CC-144**	B680
130325	**Challenger**	**Saab 17**
130326	No 412 Sqn, Lahr	**Supporter**
130327	West Germany	T401
130328	144601	T402
Lockheed	144602	T403
C-130H Hercules	**CHILE**	T404
130330	**Fuerza Aérea de Chile**	T405
130331	**Lockheed**	T406
130332	**C-130H Hercules**	T407
130333	995	T408
130334	996	T409
130335		T410
DHC CC-132		T411
Dash 7	**DENMARK**	T412
No 412 Sqn	**Kongelige Danske**	T413
Lahr, West Germany	**Flyvevaabnet**	T414
132001	**Saab A-35XD**	T415
132002	**Draken**	T417
Canadair CT-133	A001	T418
Silver Star	A002	T419
1st CAG, Sollingen	A004	T420
West Germany	A005	T421
133026	A006	T422
133052	A007	T423
133069	A008	T424
133094	A009	T425
133315	A010	T426
133345	A011	T427
133393	A012	T428
133405	A014	T429
133435	A017	T430
133450	A018	T431
133490	A019	T432
133504	A020	**Grumman**
133542	**Saab S-35XD**	**Gulfstream III**
133564	**Draken**	F249
133571	AR102	F313
133572	AR104	F330
133581	AR105	**General Dynamics**
133613	AR106	**F-16A**
133623	AR107	E174
133648	AR108	E176
Boeing CC-137	AR109	E177
(B.707-374C)	AR110	E178
13701	AR111	E179
13702	AR112	E180
13703	AR113	E181
13704	AR114	E182
13705	AR115	E183
Lockheed	AR116	E184
CP-140 Aurora	AR117	E185
140101	AR118	E186
140102	AR119	E187
140103	AR120	E188
140104	**Saab Sk-35XD**	E189
140105	**Draken**	E190
140106	AT151	E191
140107	AT152	E192
140108	AT153	E193
140109	AT154	E194
140110	AT155	E195
140111	AT156	E196
140112	AT157	E197

Serial	Serial	Serial
E198	H210	312739/CK
E199	H211	312740/CL
E200	H213	**CAARP CAP-20**
E201	H244	1 VU
E202	H245	2 VV
E203	H246	3 VW
E596		4 VX
E597	**EGYPT**	5 VY
E598	**Al Quwwat al-Jawwiya**	6 VZ
E599	**Ilmisriya**	**Cessna 310**
E600	**Lockheed**	045 AU
E601	**C-130H Hercules**	046 AV
E602	1271/SU-BAB	185 AC
E603	1272/SU-BAC	186 BI
E604	1273/SU-BAD	187 BJ
E605	1274/SU-BAE	188 BK
E606	1275/SU-BAF	190 BL
E607	1277/SU-BAI	192 BM
E608	1278/SU-BAJ	193 BG
E609	1279/SU-BAK	194 BH
E610	1280/SU-BAL	242 BW
E611	1281/SU-BAM	244 AX
General Dynamics	1282/SU-BAN	820 CL
F-16B	1283/SU-BAP	**Cessna 404**
ET204	1284/SU-BAQ	692 DX
ET205	1285/SU-BAR	**Cessna 411**
ET206	1286/SU-BAS	185 AC
ET207	1287/SU-BAT	248 AB
ET208	1288/SU-BAU	F006 AD
ET210	1289/SU-BAV	F008 AE
ET612	1290/SU-BEW	**D-BD Alpha Jet**
ET613	1291/SU-BEX	*** Patrouille de**
ET614	1292/SU-BEY	**France**
ET615		01
Sikorsky S-61A	**FRANCE**	02 F-ZWRU
U240	**Armee de l'Air**	E1
U275	**Aerospatiale TB-30**	E3 314-LY
U276	**Epsilon**	E4 118-BS
U278	01 VO	E5 118-BU
U279	02 VJ	E6 8-NW
U280	1 UA	E7 8-NW
U301	2 UB	E8 314-LC
U481	3 FZ	E9 314-LD
	4 UC	E10 8-MU
Sovaernets	5 UD	E11 8-MP
Flyvetjaeneste	6 UE	E12 8-NC
(Navy)	7 UF	E13 314-LH
Westland Lynx	8 UG	E14 F-TERD* (0)
HAS80	9 UH	E15 314-LJ
S134	10 UI	E16 314-LK
S142	11 UJ	E17 8-MR
S170	12 UK	E18 314-LM
S175	13 UL	E19 8-MK
S181	14	E20 314-LO
S187	15 UN	E21 8-NY
S191	16	E22 314-LQ
S196	17	E23 8-MQ
	18	E24 8-MA
Haerens	19	E25 314-LT
Flyvetjaeneste	20	E26 314-LU
(Army)	**Boeing KC-135F**	E27 8-MD
Hughes 500M	38470/CA	E28 314-TL
H201	38471/CB	E29 314-LV
H202	38472/CC	E30 314-LW
H203	38474/CE	E31 314-LX
H204	38475/CF	E32 314-LY
H205	312735/CG	E33 314-TA
H206	312736/CH	E34 314-LZ
H207	312737/CI	E35 314-TB
H209	312738/CJ	E36 314-TC

Serial	Serial	Serial
E37 314-TD	E114 8-NN	22 CS
E38 314-TE	E115 314-VF	49 OA
E39 314-TF	E116 8-NV	79 CT
E40 8-MB	E117 314-VG	86 CG
E41 8-MH	E118 314-VH	93 N
E42 8-MZ	E119 314-VI	104 CW
E43 314-TJ	E120 314-VJ	115 339-WL
E44 314-TN	E121 314-VK	124 CC
E45 314-TM	E122 314-VL	131 CD
E46 314-TO	E123 314-VM	138 CR
E47 8-ND	E124 8-MW	145 CV
E48 8-NZ	E125 314-VN	167 L
E49 314-TR	E126 314-VO	238 M
E50 314-TS	E127 8-MY	260 A
E51 F-TERA* (2)	E128 8-NP	268 K
E53 F-TERC* (1)	E129 314-VP	291 P
E55 F-TERE* (4)	E130 8-MT	309 U
E58 F-TERH* (7)	E131 314-VQ	422 L
E59 F-TERI* (5)	E132 314-VR	463 339-WM
E60	E133 314-VS	483
E61 F-TERJ* (8)	E134 8-NE	**Dassault Falcon 50**
E63 F-TERL* (6)	E135 314-VT	5 F-RAFI
E64 314-TT	E136 314-VU	**Dassault**
E65 314-TU	E137 8-MF	**Mirage F.1C**
E66 314-TV	E138 8-NF	2 118-AK
E67 314-TW	E139 8-MM	3 118-AL
E68 314-TX	E140 314-VV	4 118-AM
E69 314-TZ	E141 8-NY	5
E70 314-TY	E142 8-ML	6 30-MA
E72 314-UA	E143	8 5-OK
E73 118-BT	E144 314-VW	9 12-KB
E74 8-ND	E145 8-NM	10 10-SU
E75 314-UD	E146 314-VZ	12 10 ST
E76 314-UE	E147	13 30-FF
E77 8-NH	E148	14 30-MS
E79 8-NS	E149	15 30-FC
E80	E150 8-NO	16 12-ZA
E81 8-NK	E151	17 12-KC
E82 8-NX	E152 8-MC	18 12-KG
E83 314-UJ	E153	19 12-ZB
E84 314-UL	E154	20 12-YD
E85 314-UM	E155 F-TERF*	21 30-FL
E86 314-UN	E156 F-TERG*	22 118-AN
E87 314-UO	E157 8-NI	23 30-FH
E88 8-MG	E158 314-LR	24 30-ME
E89 314-UQ	E159 8-MD	25 12-ZC
E90 314-UR	E160	26 12-KF
E91 314-US	E161	27 10-SQ
E92 314-UT	E162	29 10-SN
E93 314-UU	E163	30 12-YC
E94 8-MO	E164	31 30-MB
E95	E165	32 12-KD
E96 8-MJ	E166	33 30-FJ
E97 314-UW	E167	34 30-MN
E98 314-UX	E168	35 12-ZE
E99	E169	36 12-YE
E100	E170	37 30-FB
E101	E171	38 12-KL
E102 8-ME	E172	39 12-KM
E103 314-UY	E173	40 12-YA
E104 314-UZ	E174	41 10-SG
E105 314-VA	E175	42 12-KI
E106 314-VB	E176	43 12-YK
E107 F-TERK* (3)	E177	44 12-KK
E108 314-VC	E178	45 30-MD
E109 314-VD	E179	46 10-SF
E110 8-NB	E180	47 10-SO
E111 8-NA	**Dassault**	49
E112 314-VE	**Falcon 20C**	50 12-ZH
E113 8-NJ	1 CV	52 12-YG

Overseas Serials

Serial	Serial	Serial
54 30-MF	245 5-NI	619
55 12-KH	246 5-NC	620
60 30-MJ	247 30-FR	621
62 30-MC	248 12-YF	622
63 12-YJ	249 12-ZS	623
64 30-MB	251 30-MH	624
67	252 5-ON	625
68 30-FO	253 10-SP	626
69 30-MI	254 12-ZT	627
70 10-SI	255 5-NQ	628
71 12-KJ	256 10-ST	629
72 30-MF	257 12-KO	**Dassault Mirage**
74 30-FQ	258 12-YL	**2000C**
75 30-MI	259 30-FA	01
76 12-KJ	260 5-OB	04
77 12-ZL	261 12-ZV	1 2-EP
78 30-FG	262 30-MU	2
79 10-SK	263 5-NP	3 118-AV
80 12-ZM	264 12-KN	4 2-EL
81 12-YN	265 5-NB	5 2-EB
82 10-SB	266 12-ZW	6 2-EM
83 30-MC	267 30-MP	7 2-EA
84 10-SE	268 5-OO	8 2-EC
85 12-ZN	270 12-KI	9 2-ED
87 10-SL	271 30-FM	10 2-EE
90 12-ZN	272 5-AU	11 2-EF
100 30-FK	273 12-ZX	12 2-EH
101 10-SC	274 5-AW	13 2-EI
102 10-SM	275 5-NH	14 2-EJ
103 30-MO	276 30-MA	15 2-EK
201 118-AZ	277	**Dassault Mirage**
202 5-OR	278 5-OE	**2000B**
203 30-MD	279 5-NK	501 2-EQ
204 5-OH	280 5-NF	502 2-EN
205 30-FI	281 5-NG	503 2-EO
206 5-OA	282	504 2-EG
207 30-FE	283 12-ZY	**DHC6 Twin Otter**
208 5-OJ	284	292 OW
210 30-FN	285	298 OY
211 10-SH	286	300 OZ
213 30-MG	287	603 82-PU
214 5-OG	288	730 52-LF
216 5-OL	289	742 52-LG
217 30-MK	290	743 118-ID
218 5-OM	291	745 118-IG
219 5-NL	292	786 63-VV
220 5-OD	293	790 63-VW
221 12-YT	294	**Douglas DC8F**
223 5-NM	295	45570 F-RAFE
224 5-OI		45819 F-RAFC
225 118-AO	**Dassault Mirage**	45820 F-RAFA
226 12-YO	**F.1CR**	46043 F-RAFD
227 12-KP	601	46130 F-RAFF
228 12-ZR	602	46132 F-RAFB
229 5-ND	603 33-NA	**Embraer Xingu**
230 118-AP	604 33-NB	054 118-IA
231 12-YH	605 33-NC	064 118-IB
232 30-MT	606 33-ND	072 YA
233 12-KA	607 33-NE	073 YB
234 5-OC	608 33-NF	075 YC
235 30-FP	609 33-NG	076 YD
236 5-OP	610 33-NH	078 YE
237 12-YI	611 33-NI	080 YF
238 5-NR	612 33-NJ	082 YG
239 5-NJ	613 33-NK	084 YH
240 12-YB	614 33-NL	086 YI
241 5-NE	615 33-NM	089 YJ
242 5-NA	616 33-NN	091 YK
243 5-NO	617 33-NO	092 YL
244 5-OQ	618 33-NP	

Serial	Serial	Serial
095 YM	66 AB	194 316-FP
098 YO	67 MI	196 316-FO
099 YP	68 AC	199 64-BD
100 YR	75	200 328-EK
101 BW	76 AD	201 63-VJ
102 BC	77 AK	202 63-VE
103 BY	78 AF	205 63-WR
105 CU	80 AW	206 64-BA
107 CY	81 AH	**C-160A Transall**
	83 AI	A02/61-MI
Morane Saulnier	86 MC	A04/61-BI
Paris	87 AN	A06/61-ZB
1 118-DB	88 MA	F1/61-MA
14 070-MD	89 IR	F2/61-MB
19 43-BD	91 AT	F3/61-MC
20	92 AO	F4/61-MD
23 65-LB	93 MA	F5/61-ME
24 65-LW	94 MB	F11/61-MF
25 118-DI	95 AR	F12/61-MG
26 65-LD	105 AE	F13/61-MH
27 41-AS	106 AY	F14/61-MI
29 43-BB	107 MD	F15/61-MJ
34 65-LE	108 AG	F16/61-MK
35 314-DD	109 AM	F17/61-ML
36	110 AS	F18/61-MM
38 41-AT	**Nord Noratlas**	F42/61-MN
44 44-CN	03 BT	F43/61-MO
45 41-AR	05 BS	F44/61-MP
51 43-BA	18 CR	F45/61-MQ
53 65-LO	25	F46/61-MR
54 118-DO	28 64-BM	F47/61-MS
56 65-LP	42	F48/61-MT
57 65-LV	54 63-WX	F49/61-MU
58 332-DA	66	F50/61-MV
59 65-LR	84	F51/61-MW
60 65-LQ	88 64-IX	F52/61-MX
61 65-DY	94 63-WA	F53/61-MY
62 65-DZ	96 63-VH	F54/61-MZ
65 65-LW	100 64-BZ	F55/61-ZC
68	104 118-IF	F86/61-ZD
70 65-LT	113 63-VN	F87/61-ZE
71 314-DE	114 316-FQ	F88/61-ZF
73 65-LC	120 63-VA	F89/61-ZG
75 118-DC	122 63-WD	F90/61-ZH
77 118-DF	126 64-BC	F91/61-ZI
78 65-LU	129 316-FA	F92/61-ZJ
79 65-LA	130 312-BP	F93/61-ZK
80 65-LM	132 328-ED	F94/61-ZL
81 65-LL	140 340-VB	F95/61-ZM
82 44-CM	142 63-VP	F96/61-ZN
83 NC	146 63-WV	F97/61-ZO
91 65-LN	148 328 EI	F98/61-ZP
92 118-DA	153 64-BJ	F99/61-ZQ
93 65-LJ	155 328-EG	F100/61-ZR
94 65-LH	157 63-WK	F153/61-ZS
96 65-LU	160 63-WP	F154/61-ZT
97 43-BA	161 64-IM	F155/61-ZU
100 NG	162 328-EF	F156/61-ZV
113 NI	165 63-VK	F157/61-ZW
114 NJ	169 KF	F158/61-ZX
115 OV	171 316-FR	F159/61-ZY
116 ON	177 63-WR	F160/61-ZZ
117 AZ	180 63-VB	F201/64-GA
118 NQ	185 63-VG	F202/64-GB
119 NL	187 64-IS	F203/64-GC
Nord 262 Fregate	188 316-FS	F204/64-GD
3 OH	189 316-FN	F205/64-GE
55 MH	191 63-WS	F206/64-GF
58 MJ	192 63-WI	F207/64-GG
64 AA	193 316-FU	F208/64-GH

Overseas Serials

Serial	Serial	Serial
F209/64-GI	A56 7-HI	A136 7-ND
F210/64-GJ	A58 7-ID	A137 7-NK
F211/64-GK	A59 11-YG	A138 7-NG
F212/64-GL	A60 7-HF	A139 11-MO
F213/64-GM	A61 7-PA	A140 7-NH
F214/64-GN	A63	A141 7-NI
F215/64-GO	A64 11-RO	A142
F216/64-GP	A65 7-HD	A145
F217/64-GQ	A66 11-RT	A146 11-EE
F218/64-GR	A68	A147 11-EF
F219/64-GS	A70 11-ED	A148 118-AI
F220/64-GT	A72 11-RW	A149 11-YB
F221/64-GU	A73 3-XP	A150 11-RT
F222/64/GV	A74	A151 7-NE
F223/64-GW	A75 11-YH	A152 11-RG
F224/64-GX	A76 3-XB	A153 11-MB
F225/64-GY	A77	A154 11-MP
F226/64-GZ	A79 7-HG	A155
SEPECAT	A80 7-HD	A156
Jaguar A	A82 11-RB	A157 11-MQ
A1 3-XJ	A83 11-MC	A158 11-MW
A2 3-XN	A84 11-MD	A159 11-RS
A3	A85 11-YL	A160
A4	A86 11-MG	**SEPECAT Jaguar E**
A5 7-PM	A87 11-MH	E1
A6 3-XH	A88 11-MM	E2 3-XO
A7 3-XK	A89 11-YH	E3 7-HL
A8 3-XL	A90 11-YI	E4 11-EH
A9 3-XD	A91 11-RI	E5 118-AD
A10 3-XH	A92 11-MS	E6 11-ME
A11	A93 11-MT	E7 7-PI
A12 7-PC	A94 11-MD	E8 7-IJ
A13 3-XM	A95 11-EC	E9 7-PH
A14 3-XF	A96 11-RQ	E10
A15 7-IE	A97 11-RH	E11 3-XE
A16 7-HN	A98 11-EB	E12 7-PH
A17	A99 11-EU	E13 7-PD
A19	A100 11-ED	E14
A20 3-XQ	A101 7-NE	E15 11-YZ
A21 7-1A	A102 11-YK	E16 11-RF
A22 7-HF	A103 118-AH	E17 7-PI
A23 7-HO	A104 11-EV	E18 7-YY
A24 7-HH	A105 11-EV	E19 7-PK
A25 7-IB	A107 11-YC	E20 7-IJ
A26 7-HJ	A108 11-ES	E21 11-EA
A27 3-XP	A110 118-AG	E22 11-ME
A28 11-MC	A112 11-RV	E23 11-EI
A29 7-HA	A113 11-YA	E24 7-PC
A31 7-HE	A114 11-YB	E25 7-IK
A32 3-XI	A115 11-ES	E27 11-MA
A33 7-IH	A116 11-YD	E28 7-PJ
A34 7-IL	A117 11-YE	E29 7-PB
A35 7-HA	A118 11-YF	E30 7-PL
A36 7-II	A119 11-MN	E31 7-PF
A37 7-HB	A120 11-MM	E32 7-PO
A38 3-XG	A121 11-MW	E33 11-RC
A39 7-IP	A122 11-RJ	E34
A40 3-XC	A123 11-EL	E35 7-DU
A41 11-EG	A124 11-YK	E36 11-YZ
A43 7-HK	A125 11-MD	E37 7-PF
A44 7-IF	A126 11-RB	E38 7-NN
A46 7-IM	A127 11-RK	E39 7-NO
A47	A128 11-YJ	E40 7-PN
A48 7-IG	A129 11-ER	
A49 3-XA	A130 11-MK	**Aeronavale/Marine**
A50 11-YM	A131 7-NA	**Morane Saulnier**
A51 3-XI	A132 11-MO	**Paris**
A53 7-HC	A133 11-EG	32
A54 7-HM	A134	33
A55 7-PB	A135 7-NC	40

Serial	Serial	Serial
41	37	3
42	42	4
46	43	5
47	45	6
48	47	7
85	48	9
87	49	11
88	50	15
Nord 262 Fregate	51	16
28	52	21
43	53	22
45	55	29
46	56	30
51	59	32
52	60	33
53	61	34
59	65	36
60	68	37
61	69	40
62	72	41
63	73	42
65	75	52
70	76	53
71	80	56
72	87	57
73	**Breguet 1150**	59
75	**Atlantic**	60
79	1	62
85	3	63
104	5	66
SA.321G Super	7	**Dassault**
Frelon	9	**Etendard IVP**
101	11	101
102	13	103
105	15	107
106	17	108
118	19	109
120	21	114
122	23	115
134	25	116
137	27	117
141	31	118
144	32	120
148	33	**Dassault Super**
149	35	**Etendard**
159	37	1
160	38	2
162	40	3
163	41	4
164	44	5
165	45	6
Breguet 1050	46	7
Alizé	47	8
1	48	9
2	49	10
9	50	11
11	51	12
12	52	13
13	53	14
17	54	15
24	66	16
25	67	17
26	68	18
27	ANG.01	19
28	ANG.02	20
30	ANG.03	21
31	ANG.04	23
33	**Dassault**	25
34	**Etendard IVM**	26
36	2	27

Overseas Serials

Serial	Serial	Serial
28	**LTV F-8E (FN)**	624
29	**Crusader**	625
30	1	626
31	2	627
32	3	801
33	4	802
34	6	803
37	7	804
38	8	805
39	10	806
40	11	807
41	12	808
42	14	809
43	16	810
44	17	811
45	19	812
46	20	813
47	23	814
48	24	
49	25	
50	26	**GREECE**
51	27	**Elliniki Aeroporia**
52	29	**Lockheed**
53	30	**C-130H Hercules**
54	33	741
55	34	742
57	35	743
58	37	744
59	39	745
60	40	746
61	41	747
62	42	748
63	**Piper Navajo**	749
64	227	750
70	232	751
71	903	752
	904	
Dassault Falcon	906	
10(MER)	912	**ISRAEL**
32	914	**Heyl ha'avir**
101	916	**Lockheed**
129	925	**C-130H Hercules**
133	927	4X-FBA/102
143	929	4X-FBB/106
185	931	4X-FBC/309
	Westland Lynx	**Lockheed**
Dassault Falcon	**HAS2 (FN)**	**C-130E Hercules**
Guardian	03	4X-FBE/304
48	04	4X-FBF/301
65	260	4X-FBG/310
72	261	4X-FBH/312
77	262	4X-FBI/002
80	263	4X-FBK/318
	264	4X-FBL/313
Embraer Xingu	265	4X-FBM/316
55	266	4X-FBN/307
65	267	4X-FBO/203
66	268	4X-FBP/208
67	270	**Lockeed**
68	271	**C-130H Hercules**
69	272	4X-FBQ/420
70	273	4X-FBS/427
71	274	4X-FBT/435
74	275	4X-FBU/448
77	276	4X-FBW/436
79	278	4X-FBX/428
81	620	**Lockheed**
83	621	**KC-130H Hercules**
85	622	4X-FBY/522
87	623	4X-FBZ/545
90		

Serial	Serial	Serial
ITALY	MM54465	**Panavia Tornado**
Aeronautica Militare	MM54466	***TTTE Cottesmore**
Italiano	MM54467	MM586
Aeritalia G222	MM54468	MM587
MM62101	MM54469	MM7001 RS-01
MM62102/46-20	MM54470	MM7002* I-92
MM62103/RS-35	MM54471	MM7003* I-93
MM62104/46-91	MM54472	MM7004* I-90
MM62105/46-82	MM54473	MM7005* I-91
MM62106/46-84	MM54474* 6	MM7006 S-01
MM62107/(G222VS)	MM54475* 1	MM7007 6-02
MM62108/46-30	MM54476* 11	MM7008
MM62109/	MM54477* 14	MM7009 S-04
MM62110/46-81	MM54478* 4	MM7010 6-03
MM62111/46-83	MM54479* 9	MM7011 6-10
MM62112/46-85	MM54480* 8	MM7012 6-11
MM62113/46-34	MM54481* 7	MM7013 6-05
MM62114/46-80	MM54482* 3	MM7014 6-12
MM62115/46-22	MM54483* 2	MM7015
MM62116/RS-22	MM54484* 10	MM7016
MM62117/46-25	MM54485* 13	MM7017 6-14
MM62118/46-24	MM54486* 5	MM7018 6-24
MM62119/46-21	MM54487	MM7019 6-22
MM62120/46-90	MM54488	MM7020 6-21
MM62121/46-86	MM54489	MM7021 6-30
MM62122/46-23	MM54490	MM7022 6-26
MM62123/46-28	MM54491	MM7023
MM62124/46-88	MM54492	MM7024 6-25
MM62125/46-87	MM54493	MM7025 6-31
MM62126/46-26	MM54494	MM7026 6-33
MM62126/46-26	MM54495	MM7027
MM62127/46-27	MM54496	MM7028
MM62128/46-89	MM54497	MM7029
MM62129/46-29	MM54498	MM7030 6-36
MM62130/46-31	MM54499	MM7031
MM62131/46-92	MM54500	MM7033 6-42
MM62132/46-32	MM54501	MM7034 6-41
MM62133/46-93	MM54503	MM7035
MM62134/46-33	MM54504	MM7036
MM62135/46-94	MM54505	MM7037
	MM54506	MM7038
Aeritalia G222RM	MM54507	MM7039
MM62139/	MM54508	MM7040
MM62140/	MM54509	MM7041
Aermacchi MB339	MM54510	MM7042
*Frecce Tricolori	MM54511	MM7043
MM54438	MM54512	MM7044
MM54439* 15	MM54513	MM7046
MM54440	MM54514	MM7047
MM54442	MM54515	MM7048
MM54445	MM54516	MM7049
MM54446	MM54517	MM7050
MM54447	**Lockheed**	MM7051
MM54448	**C-130H Hercules**	MM7052
MM54449	MM61988/46-02	MM7053
MM54450	MM61989/46-03	MM7054
MM54451	MM61990/46-04	MM7055
MM54452	MM61991/46-05	MM7056
MM54453	MM61992/46-06	MM7057
MM54454	MM61993/46-07	MM7058
MM54455	MM61994/46-08	MM7059
MM54456	MM61995/46-09	MM7060
MM54457	MM61997/46-11	MM7061
MM54458	MM61998/46-12	MM7062
MM54459	MM61999/46-13	MM7063
MM54460	MM62001/46-15	MM7064
MM54461	**McDonnell**	MM7065
MM54462	**Douglas DC9-32**	MM7066
MM54463	MM62012/31-12	MM7067
MM54464	MM62013/31-13	MM7068

Serial	Serial	Serial
MM7069	LX-N90444	J249
MM7070	LX-N90445	J250
MM7071	LX-N90446	J251
MM7072	LX-N90447	J253
MM7073	LX-N90448	J254
MM7074	LX-N90449	J255
MM7075	LX-N90450	J256
MM7076	LX-N90451	J257
MM7077	LX-N90452	J258
MM7078	LX-N90453	J259*
MM7079	LX-N90454	J260*
MM7080	LX-N90455	J261*
MM7081	LX-N90456	J262*
MM7082	LX-N90457	J263*
MM7083	LX-N90458	J264*
MM7084	LX-N90459	J265*
MM7085		J266*
MM7086	**NETHERLANDS**	J267*
MM7087	**Koninklijke Luchmacht**	J268*
MM7088	**Fokker F-27-100**	J269*
MM7089	**Friendship**	J270*
MM7090	C-1	J271*
MM55000* I-42	C-2	J616
MM55001* I-40	C-3	J617
MM55002* I-41	**Fokker F-27-300M**	J618
MM55003* I-43	**Troopship**	J619
MM55004 6-06	C-4	J620
MM55005 6-1	C-5	J621
MM55006 6-15	C-6	J622
MM55007 6-13	C-7	J623
MM55008 6-20	C-8	J624
MM55009 6-16	C-9	J625
MM55010	C-10	J626
MM55011	C-11	J627
MM55012	C-12	J628
MM55013	**F-27-200MPA**	J629
MM55014 6-17	M-1	J630
	M-2	J631
JORDAN	**General Dynamics**	J632
Al Quwwat Al-Jawwiya	**F-16A/F16B***	J633
Alamalakiya Al-Urduniya	J212	J635
Lockheed	J213	J636
C-130B Hercules	J214	J637
340	J215	J638
341	J218	J639
Lockheed	J219	J640
C-130H Hercules	J220	J641
344	J221	J642
345	J222	J643
346	J223	J644
347	J226	J645
	J228	J646
KUWAIT	J229	J647
Kuwait Air Force	J230	J648
McDonnell	J231	J649*
Douglas DC9-32	J232	J650*
KAF 320	J234	J651*
KAF 321	J235	J652*
Lockheed	J236	J653*
L100-30 Hercules	J238	J654*
KAF 322	J239	J655*
KAF 323	J240	J656*
KAF 324	J241	J657*
KAF 325	J242	J864
	J243	J865
LUXEMBOURG	J244	J866
NATO — Geilenkirchen	J245	J867
Boeing E-3A	J246	J868
LX-N90442	J247	J869
LX-N90443	J248	J870

Serial	Serial	Serial
J871	K3061	A383
J872	K3062	A390*
J873	K3063	A391
J874	K3065	A398*
J875	K3066	A399
J876	K3067	A407
J877	K3068	A414
J878	K3069	A451
J879	K3070	A452
J880	K3072	A453
J881	K3073	A464
J882*		A465*
J883*	**Northrop NF-5B**	A470
J884*	K4002	A471
J885*	K4003	A482
J886*	K4005	A483
J887*	K4006	A488
J888*	K4007	A489
J889*	K4008	A494
Northrop NF-5A	K4009	A495
K3001	K4010	A499*
K3003	K4011	A500
K3004	K4012	A514
K3005	K4014	A515
K3007	K4015	A521
K3008	K4017	A522
K3011	K4018	A528
K3012	K4019	A529
K3013	K4020	A535
K3014	K4021	A536
K3015	K4023	A542
K3016	K4024	A543
K3017	K4025	A550
K3018	K4026	**Marine Luchtvaartdienst**
K3019	K4027	**Breguet Atlantic**
K3020	K4028	250
K3021	K4029	251
K3022	K4030	252
K3023	**Sud Alouette III**	254
K3024	***Grasshoppers**	256
K3025	A177	258
K3026	A208	**Lockheed**
K3027	A209	**P-3C Orion**
K3028	A217	300
K3030	A218	301
K3031	A226	302
K3032	A227	303
K3033	A235	304
K3034	A246	305
K3035	A247	306
K3036	A253	307
K3039	A254	308
K3040	A260	309
K3041	A261	310
K3042	A266	311
K3043	A267	312
K3044	A275	**Westland Lynx**
K3045	A281	260 UH14A
K3046	A292	261 UH14A
K3047	A293	262 UH14A
K3048	A301	264 UH14A
K3049	A307	265 UH14A
K3050	A319	266 SH14B
K3051	A324	267 SH14B
K3052	A336	268 SH14B
K3055	A342	269 SH14B
K3056	A343	270 SH14B
K3057	A350*	271 SH14B
K3058	A351*	272 SH14B
K3060	A374	273 SH14B

Overseas Serials

Serial	Serial	Serial
274 SH14B	291	**Northrop F-5A**
276 SH14C	292	125
277 SH14C	293	128
278 SH14C	294	129
279 SH14C	295	130
280 SH14C	296	131
281 SH14C	297	132
282 SH14C	298	133
283 SH14C	299	134
	300	164
NEW ZEALAND	301*	207
Royal New Zealand Air Force	302*	208
Boeing 727-22C	303*	209
NZ7271	304*	210
NZ7272	305*	212
Lockheed	306*	214
C-130H Hercules	307*	215
NZ7001	658	220
NZ7002	659	225
NZ7003	660	227
NZ7004	661	228
NZ7005	662	369
Lockheed	663	370
P-3B Orion	664	371
NZ4201	665	372
NZ4202	666	373
NZ4203	667	374
NZ4204	668	375
NZ4205	669	376
	670	563
	671	565
NIGERIA	672	566
Federal Nigerian Air Force	673	568
Lockheed	674	569
C-130H Hercules	675	570
NAF-910	676	571
NAF-911	677	573
NAF-912	678	574
NAF-913	679	575
NAF-914	680	577
NAF-915	681	895
	682	896
NORWAY	683	897
Kongelige Norske	684	898
Luftforsvaret	685	901
Dassault	686	902
Falcon 20	687	904
041	688	905
053	689*	**Northrop RF-5A**
0125	690*	100
0151	691*	101
General Dynamics	692*	102
F-16A/*F-16B	693*	103
272	**Lockheed**	104
273	**C-130H Hercules**	105
274	952	106
275	953	107
276	954	108
277	955	109
278	956	110
279	957	112
281	**Lockheed**	113
282	**P-3B Orion**	489
284	576	490
285	583	**Northrop F-5B**
286	599	135
287	600	136
288	601	241
289	602	242
290	603	243

Serial	Serial	Serial
244	2408	1618 C-130H
387	2409	1619 C-130H
594	2410	1620 KC-130H
595	2411	1621 KC-130H
906	2412	**Lockheed Jetstar**
907	2413	101
908	2414*	102
909	2415*	
Westland	2416	**SINGAPORE**
Sea King Mk43	2417	**Republic of Singapore Air**
060	2418	**Force**
062	2419	
066	2420	**Lockheed**
068	2421*	**C-130B Hercules**
069	2422	720
070	2423*	721
071	2424	**Lockheed**
072	2425	**C-130H Hercules**
073	2426*	724
074	2427	725
189	2428	730
Westland Lynx	2429*	731
Mk86	2430	732
207	**Lockheed**	733
216	**C-130H Hercules**	
228	6801	
232	6802	**SPAIN**
235	6803	**Ejercito del Aire**
237	6804	**Dassault Falcon 20**
	6805	TM.11-1/401-02
OMAN		TM.11-2/401-03
Al Quwwat al Jawwiya al		TM.11-3/401-04
Saltanat Oman	**SAUDI ARABIA**	TM.11-4/401 05
 **BAC 1-11**	**Al Quwwat Al-Jawwiya**	**Fokker F.27M**
srs 485GD	**as Sa' udiya**	**Friendship**
551	 **Lockheed**	**400MPA**
552	**C-130 Hercules**	D.2-01
553	451 C-130E	D.2-02
Lockheed	452 C-130E	D.2-03
C-130H Hercules	455 C-130E	**Lockheed**
501	456 KC-130H	**C-130H Hercules**
502	457 KC-130H	T.10-2/312-02
503	458 KC-130H	T.10-3/311-03
Short Skyvan 3M	459 KC-130H	T.10-4/311-04
901	460 C-130H	T.10-8/311-05
902	461 C-130H	T.10-9/311-06
903	462 C-130H	T.10-10/312-04
904	463 C-130H	**Lockheed**
906	464 C-130H	**KC-130H Hercules**
907	465 C-130H	TK.10-5
908	466 C-130H	TK.10-6
910	467 C-130H	TK.10-7
911	468 C-130H	TK.10-11
912	469 C-130H	TK.10-12
913	470 C-130H	
914	1601 C-130H	
915	1602 C-130H	**SWEDEN**
916	1603 C-130H	**Kungl Svenska Flygvapnet**
	1604 C-130H	**Lockheed**
	1605 C-130H	**C-130E Hercules**
PORTUGAL	1606 C-130E	84001/841
Forca Aerea Portuguesa	1607 C-130E	84002/842
Cessna T-37C	1608 C-130E	**Lockheed**
***Asas de Portugal**	1609 C-130E	**C-130H Hercules**
2401	1610 C-130E	84003/843
2402	1611 C-130E	84004/844
2403	1612 C-130E	84005/845
2404*	1614 C-130H	84006/846
2405	1615 C-130H	84007/847
2406*	1616 KC-130H	84008/848
2407*	1617 KC-130H	

Overseas Serials

SWITZERLAND
Schweizerische Flugwaffe
    Beech E-50
    Twin Bonanza
    A-711
    A-712
    A-713

TURKEY
Turk Hava Kuvvetleri
    Lockheed
    C-130E Hercules
    ETI-00991
    ETI-01468
    ETI-01947
    ETI-13186
    ETI-13187
    ETI-13188
    ETI-13189
    ETI-17949
    Vickers V794
    Viscount
    246
    430
    431

UNITED ARAB EMIRATES
United Arab Emirates Air Force
    Abu Dhabi
    Lockheed
    C-130H Hercules
    1213
    1214
    Dubai
    Lockheed C-130H
    Hercules
    311
    312

WEST GERMANY
Luftwaffe
    Boeing 707-307C
    10+01
    10+02
    10+03
    10+04
    Lockheed L-1329
    JetStar
    11+01
    11+02
    11+03
    HFB 320 Hansa Jet
    16+01
    16+02
    16+03
    16+04
    16+05
    16+06
    16+07
    16+08
    16+22
    16+23
    16+24
    16+25
    16+26
    16+27
    16+28

VFW 614
17+01
17+02
17+03
Lockheed
F-104G Starfighter
***Marinesflieger**
20+01
20+02
20+04
20+05
20+06
20+07
20+08
20+36
20+37
20+38
20+39
20+43
20+46
20+49
20+50
20+53
20+56
20+57
20+59
20+61
20+62
20+64
20+67
20+69
20+70
20+71
20+72
20+74
20+76
21+01
21+02
21+03*
21+07*
21+09*
21+11*
21+13*
21+15*
21+16*
21+17*
21+18*
21+19*
21+21*
21+22*
21+23*
21+24*
21+25*
21+26*
21+27*
21+29*
21+30*
21+31*
21+32*
21+34
21+35
21+37
21+38
21+42
21+44
21+45
21+49
21+50
21+52
21+55

21+56
21+58
21+60
21+63
21+64
21+65
21+67
21+68
21+69
21+71
21+72
21+74
21+75
21+78
21+81
21+82
21+83
21+84
21+85
21+86
21+90
21+91
21+92
21+93
21+94
21+95
21+96
21+98
21+99
22+00
22+01
22+03
22+04
22+06
22+07
22+10
22+11*
22+12*
22+13*
22+14*
22+15*
22+16*
22+17*
22+18*
22+19*
22+20*
22+21*
22+22*
22+26*
22+28*
22+32
22+35
22+36
22+37
22+38
22+39
22+40
22+41
22+43
22+44
22+45
22+46
22+47
22+48
22+49
22+50
22+55
22+56
22+57
22+58

Serial	Serial	Serial
22+59	23+99	25+48
22+61	24+00	25+49
22+62	24+02	25+50
22+63	24+03	25+51
22+65	24+05	25+52
22+67	24+06	25+54
22+68	24+07	25+59
22+69	24+11	25+61
22+70*	24+12	25+62
22+71*	24+13	25+74
22+72*	24+19	25+78
22+73*	24+21	25+79
22+74*	24+22	25+80
22+77*	24+26	25+81
22+78*	24+27	25+86
22+80*	24+28	26+03
22+81*	24+33*	26+04
22+82*	24+38	26+05
22+83*	24+42	26+07
22+84*	24+43	26+08
22+85*	24+46	26+11
22+86*	24+49	26+12
22+87*	24+51	26+13
22+88*	24+53	26+15
22+90	24+54	26+17
22+91	24+57	26+19
22+92	24+60	26+20
22+95*	24+74	26+23
22+97*	24+77	26+24
22+98*	24+79	26+25
22+99*	24+83	26+26
23+01	24+85	26+28
23+02*	24+88	26+29
23+05	24+89	26+30
23+06*	24+90	26+31
23+07*	24+95	26+32
23+08*	24+98	26+33
23+09*	24+99	26+34
23+11*	25+02*	26+36
23+12*	25+04	26+37
23+15*	25+05	26+38
23+16*	25+09	26+39
23+17*	25+12	26+40
23+19*	25+13	26+41
23+20*	25+15	26+42
23+22*	25+17	26+43
23+23*	25+18	26+44
23+24	25+19	26+45
23+25*	25+22	26+47
23+27	25+23	26+49
23+29	25+24	26+51
23+31	25+26	26+52
23+32	25+27	26+53
23+40	25+28	26+56*
23+48	25+29	26+57*
23+50	25+30	26+58*
23+51	25+31	26+60*
23+61	25+32	26+61*
23+62	25+33	26+62*
23+65	25+34	26+63*
23+74	25+35	26+65*
23+83	25+36	26+66*
23+84	25+37	26+67*
23+87	25+40	26+69*
23+88	25+42	26+70*
23+92	25+43	26+72*
23+94	25+44	26+74*
23+95	25+45	26+75*
23+97	25+46	26+76*
23+98	25+47	26+78*

Overseas Serials

Serial	Serial	Serial
26+79*	35+66	37+49
26+80*	35+67	37+50
26+81*	35+68	37+51
26+82*	35+69	37+52
26+83*	35+71	37+53
26+85*	35+72	37+54
26+86*	35+73	37+55
26+87*	35+74	37+56
26+88*	35+75	37+57
26+89*	35+76	37+58
26+90*	35+77	37+60
McD RF-4E	35+78	37+61
Phantom	35+79	37+63
35+01	35+81	37+64
35+02	35+82	37+65
35+03	35+83	37+66
35+04	35+84	37+67
35+05	35+85	37+69
35+06	35+86	37+70
35+08	35+87	37+71
35+09	35+88	37+73
35+10	**McD F-4F**	37+75
35+11	**Phantom**	37+76
35+12	37+01	37+77
35+13	37+03	37+78
35+14	37+04	37+79
35+15	37+05	37+80
35+17	37+06	37+81
35+18	37+07	37+82
35+19	37+08	37+83
35+20	37+09	37+84
35+21	37+10	37+85
35+22	37+11	37+86
35+24	37+12	37+88
35+25	37+13	37+89
35+26	37+14	37+90
35+27	37+15	37+91
35+28	37+16	37+92
35+29	37+17	37+93
35+31	37+18	37+94
35+32	37+19	37+95
35+33	37+20	37+96
35+35	37+21	37+97
35+36	37+22	37+98
35+37	37+23	37+99
35+38	37+24	38+00
35+39	37+25	38+01
35+40	37+26	38+02
35+41	37+27	38+03
35+42	37+28	38+04
35+43	37+29	38+05
35+44	37+30	38+06
35+46	37+31	38+07
35+48	37+32	38+08
35+49	37+33	38+09
35+50	37+34	38+10
35+51	37+35	38+11
35+52	37+36	38+12
35+53	37+37	38+13
35+54	37+38	38+14
35+56	37+39	38+15
35+57	37+40	38+16
35+58	37+41	38+17
35+59	37+42	38+18
35+60	37+43	38+20
35+61	37+44	38+21
35+62	37+45	38+24
35+63	37+46	38+25
35+64	37+47	38+26
35+65	37+48	38+27

Serial	Serial	Serial
38+28	40+26	40+97
38+29	40+27	40+98
38+30	40+28	40+99
38+31	40+29	41+00
38+32	40+30	41+01
38+33	40+31	41+02
38+34	40+32	41+03
38+36	40+33	41+04
38+37	40+34	41+05
38+38	40+35	41+06
38+39	40+36	41+07
38+40	40+37	41+08
38+41	40+38	41+09
38+42	40+39	41+10
38+43	40+40	41+11
38+44	40+41	41+12
38+45	40+42	41+13
38+46	40+43	41+14
38+47	40+44	41+15
38+48	40+45	41+16
38+49	40+46	41+17
38+50	40+47	41+18
38+51	40+48	41+19
38+52	40+49	41+20
38+53	40+50	41+21
38+54	40+51	41+22
38+55	40+52	41+23
38+56	40+53	41+24
38+57	40+54	41+25
38+58	40+56	41+26
38+59	40+57	41+27
38+60	40+58	41+28
38+61	40+59	41+29
38+62	40+60	41+30
38+63	40+61	41+31
38+64	40+62	41+32
38+66	40+63	41+33
38+67	40+64	41+34
38+68	40+65	41+35
38+69	40+66	41+36
38+70	40+67	41+37
38+72	40+68	41+38
38+73	40+69	41+39
38+74	40+70	41+40
38+75	40+71	41+41
D-BD Alpha Jet	40+72	41+42
40+02	40+73	41+43
40+03	40+74	41+44
40+04	40+75	41+45
40+05	40+76	41+46
40+06	40+77	41+47
40+07	40+78	41+48
40+08	40+79	41+49
40+09	40+80	41+50
40+10	40+81	41+51
40+11	40+82	41+52
40+12	40+83	41+53
40+13	40+84	41+54
40+14	40+85	41+55
40+15	40+86	41+56
40+16	40+87	41+57
40+17	40+88	41+58
40+18	40+89	41+59
40+19	40+90	41+60
40+20	40+91	41+61
40+21	40+92	41+62
40+22	40+93	41+63
40+23	40+94	41+64
40+24	40+95	41+65
40+25	40+96	41+66

Overseas Serials

Serial	Serial	Serial
41+67	43+61*	44+33
41+68	43+62*	44+34
41+69	43+63*	44+35
41+70	43+64*	44+36
41+71	43+65*	44+37
41+72	43+67*	44+38
41+73	43+68*	44+39
41+74	43+69*	44+40
41+75	43+70*	44+41
Panavia Tornado	43+71*	44+42
*Marinesflieger	43+72*	44+43
(†TTTE Cottesmore)	43+73*	44+44
43+01/G-20†	43+74*	44+45
43+02/G-21†	43+75*	44+46
43+03/G-22†	43+76*	44+47
43+04/G-23†	43+77*	44+48
43+05/G-24†	43+78*	44+49
43+06/G-25†	43+79*	44+50
43+07/G-26†	43+80*	44+51
43+08/G-27†	43+81*	44+52
43+09/G-28†	43+82*	44+53
43+10/G-29†	43+83*	44+54
43+11/G-30†	43+84*	44+55
43+12/G-70†	43+85*	44+56
43+13/G-71†	43+86*	44+57
43+14/G-72†	43+87*	44+58
43+15/G-31†	43+88*	44+59
43+16/G-32†	43+89*	44+60
43+17/G-33†	43+90	44+61
43+18/G-77†	43+91	44+62
43+19*	43+92	44+63
43+20/G-73†	43+94	44+64
43+22	43+95	**Transall C-160**
43+23/G-34†	43+96	50+06
43+24/G-74†	43+97	50+07
43+25/G-75†	43+98	50+08
43+26/G-76†	43+99	50+09
43+27*	44+00	50+10
43+28	44+01	50+17
43+29/G-35†	44+02	50+29
43+30	44+03	50+33
43+31/G-36†	44+04	50+34
43+32	44+05	50+35
43+33	44+06	50+36
43+34	44+07	50+37
43+35/G-38†	44+08	50+38
43+36	44+09	50+39
43+37/G-37†	44+10	50+40
43+38	44+11	50+41
43+40	44+12	50+42
43+41	44+13	50+43
43+42*	44+14	50+44
43+43*	44+15	50+45
43+44*	44+16	50+46
43+45	44+17	50+47
43+46*	44+18	50+48
43+47*	44+19	50+49
43+48*	44+20	50+50
43+49*	44+21	50+51
43+50*	44+22	50+52
43+51*	44+23	50+53
43+52*	44+24	50+54
43+53*	44+25	50+55
43+54*	44+26	50+56
43+55*	44+27	50+57
43+56*	44+28	50+58
43+57*	44+29	50+59
43+58*	44+30	50+60
43+59*	44+31	50+61
43+60*	44+32	50+62

Serial	Serial	Serial
50+64	58+21	58+92
50+65	58+22	58+93
50+66	58+23	58+94
50+67	58+24	58+95
50+68	58+25	58+96
50+69	58+26	58+97
50+70	58+27	58+98
50+71	58+28	58+99
50+72	58+29	59+00
50+73	58+30	59+01
50+74	58+31	59+02
50+75	58+32	59+03
50+76	58+33	59+04
50+77	58+34	59+05
50+78	58+35	59+06*
50+79	58+36	59+07*
50+80	58+37	59+08*
50+81	58+38	59+09*
50+82	58+39	59+10*
50+83	58+40	59+11*
50+84	58+41	59+12*
50+85	58+42	59+13*
50+86	58+43	59+14*
50+87	58+44	59+15*
50+88	58+45	59+16*
50+89	58+46	59+17*
50+90	58+47	59+18*
50+91	58+48	59+19*
50+92	58+49	59+20*
50+93	58+50	59+21*
50+94	58+51	59+22*
50+95	58+52	59+23*
50+96	58+53	59+24*
50+97	58+54	59+25*
50+98	58+55	**Breguet**
50+99	58+56	**1151 Atlantic**
51+00	58+57	***Marinesflieger**
51+01	58+58	61+01*
51+02	58+59	61+02*
51+03	58+60	61+03*
51+04	58+61	61+04*
51+05	58+62	61+05*
51+06	58+63	61+06*
51+07	58+64	61+07*
51+08	58+65	61+08*
51+09	58+66	61+09*
51+10	58+67	61+10*
51+11	58+68	61+11*
51+12	58+69	61+12*
51+13	58+70	61+13*
51+14	58+71	61+14*
51+15	58+72	61+15*
Dornier Do.28D-2	58+73	61+16*
Skyservant	58+74	61+17*
*Marinesflieger	58+75	61+19*
58+05	58+76	61+20*
58+06	58+77	**Westland**
58+08	58+78	**Lynx Mk88**
58+09	58+79	***Marinesflieger**
58+10	58+80	83+01*
58+11	58+81	83+02*
58+12	58+82	83+03*
58+13	58+83	83+04*
58+14	58+84	83+05*
58+15	58+85	83+06*
58+16	58+86	83+07*
58+17	58+87	83+08*
58+18	58+89	83+09*
58+19	58+90	83+10*
58+20	58+91	83+11*

Overseas Serials

Serial	Serial	Serial
83+12*	89+56*	89+67*
Westland Sea	89+57*	89+68*
King HAS.41	89+59*	89+69*
***Marinesflieger**	89+60*	89+70*
89+50*	89+61*	89+71*
89+51*	89+62*	**English Electric**
89+53*	89+63*	**Canberra B2**
89+54*	89+65*	99+34
89+55*	89+66*	99+35

E185 General Dynamics F-16A; Royal Danish Air Force. *APM*

31-13 McDonnell Douglas DC9; Italian Air Force. *PRM*

46-34 Aeritalia G-222; Italian Air Force. *PRM*

Historic Aircraft in Overseas Markings

'Historic' aircraft carrying the markings of overseas air arms which can be seen in the UK, mainly preserved in museums and collections or taking part in air shows.

Serial	Type (alternative identity)	Owner, operator and location	Notes
Argentina			
A-517	FMA IA58 Pucara (G-BLRP)	Grampian Helicopters	
A-522	FMA IA58 Pucara (8768M)	FAA Museum, RNAS Yeovilton	
A-528	FMA IA58 Pucara (8769M)	RAF Cosford Aerospace Museum	
A-533	FMA IA58 Pucara (ZD486)	Museum of Army Flying, Middle Wallop	
A-549	FMA IA58 Pucara (ZD487)	Imperial War Museum, Duxford	
AE-406	Bell UH-1H	RNAY Fleetlands	
AE-409	Bell UH-1H	Museum of Army Flying, Middle Wallop	
AE-413	Bell UH-1H	Privately owned, Hampshire	
AE-422	Bell UH-1H	FAA Museum, RNAS Yeovilton	
AE-520	Vertol CH-47C Chinook	RAF AMS, Brize Norton	
0729	Beech T-34C Turbo Mentor [1-A-411]	FAA Museum, RNAS Yeovilton	
0767	Macchi MB339AA [4-A-116]	FAA Museum, RNAS Yeovilton	
PA-12	Sud SA330L Puma	RNAY Fleetlands	
Australia			
A2-4	Supermarine Seagull V (VH-ALB)	Battle of Britain Museum, Hendon	
A16-199	Lockheed Hudson IV (G-BEOX) [SF-R]	RAF Museum, Hendon	
Belgium			
FT-36	Lockheed T-33A	Dumfries & Galloway Aviation Museum, Tinwald Downs	
FT-37	Lockheed T-33A	RAF Alconbury	
FU-6	Republic F-84F Thunderstreak (52-7133)	RAF Museum, at Rochester for restoration	
HD-75	Hanriot HD1 (OO-APJ/G-AFDX/N75)	RAF Museum, Hendon	
Cambodia			
125	Morane MS733 Alcyon (G-SHOW/ F-BMQJ)	Privately owned, Booker	
Canada			
920	VS Stranraer (CF-BXO) [Q-N]	RAF Museum, Hendon	
5547	Hawker Hurricane II (G-HURI)	Privately owned, Coventry	
9059	Bristol Bolingbroke IVT	Privately owned, Portsmouth	
9893	Bristol Bolingbroke IVT	Privately owned, Duxford	
9940	Bristol Bolingbroke IVT	Royal Scottish Museum of Flight, East Fortune	
10038	Bristol Bolingbroke IVT (G-MKIV)	Privately owned, Duxford	
10201	Bristol Bolingbroke IVT	Strathallan Aircraft Collection	
18393	Avro Canada CF-100 (G-BCYK)	Imperial War Museum, Duxford	
20385	CCF AT-16 Harvard IV (G-BGPB)	Privately owned, Duxford	
Denmark			
E-402	Hawker Hunter F51	Privately owned, Macclesfield	
E-407	Hawker Hunter F51	Phoenix Aviation Museum, Bruntingthorpe	
E-408	Hawker Hunter F51 (8565M) [B]	RAF Brawdy, main gate	
E-412	Hawker Hunter F51	Tangmere Military Aviation Museum	
E-419	Hawker Hunter F51	North East Aircraft Museum, Usworth	
E-421	Hawker Hunter F51	Brooklands College of Technology, Surrey	
E-424	Hawker Hunter F51	Lincolnshire Aviation Museum, Tattershall	
E-425	Hawker Hunter F51	Midland Air Museum, Coventry	
E-427	Hawker Hunter F51 (G-9-447)	BAe Apprentice School, Brough	
ET-271	Hawker Hunter T53	Warbirds of GB, Blackbushe	

Historic Aircraft

Notes	Serial	Type (alternative identity)	Owner, operator and location
	ET-273	Hawker Hunter T7	Bomber County Aviation Museum, Cleethorpes
	L866	Consolidated Catalina (8466M)	RAF Cosford Aerospace Museum
	P122	DH Chipmunk 22 (G-ALUL)	Privately owned, Northants
Eire			
	177	Percival Provost T1	Privately owned, Shobdon
	178	Percival Provost T1 (G-BKOS)	Privately owned, Woodvale
France			
	9	Dassault Mystere IVA	RAF Woodbridge
	19	Deperdussin Replica (BAPC136)	Leisure Sport, Thorpe Park
	25	Dassault Mystere IVA	RAF Woodbridge
	36	Dassault Mystere IVA [EABDR 8]	RAF Upper Heyford
	45	SNCAN Stampe SV4C (G-BHFG)	Privately owned, Enstone
	46	Dassault Mystere IVA [EABDR 6]	RAF Upper Heyford
	50	Dassault Mystere IVA	RAF Woodbridge
	57	Dassault Mystere IVA [8-MT]	Imperial War Museum, Duxford
	59	Dassault Mystere IVA [314-TH]	Wales Aircraft Museum, Cardiff
	70	Dassault Mystere IVA	Midland Air Museum, Coventry
	75	Dassault Mystere IVA	RAF Lakenheath
	79	Dassault Mystere IVA [8-NB]	Norfolk & Suffolk Aviation Museum, Flixton
	83	Dassault Mystere IVA [8-MS]	Newark Air Museum, Winthorpe
	84	Dassault Mystere IVA	Lashenden Air Warfare Museum, Headcorn
	85	Dassault Mystere IVA [8-MV]	Phoenix Aviation Museum, Bruntingthorpe
	92	MH Broussard (G-BJGW) [31-GW]	Privately owned, Duxford
	97	Dassault Mystere IVA	RAF Lakenheath
	99	Dassault Mystere IVA	RAF Lakenheath
	101	Dassault Mystere IVA [8-MN]	Bomber County Aviation Museum, Cleethorpes
	104	Dassault Mystere IVA	RAF Woodbridge
	120	Stampe SV4C (G-AZGC)	Privately owned, Booker
	121	Dassault Mystere IVA [8-MY]	City of Norwich Aviation Museum
	126	Dassault Mystere IVA [EABDR 7]	RAF Lakenheath
	127	Dassault Mystere IVA	RAF Upper Heyford
	133	Dassault Mystere IVA	RAF Woodbridge
	139	Dassault Mystere IVA [EABDR 9]	RAF Upper Heyford
	146	Dassualt Mystere IVA [8-MC]	North East Aircraft Museum, Usworth
	184	Dassault Mystere IVA	RAF Lakenheath, BDRT
	217	MH Broussard (G-BKPU)	Privately owned, Shawdene
	276	Dassault Mystere IVA	RAF Woodbridge
	309	Dassault Mystere IVA	RAF Lakenheath
	318	Dassault Mystere IVA	Dumfries & Galloway Aviation Museum, Tinwald Downs
	319	Dassault Mystere IVA [8-ND]	Rebel Air Museum, Andrewsfield
	1049	Morane MS230 (G-BJCL)	Privately owned, Booker
	1076	Morane MS230 (G-AVEB)	Privately owned, Booker
	3398	Spad XII Replica (G-BFYO) [2]	Privately owned, St Just
	133722	Vought F4U-7 Corsair (NX1337A) [15F22]	Privately owned, Duxford
Germany			
	C19/18	Albatross replica (BAPC 118)	Privately owned, North Weald
	D5397/17	Albatross D.VA Replica (G-BFXL)	Privately owned, St Just
	5036	Bucker Jungmann (G-ATJX) [AT+JX]	Privately owned, Stapleford Tawney
	AX+IH	Bucker Jungmeister (G-AXIH)	Privately owned, White Waltham
	D2+600	CASA 352L (G-BFHG)	Aces High, Duxford
	1Z+EK	CASA 352L (N9012P)	Privately owned, Rochester
	N8+AA	CASA 352L (G-BFHD)	Warbirds of GB, Blackbushe
	N9+AA	CASA 352L (G-BECL)	Warbirds of GB, Blackbushe
	6J+PR	CASA 2-111 (G-AWHB)	Privately owned, London
	475081	Fieseler Fi156C Storch (VP546/7362M)	RAF St Athan Historic Aircraft Collection
	CB+VD	Fieseler Fi156C Storch (D-EKMU)	Whitehall Theatre of War, London
	28368	Flettner Fl282V Kolibri	Midland Air Museum, Coventry
	100143	Focke-Achgelis Fa330	Imperial War Museum, Duxford

Serial	Type (alternative identity)	Owner, operator and location	Notes
100406	Focke-Achgelis Fa330	Institute of Technology, Cranfield	
100502	Focke-Achgelis Fa330	The Aeroplane Collection, Wigan	
100509	Focke-Achgelis Fa330	Science Museum, South Kensington	
100545	Focke-Achgelis Fa330	Torbay Aircraft Museum, Paignton	
100549	Focke-Achgelis Fa330	Manchester Air & Space Museum	
04	Focke Wulf FW190 Replica (G-WULF)	Privately owned, Elstree	
7334	Focke Wulf Fw190 replica (G-SYFW) [2+1]	Privately owned, Guernsey	
584219/38	Focke Wulf FW190F-8/UI (8470M)	RAF St Athan Historic Aircraft Collection	
733682	Focke Wulf FW190A-8/R6	Imperial War Museum, Lambeth	
4253/18	Fokker D.VII (G-BFPL)	Privately owned, Sandown	
5125/18	Fokker D.VII Replica (BAPC 110)	Leisure Sport, Thorpe Park	
8417/18	Fokker D.VII	RAF Museum Restoration Centre, Cardington	
150/17	Fokker Dr.1 Dreidekker Replica (BAPC 139)	Leisure Sport, Thorpe Park	
152/17	Fokker Dr.1 Dreidekker Replica (G-ATJM)	British Aerial Museum, Duxford	
425/17	Fokker Dr.1 Dreidekker Replica (BAPC 133)	Torbay Aircraft Museum, Paignton	
425/17	Fokker Dr.1 Dreidekker replica (G-BEFR)	Privately owned, St Athan	
422/15	Fokker EIII replica (G-AVJO)	Privately owned, Booker	
22912	Hansa Brandenburg W.29 Replica (BAPC 138)	Leisure Sport, Thorpe Park	
701152	Heinkel He111H-23 (8471M) [NT+SL]	Battle of Britain Museum, Hendon	
120227	Heinkel He162 Salamander (8472M) [2]	RAF St Athan Historic Aircraft Collection	
120235	Heinkel He162 Salamander	Imperial War Museum, Lambeth	
14	Hispano HA1112 (C4K-235/ G-BJZZ)	Whitehall Theatre of War, London	
1Z+NK	Junkers Ju52/3M (6316)	Imperial War Museum, Duxford	
494083	Junkers Ju87 D-3 (8474M) [RI+,lK]	Battle of Britain Museum, Hendon	
360043	Junkers Ju88R-1 (PJ876/8475M) [D5+EV]	Battle of Britain Museum, Hendon	
7198/18	LVG C.VI (G-AANJ)	Shuttleworth Collection, Old Warden	
1190	Messerschmitt Bf109E-3	Privately owned, Hurn	
4101	Messerschmitt Bf109E-4 (DG200/ 8477M)	Battle of Britain Museum, Hendon	
10639	Messerschmitt Bf109G-2 (RN228/ 8478M)	RAF Benson, under restoration	
730301	Messerschmitt Bf110C-4 (AX772/ 8479M)	Battle of Britain Museum, Hendon	
191316	Messerschmitt Me163B Komet	Science Museum, South Kensington	
191614	Messerschmitt Me163B Komet (8481M)	RAF Cosford Aerospace Museum	
191659	Messerschmitt Me163B Komet	Royal Scottish Museum of Flight, East Fortune	
191660	Messerschmitt Me163B Komet	Imperial War Museum, Duxford	
191904	Messerschmitt Me163B Komet (8480M) [25]	RAF St Athan Historic Aircraft Collection	
112372	Messerschmitt Me262A-1 (VK893/ 8482M)	RAF Cosford Aerospace Museum	
420430	Messerschmitt Me410A-1/U2 (8483M) [PD+VO]	RAF Cosford Aerospace Museum	
ZA+WN	Morane 500 (G-AZMH)	Privately owned, Booker	
FI+S	Morane 505 (G-BIRW)	Royal Scottish Museum of Flight, East Fortune	
17	Nord 1002 (G-ATBG)	Privately owned, Sutton Bridge	
16+RF	Pilatus P-2 (U-110/G-PTWO)	Privately owned, Duxford	
1480	SNCAN Noralpha (G-BAYV)	Booker Aircraft Museum	
Italy			
MM5701	Fiat CR42 (BT474/8468M) [13-95]	Battle of Britain Museum, Hendon	
MM53211	Fiat G.46-4 (BAPC 79)	Privately owned, Lympne	
MM53432	NA T-6D (RM-11)	Privately owned, Staverton	

Historic Aircraft

Notes	Serial	Type (alternative identity)	Owner, operator and location
	MM54137	NA T-6G Texan (G-CTKL)	Privately owned, Dorchester
	MM542540	Piper Super Cub	RAF Woodbridge, stored
	146	Dassault Mystere IVA [8-MC]	North East Aircraft

Netherlands

	E-15	Fokker S-11 Instructor (G-BIYU)	Privately owned, Denham
	R-163	Piper Super Cub (G-BIRH)	Privately owned, Lee-on-Solent
	204/V	Lockheed SP-2H Neptune	RAF Cosford Aerospace Museum

Norway

| | 56321 | Saab Safir (G-BKPY) | Newark Air Museum, Winthorpe |

South Africa

| | 6130 | Lockheed Ventura II (AJ469) | RAF Museum store, Henlow |
| | 7185 | NA AT-6C Harvard IIA (G-BGOU) | Privately owned, Audley End |

Spain

| | T2B-272 | CASA C.352L | RAF Cosford Aerospace Museum |
| | HD5-1 | Dornier Do24T-3 [58-1] | RAF Museum, Hendon |

Sweden

| | 35075 | Saab J-35J Draken [40] | Duxford Aviation Society |
| | 29640 | Saab J-29F [08] | RAF Cosford Aerospace Museum |

Switzerland

	J-108	Pilatus P-2 (G-BJAX)	Privately owned, Cranwell
	U-125	Pilatus P-2 (G-BLKZ)	Warbirds of GB, Blackbushe
	U-142	Pilatus P-2 (G-BONE)	Privately owned, Southend
	U-143	Pilatus P-2 (G-CJCI)	Warbirds of GB, Blackbushe
	J-1008	DH Vampire FB6	Mosquito Aircraft Museum, London Colney
	J-1172	DH Vampire FB6 (8487M)	Manchester Air & Space Museum
	J-1523	DH Venom FB50 (G-VENI)	Privately owned, Cranfield
	J-1542	DH Venom FB50 (G-GONE)	Privately owned, Hurn
	J-1601	DH Venom FB50 (G-VIDI)	Privately owned, Cranfield
	J-1605	DH Venom FB50 (G-BLID)	Aces High, Duxford
	J-1614	DH Venom FB50 (G-BLIE)	Aces High, Duxford
	J-1616	DH Venom FB50 (G-BLIF)	Aces High, Duxford
	J-1632	DH Venom FB50 (G-VNOM)	Privately owned, Cranfield
	J-1704	DH Venom FB4	RAF Cosford Aerospace Museum
	J-1790	DH Venom FB54 (G-BLKA)	Privately owned, Cranfield
	J-1799	DH Venom FB54 (G-BLIC)	Aces High, Duxford

USA

	0-17899	Convair VT-29B	Imperial War Museum, Duxford
	111989	Cessna L-19A Bird Dog (N33600)	Museum of Army Flying, Middle Wallop
	115042	NA T-6G Texan (G-BGHU) [TA-042]	Privately owned, Wellesbourne Mountford
	115227	NA AT-6G Harvard (G-BKRA)	Privately owned, Shoreham
	115302	Piper L-18C (G-BJTP)	Privately owned, Sywell
	12392	NA AT-6D Harvard III (FE905/LN-BNM)	Privately owned, London
	133722	C-V F4U-7 Corsair (NX1337A) [15F22]	Privately owned, Duxford
	133854	NA Harvard III (G-SUES)	Privately owned, Biggin Hill
	14060	Lockheed T-33A [LN]	RAF Lakenheath
	14286	Lockheed T-33A [WK]	Imperial War Museum, Duxford
	14419	Lockheed T-33A [30-QC]	Midland Air Museum, Coventry
	146289	NA T-28 Trojan (N99153)	Norfolk & Suffolk Aviation Museum, Flixton
	151632	NA TB-25N Mitchell (NL9494Z)	Privately owned, Blackbushe
	164	Beech 18 (G-BKGL)	British Aerial Museum, Duxford
	16718	Lockheed T-33A	RAF Sculthorpe
	16769	Lockheed T-33A	RAF Mildenhall
	17473	Lockheed T-33A	RAF Cosford Aerospace Museum
	181528	Piper J-3C-65 Cub	Privately owned, Southampton
	19252	Lockheed T-33A [314-UY]	Tangmere Military Aviation Museum
	231983	Boeing B-17G [IY-G]	Imperial War Museum, Duxford

Serial	Type (alternative identity)	Owner, operator and location	Notes
24535	Kaman HH-43F Huskie	Midland Air Museum, Coventry	
26	Boeing Stearman (G-BAVO)	Privately owned, Liverpool	
27767	Aeronca L-3A (G-BIHW)	Privately owned, Shobdon	
2807	NA T-6G Texan (G-BHTH)	Privately owned, Liverpool	
29963	Lockheed T-33A	Wales Aircraft Museum, Cardiff	
315509	Douglas C-47D (G-BHUB)	Imperial War Museum, Duxford	
329417	Piper J-3C-65 Cub (G-BDHK)	Privately owned, Coleford	
329601	Piper J-3C-65 Cub (G-AXHR) [D-44]	Privately owned, Old Warden	
329934	Piper J-3C-65 Cub (G-BCPH) [72-B]	Privately owned, Booker	
34037	NA TB-25N Mitchell (429366/ N9115Z/151645/8838M)	Bomber Command Museum, Hendon	
413048	Piper J-3C-65 Cub (G-BCXJ) [39-E]	Privately owned, Compton Abbas	
414	NA P-51D Mustang (IDAF-48) [C5-E]	Whitehall Theatre of War, London	
42157	NA F-100D Super Sabre	North East Aviation Museum, Usworth	
42160	NA F-100D Super Sabre [FW-OOO]	Wales Aircraft Museum, Cardiff	
42163	NA F-100D Super Sabre [11-YG]	Dumfries & Galloway Aviation Museum, Tinwald Downs	
42165	NA F-100D Super Sabre [11-ML]	Imperial War Museum, Duxford	
42174	NA F-100D Super Sabre [11-YF]	Midland Air Museum, Coventry	
42196	NA F-100D Super Sabre [LT]	Norfolk & Suffolk Aviation Museum, Flixton	
42204	NA F-100D Super Sabre [11-MQ]	RAF Alconbury	
42212	NA F-100D Super Sabre [LN]	RAF Sculthorpe	
42223	NA F-100D Super Sabre	Newark Air Museum, Winthorpe	
42239	NA F-100D Super Sabre [FW-239]	Phoenix Aviation Museum, Bruntingthorpe	
430210	NA TB-25N Mitchell (N9455Z)	Privately owned, France	
431171	NA B-25J Mitchell (N7614C)	Imperial War Museum, Duxford	
44	Piper L-18 Super Cub (G-BJLH) [K-33]	Privately owned, Liverpool	
454537	Piper L-4J Cub (G-BFDL) [04-J]	Privately owned, Prestwick	
461748	Boeing B-29A Superfortress (G-BHDK) [Y]	Imperial War Museum, Duxford	
463221	NA P-51D Mustang (N6340T) (really 473149)	Privately owned, Duxford	
472028	NA P-51D Mustang	Privately owned, Teesside	
472216	NA P-51D Mustang (G-BIXL) [WZ-I]	Privately owned, Duxford	
472258	NA P-51D Mustang (really 473979) [WZ-I]	Imperial War Museum, Duxford	
473543	NA P-51D Mustang	Privately owned, Woburn Green, Bucks	
479609	Piper J-3C-65 Cub (G-BHXY)	Privately owned, Barton	
479865	Piper J-3C-65 Cub (G-BHPK) [A-44]	Privately owned, Sywell	
480594	Piper J-3C-65 Cub (G-BEDJ)	Privately owned, Ashford Hill	
483009	NA AT-6 Harvard (really 244540)	Epping Museum, North Weald	
483868	Boeing B-17G Fortress (N5237V)	Bomber Command Museum, Hendon	
485784	Boeing B-17G (G-BEDF) [K-G]	Privately owned, Duxford	
51-15227	NA T-6G Harvard (G-BKRA)	Privately owned, Shoreham	
540	Piper L-4 Cub (G-BCNX)	Privately owned, Monewden	
54048	NA F-100D Super Sabre (really 42269) [LN]	RAF Lakenheath, at gate	
542265	NA F-100D Super Sabre [FW-2265]	RAF Wethersfield, at gate	
542447	Piper PA18-135 Super Cub (G-SCUB)	Privately owned, Anwick	
542457	Piper PA18-135 Super Cub (G-LION/R-167)	Privately owned, Orsett	
542474	Piper PA18-135 Super Cub (G-PCUB/R-164)	Privately owned, Redhill	
54433	Lockheed T-33A [WD]	Norfolk & Suffolk Aviation Museum, Flixton	
54439	Lockheed T-33A	North East Aviation Museum, Usworth	
549205	Republic P-47D Thunderbolt (N47DE)	Warbirds of GB, Blackbushe	
5547	Lockheed T-33A (really 19036)	Newark Air Museum, Winthorpe	
60689	Boeing B-52D Stratofortress	Imperial War Museum, Duxford	
63935	NA F-100F Super Sabre [11-MN]	RAF Alconbury	

Historic Aircraft

Notes	Serial	Type (alternative identity)	Owner, operator and location
	63938	NA F-100F Super Sabre [11-MU]	Lashenden Air Warfare Museum, Headcorn
	7797	Aeronca L-16A (G-BFAF)	Privately owned, Finmere
	82062	DHC U-6A Beaver	Midland Air Museum, Coventry
	8810677	NA AT-6C Harvard (G-VALE) [LTA-584]	Privately owned, Cardiff
	P51D	NA P-51D Mustang (G-PSID) (really 4472258)	Warbirds of GB, Blackbushe

584219 Focke Wulf Fw190F-8/UI; RAF St Athan Historic Aircraft Collection. *PRM*

16+RF Pilatus P-2; Privately owned, Duxford. *PRM*

7185 North American Harvard IIA; Privately owned, Audley End. *PRM*

US Military Aircraft Markings

All USAF aircraft have been allocated a fiscal year (FY) number since 1921. Individual aircraft are given a serial according to the fiscal year in which they are ordered. The numbers commence at 0001 and are prefixed with the year of allocation. For example F-111E 68-0001 was the first aircraft ordered in 1968. The fiscal year (FY) serial is carried on the technical bloc which is usually stencilled on the left-hand side of the aircraft just below the cockpit. The number displayed on the fin is a corruption of the FY serial. Most tactical aircraft carry the fiscal year in small figures followed by the last three digits of the serial in large figures. For example F-111F 70-2362 carries 70362 on its tail. An exception to this practice is the F-5E which carries the five digits of the production serial without the fiscal year. For example the FY serial of the F-5E which displays 01532 is 74-01532. Large transport and tanker aircraft such as C-130s and KC-135s usually display a five-figure number commencing with the last digit of the appropriate fiscal year and four figures of the production number. An example of this is EC-135H 61-0282 which displays 10282 on its fin. Aircraft of more than 10 years vintage which might duplicate a five-figure number of a more modern type in service, are prefixed 0-.

USN serials follow a straightforward numerical sequence which commenced, for the present series, with the allocation of 00001 to an SB2C Helldiver by the Bureau of Aeronautics in 1940. Numbers in the 16000 series are presently being issued. They are usually carried in full on the rear fuselage of the aircraft and displayed either as a four- or five-figure sequence or in full on the fin.

UK based USAF Aircraft

The following aircraft are normally based in the UK. They are listed in alphabetical order of type with individual aircraft in serial number order, as depicted on the aircraft. The number in brackets is either the alternative presentation of the five-figure number commencing with the last digit of the fiscal year, or the fiscal year where a five-figure serial is presented on the aircraft. Where it is possible to identify the allocation of aircraft to individual squadrons by means of colours carried on fin or cockpit edge, this is also provided.

Notes	Serial	Serial	Notes
	Boeing EC-135H	79-220 (90220) gy	
	(513TAW/10 ACCS, Mildenhall)	79-221 (90221) pr	
	FY61	79-224 (90224) gy	
	10282 EC-135H	79-225 (90225) bl	
	10285 EC-135H	80-143 (00143) r	
	10286 EC-135H	80-144 (00144) gy	
	10291 EC-135H	80-145 (00145) y	
		80-146 (00146) bk	
	Fairchild A-10A Thunderbolt II	80-147 (00147) pr	
	WR: 81TFW:	80-155 (00155) pr	
	78TFS red (r) Woodbridge	80-156 (00156) bk	
	91TFS blue (bl) Woodbridge	80-157 (00157) bk	
	92TFS yellow (y) Bentwaters	80-158 (00158) bl	
	509TFS grey (gy) Bentwaters	80-159 (00159) y	
	510TFS purple (pr) Bentwaters	80-160 (00160) pr	
	511TFS black (bk) Bentwaters	80-167 (00167) r	
	79-217 (90217)	80-168 (00168) y	
	79-218 (90218) y	80-169 (00169) pr	
	79-219 (90219) bk	80-170 (00170) gy	

Notes	Serial	Serial	Notes
	80-171 (00171) bl	81-967 (10967) bk	
	80-172 (00172) bk	81-976 (10976)	
	80-179 (00179) r	81-977 (10977) y	
	80-180 (00180) bl	81-978 (10978) r	
	80-181 (00181)	81-979 (10979) gy	
	80-183 (00183) pr	81-980 (10980) pr	
	80-184 (00184) gy	81-981 (10981) bk	
	80-192 (00192) y	81-982 (10982) r	
	80-194 (00194) gy	81-983 (10983) bl	
	80-195 (00195) pr	81-984 (10984) r	
	80-196 (00196)	81-985 (10985) y	
	80-203 (00203) r	81-986 (10986) bk	
	80-204 (00204) bl	81-987 (10987) gy	
	80-205 (00205) bl	81-988 (10988) pr	
	80-206 (00206) y	81-990 (10990) gy	
	80-207 (00207) y	81-991 (10991) bl	
	80-208 (00208)	81-992 (10992) y	
	80-215 (00215) pr	82-646 (20646) pr	
	80-216 (00216) pr	82-647 (20647) bk	
	80-217 (00217) y	82-649 (20649) bl	
	80-218 (00218) gy	82-650 (20650) pr	
	80-219 (00219) gy	82-654 (20654) r	
	80-220 (00220) bl	82-655 (20655) bl	
	80-227 (00227) gy	82-656 (20656) y	
	80-228 (00228) pr	82-657 (20657) gy	
	80-229 (00229) bk	82-658 (20658) r	
	80-230 (00230) bk	82-659 (20659) bk	
	80-231 (00231) gy		
	80-232 (00232) bl	**General Dynamics EF-111A**	
	80-233 (00233) r	**Raven**	
	80-234 (00234) bl	(UH: 20TFW/42ECS, RAF Upper	
	80-235 (00235) r	Heyford)	
	80-236 (00236) r	66-033 (60033)	
	80-237 (00237) bk	66-037 (60037)	
	80-270 (00270) r	66-039 (60039)	
	80-271 (00271) bl	66-041 (60041)	
	80-272 (00272) y	66-056 (60056)	
	80-273 (00273) gy	67-041 (70041)	
	80-274 (00274) pr		
	80-275 (00275) bk	**General Dynamics F-111E**	
	80-276 (00276) y	(UH: 20TFW, RAF Upper Heyford)	
	80-277 (00277) bk	42ECS grey (gy)	
	80-278 (00278) r	55TFS blue (bl)	
	80-279 (00279) pr	77TFS red (r)	
	80-280 (00280) bl	79TFS yellow (y)	
	80-281 (00281) y	67-119 (70119) r	
	81-939 (10939) gy	67-120 (70120) gy	
	81-940 (10940) bk	67-121 (70121) gy	
	81-941 (10941) r	67-122 (70122) gy	
	81-942 (10942)	67-123 (70123) r	
	81-943 (10943) y	68-001 (80001) gy	
	81-944 (10944) pr	68-002 (80002) y	
	81-947 (10947) gy	68-004 (80004) bl	
	81-948 (10948) gy	68-005 (80005) bl	
	81-949 (10949) bk	68-006 (80006) bl	
	81-950 (10950) bl	68-007 (80007) r	
	81-951 (10951) bl	68-009 (80009) r	
	81-952 (10952) pr	68-010 (80010) y	
	81-953 (10953) gy	68-011 (80011) gy	
	81-954 (10954) y	68-013 (80013) y	
	81-955 (10955) bk	68-014 (80014) bl	
	81-956 (10956) bl	68-015 (80015) bl	
	81-957 (10957) y	68-016 (80016) bl	
	81-960 (10960) r	68-017 (80017) r	
	81-961 (10961)	68-020 (80020) multi	
	81-962 (10962) bl	68-021 (80021) gy	
	81-963 (10963) y	68-022 (80022) y	
	81-964 (10964) gy	68-023 (80023) y	
	81-965 (10965) pr	68-025 (80025) bl	
	81-966 (10966) pr		

Serial	Serial
68 026 (80026) bl	70-375 (02375) bl
68-027 (80027) r	70-376 (02376) y
68-028 (80028) r	70-378 (02378) r
68-029 (80029) r	70-379 (02379) r
68-030 (80030) y	70-381 (02381) y
68-031 (80031) gy	70-382 (02382) y
68-032 (80032) y	70-383 (02383) y
68-033 (80033) y	70-384 (02384) r
68-034 (80034) bl	70-385 (02385) gn
68-035 (80035) bl	70-386 (02386) y
68-036 (80036) bl	70-387 (02387) gn
68-037 (80037) r	70-389 (02389) r
68-038 (80038) r	70-390 (02390) gn
68-039 (80039) r	70-391 (02391) gn
68-040 (80040) y	70-392 (02392) gn
68-041 (80041) gy	70-394 (02394) bl
68-043 (80043) y	70-396 (02396) bl
68-044 (80044) bl	70-397 (02397) y
68-046 (80046) bl	70-398 (02398) gn
68-047 (80047) r	70-399 (02399) bl
68-048 (80048) r	70-401 (02401) r
68-049 (80049) r	70-402 (02402) y
68-050 (80050) y	70-403 (02403) bl
68-051 (80051) gy	70-404 (02404) y
68-052 (80052) y	70-405 (02405) r
68-053 (80053) y	70-406 (02406) bl
68-054 (80054) bl	70-408 (02408) r
68-055 (80055) bl	70-409 (02409) r
68-056 (80056) bl	70-411 (02411) bl
68-059 (80059) r	70-412 (02412) gn
68-061 (80061) gy	70-413 (02413) r
68-062 (80062) y	70-414 (02414) gn
68-063 (80063) y	70-415 (02415) y
68-064 (80064) bl	70-416 (02416) r
68-065 (80065) bl	70-417 (02417) r
68-066 (80066) bl	70-418 (02418) bl
68-067 (80067) r	70-419 (02419) gn
68-068 (80068) r	71-883 (10883) bl
68-069 (80069) r	71-884 (10884) gn
68-071 (80071) gy	71-885 (10885) gn
68-072 (80072) y	71-886 (10886) gn
68-073 (80073) y	71-887 (10887) r
68-074 (80074) bl	71-888 (10888) bl
68-075 (80075) bl	71-889 (10889) y
68-076 (80076) bl	71-890 (10890) y
68-077 (80077) r	71-891 (10891) gn
68-078 (80078) r	71-892 (10892) y
68-079 (80079) y	71-893 (10893) bl
68-080 (80080) y	71-894 (10894) gn
68-082 (80082) y	72-442 (21442) r
68-083 (80083) y	72-443 (21443) r
68-084 (80084) bl	72-444 (21444) r
	72-445 (21445) gn
	72-446 (21446) r
General Dynamics F-111F	72-448 (21448) y
(LN: 48TFW, RAF Lakenheath)	72-449 (21449) y
492 TFS blue (bl)	72-450 (21450) y
493 TFS yellow (y)	72-451 (21451) y
494 TFS red (r)	72-452 (21452) r
495 TFS green (gn)	73-707 (30707) r
	73-708 (30708) r
70-362 (02362) bl	73-710 (30710) r
70-363 (02363) y	73-711 (30711) gn
70-364 (02364) bl	73-712 (30712) gn
70-365 (02365) bl	73-713 (30713) gn
70-368 (02368) bl	74-177 (40177) bl
70-369 (02369) bl	74-178 (40178) gn
70-370 (02370) bl	74-180 (40180) bl
70-371 (02371) gn	74-181 (40181) bl
70-373 (02373) bl	74-182 (40182) bl
70-374 (02374) y	

Notes	Serial	Serial	Notes

74-183 (40183) gn
74-184 (40184) y
74-185 (40185) r

Lockheed C-130 Hercules
(67ARRS/39 ARRW, RAF
Woodbridge)

50962 (FY65) HC-130H
60220 (FY66) HC-130P
95820 (FY69) HC-130N
95823 (FY69) HC-130N
95826 (FY69) HC-130N
95827 (FY69) HC-130N

Lockheed TR-1A
(95RS/17RW, RAF Alconbury)

01068 (FY80)
01069 (FY80)
01070 (FY80)

**McDonnell-Douglas RF-4C
Phantom**
(AR: TRS/10TRW, RAF Alconbury)

68-553 (80553)
68-554 (80554)
68-555 (80555)
68-557 (80557)
68-561 (80561)
68-562 (80562)
68-563 (80563)
68-564 (80564)
68-565 (80565)
68-567 (80567)
68-568 (80568)
68-570 (80570)
68-571 (80571)
68-580 (80580)
68-583 (80583)
68-589 (80589)
69-369 (90369)

69-370 (90370)
69-378 (90378)
69-380 (90380)
69-381 (90381)
69-384 (90384)
69-382 (90382)
69-383 (90383)
71-259 (10259)
72-146 (20146)

Northrop F-5E Tiger II
(527AS/10TRW, RAF Alconbury)
FY74

01532
01534
01534 Replica at
     Alconbury gate
01535
01542
01543
01544
01545
01547
01549
01551
01553
01554
01556
01559
01560
01563
01566
01568
01569

Sikorsky HH-53C
(67 ARRS, RAF Woodbridge)

5784 (FY69)
5785 (FY69)
5796 (FY69)
5797 (FY69)
8284 (FY68)

US Navy aircraft based in the UK

Serial

Beech UC-12B
(Naval Air Facility, RAF Mildenhall)
1322/8D (161322)
1503/8G (161503)

80-205 Fairchild A-10A Thunderbolt II; 81TFW, RAF Woodbridge. *APM*

67-041 General Dynamics EF-111A Raven; 20TFW, RAF Upper Heyford. *PRM*

161503 Beech UC-12B; Naval Air Facility, RAF Mildenhall. *PRM*

European based USAF Aircraft

These aircraft are normally based in Western Europe with the USAFE. They are shown in numerical order of type designation, with individual aircraft in serial number order as carried on the aircraft. An alternative five-figure presentation of the serial is shown in brackets where appropriate. Fiscal year (FY) details are also provided if necessary. The unit allocation and operating bases are given for most aircraft.

Serial	Serial	Serial
Bell UH-1N	**McDonnell Douglas**	68-536 (80536) RS
67ARRS	**F-4E Phantom**	68-538 (80538) RS
Det 2 Ramstein*	(RS: 86TFW Ramstein	69-244 (90244) RS
Det 9 Zaragoza†	SP: 52TFW	69-249 (90249) RS
FY69	Spangdahlem)	69-260 (90260) RS
96603†	67-343 (70343) RS	69-264 (90264) RS
96606*	68-370 (80370) RS	69-278 (90278) RS
96607*	68-372 (80372) RS	7-1247 (10247) SP
96608*	68-375 (80375) RS	71-079 (11079) SP
96609*	68-377 (80377) RS	72-139 (20139) SP
96611†	68-378 (80378) RS	72-159 (20159) SP
96630†	68-379 (80379) RS	72-165 (20165) SP
	68-381 (80381) RS	72-166 (20166) SP
	68-384 (80384) RS	72-167 (20167) SP
McDonnell Douglas	68-386 (80386) RS	72-407 (21407) SP
RF-4C Phantom	68-388 (80388) RS	72-477 (21477) SP
(ZR: 26TRW/38TRS	68-392 (80392) RS	72-482 (21482) SP
Zweibrucken)	68-393 (80393) RS	72-483 (21483) SP
64-001 (41001)	68-394 (80394) RS	72-485 (21485) SP
67-469 (70469)	68-401 (80401) RS	74-044 (41044) SP
68-569 (80369)	68-403 (80403) RS	74-045 (41045) SP
69-356 (90356)	68-404 (80404) RS	74-048 (41048) SP
69-360 (90360)	68-406 (80406) RS	74-049 (41049) SP
69-361 (90361)	68-408 (80408) RS	74-050 (41050) SP
69-364 (90364)	68-411 (80411) RS	740-52 (41052) SP
69-365 (90365)	68-413 (80413) RS	74-053 (41053) SP
69-366 (90366)	68-438 (80438) RS	74-055 (41055) SP
69-367 (90367)	68-440 (80440) RS	74-056 (41056) SP
69-368 (90368)	68-441 (80441) RS	74-057 (41057) SP
69-371 (90371)	68-442 (80442) RS	74-059 (41059) SP
69-372 (90372)	68-444 (80444) RS	74-060 (41060) SP
69-374 (90374)	68-445 (80445) RS	74-622 (41622) SP
69-381 (90381)	68-459 (80459) RS	74-628 (41628) SP
71-249 (10249)	68-460 (80460) RS	74-630 (41630) SP
71-251 (10251)	68-464 (80464) RS	74-633 (41633) SP
71-254 (10254)	68-465 (80465) RS	74-634 (41634) SP
72-152 (20152)	68-467 (80467) RS	74-635 (41635) SP
72-153 (20153)	68-476 (80476) RS	74-636 (41636) SP
	68-480 (80480) RS	74-638 (41638) SP
	68-481 (80481) RS	74-639 (41639) SP
McDonnell Douglas	68-496 (80496) RS	74-641 (41641) SP
F-4E Phantom	68-506 (80506) RS	74-642 (41642) SP
(57FIS Keflavik)	68-507 (80507) RS	74-644 (41644) SP
66-300 (60300)	68-508 (80508) RS	74-645 (41645) SP
66-304 (60304)	68-509 (80509) RS	74-647 (41647) SP
66-314 (60314)	68-512 (80512) RS	74-648 (41648) SP
66-328 (60328)	68-516 (80516) RS	74-650 (40650) SP
66-330 (60330)	68-517 (80517) RS	74-650 (41650) SP
66-334 (60334)	68-526 (80526) RS	74-651 (41651) SP
66-336 (60336)	68-527 (80527) RS	74-652 (40652) SP
66-344 (60344)	68-528 (80528) RS	74-652 (41652) SP
66-345 (60345)	68-529 (80529) RS	74-653 (40653) SP
66-346 (60346)	68-530 (80530) RS	74-653 (41653) SP
66-370 (60370)	68-531 (80531) RS	74-654 (40654) SP
66-382 (60382)	68-533 (80533) RS	74-656 (40656) SP
67-224 (70224)	68-534 (80534) RS	74-657 (40657) SP
67-315 (70315)	68-535 (80535) RS	74-659 (40659) SP

Serial	Serial	Serial

74-662 (40662) SP
74-663 (40663) SP
74-664 (40664) SP

**McDonnell Douglas
F-4G Phantom**
(SP 52TFW
Spangdahlem)
69-202 (97202)
69-212 (97212)
69-234 (97234)
69-236 (97236)
69-247 (90247)
69-248 (90248)
69-250 (90250)
69-253 (90253)
69-255 (90255)
69-262 (97262)
69-268 (97268)
69-269 (90269)
69-270 (97270)
69-285 (90285)
69-286 (90286)
69-293 (97293)
69-295 (97295)
69-546 (97546)
69-556 (97556)
69-558 (97558)
69-566 (97566)
69-579 (97579)
69-582 (97582)
69-587 (97587)

**McDonnell Douglas
C-9A Nightingale**
(435TAW Rhein Main)
FY71
10876
10878
10879
10880
10881
10882

Beech C-12
(*58 MAS Ramstein
†7005ABS Stuttgart
‡JUSMG Madrid)
**MAAG Athens
‡‡JUSMG Turkey
22549 (FY76)† C12A
22550 (FY76)† C-12A
22932 (FY77)† C-12A
22933 (FY77)† C-12A
30498 (FY83) C-12A
31212 (FY83)‡ C-12A
31216 (FY73)* C-12A
31218 (FY73)** C-12A
40161 (FY84)* C-12F
40162 (FY84)* C-12F
40163 (FY84)* C-12F
40164 (FY84)* C-12F
40165 (FY84)* C-12F
40166 (FY84)* C-12F
60166 (FY76)* C-12A
60171 (FY76)* C-12A

**McDonnell Douglas
F-15C/F-15D ‡Eagle**
(CR 32TFS Soesterberg
BT 36TFW Bitburg)
22TFS red (r)
53TFS yellow (y)
525TFS blue (bl)
79-004 (90004) CR‡
79-005 (90005) CR‡
79-006 (90006) BT‡ bl
79-007 (90007) BT‡ y
79-008 (90008) BT‡ bl
79-009 (90009) BT‡ y
79-010 (90010) BT‡ y
79-011 (90011) BT‡ r
79-012 (90012) BT‡ r
79-015 (90015) CR
79-016 (90016) CR
79-017 (90017) CR
79-018 (90018) CR
79-019 (90019) CR
79-020 (90020) CR
79-021 (90021) CR
79-022 (90022) BT r
79-023 (90023) CR
79-024 (90024) CR
79-025 (90025) BT bl
79-026 (90026) CR
79-027 (90027) CR
79-028 (90028) CR
79-029 (90029) CR
79-030 (90030) CR
79-031 (90031) CR
79-032 (90032) CR
79-033 (90033) CR
79-034 (90034) CR
79-035 (90035) BT bl
790-36 (90036) BT multi
79-037 (90037) BT bl
79-038 (90038) BT bl
79-039 (90039) BT bl
79-041 (90041) BT bl
79-042 (90042) BT bl
79-043 (90043) BT bl
79-045 (90045) BT bl
79-046 (90046) BT bl
79-047 (90047) BT bl
79-048 (90048) BT y
79-049 (90049) BT r
79-050 (90050) BT bl
79-051 (90051) BT r
79-052 (90052) BT r
790-53 (90053) BT y
79-054 (90054) BT r
79-055 (90055) BT bl
79-056 (90056) BT r
79-057 (90057) BT r
79-058 (90058) BT bl
79-059 (90059) BT r
79-060 (90060) BT r
79-061 (90061) BT r
79-062 (90062) BT bl
79-063 (90063) BT r
79-064 (90064) BT r
79-065 (90065) BT r
79-066 (90066) BT y
79-067 (90067) BT y
79-068 (90068) BT y
79-069 (90069) BT y
79-070 (90070) BT y

79-072 (90072) BT y
79-073 (90073) BT y
79-074 (90074) BT y
79-075 (90075) BT y
79-076 (90076) BT y
79-077 (90077) BT y
79-078 (90078) BT y
79-079 (90079) BT r
79-080 (90080) BT y
79-081 (90081) BT y
80-002 (00002) BT bl
80-003 (00003) BT y
80-004 (00004) BT multi
80-005 (00005) BT r
80-006 (00006) BT r
80-009 (00009) BT multi
80-010 (00010) BT r
80-011 (00011) BT y
80-012 (00012) BT y
80-013 (00013) BT y
80-014 (00014) BT y
80-015 (00015) BT y
80-016 (00016) BT r
80-017 (00017) BT bl
80-018 (00018) BT bl
80-019 (00019) BT bl
80-020 (00020) BT bl
80-021 (00021) BT r
80-022 (00022) BT r
80-023 (00023) BT r
80-024 (00024) BT bl
80-026 (00026) BT r
80-028 (00028) BT y
80-029 (00029) BT bl
80-031 (00031) BT r
80-032 (00032) BT bl
81-045 (10045) CR
81-046 (10046) CR
81-047 (10047) CR
81-048 (10048) CR
81-049 (10049) CR
81-065 (10065) CR‡
81-066 (10066) CR‡

**General Dynamics
F-16A/F16B‡**
(HR: 50TFW Hahn)
10TFS blue (bl)
313TFS white (w)
496TFS red (r)
(TJ: 401TFW Torrejon)
612TFS blue/white
(bl/w)
613TFS yellow/black
(y/bk)
614TFS red/black (r/bk)
80-543 (00543) HR w
80-544 (00544) HR w
80-545 (00545) HR w
80-546 (00546) HR w
80-555 (00555) HR w
80-556 (00556) HR bl
80-558 (00558) HR bl
80-559 (00559) HR bl
80-560 (00560) HR
80-561 (00561) HR r
80-562 (00562) HR r
80-563 (00563) HR r
80-565 (00565) HR r
80-572 (00572) HR w

USAF (EUR based)

Serial	Serial	Serial
80-574 (00574) HR w	81-791 (10791) TJ bl/w	82-988 (20988) TJ bl/w
80-575 (00575) HR w	81-792 (10792) TJ bl/w	82-991 (20991) TJ bl/w
80-577 (00577) HR bl	81-794 (10794) TJ bl/w	82-992 (20992) TJ bl/w
80-585 (00585) HR w	81-796 (10796) TJ bl/w	82-993 (20993) TJ bl/w
80-586 (00586) HR bl	81-798 (10798) TJ bl/w	82-996 (20996) TJ bl/w
80-587 (00587) HR bl	81-800 (10800) TJ r/bk	82-998 (20998) TJ bl/w
80-588 (00588) HR bl	81-802 (10802) TJ r/bk	82-999 (20999) TJ r/bk
80-589 (00589) HR bl	81-804 (10804) TJ r/bk	83-066 (31066) TJ bl/w
80-590 (00590) HR bl	81-806 (10806) TJ r/bk	83-067 (31067) TJ bl/w
80-592 (00592) HR r	81-808 (10808) TJ r/bk	83-068 (31068) TJ bl/w
80-601 (00601) HR r	81-810 (10810) TJ r/bk	83-069 (31069) TJ bl/w
80-602 (00602) HR r	81-818 (10818)‡ HR bl	83-074 (31074) TJ y/bk
80-603 (00603) HR r	81-819 (10819)‡ HR w	83-079 (31079) TJ y/bk
80-604 (00604) HR r	81-820 (10820)‡ HR r	83-166 (31166)‡ TJ y/bk
80-605 (00605) HR r	81-821 (10821)‡ TJ r/bk	83-167 (31167)‡ TS y/bk
80-606 (00606) HR r	81-822 (10822)‡ TJ r/bk	
80-607 (00607) HR r	82-002 (21002) TJ r/bk	**Gates C-21A**
80-608 (00608) HR r	82-004 (21004) TJ r/bk	**Learjet**
80-610 (00610) HR w	82-007 (21007) TJ r/bk	(*58MAS Ramstein
80-612 (00612) HR w	82-009 (21009) TJ y/bk	†7005ABS Stuttgart)
80-613 (00613) HR bl	82-011 (21011) TJ y/bk	*FY84*
80-614 (00614) HR bl	82-013 (21013) TJ bl/w	40081†
80-615 (00615) HR bl	82-015 (21015) TJ bl/w	40082†
80-616 (00616) HR bl	82-017 (21017) TJ r/bk	40083†
80-618 (00618) HR w	82-020 (21020) TJ y/bk	40084*
80-619 (00619) HR w	82-022 (21022) TJ	40085*
80-620 (00620) HR bl	82-025 (21025) TJ bl/w	40086*
80-622 (00622) HR w	82-031 (21031)‡ HR r	
80-636 (00636)‡ HR w	82-035 (21035)‡ HR bl	**Shorts C-23A**
80-637 (00637)‡ HR bl	82-039 (21039)‡ TJ	**Sherpa**
81-665 (10665) HR w	82-047 (21047)‡ TJ r/bk	(322MAW/10MAS
81-666 (10666) HR r	82-900 (20900) TJ r/bk	Zweibrucken)
81-669 (10669) HR bl	82-902 (20902) TJ r/bk	*FY83*
81-671 (10671) HR w	82-904 (20904) TJ r/bk	30512
81-672 (10672) HR bl	82-906 (20906) TJ r/bk	30513
81-673 (10673) HR bl	82-908 (20908) TJ r/bk	*FY84*
81-674 (10674) HR r	82-911 (20911) TJ r/bk	40458
81-675 (10675) HR bl	82-914 (20914) TJ r/bk	40459
81-680 (10680) HR r	82-918 (20918) TJ r/bk	40460
81-681 (10681) HR w	82-920 (20920) TJ r/bk	40461
81-682 (10682) HR w	82-922 (20922) TJ r/bk	40462
81-694 (10694) HR r	82-924 (20924) TJ r/bk	40463
81-695 (10695) HR w	82-927 (20927) TJ r/bk	40464
81-696 (10696) HR w	82-928 (20928) TJ bl/w	40465
81-697 (10697) HR r	82-931 (20931) TJ bl/w	
81-698 (10698) HR r	82-933 (20933) TJ y/bk	**North American**
81-699 (10699) HR bl	82-936 (20936) TJ y/bk	**T-39A/CT-39A**
81-700 (10700) HR bl	82-938 (20938) TJ y/bk	(*58MAS Ramstein;
81-707 (10707) HR r	82-941 (20941) TJ y/bk	†1868FCS Rhein
81-709 (10709) HR r	82-943 (20943) TJ y/bk	Main
81-710 (10710) HR bl	82-944 (20944) TJ y/bk	‡7005ABS Stuttgart)
81-711 (10711) HR bl	82-946 (20946) TJ y/bk	03483 (FY60)*
81-712 (10712) HR w	82-948 (20948) TJ y/bk	03485 (FY60)*
81-713 (10713) HR w	82-949 (20949) TJ y/bk	10651 (FY60)‡
81-721 (10721) HR w	82-952 (20952) TJ y/bk	10684 (FY61)‡
81-722 (10722) HR	82-954 (20954) TJ y/bk	24453 (FY62)†
multi	82-955 (20955) TJ y/bk	24461 (FY62)*
81-723 (10723) HR r	82-957 (20957) TJ y/bk	24471 (FY62)*
81-731 (10731) HR w	82-959 (20959) TJ y/bk	
81-732 (10732) HR w	82-962 (20962) TJ y/bk	**Sikorsky CH-53C**
81-737 (10737) HR bl	82-965 (20965) TJ y/bk	(601TCW Sembach)
81-738 (10738) HR bl	82-966 (20966) TJ	01625 (FY70)
81-757 (10757) HR bl	82-968 (20968) TJ y/bk	01626 (FY70)
81-758 (10758) HR bl	82-970 (20970) TJ y/bk	01629 (FY70)
81-759 (10759) HR	82-971 (20971) TJ y/bk	01630 (FY70)
81-762 (10762) TJ bl/w	82-975 (20975) TJ y/bk	10924 (FY68)
81-772 (10772) TJ bl/w	82-977 (20977) TJ y/bk	10928 (FY68)
81-773 (10773) TJ bl/w	82-980 (20980) TJ y/bk	10930 (FY68)
81-788 (10788) TJ bl/w	82-982 (20982) TJ bl/w	10932 (FY68)
81-790 (10790) TJ bl/w	82-986 (20986) TJ bl/w	

Serial	Serial	Serial

Lockheed C-130E
Hercules

(37TAS Rhein Main)
(*7405 OS Rhein Main)
01260 (FY70)
01264 (FY70)
01271 (FY70)
01274 (FY70)
10935 (FY68)
10938 (FY68)
10943 (FY68)
10946 (FY68)
10947 (FY68)
17681 (FY64)

18240 (FY64)
21819 (FY62)*
21822 (FY62)*
21828 (FY62)*
37885 (FY63)
40502 (FY64)
40527 (FY64)
40550 (FY64)
96566 (FY69)
96582 (FY69)
96583 (FY69)

Lockheed MC-130E
Hercules
(7SOS Rhein Main)

40523 (FY64)
40551 (FY64)
40555 (FY64)
40561 (FY64)
40566 (FY64)

Lockheed VC-140B
Jetstar
(58MAS Ramstein)
12489 (FY61)
12491 (FY61)
24198 (FY62)
24200 (FY62)
24201 (FY62)

European based US Army Aircraft

Bell AH-1S (FM)
Cobra
2nd Armoured Cavalry
  Regiment: Feucht
11th Armoured Cavalry
  Regiment: Fulda
3rd Aviation Battalion
  (Combat), 'B' Co:
  Giebelstadt
3rd Aviation Battalion
  (Combat), 'C' Co:
  Schweinfurt
8th Aviation Battalion
  (Combat), ''B' Co:
  Mainz-Finthen
8th Aviation Battalion
  (Combat), 'C' Co:
  Mainz-Finthen
501st Aviation
  Battalion (Combat),
  'B' Co: Ansbach
501st Aviation
  Battalion (Combat),
  'C' Co: Illesheim
503rd Aviation
  Battalion (Combat),
  'B' Co: Hanau
503rd Aviation
  Battalion (Combat),
  'C' Co: Hanau
FY68
15007 8 B Co
15015 3 C Co
15036 503 C Co
15038 501 B Co
15045 8 B Co
15046 501 B Co
15057 501 C Co
15069 501 B Co
15084 503 B Co
15085 2 ACR
15092 503 B Co
15093 8 B Co

15104 503 C Co
15105 2 ACR
15106 3 B Co
15110 503 B Co
15112 501 C Co
15113 503 C Co
15116 2 ACR
16131 8 C Co
15134 501 B Co
15142 11 ACR
15152 501 B Co
15167 501 B Co
15173 501 B Co
15180 503 B Co
15208 503 C Co

FY66
15249 503 B Co
15250 2 ACR
15252 11 ACR
15254 2 ACR
15261 2 ACR
15263 8 B Co
15264 3 B Co
15266 2 ACR
15273 11 ACR
15275 503 C Co
15286 2 ACR
15289 8 B Co
15290 2 ACR
15292 8 C Co
15293 501 C Co
15295 2 ACR
15315 503 B Co
15316 3 C Co
15321 8 C Co
15322 501 B Co
15324 501 C Co
15328 503 B Co
15335 11 ACR
15348 3 C Co
15350 3 C Co
15356 11 ACR

FY67
15450 2 ACR
15452 8 C Co
15455 2 ACR
15456 501 C Co
15457 503 C Co
15459 2 ACR
15460 8 B Co
15470 11 ACR
15473 11 ACR
15475 11 ACR
15477 3 C Co
15479 3 B Co
15480 503 B Co
15489 8 B Co
15490 503 B Co
15491 8 C Co
15497 2 ACR
15506 3 B Co
15508 501 C Co
15512 3 B Co
15520 501 C Co
15522 3 B Co
15528 3 B Co
15530 3 B Co
15535 3 C Co
15540 8 C Co
15548 3 B Co
15551 501 C Co
15565 3 C Co
15571 8 B Co
15572 11 ACR
15587 501 C Co
15593 11 ACR
15610 2 ACR
15613 8 C Co
15614 8 B Co
15617 503 B Co
15621 2 ACR
15624 501 B Co
15633 501 C Co
15642 8 C Co
15643 2 ACR

143

US Army (EUR based)

Serial	Serial	Serial
15650 503 B Co	*FY68*	14247 (FY64)*
15652 503 B Co	17023 503 C Co	14248 (FY64)*
15658 11 ACR	17028 503 B Co	14256 (FY64)*
15659 2 ACR	17047 11 ACR	14258 (FY64)*
15662 11 ACR	17049 8 B Co	14261 (FY64)*
15664 3 C Co	17062 503 C Co	14268 (FY64)*
15665 8 C Co	17063 503 B Co	14269 (FY64)*
15666 11 ACR	17066 501 C Co	14270 (FY64)*
15675 11 ACR	17067 501 C Co	15930 (FY68)†
15679 8 C Co	17070 501 C Co	15938 (FY68)†
15682 8 B Co	17074 503 C Co	15940 (FY68)†
15683 501 B Co	17076 501 B Co	15951 (FY68)†
15701 2 ACR	17078 8 B Co	16996 (FY68)†
15710 503 B Co	17079 503 B Co	17004 (FY69)†
15716 503 C Co	17082 503 C Co	17007 (FY69)†
15717 3 B Co	17085 503 C Co	17008 (FY69)†
15721 3 C Co	17087 501 C Co	18898 (FY67)‡
15736 3 C Co	17088 11 ACR	18899 (FY67)‡
15741 503 C Co	17092 503 B Co	18905 (FY67)‡
15745 8 B Co	17095 8 C Co	18909 (FY67)‡
15757 503 C Co	17100 501 B Co	18919 (FY67)‡
15762 501 B Co	17101 503 C Co	18921 (FY67)‡
15764 3 B Co	17104 501 B Co	25886 (FY62)*
15769 8 C Co	17105 501 C Co	25891 (FY62)§
15771 503 B Co	17108 501 C Co	25897 (FY62)§
15772 8 B Co	17111 8 C Co	
15775 503 C Co	17112 503 B Co	**Beech C-12A Super King Air**
15776 503 C Co		($=C-12C, @=RC-12D)
15784 8 B Co	*FY71*	(* 25AvCo, Stuttgart;
15789 501 C Co	20998 11 ACR	† HQ/USEUCOM;
15790 3 C Co	21014 503 C Co	‡ 56AvCo, Vicenza
15805 501 B Co	21028 503 C Co	§ 207AvCo
15815 501 B Co	21035 2 ACR	**1MIB, Wiesbaden)
15822 2 ACR		22250 (FY73)†
15829 501 C Co	*FY78*	22253 (FY73)*
15833 8 C Co	23118 3 B Co	22254 (FY73)§
15842 501 B Co		22255 (FY73)†
15852 503 C Co	*FY79*	22256 (FY73)
15860 8 C Co	23189 3 B Co	22257 (FY73)†
15863 3 C Co	23190 3 B Co	22260 (FY73)‡
	23194 3 B Co	22261 (FY73)†
FY70	23199 3 C Co	22262 (FY73)§
15947 501 C Co	23200 3 C Co	22556 (FY76)‡
15950 501 C Co	23235 3 C Co	22557 (FY76)§
15951 503 C Co		22558 (FY76)†
15952 11 ACR	*FY81*	22564 (FY76)‡
15958 11 ACR	23526 11 ACR	22931 (FY77)†
15959 8 C Co	23527 11 ACR	22944 (FY77)‡
15961 8 C Co	23528 8 C Co	22950 (FY78)§
15970 3 B Co	23529 8 C Co	23126$ (FY78)†
15971 3 C Co	23530 8 C Co	23127$ (FY78)†
15995 2 ACR	23531 8 B Co	23128$ (FY78)†
16012 3 C Co	23532 8 C Co	23132$ (FY78)
16016 3 C Co	23533 8 B Co	23141@ (FY78)**
16048 3 C Co	23534 8 B Co	23143@ (FY78)**
16054 501 B Co	23535 8 B Co	23142@ (FY78)**
16091 501 B Co	23536 8 B Co	23375@ (FY79)**
	23537 3 B Co	23377@ (FY79)**
FY69	23538 3 B Co	23542@ (FY81)**
16411 3 C Co	23539 3 C Co	23638@ (FY82) Athens
16422 501 B Co	23540 3 B Co	23639@ (FY82)
16426 501 B Co		23640@ (FY82)
16429 3 B Co	**Grumman V-1 Mohawk**	23641 @ (FY82)
16431 3 B Co	(*OV-1B; ‡OV-1C,	23642@ (FY82) Athens
16432 503 B Co	†OV-1D, §RV-1D)	
16433 8 B Co	73CIC, Stuttgart	**Beech U-21A King Air**
16434 503 B Co	14239 (FY64)*	(56AvCo)
16436 503 C Co	14244 (FY64)*	(* EU-21A; 7th Signals Bgde)
16445 8 B Co	14246 (FY64)*	

Serial	Serial	Serial
18000 (FY66)*	15028 (FY70)†	18531 (FY67)†
18010 (FY66)	15029 (FY70)†	18533 (FY67)‡
18013 (FY66)*	15030 (FY70)†	18540 (FY67)*
18014 (FY66)	15032 (FY70)†	18548 (FY67)*
18019 (FY66)	15829 (FY68)‡	20946 (FY71)†
18025 (FY66)	15831 (FY68)‡	20950 (FY71)†
18027 (FY66)*	15838 (FY68)†	20951 (FY71)†
18037 (FY66)	15846 (FY68)*	20952 (FY71)†
18040 (FY66)	15847 (FY68)†	20953 (FY71)†
18048 (FY67)	15849 (FY68)†	20954 (FY71)‡
18049 (FY67)	15851 (FY68)†	22277 (FY74)†
18050 (FY67)	15856 (FY68)*	22281 (FY74)*
18058 (FY67)	15865 (FY68)*	22283 (FY74)‡
18078 (FY67)	15867 (FY68)*	22284 (FY74)‡
18080 (FY67)	15868 (FY68)*	22285 (FY74)†
18116 (FY67)	15990 (FY68)‡	22286 (FY74)†
Boeing-Vertol	15995 (FY68)*	22291 (FY74)†
CH-47C Chinook	15997 (FY68)*	22293 (FY74)‡
(* 180AvCo,	16005 (FY68)†	22676 (FY76)†
Schwabisch Hall;	16006 (FY68)*	22677 (FY76)‡
† 205AvCo,	16008 (FY68)‡	22678 (FY76)‡
Mainz-Finthen;	16009 (FY68)†	22679 (FY76)‡
‡ 295AvCo,	17106 (FY69)†	22681 (FY76)*
Coleman Barracks)	17114 (FY69)‡	22683 (FY76)†
15002 (FY70)*	17116 (FY69)*	22684 (FY76)‡
15005 (FY70)†	17117 (FY69)*	23394 (FY79)*
15007 (FY70)†	17118 (FY69)*	23395 (FY79)†
15012 (FY70)‡	17126 (FY69)†	23396 (FY79)*
15020 (FY70)*	18516 (FY67)‡	23398 (FY79)‡

US Navy Aircraft based in Europe

Grumman C-1A Trader
(VR-24 Sigonella)
136756 [JM46]
136757 [JM45]
146025 [JM41]
146028 [JM42]
146034 [JM43]
146049 [JM44]
146051 [JM51]

Grumman C-2A Greyhound
(VR-24 Sigonella)
148148 [JM20]
152786 [JM21]
152791 [JM22]
155123 [JM23]
155124 [JM24]

Douglas EA-3B Skywarrior
(VQ-2 Rota)
144850 [JQ12]
144852 [JQ18]
146448 [JQ14]
146453 [JQ15]
146454 [JQ16]
146455 [JQ17]

Beech UC-12B Super King Air
(8C) NAF Sigonella;
(8D) NAF Rota
1197 [8D] (161197)
1323 [8C] (161323)
1517 [8D] (161517)

NA CT-39G Sabreliner
(VR-24 Sigonella)
159361 [JM30]
159362 [JM31]
159363 [JM32]

Sikorsky RH-53D Sea Stallion
(VR-24 Sigonella)
158690 [JM50]
158691 [JM51]

Lockheed C-130F Hercules
(VR-24: JL: Rota; JM: Sigonella)
149790 [JL790]
149794 [JM794]
149797 [JL797]
149801 [JM801]

Although only a small number of the following Lockheed P-3 Orions are based in Europe, more than half of the aircraft listed have visited or detached during the past two years.

Lockheed P-3 Orion
Brunswick NAS
VP-8; VP-10; VP-11; VP-23; VP-26; VP-44
Jacksonville NAS
CNO; CinC LANT; VP-5; VP-16; VP-24; VP-30; VP-45; VP-49; VP-56; VP-62
Moffett Field NAS
VP-91
New Orleans NAS
VP-94
Patuxent River NAS
NRL; VP-68; VX-1; VXN-8
Rota NAS (Spain)
VQ-2
South Weymouth NAS
VP-92

US Navy (EUR based)

Willow Grove NAS
VP-64; VP-66

P-3A
(‡EP-3A; †EP-3E;
*RP-3A; §VP-3A)

Serial	Unit
148883	NADC
148888 [JQ-23]†	VQ-2
148889	NADC
149667*	VXN-8
149668 [JQ-21]†	VQ-2
149670*	NRL
149673 [JA-6]‡	VX-1
149674‡	NRL
149676§	CNO
149677 [JQ-20]	VQ-2
150494 [JQ-25]†	VQ-2
150495	Keflavik
150496§	CinC LANT
150500*	VXN-8
150502 [JQ-22]†	VQ-2
150503 [JQ-26]†	VQ-2
150505 [JQ-24]†	VQ-2
150511§	CinC AFSE
150514 [LZ-4]	VP-94
150515§	HQ USMC
150517 [LL-17]	VP-30
150527 [JB]	VXN-8
150528 [JB]†	VXN-8
150604 [LV-00]	VP-66
150605 [LW-10]	VP-68
150607	NRL
151349 [LZ-1]	VP-94
151351 [LZ-3]	VP-94
151354 [LW-15]	VP-68
151359 [LZ-2]	VP-94
151360 [LW-12]	VP-68
151361 [LW-1]	VP-68
151364 [LZ-7]	VP-94
151366 [LW-5]	VP-68
151369 [LW-9]	VP-68
151370 [LZ-6]	VP-94
151371 [LZ-00]	VP-94
151376 [LZ-10]	VP-94
151382 [LZ-11]	VP-94
151384 [LW-4]	VP-68
151387 [LZ-5]	VP-94
151389 [LW-6]	VP-68
151390 [LU-0]	VP-64
151392 [LW-2]	VP-68
151395 [LW-14]	VP-68
152140 [LV-12]	VP-66
152141 [LY-11]	VP-92
152143 [LU-2]	VP-64
152146 [LV-1]	VP-66
152147 [LU-5]	VP-64
152148 [LV-11]	VP-66
152150 [LY-7]	VP-92
152152 [LU-10]	VP-64
152154 [LU-7]	VP-64
152156 [LV-10]	VP-66
152157 [LU-1]	VP-64
152158 [LU-4]	VP-64
152160 [LV-3]	VP-66
152162 [LV-7]	VP-66
152163 [LV-5]	VP-66
152165 [LU-11]	VP-64
152166 [LY-1]	VP-92
152168 [LY-6]	VP-92
152169 [LY-3]	VP-92

Serial	Unit
152170 [LY-10]	VP-92
152174 [LU-3]	VP-64
152178 [LY-2]	VP-92
152179 [LY-4]	VP-92
152180 [LV-6]	VP-66
152181 [LU-6]	VP-66
152183 [LV-14]	VP-66
152184 [LU-12]	VP-64
152185 [LV-2]	VP-66
152186 [LY-5]	VP-92

P-3B
(†EP-3B; *YP-3C)

Serial	Unit
152718 [LT-1]	VP-62
152725 [PM-6]	VP-91
152726 [PM-4]	VP-91
152727 [LT-62]	VP-62
152728 [LT-3]	VP-62
152730 [LT-4]	VP-62
152736 [LL-22]	VP-30
152737 [PM-2]	VP-91
152738 [LT-5]	VP-62
152740 [PM-1]	VP-91
152743 [LT-6]	VP-62
152744 [PM-3]	VP-91
152746 [PM-12]	VP-91
152747 [PM-10]	VP-91
152750 [LT-7]	VP-62
152752 [PM-5]	VP-91
152756 [PM-11]	VP-91
152760 [LL-23]	VP-30
152762 [LT-10]	VP-62
152763 [PM-7]	VP-91
153414 [LT-12]	VP-62
153426 [LT-11]	VP-62
153430 [LL-25]	VP-30
153434 [LL-24]	VP-30
153442†	NRL
153443*	NADC

P-3C
(*RP-3D)

Serial	Unit
156507 [LL-39]	VP-30
156510 [LN-40]	VP-45
156511 [LL-37]	VP-30
156516 [LR-4]	VP-24
156517 [JA-2]	VX-1
156518 [LQ-1]	VP-56
156520 [LQ-7]	VP-56
156521 [LL-34]	VP-30
156522 [LQ-3]	VP-56
156523 [LQ-9]	VP-56
156524 [LL-33]	VP-30
156525 [LL-32]	VP-30
156526 [LL-31]	VP-30
156527 [LP-2]	VP-49
156528 [LL-40]	VP-30
156529 [LL-41]	VP-30
156530 [LQ-5]	VP-56
157310 [LR-1]	VP-24
157311 [LR-2]	VP-24
157312 [LR-3]	VP-24
157313 [LP-4]	VP-49
157314 [LP-3]	VP-49
157315 [LP-5]	VP-49
157316 [LL-36]	VP-30
157318 [LL-30]	VP-30
157319 [LP-1]	VP-49
157321 [LQ-6]	VP-56
157323 [LQ-8]	VP-56

Serial	Unit
157324 [LQ-2]	VP-56
157326 [JA-5]	VX-1
158204	NADC
158206 [JA-3]	VX-1
158227*	VXN-8
158563 [JA-4]	VX-1
158564 [LR-5]	VP-24
158565 [LA-1]	VP-5
158566 [LA-4]	VP-5
158567 [LA-6]	VP-5
158568 [LP-9]	VP-49
158569 [LN-41]	VP-45
158570 [LN-42]	VP-45
158571 [LA-8]	VP-5
158572 [LN-43]	VP-45
158573 [LN-44]	VP-45
158920 [LP-7]	VP-49
158923 [LA-9]	VP-5
158924 [LA-5]	VP-5
158926 [LN-45]	VP-45
158927 [LP-8]	VP-49
158929 [LP-6]	VP-49
158931 [LA-3]	VP-5
158932 [LA-2]	VP-5
158933 [LN-46]	VP-45
158934 [LR-6]	VP-24
158935 [LR-7]	VP-24
159318 [LN-47]	VP-45
159319 [LN-48]	VP-45
159320 [LR-8]	VP-24
159322 [LR-9]	VP-24
159889 [JA-8]	VX-1
160291	NADC
160292 [LL-50]	VP-30
160293 [LL-51]	VP-30
160610 [LM-9]	VP-44
160611 [LM-8]	VP-44
160612 [LM-7]	VP-44
160761 [LM-1]	VP-44
160762 [LM-2]	VP-44
160763 [LM-3]	VP-44
160764 [LM-4]	VP-44
160765 [LM-5]	VP-44
160766 [LM-6]	VP-44
160767 [LJ-7]	VP-23
160768 [LJ-8]	VP-23
160769 [LJ-9]	VP-23
160770 [LJ-5]	VP-23
160999 [LJ-6]	VP-23
161000 [LJ-1]	VP-23
161001 [LL-52]	VP-30
161002 [LJ-2]	VP-23
161003 [LJ-3]	VP-23
161004 [LJ-4]	VP-23
161005 [LK-5]	VP-26
161006 [LK-6]	VP-26
161007 [LK-7]	VP-26
161008 [LK-8]	VP-26
161009 [LK-9]	VP-26
161010 [LK-4]	VP-26
161011 [LK-1]	VP-26
161012 [LK-2]	VP-26
161013 [LK-3]	VP-26
161014 [LL-53]	VP-30
161121 [LL-54]	VP-30
161122 [JA-7]	VX-1
161123 [LD-3]	VP-10
161124 [LD-4]	VP-10
161125 [LD-5]	VP-10
161126 [LD-6]	VP-10

Serial		Serial		Serial	
161127 [LD-7]	VP-10	161337 [LE-7]	VP-11	161585 [JA-1]	VX-1
161128 [LD-8]	VP-10	161338 [LC-81]	VP-8	161586 [LF-6]	VP-16
161129 [LD-9]	VP-10	161339 [LC-82]	VP-8	161587 [LF-7]	VP-16
161130 [LD-2]	VP-10	161340 [LC-83]	VP-8	161588 [LF-8]	VP-16
161131 [LD-1]	VP-10	161404 [LC-84]	VP-8	161589 [LF-9]	VP-16
161132 [LL-55]	VP-30	161405 [LC-85]	VP-8	161590 [LL-65]	VP-30
161329 [LE-9]	VP-11	161406 [LC-86]	VP-8	161591 [LF-1]	VP-16
161330 [LE-8]	VP-11	161407 [LC-87]	VP-8	161592 [LF-2]	VP-16
161331 [LE-1]	VP-11	161408 [LC-88]	VP-8	161593 [LF-3]	VP-16
161332 [LE-2]	VP-11	161409 [LC-89]	VP-8	161594 [LF-4]	VP-16
161333 [LE-3]	VP-11	161412 [LL-61]	VP-30	161595 [LF-5]	VP-16
161334 [LE-4]	VP-11	161413 [LL-62]	VP-30	161596 [LL-66]	VP-30
161335 [LE-5]	VP-11	161414 [LL-63]	VP-30		
161336 [LE-6]	VP-11	161415 [LL-64]	VP-30		

79-038 McDonnell Douglas F-15C Eagle; 36TFW Bitburg AFB. *APM*

50125 Boeing E-4B; 1ACCS USAF. *APM*

10321 KC-135A Stratotanker; 19BW USAF. *PRM*

50276 Lockheed C-141B Starlifter; 437MAW USAF. *APM*

US based USAF Aircraft

The following aircraft are normally based in the USA but are likely to be seen visiting the UK from time to time. They are listed in numerical progression by the serial actually carried on the aircraft externally. Fiscal year information is provided, together with details of mark variations and in some cases operating units. The types are also in numerical order, commencing with the E-3B and concluding with the C-141B.

Serial		Serial	Wing	Serial	Wing
Boeing E-3B/C		00446	60 MAW	90002	60 MAW
Sentry		00447	436 MAW	90003	436 MAW
(552AW&CD)		00448	436 MAW	90004	436 MAW
00137 (FY80) C		00449	60 MAW	90005	60 MAW
00138 (FY80) C		00450	60 MAW	90006	436 MAW
00139 (FY80) C		00451	60 MAW	90007	60 MAW
10004 (FY81) C		00452	436 MAW	90008	436 MAW
10005 (FY81) C		00453	436 MAW	90009	60 MAW
11407 (FY71) B		00454	436 MAW	90010	60 MAW
11408 (FY71) B		00455	436 MAW	90011	60 MAW
20006 (FY82) C		00456	436 MAW	90012	60 MAW
20007 (FY82) C		00457	60 MAW	90013	60 MAW
30008 (FY83) C		00458	60 MAW	90014	60 MAW
30009 (FY83) C		00459	60 MAW	90015	436 MAW
31674 (FY73) C		00460	436 MAW	90016	60 MAW
31675 (FY73) B		00461	60 MAW	90017	436 MAW
50556 (FY75) B		00462	60 MAW	90018	60 MAW
50557 (FY75) B		00463	436 MAW	90019	436 MAW
50558 (FY75) B		00464	436 MAW	90020	60 MAW
50559 (FY75) B		00465	436 MAW	00021	436 MAW
50560 (FY75) B		00466	443 MAW	90022	60 MAW
61604 (FY76) B		00467	443 MAW	90023	60 MAW
61605 (FY76) B				90024	60 MAW
61606 (FY76) B		*FY66*		90025	60 MAW
61607 (FY76) B		68304	436 MAW	90026	436 MAW
70351 (FY77) B		68305	60 MAW	90027	436 MAW
70352 (FY77) B		68306	60 MAW		
70353 (FY77) B		68307	436 MAW	**McDonnell-**	
70354 (FY77) B				**Douglas KC-10A**	
70355 (FY77) B		*FY67*		**Extender**	
70356 (FY77) B		70167	60 MAW	(2 BW* 22 ARW†)	
80576 (FY78) B		70168	436 MAW	20190 (FY82)*	
80577 (FY78) B		70169	60 MAW	20191 (FY82)†	
80578 (FY78) B		70170	436 MAW	20192 (FY82)*	
90001 (FY79) B		70171	60 MAW	20193 (FY82)†	
90002 (FY79) B		70173	436 MAW	30075 (FY83)*	
90003 (FY79) B		70174	436 MAW	30076 (FY83)†	
				30077 (FY83)*	
Boeing E-4A/B		*FY68*		30078 (FY83)†	
(1ACCS)		80211	60 MAW	30079 (FY83)*	
31676 (FY73) A		80212	436 MAW	30080 (FY83)†	
31677 (FY73) A		80213	60 MAW	30081 (FY83)*	
40787 (FY74) A		80214	436 MAW	30082 (FY83)†	
50125 (FY75) B		80215	436 MAW	40185 (FY84)†	
		80216	60 MAW	40186 (FY84)	
		80217	436 MAW	40187 (FY84)	
Lockheed C-5A		80219	60 MAW	90433 (FY79)*	
Galaxy		80220	436 MAW	90434 (FY79)*	
(60 MAW: Travis		80221	60 MAW	91710 (FY79)*	
AFB, California		80222	436 MAW	91711 (FY79)*	
436 MAW: Dover		80223	60 MAW	91712 (FY79)*	
AFB, Delaware		80224	436 MAW	91713 (FY79)*	
443 MAW: Altus		80225	436 MAW	91946 (FY79)*	
AFB, Oklahoma)		80226	60 MAW	91947 (FY79)*	
		80228	60 MAW	91948 (FY79)*	
FY70				91949 (FY79)†	
00445	436 MAW	*FY69*		91950 (FY79)†	
		90001	443 MAW	91951 (FY79)†	

149

USAF (US based)

Serial	Serial	Serial
Boeing EC-18B	*FY58*	80239
	80158	80240
FY81	80159	80241
10891	80160	80242
10892	80161	80243
10893	80162	80244
10894	80163	80245
10895	80164	80247
10896	80165	80248
10897	80166	80249
10898	80167	80250
	80168	80251
Grumman C-20A	80170	80252
Gulfstream II	80171	80253
FY83	80172	80254
30500	80173	80255
30501	80175	80257
	80176	80258
Boeing B-52G	80177	
Stratofortress	80178	*FY59*
	80179	92564
FY57	80181	92565
76468	80182	92566
76469	80183	92567
76470	80184	92568
76471	80185	92569
76472	80186	92570
76473	80189	92571
76474	80190	92572
76475	80191	92573
76476	80192	92575
76477	80193	92577
76478	80194	92578
76479	80195	92579
76480	80197	92580
76483	80199	92581
76484	80200	92582
76485	80202	92583
76486	80203	92584
76487	80205	92585
76488	80206	92586
76489	80207	92587
76490	80210	92588
76491	80211	92589
76492	80212	92590
76494	80213	92591
76495	80214	92592
76497	80216	92593
76499	80217	92594
76500	80218	92595
76501	80219	92596
76502	80220	92597
76503	80221	92598
76504	80222	92599
76505	80223	92601
76506	80224	92602
76508	80225	
76509	80226	**Boeing B-52H**
76510	80227	**Stratofortress**
76511	80229	
76512	80230	*FY60*
76513	80231	00001
76514	80232	00002
76515	80233	00003
76516	80234	00004
76517	80235	00005
76518	80236	00007
76519	80237	00008
76520	80238	00009

Serial	Serial	Serial
00010	10017	01266
00011	10018	01267
00012	10019	01268
00013	10020	01269
00014	10021	01270
00015	10022	01271
00016	10023	01272
00017	10024	01273
00018	10025	01274
00019	10026	01275
00020	10027	01276
00021	10028	
00022	10029	*FY68*
00023	10030	10934
00024	10031	10935
00025	10032	10937
00026	10034	10938
00028	10035	10939
00029	10036	10940
00030	10037	10941
00031	10038	10942
00032	10039	10943
00033	10040	10945
00034		10946
00035		10947
00036	**Lockheed SR-71A**	10948
00037	(9SRW)	10949
00038	(No 4 Detachment:	10950
00040	RAF Mildenhall)	
00041		*FY61*
00042	*FY64*	12358*
00043	17950	12359*
00044	17952	12360‡
00045	17953	12361
00046	17958	12362
00047	17959	12363
00048	17960	12364
00049	17961	12365‡
00050	17962	12366‡
00051	17964	12367*
00052	17967	12368
00053	17968	12369
00054	17969	12370*
00055	17970	12371
00056	17971	12372*
00057	17972	12373*
00058	17974	
00059	17975	*FY64*
00060	17976	17680
00061	17979	17681
00062	17980	18240
FY61		*FY72*
10001	**Lockheed C-130E**	21288
10002	**Hercules/WC-**	21289
10003	**130E ‡/MC-130E**	21290
10004	(*ANG, Air National	21291
10005	Guard;	21292
10006	†AFRES, Air Force	21293
10007	Reserve)	21294
10008		21295
10009	*FY70*	21296
10010	01259	21298
10011	01260	21299
10012	01261	
10013	01262	
10014	01263	*FY62*
10015	01264	21784*
10016	01265	21786*
		21787*

USAF (US based)

Serial	Serial	Serial
21788*	37786	37874
21789†	37788	37876
21790*	37790	37877
21792*	37791	37879
21793*	37792	37880
21794†	37793	37881
21795*	37794	37882
21798*	37795	37883†
21799*	37796	37884
21801*	37799	37885
21803†	37800	37887
21804*	37803	37888
21806†	37804	37889
21807†	37805*	37890
21808†	37806	37891
21810†	37807	37892†
21811*	37808	37893
21812*	37809	37894
21816†	37811	37895
21817*	37812	37896
21819	37813	37897
21820†	37814	37898
21821	37817†	37899
21822	37818	39810
21823†	37819	39811
21824*	37820	39812
21826*	37821	39813
21827	37822*	39814
21828	37823	39815
21829*	37824	39816*
21830†	37825	
21833*	37826†	*FY64*
21834†	37829	40495
21835†	37830	40496
21837*	37831	40497
21838†	37832†	40498
21839†	37833†	40499
21842*	37834†	40500
21844†	37835	40501
21846*	37836	40502
21847†	37837	40503
21848†	37838	40504
21849†	37839	40510
21850†	37840	40512
21851*	37841	40513
21852†	37842	40514
21855	37845	40515
21856*	37846	40517
21858†	37847	40518
21859	37848†	40519
21860†	37849	40520
21862*	37850	40521
21864*	37851	40523§
21866†	37852†	40524
	37853†	40525
FY63	37854	40526
37764*	37856*	40527
37765	37857	40529
37767	37858	40530
37768	37859	40531
37769	37860	40533
37770†	37861	40534
37771	37863†	40535
37776	37864	40537
37777	37865	40538
37778	37866	40540
37779	37867†	40541
37781	37868	40542
37782	37871	40544
37784	37872	40549

152

Serial		Serial		Serial	Type
40550		*FY73*		80812*	
40551§		31580		80813*	
40552‡		31582			
40553‡		31590		*FY79*	
40554‡		31597		90473*	
40555§		31598		90474*	
40556				90475*	
40557		*FY74*		90476*	
40560		41658		90477*	
40561§		41659		90478*	
40566§		41660		90479*	
40569		41661		90480*	
40570		41662			
		41663		**Boeing C-135**	
FY69		41664		**Stratotanker**	
96566		41665		(*ANG, Air National	
96579		41666		Guard;	
96580		41667		†AFRES, Air Force	
96582		41668		Reserve)	
96583		41669		*FY60*	
		41670		00313	KC-135A
		41671		00314	KC-135A
Lockheed C-130H/		41673		00315	KC-135A
Hercules/		41674		00316	KC-135A
WC-130H‡		41675		00317	KC-135A
(*ANG, Air National		41676		00318	KC-135A
Guard; †AFRES,		41677		00319	KC-135A
Air Force Reserve)		41679		00320	KC-135A
		41680		00321	KC-135A
FY80		41681		00322	KC-135A
00320*		41682		00323	KC-135A
00321*		41684		00324	KC-135A
00322*		41686		00325	KC-135A
00323*		41687		00326	KC-135A
00324*		41688		00327	KC-135A
00325*		41689		00328	KC-135A
00326*		41690		00329	KC-135A
00332*		41691		00330	KC-135A
		41692		00331	KC-135A
FY81		42061		00332	KC-135A
10626†		42062		00333	KC-135A
10627†		42063		00334	KC-135A
10628†		42065		00335	KC-135Q
10629†		42066		00336	KC-135Q
10630†		42067		00337	KC-135Q
10631†		42069		00339	KC-135Q
		42070		00341	KC-135A
FY64		42071		00342	KC-135Q
14861‡		42072		00343	KC-135Q
		42130		00344	KC-135Q
FY82		42131		00345	KC-135Q
20054*		42132		00346	KC-135Q
20055*		42133		00347	KC-135A
20056*		42134		00348	KC-135A
20057*				00349	KC-135A
20058*		*FY65*		00350	KC-135A
20059*		50963‡		00351	KC-135A
20060*		50966‡		00353	KC-135A
20061*		50968‡		00355	KC-135A
		50976‡		00356	KC-135A
FY83		50984‡		00357	KC-135A
30483†		50985‡		00358	KC-135A
30487†				00359	KC-135A
30488†		*FY78*		00360	KC-135A
30489†		80806*		00361	KC-135A
30490*		80807*		00362	KC-135A
30491*		80808*		00363	KC-135A
30492*		80809*		00364	KC-135A
30493*		80810*		00365	KC-135A
31212§		80811*		00366	KC-135A

USAF (US based)

Serial	Type	Serial	Type	Serial	Type
00367	KC-135A	12662	RC-135S	23530	KC-135A
00372	C-135E	12663	RC-135S	23531	KC-135A
00374	EC-135E	12665	WC-135B	23532	KC-135A
00375	C-135E	12666	WC-135B	23533	KC-135A
00376	C-135E	12667	WC-135B	23534	KC-135A
		12668	C-135C	23537	KC-135A
FY61		12669	C-135C	23538	KC-135A
10261	EC-135L	12670	WC-135B	23539	KC-135A
10262	EC-135A	12671	C-135C	23540	KC-135A
10263	EC-135L	12672	WC-135B	23541	KC-135A
10264	KC-135A	12673	WC-135B	23542	KC-135A
10266	KC-135A	12674	WC-135B	23543	KC-135A
10267	KC-135A			23544	KC-135A
10268	KC-135A	*FY64*		23545	KC-135A
10269	EC-135L	14828	KC-135A	23546	KC-135A
10270	KC-135A	14829	KC-135A	23547	KC-135A
10271	KC-135A	14830	KC-135A	23548	KC-135A
10272	KC-135A	14831	KC-135A	23549	KC-135A
10274	EC-135H	14832	KC-135A	23550	KC-135A
10275	KC-135A	14833	KC-135A	23551	KC-135A
10276	KC-135A	14834	KC-135A	23552	KC-135A
10277	KC-135A	14835	KC-135A	23553	KC-135A
10278	EC-135A	14836	KC-135A	23554	KC-135A
10279	EC-135L	14837	KC-135A	23555	KC-135A
10280	KC-135A	14838	KC-135A	23556	KC-135A
10281	KC-135A	14839	KC-135A	23557	KC-135A
10282	EC-135H	14840	KC-135A	23558	KC-135A
10283	EC-135L	14841	RC-135V	23559	KC-135A
10284	KC-135A	14842	RC-135V	23560	KC-135A
10285	EC-135H	14843	RC-135V	23561	KC-135A
10286	EC-135H	14844	RC-135V	23562	KC-135A
10287	EC-135A	14845	RC-135V	23563	KC-135A
10288	KC-135A	14846	RC-135V	23564	KC-135A
10289	EC-135A	14847	RC-135U	23565	KC-135A
10290	KC-135A	14848	RC-135V	23566	KC-135A
10291	EC-135H	14849	RC-135U	23567	KC-135A
10292	KC-135A			23568	KC-135A
10293	KC-135R	*FY62*		23569	KC-135A
10294	KC-135A	23497	KC-135A	23570	EC-135G
10295	KC-135A	23498	KC-135A	23571	KC-135A
10297	EC-135A	23499	KC-135A	23572	KC-135A
10298	KC-135A	23500	KC-135A	23573	KC-135A
10299	KC-135A	23501	KC-135A	23574	KC-135A
10300	KC-135A	23502	KC-135A	23575	KC-135A
10302	KC-135A	23503	KC-135A	23576	KC-135A
10303	KC-135A	23504	KC-135A	23577	KC-135A
10304	KC-135A	23505	KC-135A	23578	KC-135A
10305	KC-135A	23506	KC-135A	23579	EC-135G
10306	KC-135A	23507	KC-135A	23580	KC-135A
10307	KC-135A	23508	KC-135A	23581	EC-135C
10308	KC-135A	23509	KC-135A	23582	EC-135C
10309	KC-135A	23510	KC-135A	23583	EC-135C
10310	KC-135A	23511	KC-135A	23584	EC-135J
10311	KC-135A	23512	KC-135A	23585	EC-135C
10312	KC-135A	23513	KC-135A	24125	C-135B
10313	KC-135A	23514	KC-135A	24126	C-135B
10314	KC-135A	23515	KC-135A	24127	C-135B
10315	KC-135A	23516	KC-135A	24128	RC-135X
10316	KC-135A	23517	KC-135A	24129	C-135B
10317	KC-135A	23518	KC-135A	24130	C-135B
10318	KC-135A	23519	KC-135A	24131	RC-135W
10320	KC-135A	23520	KC-135A	24132	RC-135M
10321	KC-135A	23521	KC-135A	24133	EC-135B
10323	KC-135A	23523	KC-135A	24134	RC-135W
10324	KC-135A	23524	KC-135A	24135	RC-135W
10325	KC-135A	23525	KC-135A	24138	RC-135W
10326	EC-135N	23526	KC-135A	24139	RC-135M
10327	EC-135N	23527	KC-135A	26000	VC-137C
10329	EC-135E	23528	KC-135A	*FY72*	
10330	EC-135E	23529	KC-135A	27000	C137C

Serial	Type	Serial	Type	Serial	Type
		38046	EC-135C	63619	KC-135A
FY63		38047	EC-135C	63620	KC-135A
37976	KC-135A	38048	EC-135C	63621	KC-135A
37977	KC-135A	38049	EC-135C	63622*	KC-135A
37978	KC-135A	38050	EC-135C	63623†	KC-135A
37979	KC-135A	38051	EC-135C	63624	KC-135A
37980	KC-135A	38052	EC-135C	63625	KC-135A
37981	KC-135A	38053	EC-135C	63626*	KC-135E
37982	KC-135A	38054	EC-135C	63627	KC-135A
37983	KC-135A	38055	EC-135J	63630*	KC-135A
37984	KC-135A	38056	EC-135J	63631*	KC-135E
37985	KC-135A	38057	EC-135J	63632	KC-135A
37986	KC-135A	38058	KC-135D	63633	KC-135A
37987	KC-135A	38059	KC-135D	63634	KC-135A
37988	KC-135A	38060	KC-135D	63635	KC-135A
37990	KC-135A	38061	KC-135D	63636	KC-135A
37991	KC-135A	38871	KC-135A	63637	KC-135A
37992	KC-135A	38872	KC-135A	63638*	KC-135E
37993	KC-135A	38873	KC-135A	63639	KC-135A
37994	EC-135G	38874	KC-135A	63640*	KC-135A
37995	KC-135A	38875	KC-135A	63641*	KC-135A
37996	KC-135A	38876	KC-135A	63642	KC-135A
37997	KC-135A	38877	KC-135A	63643*	KC-135E
37998	KC-135A	38878	KC-135A	63644	KC-135A
37999	KC-135A	38879	KC-135A	63645	KC-135A
38000	KC-135A	38880	KC-135A	63646	KC-135A
38001	EC-135G	38881	KC-135A	63647	KC-135A
38002	KC-135A	38883	KC-135A	63648*	KC-135E
38003	KC-135A	38884	KC-135A	63649	KC-135A
38004	KC-135A	38885	KC-135A	63650*	KC-135A
38005	KC-135A	38886	KC-135A	63651	KC-135A
38006	KC-135A	38887	KC-135A	63652	KC-135A
38007	KC-135A	38888	KC-135A	63653	KC-135A
38008	KC-135A	39792	RC-135V	63654*	KC-135A
38009	KC-135A			63656	KC-135A
38010	KC-135A	*FY55*		63658*	KC-135A
38011	KC-135A	53118	EC-135K		
38012	KC-135A	53125	EC-135Y	*FY57*	
38013	KC-135A	53129	EC-135P	71418	KC-135A
38014	KC-135A	53130	KC-135A	71419	KC-135A
38015	KC-135A	53136	KC-135A	71420	KC-135A
38016	KC-135A	53137	KC-135A	71421	KC-135A
38017	KC-135A	53139	KC-135A	71422†	KC-135A
38018	KC-135A	53141*	KC-135A	71423*	KC-135A
38019	KC-135A	53142	KC-135A	71425*	KC-135E
38020	KC-135A	53143*	KC-135E	71426*	KC-135A
38021	KC-135A	53145†	KC-135A	71427	KC-135A
38022	KC-135A	53146*	KC-135A	71428*	KC-135A
38023	KC-135A			71429*	KC-135A
38024	KC-135A	*FY56*		71430	KC-135A
38025	KC-135A	63591	KC-135A	71431*	KC-135E
38026	KC-135A	63592	KC-135A	71432	KC-135A
38027	KC-135A	63593*	KC-135A	71433*	KC-135E
38028	KC-135A	63594	KC-135A	71434*	KC-135A
38029	KC-135A	63595	KC-135A	71435	KC-135A
38030	KC-135A	63600	KC-135A	71436	KC-135A
38031	KC-135A	63601	KC-135A	71437	KC-135A
38032	KC-135A	63603	KC-135A	71438†	KC-135A
38033	KC-135A	63604*	KC-135A	71439	KC-135A
38034	KC-135A	63606*	KC-135A	71440	KC-135A
38035	KC-135A	63607*	KC-135E	71441	KC-135A
38036	KC-135A	63608	KC-135A	71443*	KC-135A
38037	KC-135A	63609*	KC-135E	71445*	KC-135A
38038	KC-135A	63610	KC-135A	71447	KC-135A
38039	KC-135A	63611*	KC-135A	71448*	KC-135A
38040	KC-135A	63612*	KC-135E	71450*	KC-135A
38041	KC-135A	63614	KC-135A	71451	KC-135A
38043	KC-135A	63615	KC-135A	71452*	KC-135E
38044	KC-135A	63616	KC-135A	71453	KC-135A
38045	KC-135A	63617	KC-135A	71454	KC-135A

USAF (US based)

Serial	Type	Serial	Type	Serial	Type
71455*	KC-135E	72605	KC-135A	80070	KC-135A
71456	KC-135A	72606*	KC-135E	80071	KC-135Q
71458*	KC-135E	72607*	KC-135E	80072	KC-135Q
71459	KC-135A	72608*	KC-135E	80073	KC-135A
71460*	KC-135A	72609	KC-135A	80074	KC-135Q
71461	KC-135A			80075	KC-135A
71462	KC-135A	*FY58*		80076	KC-135A
71463*	KC-135A	80001	KC-135A	80077	KC-135Q
71464*	KC-135A	80003*	KC-135E	80078*	KC-135E
71465*	KC-135A	80004	KC-135A	80079	KC-135A
71467	KC-135A	80005	KC-135A	80080*	KC-135E
71468†	KC-135A	80006*	KC-135E	80081	KC-135A
71469	KC-135A	80008*	KC-135A	80082*	KC-135A
71470	KC-135A	80009	KC-135A	80083	KC-135A
71471	KC-135A	80010	KC-135A	80084	KC-135Q
71472	KC-135A	80011	KC-135A	80085†	KC-135A
71473	KC-135A	80012*	KC-135E	80086	KC-135Q
71474	KC-135A	80013†	KC-135A	80087*	KC-135E
71475*	KC-135E	80014	KC-135A	80088	KC-135Q
71476	KC-135A	80015	KC-135A	80089	KC-135Q
71477	KC-135A	80016	KC-135A	80090†	KC-135A
71478*	KC-135E	80017*	KC-135A	80091	KC-135A
71479†	KC-135A	80018	KC-135A	80092	KC-135A
71480*	KC-135E	80019	EC-135P	80093	KC-135A
71481*	KC-135A	80020*	KC-135A	80094	KC-135Q
71482*	KC-135A	80021	KC-135A	80095	KC-135Q
71483	KC-135A	80022	EC-135P	80096†	KC-135A
71484*	KC-135E	80023	KC-135A	80097	KC-135A
71485*	KC-135E	80024*	KC-135E	80098	KC-135A
71486	KC-135A	80025	KC-135A	80099	KC-135Q
71487*	KC-135A	80027	KC-135A	80100	KC-135A
71488	KC-135A	80028	KC-135A	80102	KC-135A
71490	KC-135A	80029	KC-135A	80103	KC-135Q
71491*	KC-135A	80030	KC-135A	80104	KC-135A
71492	KC-135A	80032*	KC-135E	80105	KC-135A
71493	KC-135A	80033	KC-135A	80106	KC-135A
71494*	KC-135A	80034	KC-135A	80107*	KC-135E
71495*	KC-135E	80035	KC-135A	80108†	KC-135A
71496*	KC-135E	80036	KC-135A	80109	KC-135A
71497	KC-135A	80037	KC-135A	80110	KC-135A
71499	KC-135A	80038	KC-135A	80111*	KC-135E
71501*	KC-135A	80040*	KC-135E	80112	KC-135Q
71502	KC-135A	80041†	KC-135A	80113	KC-135A
71503*	KC-135E	80042	KC-135A	80114	KC-135A
71504†	KC-135A	80043*	KC-135E	80115*	KC-135E
71505*	KC-135A	80044	KC-135A	80116	KC-135A
71506	KC-135A	80045	KC-135Q	80117	KC-135Q
71507*	KC-135A	80046	KC-135Q	80118	KC-135A
71508	KC-135A	80047	KC-135Q	80119	KC-135A
71509*	KC-135E	80049	KC-135Q	80120	KC-135A
71510*	KC-135E	80050	KC-135Q	80121	KC-135A
71511†	KC-135A	80051	KC-135A	80122	KC-135A
71512†	KC-135A	80052†	KC-135A	80123	KC-135A
71514	KC-135A	80053†	KC-135A	80124	KC-135A
72589	KC-135E	80054	KC-135Q	80125	KC-135Q
72590	KC-135A	80055	KC-135Q	80126	KC-135A
72591	KC-135A	80056	KC-135Q	80128	KC-135A
72592	KC-135A	80057*	KC-135E	80129	KC-135Q
72593	KC-135A	80058†	KC-135A	80130	KC-135A
72594*	KC-135E	80059	KC-135A	86970	EC-137B
72595*	KC-135E	80060	KC-135Q	86971	EC-137B
72596	KC-135A	80061	KC-135Q	86972	EC-137B
72597	KC-135A	80062	KC-135Q		
72598†	KC-135A	80063	KC-135A	*FY59*	
72599	KC-135A	80064†	KC-135A	91443	KC-135A
72600*	KC-135E	80065	KC-135A	91444	KC-135A
72601	KC-135A	80066	KC-135A	91445*	KC-135A
72602	KC-135A	80067*	KC-135E	91446	KC-135A
72603†	KC-135A	80068*	KC-135E	91447†	KC-135A
72604*	KC-135E	80069	KC-135Q	91448*	KC-135A

Serial	Type	Serial	Wing	Serial	Wing
91449	KC-135A	91522	KC-135A	40648	443 MAW
91450*	KC-135A	91523	KC-135Q	40649	437 MAW
91451†	KC-135A			40650	438 MAW
91452*	KC-135A			40651	437 MAW
91453	KC-135A	**Lockheed C-141B Starlifter**		40653	63 MAW
91454	KC-135A	(60 MAW: Travis AFB, California			
91455	KC-135A	62 MAW: McChord AFB, Washington		*FY65*	
91456*	KC-135E	63 MAW: Norton AFB, California		50216	63 MAW
91457*	KC-135E	437 MAW: Charleston AFB, S Carolina		50217	437 MAW
91458	KC-135A	438 MAW: McGuire AFB, New Jersey		50218	437 MAW
91459	KC-135A	443 MAW: Altus AFB, Oklahoma)		50219	60 MAW
91460	KC-135Q			50220	437 MAW
91461	KC-135Q	*FY61*		50221	438 MAW
91462	KC-135Q	12778*	438MAW	50222	437 MAW
91463	KC-135A			50223	438 MAW
91464	KC-135Q	*FY63*		50224	438 MAW
91466	KC-135A	38075	60 MAW	50225	63 MAW
91467	KC-135Q	38076	438 MAW	50226	443 MAW
91468	KC-135Q	38078	437 MAW	50227	62 MAW
91469	KC-135A	38079	437 MAW	50228	62 MAW
91470	KC-135Q	38080	438 MAW	50229	62 MAW
91471	KC-135Q	38081	62 MAW	50230	60 MAW
91472	KC-135A	38082	62 MAW	50231	60 MAW
91473*	KC-135E	38083	438 MAW	50232	62 MAW
91474	KC-135Q	38084	63 MAW	50233	60 MAW
91475	KC-135A	38085	63 MAW	50234	60 MAW
91476	KC-135A	38086	62 MAW	50235	62 MAW
91477†	KC-135A	38087	63 MAW	50236	60 MAW
91478	KC-135A	38088	60 MAW	50237	62 MAW
91479*	KC-135E	38089	438 MAW	50238	60 MAW
91480	KC-135Q	38090	438 MAW	50239	60 MAW
91482	KC-135A			50240	62 MAW
91483	KC-135A	*FY64*		50241	62 MAW
91484*	KC-135E	40609	62 MAW	50242	60 MAW
91485*	KC-135E	40610	437 MAW	50243	62 MAW
91486	KC-135A	40611	437 MAW	50244	62 MAW
91487*	KC-135E	40612	437 MAW	50245	60 MAW
91488	KC-135A	40613	437 MAW	50246	60 MAW
91489*	KC-135E	40614	63 MAW	50247	60 MAW
91490	KC-135Q	40615	437 MAW	50248	62 MAW
91492	KC-135A	40616	438 MAW	50249	60 MAW
91493	KC-135A	40617	63 MAW	50250	60 MAW
91494*	KC-135A	40618	437 MAW	50251	60 MAW
91495*	KC-135E	40619	443 MAW	50252	60 MAW
91496*	KC-135E	40620	438 MAW	50253	62 MAW
91497*	KC-135E	40621	438 MAW	50254	60 MAW
91498	KC-135A	40622	438 MAW	50255	62 MAW
91499*	KC-135A	40623	438 MAW	50256	60 MAW
91500	KC-135A	40624	437 MAW	50257	62 MAW
91501	KC-135A	40625	438 MAW	50258	62 MAW
91502	KC-135A	40626	438 MAW	50259	60 MAW
91503	KC-135A	40627	438 MAW	50260	60 MAW
91504	KC-135Q	40628	438 MAW	50261	438 MAW
91505*	KC-135A	40629	437 MAW	50262	60 MAW
91506*	KC-135E	40630	437 MAW	50263	62 MAW
91507	KC-135A	40631	437 MAW	50264	62 MAW
91508	KC-135A	40632	60 MAW	50265	438 MAW
91509*	KC-135A	40633	438 MAW	50266	437 MAW
91510	KC-135Q	40634	63 MAW	50267	437 MAW
91511	KC-135A	40635	62 MAW	50268	60 MAW
91512	KC-135Q	40636	63 MAW	50269	437 MAW
91513	KC-135Q	40637	60 MAW	50270	437 MAW
91514	KC-135A	40638	438 MAW	50271	438 MAW
91515	KC-135A	40639	438 MAW	50272	437 MAW
91516	KC-135A	40640	60 MAW	50273	437 MAW
91517	KC-135A	40642	60 MAW	50275	437 MAW
91518	EC-135K	40643	60 MAW	50276	437 MAW
91519*	KC-135E	40644	437 MAW	50277	62 MAW
91520	KC-135Q	40645	60 MAW	50278	60 MAW
91521	KC-135A	40646	437 MAW	50279	437 MAW

USAF (US based)

Serial	Wing	Serial	Wing	Serial	Wing
50280	62 MAW	60158	62 MAW	60209	437 MAW
59397	63 MAW	60159	62 MAW	67944	60 MAW
59398	60 MAW	60160	63 MAW	67945	437 MAW
59399	62 MAW	60161	62 MAW	67946	63 MAW
59400	63 MAW	60162	438 MAW	67947	437 MAW
59401	437 MAW	60163	437 MAW	67948	438 MAW
59402	63 MAW	60164	62 MAW	67949	63 MAW
59403	60 MAW	60165	62 MAW	67950	438 MAW
59404	63 MAW	60166	438 MAW	67951	62 MAW
59405	60 MAW	60167	437 MAW	67952	63 MAW
59406	63 MAW	60168	437 MAW	67953	438 MAW
59408	437 MAW	60169	438 MAW	67954	438 MAW
59409	438 MAW	60170	438 MAW	67955	437 MAW
59410	62 MAW	60171	63 MAW	67956	437 MAW
59411	438 MAW	60172	63 MAW	67957	63 MAW
59412	438 MAW	60173	438 MAW	67958	63 MAW
59413	438 MAW	60174	443 MAW	67959	63 MAW
59414	63 MAW	60175	63 MAW		
		60176	62 MAW	*FY67*	
FY66		60177	63 MAW	70001	63 MAW
60126	438 MAW	60178	437 MAW	70002	437 MAW
60128	63 MAW	60179	63 MAW	70003	443 MAW
60129	62 MAW	60180	63 MAW	70004	437 MAW
60130	63 MAW	60181	63 MAW	70005	63 MAW
60131	437 MAW	60182	63 MAW	70007	438 MAW
60132	438 MAW	60183	438 MAW	70009	63 MAW
60133	438 MAW	60184	63 MAW	70010	437 MAW
60134	63 MAW	60185	443 MAW	70011	437 MAW
60135	437 MAW	60186	443 MAW	70012	437 MAW
60136	63 MAW	60187	437 MAW	70013	438 MAW
60137	63 MAW	60188	443 MAW	70014	437 MAW
60138	63 MAW	60189	443 MAW	70015	63 MAW
60139	63 MAW	60190	63 MAW	70016	437 MAW
60140	438 MAW	60191	60 MAW	70018	62 MAW
60141	62 MAW	60192	62 MAW	70019	438 MAW
60142	62 MAW	60193	63 MAW	70020	438 MAW
60143	63 MAW	60194	437 MAW	70021	438 MAW
60144	437 MAW	60195	437 MAW	70022	443 MAW
60145	62 MAW	60196	437 MAW	70023	62 MAW
60146	438 MAW	60197	62 MAW	70024	438 MAW
60147	60 MAW	60198	63 MAW	70025	60 MAW
60148	63 MAW	60199	443 MAW	70026	437 MAW
60149	438 MAW	60200	63 MAW	70027	438 MAW
60150	63 MAW	60201	63 MAW	70028	63 MAW
60151	60 MAW	60202	437 MAW	70029	63 MAW
60152	437 MAW	60203	437 MAW	70031	60 MAW
60153	63 MAW	60204	438 MAW	70164	62 MAW
60154	438 MAW	60205	63 MAW	70165	438 MAW
60155	438 MAW	60206	62 MAW	70166	443 MAW
60156	63 MAW	60207	438 MAW		
60157	438 MAW	60208	63 MAW		

Civil Registered Aircraft in Military Service

Serial	Serial
Dassault Falcon 20 (Flight Refuelling Ltd/FRADU, RNAS Yeovilton)	N53 N54 N55
N2FE	N56
N3FE	N57
N5FE	N58
N22FE	N59
N26FE	N60
N32FE	N61
N33FE	N62
N37FE	N63
	N64
Grumman Gulfsteam III (Government of Saudi Arabia)	N65
HZ108	**North American F-100F Super Sabre** (Flight Refuelling Ltd, Hurn/Flight Systems, Decimomannu)
Lockheed C-130H Hercules (Government of Saudi Arabia)	
HZ114	N414FS
HZ115	N415FS
HZ116	N416FS
HZ117	N417FS
	N418FS
	N419FS
North American Sabre 75A (Federal Aviation Adminiatration)	**Lockheed P-3 Orion** (NOAA)
N51	N42RF (159773) WP-3D
N52	N43RF (159875) WP-3D

N417FS NA F-100F Super Sabre; Flight Systems/FRL, Hurn. *PRM*

Addenda

Notes	Serial	Type (alternative identity)	Owner, Operator or Location
	KE418	Hawker Tempest (rear fuselage only)	RNEC, Manadon
	LH208	Airspeed Horsa 1	Museum of Army Flying, Middle Wallop
	RA897	Slingsby Cadet TX1	Newark Air Museum store, Hucknall
	VP961	DH Devon C2 (G-ALFM)	Privately owned, Leavesden
	VT475	Fairey Firefly AS5 (fuselage only)	Privately owned, St Merryn
	WD379	DH Chipmunk T10 (WB696/ G-ALPO)	Privately owned, Jersey
	WH742	EE Canberra T19 (nose only)	RAF Shawbury, fire section
	WH777	EE Canberra PR7 (tail only)	BAe Samlesbury, stored
	WM223	AW Meteor TT22 (4X-FNA)	Second World War Aircraft Preservation Society, Lasham
	WM367	AW Meteor NF13	Privately owned, Worcester
	WP778	DH Chipmunk T10 (G-BBNF)	Privately owned, Botney, Essex
	WT212	EE Canberra B6	Privately owned, Macclesfield
	XA571	Gloster Javelin FAW1 (nose only/7663M)	Nene Valley Aviation Society, Sibson
	XD816	Vickers Valiant B(K)1 (nose only)	RAF Abingdon, BDRF
	XE797	Slingsby Cadet TX3 PAX	RAF No 645 VGS, Dishforth
	XG195	Hawker Hunter FGA9	Bomber County Aviation Museum, Cleethorpes
	XH134	EE Canberra PR9	RAF No 1 PRU, Wyton
	XJ494	DH Sea Vixen FAW2	Privately owned, Kings Langley, Herts
	XL384	Avro Vulcan (nose only/ 8670M)	Lincolnshire Aviation Museum, Tattershall
	XM379	Hunting Jet Provost T3	Army Apprentice College, Arborfield
	XM413	Hunting Jet Provost T3	Army Apprentice College, Arborfield
	XN473	Hunting Jet Provost T3A [98]	RAF Cranwell
	XN592	Hunting Jet Provost T3 (nose only)	No 1105, ATC, Winchester
	XN651	DH Sea Vixen FAW2 (nose only/A2616)	The Winbolt Collection, Pucklechurch, Avon
	XX344	HS Hawk T1	RAF BDRF, Abingdon
	XX477	SA Jetstream T1 (8462M)	RAF No 6 FTS, Finningley, ground instruction
	XZ395	SEPECAT Jaguar GR1 [GJ]	RAF ASF, Coltishall
	ZD559	Westland Lynx AH5	MoD(PE) RAE, Farnborough
	ZD560	Westland Lynx HAS3	MoD(PE) ETPS, Boscombe Down
	ZE154	Panavia Tornado F2	MoD(PE) for RAF
	ZE155	Panavia Tornado F2	MoD(PE) for RAF
	ZE156	Panavia Tornado F2	MoD(PE) for RAF
	ZE157	Panavia Tornado F2	MoD(PE) for RAF
	ZE158	Panavia Tornado F2	MoD(PE) for RAF
	ZE159	Panavia Tornado F2	MoD(PE) for RAF
	ZE160	Panavia Tornado F2	MoD(PE) for RAF
	ZE700	BAe 146 CC2	MoD(PE) for RAF Queens Flight, Benson
	ZE701	BAe 146 CC2	MoD(PE) for RAF Queens Flight, Benson